Terror Down Under

Terror Down Under

A History of Horror Film in Australia, 1897–1973

Daniel Best

McFarland & Company, Inc., Publishers
Jefferson, North Carolina

LIBRARY OF CONGRESS CATALOGUING-IN-PUBLICATION DATA

Names: Best, Daniel, 1967– author.
Title: Terror down under : a history of horror film in Australia, 1897–1973 / Daniel Best.
Description: Jefferson, North Carolina : McFarland & Company, Inc., Publishers, 2023 | Includes bibliographical references and index.
Identifiers: LCCN 2023010370 | ISBN 9781476688411 (paperback : acid free paper) ∞
ISBN 9781476648316 (ebook)
Subjects: LCSH: Horror films—Australia—History and criticism. | Motion pictures—Censorship—Australia. | BISAC: PERFORMING ARTS / Film / Genres / Horror | HISTORY / Australia & New Zealand
Classification: LCC PN1995.9.H6 B4845 2023 | DDC 791.43/6164—dc23
LC record available at https://lccn.loc.gov/2023010370

BRITISH LIBRARY CATALOGUING DATA ARE AVAILABLE

ISBN (print) 978-1-4766-8841-1
ISBN (ebook) 978-1-4766-4831-6

© 2023 Daniel Best. All rights reserved

No part of this book may be reproduced or transmitted in any form or by any means, electronic or mechanical, including photocopying or recording, or by any information storage and retrieval system, without permission in writing from the publisher.

Front cover images © 2022 Shutterstock

Printed in the United States of America

McFarland & Company, Inc., Publishers
Box 611, Jefferson, North Carolina 28640
www.mcfarlandpub.com

To my mother and uncle, Geoff, both of whom always had time to talk to me about cinema and classic horror films.

∼

I still miss you, Geoff. This one is for you.

Acknowledgments

Books such as these are never written in a true vacuum. Some sections of this work were published (in their earliest form) in *Monster!* This resulted in those articles being nominated for Rondo Awards and those nominations, and feedback that I received, gave me the motivation to expand upon my work and produce the book you now hold.

I want to thank all the following:

Stephen Bissette for his unending encouragement, support and for helping me along the way. His ability to be a sounding board and his willingness to share the knowledge of decades of writing and publishing has been essential.

Chad Eglinton, without whom everyone would see my dyslexic writing flaws.

Tim Paxton, Brian Strauss, Steve Fenton and Brian Harris, the publishers and editors of Monster! and my first horror-themed book, *Australian Gothic*. They took a punt on an otherwise unpublished Australian writing about horror films in the Australian context.

John Harrison who pushed me to write about historical horror films in the Australian setting.

Gary Chaloner, who has been an amazing chum and always there at the right time.

Others have contributed to this work in some form, most without knowing it. They include the National Archives of Australia, the National Library of Australia, the South Australian State Library, Martin Dunne and Steven Smith.

I want to thank the writers who have inspired me along the way: Gideon Haigh, Ina Bertrand, Ross Thorne, David J. Skal, Gary D. Rhodes, Scott Nollen, Kevin Barlow, David Robinson and Tom Weaver. If I could be a third as good as any of you, I would be happy.

And the mighty Gregory Mank, who set me on this path back in 1984 without ever knowing it.

I want to thank my amazing family, my partner in life Lyndal and my children, Kat and Geoffrey, all of whom, along with the rest of my family and friends, endure me talking about topics that must bore them senseless at times.

This is for all of you!

Table of Contents

Acknowledgments — vi
Introduction — 1

1. Early Cinema: 1894–1900 — 3
2. The Silent Era: 1909–1929 — 13
3. The Golden Age: 1930–1948 — 53

*Intermission: The Fall of the Cinema,
 the Rise of the Drive-In* — 105

4. The Ban Years: 1949–1969 — 108
5. Television: 1956–1973 — 136
6. Rebirth: The '70s and Beyond — 147

Epilogue — 165
Filmography, 1897–1973 — 169
Chapter Notes — 287
Bibliography — 297
Index — 299

Introduction

The first time the phrase "horror film" was used in Australia in conjunction with cinema came on July 20, 1912. Newspapers across the country reported on a suspicious case of death by gunshot in England, in which the magistrate denounced the victim's practice of immoderately seeing films focusing on the crime genre. The magistrate ruled that George Porter's death was due to suicide by insanity and that the films he had seen were a direct cause. This would not be the last time that cinema was blamed for a death, or even a murder. What made the case notable was the title "Coroner Condemns 'Horror' Films."[1]

Even though it became clear that Porter's films of choice fell squarely into the crime genre, the media decided that any film that contained stabbings, shootings and otherwise terrifying subjects, were horror films.

Once coined, the phrase stuck, and it moved with the times. Horror in the teens was crime. In the '20s, it covered everything from supernatural themes to fallen women (vampires), drinking bootleg alcohol and dancing to jazz. By the 1930s, the horror genre was as we know it today, although the phrase was occasionally used to describe movies that otherwise defied description.

In the early 1940s, the phrase was used to describe films that emerged from World War II, those films showing German concentration camps and the people affected within. Those movies featured real-life horrors; the types that were produced by studios such as Universal, Republic, Columbia *et al.* couldn't compete.

In 1948, the Australian government, responding to pressure from various community and religious groups, banned all horror movies in the country. Although movies that were already in the country could still be screened, no new horror movie would be allowed in. Australia was already one of the most conservative countries when it came to entertainment, and movies had been censored and banned in substantial numbers before this move, so the block banning came as no great surprise. The ban remained in place for decades.

The 1950s brought the world atomic age monsters, which became a subgenre. A movie such as *The Day the Earth Stood Still* was no more a horror film than any other science fiction film. Indeed, even though the ban was firmly in place, some horrors, such as *Creature from the Black Lagoon* (1954, Universal) and *The Mummy* (1959, Hammer) circumvented the ban. How this was done is explained in this book.

In 1969, the horror ban was lifted. One of the main victims of the ban had been the Australian film industry, which could not make a simple thriller, let alone a full-blown horror film. Nineteen seventy-one's *Wake in Fright*, a suspense film with horror overtones, broke the ice. In 1973, director Terry Bourke released *Night of Fear*, the first real horror film made in Australia since the silent era. With that film, the last remaining shackles of the horror ban were snapped. An all-new era was ushered in, and Australian cinema, and the Australian cinema-going public, embraced it.

This book details what happened from the introduction of cinema in Australia in 1897 through to 1973, when the Australian film industry was able to properly establish a local horror film scene. Post–1973 events are for another book.

1

Early Cinema: 1894–1900

Much has been written about the birth of cinema in Australia, almost 130 years ago, but exactly how much of it is accurate? The accepted story of Australian cinema is that Carl Hertz, a magician, gave the first exhibition of motion pictures, via the Kinematograph, at the Melbourne Town Hall on Saturday, August 22, 1896, 17 months after its Paris debut on March 22, 1895. Hertz fired up his Kinematograph shortly after the intermission of an otherwise nondescript vaudeville performance, to an audience of patrons who had no idea what was about to happen. The screening ran for around 20 minutes and stunned the audience into silence. This has been accepted as gospel for the past 114 years. But history tells a different story.

The Kinetoscope

The precursor to the Kinematograph, the Kinetoscope, as developed by Thomas Edison, first appeared in Australia in 1894. The Kinetoscope was brought to Australia by theater impresario J.C. Williamson, after he had viewed an exhibition of it in America earlier that year. Williamson quickly snapped up the Australian rights from Edison and arranged for five machines and film to be sent to Australia at the earliest opportunity.[1] He exhibited in Sydney on November 30, 1894, at 144 Pitt Street. Audience members paid one shilling to view the program of five films.[2]

Kinetoscopes were a single unit with a viewing window in the top which enabled a single viewer to see a clear but tiny image, from a 50-foot loop of film running at the surprisingly high speed of about 40 pictures a second and lasting about 30 seconds. It was a roaring success, with 25,000 patrons recorded in the first month of business.

Williamson then sent his five machines out on tour and supplemented the original five films with another 16.[3] From Sydney the show visited Hobart from February to March 1895, then on to Melbourne, Bendigo, Ballarat, Geelong, Sydney, Brisbane and Townsville.

It was in Queensland, at Charter Towers, that the first synchronized sound Kinetoscope was exhibited. Combining the Kinetoscope with the phonogram, a motor rotated the phonograph mechanism through a belt drive. This ensured that the two mechanisms would start and stop simultaneously, although the sync was hit and miss at best. Most exhibitions of this combination only provided rough musical backing for the films, heard through special ear tubes, an early form of modern headphones.[4]

Although primitive, they proved to be another hit, and the three machines toured from Rockhampton to Adelaide, to Ballarat, back to Adelaide, to Broken Hill and then to Sydney where they were installed in Pitt Street.[5] But they were soon overshadowed by the introduction of something more amazing: moving pictures on a screen.

The Kinematograph

To say that Carl Hertz was an unusual man would be an understatement. Born to Russian immigrants in America in 1859, he began his career in California, performing simple conjuring tricks for miners. As his career progressed, he began to tour the world. Playing in England and Europe, he refined his act. He was best known for his "Flying Birdcage" trick; he could produce flowers from a simple paper bag, and he presented the "Vanishing Lady" trick before anyone in England.

Thanks to media reports regarding his Vanishing Birdcage trick, he was known to Australians as early as 1888. As a magician, he toured Australia in 1892. In 1896, he toured again, bringing with him the Kinematograph.

Hertz is credited with being the first person to bring the machine to Australia. He was not. In 1896, he badgered Robert W. Paul[6] into selling him one of the two machines operating in England, and then bought several hundred feet of film hoping to make a healthy profit on his £100 outlay. Hertz's vision of riches exceeded his imagination: He later estimated that he had realized over £10,000[7] in pure profit over the next few years.

Hertz was a Kinematograph pioneer, inadvertently becoming the first man to successfully screen a moving picture at sea on his voyage to South Africa, then the first to screen film there. While in Johannesburg, he bought yet more film. This was Kinescope film, and incompatible with his equipment, so he modified the reels by hand to show them. Thus, armed with a variety of films, he landed in Hobart, Tasmania, on August 7, 1896.

In the race to land a kinematograph in Australia, Hertz lost to A.J. Perier, who had imported one in July 1896. Perier said in 1955,

> The great news came through that the cinématographe or moving pictures had at last reached a point where they could be exhibited in public. My friend Gustave Neymark was a French artist sent out by the French government to look upon the art possibilities in Australia and had relations in Paris. We wrote to his sister, suggesting to her that she should send us one of those [cine] instruments, together with pictures to display. This projector duly arrived in Sydney in the middle part of 1896.[8]

Perier had his machine, and 12 films, but elected to wait for further stock to arrive before exhibiting.

Hertz was in Tasmania for four days as he made his way to Melbourne, where he began performing on Saturday, August 15, at the Melbourne Opera House. His show, promoted by Harry Rickards as "Carl Hertz—the Premier Prestidigitator and Illusionist of the World in his Conflux of Apparent Miracles including the Most Marvelous Illusion ever seen," got tepid reviews and played to average houses. The reference to the "Most Marvelous Illusion" was not the Kinematograph, but a trick called "Steoubaika," a disappearing lady act.

Hertz had been talking up his Kinematograph and wanted to unveil it as soon as it was practical to do so, but there were issues to contend with.

On Monday, August 17, after that evening's show had ended, Hertz cleared the theater and fired up the Kinematograph for a select audience of reporters, members of the theater world and some public.[9] Accounts describe about the slowness of the action on the screen, understandable as the film was hand-cranked, and there were other, undefined defects. Nevertheless, what the press and guests saw clearly amazed them.

A representative from *The Free-Lance* was present that night. The review was notable for appearing on the day of the first public performance, and for accurately predicting the eventual decline of live theater should moving pictures capture the public's imagination:

> At the end of the show at the Opera House on Monday night, the press was invited to a private view of the Cinematographs—a weird and wonderful machine that deserves a weird and wonderful name. Under the charge of Karl Hertz, it turned a white screen into various scenes, occupied appropriately by ballet dancers, pugilists, nurses, gallant militaries, and various other things of joy. These figures were life size and moved and seemed to have a being. The action was a little slow, but capable of amendment. When a few slight defects are obliterated and the machine worked for the public, it should prove one of Rickard's greatest draws. Indeed, with it and the phonograph, a manager will be able to give a whole variety show, carrying it in a box. and saving all wages. Alas a bad time is coming for pros.[10]

Hertz was primarily a magician. He knew that if an act had flaws, then it needed to be rehearsed until it ran perfectly. Timing was all-important. It would serve no use unveiling the Kinematograph mid-week to a half-full house; better to begin promoting it for a Saturday night, when the evening began, and a full house was all but guaranteed.

By putting the unveiling back to Saturday, Hertz had four nights to perfect the Kinematograph. Every evening, after the show, he practiced his performance.

While it is true that the August 22 exhibition at the Melbourne Opera House was the first time the Kinematograph was demonstrated before a *paying*, public audience in a theater, the actual date for the first exhibition of moving pictures had come five days earlier to a non-paying, private audience. Reviews in *The Free-Lancer* and *Table Talk* reported the Monday evening screening in their Saturday editions, and advertisements in all newspapers made mention of the unveiling of the Kinematograph that night. This meant that those attending the show on the 22nd could have, and in some cases more than likely did, read about what was planned for that evening, even if they did not fully comprehend the importance.

On August 21, an unnamed critic wrote in *Table Talk*,

> Tomorrow night ... Mr. Carl Hertz will produce his "inematographe" described as the latest invention of photography, but which is more wonderful than the Rontgen X-rays. The first glimpse of this novelty was given last Monday night after the ordinary performance had terminated, and the spectators wore astonished at what they saw. It is the kinetoscope on an extended scale, in one sense, combined with all the glory of a limelight view. The groups thus have the charm of dramatis tableaux, particularly as they retain all the finish and completeness of the subjects of the kinetoscope. The action of the figures is not less natural than the effect of a storm at sea. As a novelty, the Cinematographe is the smartest and most up-to-date process yet invented for picture views.[11]

On August 22, the evening audience was entertained by the Durham Dancers, the New Tivoli Minstrels, comedians Sonny Parlatto, Harry Shine and Will Whitburn ("Melbourne's Greatest, Favorite, Versatile, Original and Eccentric Comedian"), Clarence Lyon ("Australian Song and Dance Man"), Madame Jessica (billed as "The Beautiful Jessica[12]") a plump woman who performed a serpentine dance on a wire rope, singer Amy Dewhurst ("Direct from London") and baritone Thomas Brew.

As the intermission ended and the audience once more found their seats, a screen was wheeled onto the stage. Audiences had become used to limelight slideshows and paid little attention as the lights dimmed. The auditorium rapidly quietened as the screen illuminated and for the first time in Australia, the moving image of a London street flickered before their eyes. Hertz had achieved another first.

The titles of the multiple short films Hertz showed on both nights are now lost to time. The Kinematograph he operated was hand-cranked; the audience would have been enthralled by the sight of Hertz, silhouetted by his machine, as he cranked the films through by hand, while offering up his stage banter and commentary. *Table Talk* wrote of the performance:

> The "Cinomatographe," which nobody can pronounce straight off, and which so many bewildered people are describing as "that new picture in motion they've got at the Opera House," is having just the same kind of boom as that created by the *tableaux vivants*. The series of views include Westminster Bridge, a military spectacle, a Trilby incident, a glimpse of Kempton Park races, and a graphic bit of London Life, with all sorts of accessories to add to the realism. In addition, there are representations of famous dancers, and a variety of illustrations, some quaint, some serious, some wildly comic, but all entertaining. What the kinetoscope does on a few inches scale, the cinematographe does with life-size figures.[13]

The Leader also sang the invention's praise:

> The cinematographe is a combination by which the effects of the kinetoscope are imparted to limelight views, producing scenes of amazing realism, and giving them all the characteristics of actual moving life. All the accuracy of detail belonging to modern photography, which is, of course, the groundwork of the views, is strikingly manifested. Amongst the most vivid views were an Italian skirt dance, in which the danseuse was seen with the same clearness as if she had been actually on the stage; a pugilistic encounter, street scenes of London and London-bridge, showing hansoms, market wagons, buses and coster carts threading their way at various rates of speed through a maze of traffic, the drivers gesticulating and apparently reviling each other, just as they did one morning months ago, when the original

photograph was taken. The most perfect of the scenes is the seascape, a flowing tide and a rocky foreshore. The rhythmic motion of the waves, the spray and foam and broken waters where the waves were raft by the boulders, were so intensely natural that the audience who had been growing enthusiastic over the display, broke into a storm of applause, but the cinematographe is not educated up to encores.[14]

Rickards, impressed by the reaction, and more importantly the profits, quickly secured exclusive Kinematograph exhibition rights in Australia for £3000. A.J. Perier began showing films at the Melbourne Cine Salon on October 26, 1896. Unlike Hertz's efforts, Perier's were not met with praise.

"The cinématographe is responsible for some exhibition of colossal 'cheek' by amateur showmen," wrote *The Bulletin*. "A Cine Salon—a long, thin, ill-ventilated room—was opened in Collins Street, Melbourne, the other week. The entertainment consisted of 16 views displayed in a small frame, very little better, as works of photography, than those which Rickards includes in his variety entertainment. Yet the public were asked to pay 1 [shilling] at a time for the periodical production of those 16 second-rate samples of a stale novelty.[15]"

The "stale novelty" closed on November 9, traveled to country Victoria and finished up in Sydney.

Hertz and his Kinematograph traveled across Australia, but he did not bring the Kinematograph to each show, instead concentrating on Melbourne and Sydney. Before he left Melbourne, a rival show was established in Sydney by the MacMahon brothers with a Vitascope.

Joseph MacMahon was familiar with the concept of film due to his involvement with the J.C. Williamson tour of the Kinetoscope. MacMahon was keen to get film into Australia and, in May 1896, traveled to England to purchase the new Armat-Edison Vitascope projector. While in Europe, he cut a deal with Marius Sestier, an agent for *frères* Lumière. The deal was simple: Lumière promised to hand over film stock in return for the MacMahon brothers agreeing not to make any movies locally.

Using the Vitascope in combination with Edison film, MacMahon, on August 27, 1896, gave a private show and became the first man to screen film in Sydney, and then Brisbane. In contrast to Melbourne and later in Adelaide, Sydney screenings ran smoother. The only problem reported was a flickering of the overall image, causing some distraction.

The MacMahon brothers and Sestier threatened Hertz with legal action and hit him with a cease-and-desist notice. But Hertz was not going to be stopped just as the cash was beginning to roll in, so he simply ignored them. This series of events marked the first battle between film distributors in Australia. It is apt that such a fight should erupt at the same time as cinema was introduced. It set the stage for the many other battles and lawsuits that followed for the next 120 years.

Critics and reporters raved about Hertz and his "demon machine" playing to packed houses. Hertz's success in Melbourne and Sydney left it to others to show motion pictures to the rest of the country.

In partnership with Marius Sestier and H. Walter Barnett, Wybert Reeve brought the cinematograph to Adelaide. The first Adelaide screening, at the Theatre

Royal on October 19, had to be aborted when the equipment malfunctioned. Adding to the trouble was that the film was being shown at 1:00 p.m. and the windows were not properly blacked out, so the picture could not be properly seen. After that first screening, the show was rushed down nearby Hindley Street, on foot, for subsequent screenings at the Beehive Building on the corner of King William and Rundle.

On November 12, the process was reversed, and the film and apparatus were taken back down Hindley Street and re-installed in the Theatre Royal where they stayed until the end of January 1897. This time the apparatus was a Lumière cinématographe, the second one to enter the country.

Reeve, now working with Sestier, moved back to the Theatre Royal on Boxing Day, 1896, and remained there until the end of January 1897. Reeve toured regional South Australia and Victoria until October 1897, then toured New Zealand for the remainder of the year.

Of interest is that Hertz landed in Adelaide as part of his tour and began his stage production on Boxing Day, 1896. His residency lasted until January 15, 1897, but he did not use his cinematographe at the shows. Instead, the Lumière machine owned and operated by Reeve was utilized.

Reeve returned to Adelaide in January 1898 and he attempted to sell his equipment and 63 films, to no avail. He continued to tour South Australia, visiting Victor Harbor, Goolwa, Port Elliot and other towns, and contributed to the first Cyclorama in Adelaide in August and September of that year. Despite the fame he was acquiring and the acceptance of the cinematographe as entertainment, he was unsuccessful in selling his equipment, even at the discounted price of £150. No record of his cinematographe exist beyond January 1899.

Most early movies were short films: slapstick comedies, newsreels, melodramas and industrial films, each lasting no longer than a few minutes. As thrilling as these were, not everybody was enamored. Across the country, church officials denounced moving pictures as the work of Satan and warned that their viewing would condemn people to eternal damnation. The risk to their souls did not deter the public from flocking to see what the fuss was all about.

Early screenings often suffered from an overabundance of light, resulting in poor image quality, and the very real fear that the entire building could erupt into an explosion at any time. For those who braved the risks, real and imagined, the result was breathtaking, as people could finally see a world they could barely imagine, moving before their eyes.

At one screening, the film was run backwards by mistake, showing a carriage gradually growing larger and larger until it looked as if it would burst through the screen. This caused a mild panic as people ducked and moved, but the carriage vanished into thin air.[16] People reportedly threw up after watching a boat navigate through rough seas.[17] Naturally, these reports only made people want to see the new phenomena even more.

The MacMahons set up a "Salon Lumière" at 237 Pitt Street, Sydney, and by default it became the first cinema in Australia.[18] Located opposite the Lyceum Theatre, the Salon was open from midday to late in the evenings and showed films on a large screen every 30 minutes. The Salon even provided musical accompaniment, using musicians from the Lyceum.[19]

The Age of Cinema Begins

The equipment that Hertz had brought over only allowed for the screening of film. The Lumière equipment, carried by Sestier, also allowed for filming, and in 1896 he shot Australia's first film: *Patineur Grotesque*, a one-minute study of a roller skater performing before a crowd in Sydney's Prince Alfred Park. Although filmed in Sydney, this film was not shown in Australia until 114 years later. Sestier sent the film to France where it was exhibited, after which time it vanished. A copy was found in Hungary in 1966 and, after a long and often tortuous process, it was eventually restored and sent back to Australia where it now resides in the National Film and Sound Archive's Marius Sestier Collection.

The first Australian-made film to be shown domestically depicted the 1896 Melbourne Cup. Sestier supervised the filming, thus allowing people outside of Melbourne to see what the fuss was all about. Sestier also filmed passengers disembarking the S.S. *Brighton*, horses at the Victoria Barracks, Derby Day at Flemington Racecourse,[20] and trains.

Other pioneering filmmakers emerged: Ernest Thwaites, G.W. Heller, Georges Boivin, Mark Blow, Auguste Plane and Charles Lomet began to film anything and everything they could. These men, along with others whose names are lost to history, began the film industry in Australia.

The Haunted Castle and *The Vanishing Lady*: The First Horror Films

Early cinema was, by large, dominated by French pioneer Georges Méliès. He made films by the dozen, firing them out as quickly as he could to capitalize on the new medium. The bulk of those early films are now lost, but those that remain show incredible vision and some, for the time, startling special effects. Anyone who saw Méliès' four-minute masterpiece *The Astronomers Dream* (France, 1898) was mesmerized by the sight of a rocket plunging into the eye of a laughing moon. Theatergoers were also terrified by the Lumière Brothers' *Train Pulling into a Station* (1896): The sight of a steam train roaring towards viewers was a bit too much for some delicate souls.

The first horror movies to be shown in Australia, verified via advertisements and contemporary reviews, were *The Haunted Castle* and *The Vanishing Lady* (both France 1896). While Hertz was moving his sights to New Zealand, Rickards and Sestier busily imported as many films as they could from England and France. Méliès' rapidly growing catalogue was an obvious source.

The Méliès film library and contemporary accounts record that both films were shown in Sydney. Méliès intended for *The Haunted Castle* to be a comedy of sorts, but because of the supernatural themes and a scene of a bat transforming into a man (vampirism), the movie is considered a horror.

Méliès' short films ran for a minute or two, while *The Haunted Castle* boasted a running time of three minutes. It is near impossible to track down all the Méliès movies that were shown in Australia as the titles lost a lot in the translation from French to English and sometimes films were assigned new titles.

Another problem: Advertisements of the day noted only that a Kinematograph show was taking place that day. While promising the theatergoer previously unseen delights, the actual film content was rarely recorded. Very few films were named in ads, instead being described in broad terms, such as "a great pastoral scene" or "scenes of London street life."

In 1897, Rickards sent Australian stage producer Edwin Geach on tour to New Zealand with a selection of Méliès films and a Kinematograph. One of these films was *The Haunted Castle*. After the New Zealand run, the film was thought to be lost until a copy surfaced in the New Zealand Film Archives in 1988; it is the copy that Rickards had received from Méliès and subsequently passed on to Geach in 1897. It's impossible to believe that Rickards would import a film and not show it in Australia before New Zealand. The public, at the time, could not get enough of the new sensation, and they would eagerly return to theaters on an almost daily basis if they were promised variety.

The (Other) *Haunted Castle*

When Hertz returned to Australia in mid–1896, he too brought a film titled *The Haunted Castle*. While in England, he had secured the rights to exhibit several films by English filmmaker George Albert Smith. These titles included a trio of films, described at the time as comedy mysteries, but now recognized as early horrors: *The Haunted Castle, Photographing a Ghost* and *The X-Rays*. These films were all praised for their trick photography and dazzling special effects.

Smith's *Haunted Castle* was a copy of the Méliès film, featuring the same basic plot. Ghosts haunted an inn and, to the horror of actress Laura Bayley, they made objects move around. The effects were simple but highly effective.

Early film copyright and ownership was a debacle, with filmmakers in England, America, France and even Australia all making the same movies and, at times, taking an existing film and inserting their own title card to change the theme and passing it off as their own.

The Haunted Castle was screened as part of a vaudeville show in Hobart, Tasmania, as late as 1901.

Soldiers of the Cross

By 1900, filmmaking in Australia had gone beyond a hobby and was now becoming a business. Most Australian-made films in the early part of the 20th century were actuality or "newsreels," showing important or attention-getting events of the day. State governments, and later the federal government, commissioned the production of films for propaganda purposes, specifically to show Australia's resources and opportunities for immigrants. These films were mixed in with other fictional films and proved to be popular with the public, providing a glimpse into an Australia they might never have seen before.

The Salvation Army entered the business of filmmaking in 1897 when it established its Limelight Department. Headed by Herbert Booth and Joe Perry, it had become the first major producer of motion pictures in Australia, making and releasing over 300 films before closing in 1909. The Limelight Department established a film processing unit which, at reasonable rates, was available to anyone who wanted to process their own films.

Designed to accompany lectures, most of the Limelight Department's early films were a combination of glass slides and narrative film.[21] Booth and Perry shot propaganda and slice-of-life scenes. In January 1900, they began to accept commissions (starting with coverage of Victoria's Second Boer War Contingent departing for South Africa) to raise fighting funds at a Melbourne Town Hall patriotic concert. The commissions earned enabled the Limelight Department to expand and the revenue was used to make longer, more adventurous films.

In 1901, the Limelight Department embarked on an adaptation of the production *Passion Play,* based on the life of Jesus Christ. It was a combination of both film and glass slides, never meant to be a narrative, stand-alone film, but to accompany a lecture on Christ. The project itself appears to have been influenced by Georges Hàtot's *La Vie et la Passion de Jésus-Christ* (Lumière, 1898), another adaptation of the *Passion Play,* exhibited in Victoria in 1900 by the adjutant of the Limelight Department, James Dutton.

Soldiers of the Cross raised the bar for filmmaking in Australia, and indeed the world. Costing an incredible £500, it was the first such presentation to feature a consistent narrative theme. It contained a scene of pure horror, showing Christians being eaten by lions.[22] This very realistic effect was achieved by a combination of real lions tearing apart dummies with meat packed inside, intermixed with live people, giving off one of the most powerful images put on film at the time. This scene, in an otherwise tame religious story, was one of the few times that Australia produced effective, and realistic, horror cinema before 1972.

Even though *Cross* is considered the world's first full-length narrative feature film, the use of slides means it must be denied that honor. But *The Story of the Kelly Gang* (Australia, 1906) is a strong contender. Running just over an hour, and using the story of Ned Kelly, Australia's most famous bushranger, the movie is now considered the world's first full-length narrative film. Today, only fragments survive.

For all the early experimentation in making movies, Australians did not make horror movies, preferring to film local events as they happened or to film stories that were familiar to all Australians. Despite having scenes of violence and suspense, there was no hint of horror in *Ned Kelly.*

With all this activity, both at home and abroad, it did not take long for cinema to gain traction. By 1900, there were halls dedicated to the screening of film in all the major capital cities. Theaters that were previously reserved for vaudeville were adapted with rudimentary screens and screening booths and film were shown as part of the evening's entertainment.

Another byproduct: the traveling Picture Show Man. He would haul his wares across the country to rural towns, set up and show films to packed houses. Live theater was still preferred, but film was a valuable novelty.

2

The Silent Era: 1909–1929

Griffith, Porter, Turner and the American Invasion

By virtue of location and nationality, the first films in Australia were sourced from England and Europe. At the time, Australians were not looking towards America as a cultural leader, nor was America looking at Australia as an important export partner.[1]

That all changed when the American film industry began to take shape. Companies such as Biograph, American Vitagraph, Kale, Essanay, Edison, Star Films, American Pathe and Selig Polyscope were all competing and reaping sizable profits. As European films began to lose traction, American studios saw opportunity and seized it, establishing offices in Australia and flooding the market with as much film as could be shipped. This flooding prompted the establishment of excise taxes and censorship in a failed attempt to save the local film industry.

The industry was new and, as such, no controls were in place, leaving the studios leaps ahead of the government. The latter was trying to understand what was happening.

As soon as legislation was drafted, situations and circumstances changed, leaving the lawmakers playing a never-ending game of catch up. It was a game that the government always lost until they stopped everything with the Royal Commission of 1929.

The first American horrors exhibited in Australia included *The Sealed Room* by D.W. Griffith, *Dr. Jekyll and Mr. Hyde* by Otis Turner and *Faust and Marguerite* by Edwin S. Porter. The latter, made in 1901, was not released in Australia until 1907.

The French film *Les Vampires de la Côte*, aka *Vampires of the Coast*, was also shown. Despite the title, it was anything but a vampire movie, instead telling the story of pirates who lure ships from their course to be wrecked on rocks, after which they would be looted and the crews killed. This was more an adaptation of the famous Alexander "Sawney" Bean[2] legend (with all the gory bits, cannibalism and incest removed) than a vampire film.

One American movie imported and given a full release across the country was Thomas Edison's 1910 *Frankenstein*. Very likely the first horror film to be exhibited across Australia, it began its run in June 1910, on a bill that featured other Edison films: *The Heart of the Outlaw, A Rich Revenge* and *The Twisted Tale*, now all lost to the world.

Edison's *Frankenstein* was mentioned in contemporary reviews, described as a "representation of Mrs. Shelley's classic in tales of horror and imagination. The formation of a hideous monstrosity from the chemicals the medical student Frankenstein imagined would produce a human being of marvelous grace and beauty, showed Mr. Edison's capacity for cinematography jugglery at its best."[3] One reviewer called the laboratory scene "one of the weirdest scenes ever shown,"[4] while describing the Monster as "ghastly abhorrent." The movie delighted and scared audiences as it moved from capitol to capitol, before settling into a run in the regional centers.

Although the Edison *Frankenstein* was released in Australia, Joseph W. Smiley's 1915 *Life Without Soul* starring English actor Percy Standing[5] as the Monster, here called "The Brute," was not. Despite extensive searching, no trace of that film's exhibition in Australia or New Zealand can be found.

The Strangler's Grip

The Strangler's Grip was the first Australian-made movie that can be classified as a horror film. Reviews show that it was less a horror film and more of a thriller-suspense.

Its plot was simple: John Dalton, a squatter, is having a quiet evening with his wife when he receives a telegram calling him away on business. His wife begs him to stay as she has a premonition of impending danger. Dalton reassures her that Simon, the butler, is there to protect her and she can use the telephone (at the time still a novelty in Australia) to reach him, if necessary. Not long after he has gone, a tramp appears and begins to terrorize the wife. She rings her husband and screams, via title card, "Help!" Her husband leaps into his car and speeds home, in a sequence that was described as the most exciting of its type ever filmed to that point. As car chases were new to the Australian screen, this was not an exaggeration. The tramp disposes of the butler and begins to fight with the wife, wrapping his hands around her neck (hence the title). Dalton reaches home, rushes into the house just in time, punches the tramp's lights out. He and his wife embrace and kiss as the camera irises out. The End.

The movie was one of four films made by actors Arthur Shirley, Cyril Mackay, Leonard Willey and Sydney Stirling for West's Pictures. Mackay was born in London and brought to Australia around 1906 by J.C. Williamson to appear in stage productions. He returned to the stage, briefly, and died in Brisbane in July 1923 at the age of 43. Leonard Willey and his wife, Irby Marshall, went to the U.S. in 1914 to further their careers, and both found extensive work on the stage there.

The script was written with the sole purpose of making a movie, unusual for the time as most films were written with the stage in mind or were adaptations of stage productions. It had no credited director, but was filmed by Franklyn Barren, who also shot the trio's other movies; Barren claimed to have directed one of them, *The*

Silent Witness. *The Stranger's Grip* was most likely a collaborative effort between the four men.

The Strangler's Grip opened at the Victoria Theatre, Sydney, on February 5, 1912. Reviews were positive, with the film being described as "exciting"[6] and being sure to "appeal to those who like their blood curdled."[7] It ran until mid–1912 and is now considered to be a lost film.

One thing *The Strangler's Grip* did was show that Australian audiences had no interest in seeing a fully realized, locally made horror film.

Universal Films Ltd. (Australia)

Universal became synonymous with horror films in the years between world wars. It was Universal that launched the careers of actors Boris Karloff, Bela Lugosi and Lon Chaney Jr., and moved the latter's father Lon Chaney into the stratosphere. But the Universal that everyone knows was not the first company to bear that title.

The formation of Universal Films Ltd. (Australia) was announced on March 23, 1912, via a prospectus being launched in the pages of Sydney newspapers. The prospectus gave investors the opportunity to purchase 65,000 shares at a cost of £1 each. Twenty-five thousand shares were available to the public, an equal number held in reserve. At the time, putting money in motion pictures was considered a sound investment as the risks were low and returns were often high. An offer to get in on the ground floor of a new company was highly appealing. Universal Studios (U.S.) was incorporated a month later, on April 30, 1912.[8]

The launch of Universal Films Ltd. (Australia) was successful and the company was soon fully subscribed. The money raised went into the purchase of the ailing American-Australian Film Service and the Australian Life Biograph film companies. The former held distribution rights for American-made films, and the latter had real estate in the form of theaters along with equipment such as projectors. Universal Films also held leases on theaters already set up to show their movies.

It was not to be. The company had invested, heavily, in two companies that were struggling for both finances and market share. The American-Australian Film Service vanished as quickly as it had appeared and, despite a promising start, Australian Life Biograph had fallen over with very few assets and a lot of debt. The money raised from the prospectus went to Australian Life Biograph's many creditors, leaving Universal Films Ltd. (Australia) with a few buildings, some contracts, some films (from which money was owed to investors) and not enough capital to make it through a depressed market.

The courts found against Universal for failure to pay employees. A further hit came at the end of 1913 when the building that housed their headquarters burned to the ground, resulting in a total loss of more than £100,000. The insurance was not enough to keep the company afloat and in 1914 it went into liquidation. It took until mid–1918 for the company to finally be dissolved and wound up.

In 1920, Universal Studios (U.S.) began to distribute its own films in Australia.

The company appointed a local, Hercules Christian McIntyre,[9] to oversee the company. McIntyre had entered the business in 1912, after he and his brothers, Gus and Hughie, quit their jobs working on the Panama Canal.[10] In New York, they witnessed the popularity and financial success of the early Biograph machines. The brothers bought a machine and set up shop in a tin shed on Sydney's North Shore and called it the McIntyre Bros. Cinema. The machine was hauled through the bush in a horse-drawn wagon. Despite the novelty of cinema at the time in country areas, they went broke. Funded by their aunt, the brothers set up another cinema, in a tent this time, in North Sydney and began screening films. This time it was a success. Herc became a film buyer for McIntyre's Pictures, then Paramount as a salesman. Hughie formed the Haymarket Theatres Ltd. (now part of the Greater Union Organization), and Gus the Broadway Theatres chain.

Although a relative youth when appointed (in his early thirties),[11] Herc was a giant of a man, standing at just over six foot three. He was powerfully built and projected a personality to match. He had an appreciation for the Australian film industry and fought the mass importation of American films at every opportunity. If Universal had ever thought that they were hiring a "yes man," they were about to find out that Herc McIntyre was his own man. From the start of his tenure, he established a pattern of disregarding most of the edicts handed down to him from America and made no apologies.

Shortly after joining, McIntyre was ordered to cut salaries, lay off staff and curtail all office expenses, bringing spending to a bare minimum. He ignored the order and instead raised the salaries of his staff, encouraged them to do whatever they needed to do to sell films and publicize them, and later told people that within five months he had raised the weekly gross from £700 to £4800.

McIntyre had good reasons to see Universal succeed in Australia. To start with, continued success would see him remain in a job. Secondly, Universal had allowed McIntyre to negotiate his own contract that would see him collect a percentage[12] on all films sold in Australia alongside his salary.[13] The more films sold, the more money for both Universal and McIntyre. Universal would never be able to remove this clause from McIntyre's contract.

His organizational skills won him much praise from industry insiders in both Australia and America. Carl Laemmle later claimed that McIntyre was the best salesman in motion pictures.[14]

Entering Australia was an essential but long-term headache for Universal, which had begun to make a strong impact by the mid–1920s. And McIntyre would, despite his parochialism, prove to be a strong advocate for the horror era that was to be launched at the beginning of the 1930s.

Film Censorship: Take 1

Film censorship began in earnest in Australia in 1917, 21 years after the first film was screened in Melbourne, and it focused only on imported films until 1926.

A Commonwealth Film Censorship Board was established and based in Melbourne; its function was to screen movies for suitability to Australian audiences. Often films were released with minor cuts, although State Censors could, if required, override their federal counterparts, much to the annoyance of the Motion Pictures Exhibitor Association, a board established to protect the interests of all film studios, both domestic and abroad.

Where most of the states fell in line with this practice, South Australia was an exception. As early as 1907, controls over entertainment and the film industry had been raised in Parliament and entered legislation. These discussions continued throughout the years; in 1910, the premier of South Australia lobbied for an adjustment in the legislation specifically designed to prevent the screening of the Jack Johnson-Jim Jeffries heavyweight fight. Officially the ban was on the grounds of violence, but unofficially it had more to do with the fact that a black man beat up a white man, cheerfully and with ease.

In 1911, an inspector of places of public entertainment was appointed, and immediately wrote to the Chief Secretary about the importation of indecent films into Adelaide. In November 1911, the Chief Secretary, drawing criteria from the New South Wales censorship model, announced that any objectionable film would be prohibited from Federal exhibition, but that individual state censorship boards could elect to ban films that had been passed on a federal level. The criteria included the familiar morals clauses and an 1888 clause which allowed prohibition on the grounds that the entertainment might provoke a breach of the peace.

In setting down the new model, the South Australian censors had provided the means to remove themselves from the federal censor and thus be able to ban films as they saw fit. Every movie, from 1912 onwards, had to be screened before the state censor—including any film approved for release federally.

The Commonwealth left it to the states to regulate exhibition and thereby effectively censor both local and imported films, but the best that New South Wales could devise was a plan to make local police responsible for the censorship of their local picture shows. The *Newcastle Morning Herald* pointed out the obvious flaw in this model, questioning whether police were "competent to take up this duty of censorship"[15] due to each individual's own set of morals and views on decency.

The financial issues of having each state control censorship also came to the fore. It was argued that a central, Commonwealth censor could not take account of the different definitions of decency for each individual state, so a combination of the two systems was adopted, with Customs taking charge of film censorship while the states remained responsible for overseeing the operation of the cinemas.

In May 1917, the first Advisory Board of Film Censors for South Australia was established. Its role was to advise the state censor as to what films should be banned, thus removing the state censor from screening movies. Although the board was not a statutory body, it soon became powerful and virtually every film judged unsuitable for Adelaide audiences was banned. The board ran to 1938, when it was retired after conflicts between the federal and state governments became too obstructive and the powers to prohibit films were handed back to the federal censor.

The Board in South Australia conducted itself much the same as other state boards. They gathered, had a short meeting and then went to the cinema and watched the film. After viewing it, another short meeting was held, and they promptly issued their findings and any restrictions they saw fit to make.

In New South Wales, the focus was more on the Commonwealth model than a state level. This was due to most films entering the country via Sydney, so a film could be viewed, censored, banned or restricted from there.

In 1917, Sir Harry Wollaston, a recently retired comptroller-general, became the first Chief Censor of the Commonwealth Film Censorship Board. Upon announcement of his new role, he laid out his criteria for banning films, warning film importers that he would be watching for scenes

> showing indecent, suggestive or insufficient dress; embraces overstepping the limits of affection, nude figures, and positions of the actors which are suggestive of sexual passion or desire; any scenes which might be offensive to the religious feelings of any class of the community; or which might be thought subversive of morality or virtue, or which might seem to encourage perpetration of crime; and any scene which treated lightly those laws or rules which govern the relations of the sexes, in married and single life.

Despite his stern words, history shows that Wollaston rarely, if ever, bothered to watch a film, instead relying on written synopses that were legally required to accompany them. As these synopses rarely, if ever, mentioned the very things that Wollaston was looking for, very few films were banned.

Starting in 1919, all imported films had to be viewed by the censors, now headed by Prof. Archibald Strong, the acting professor of English at Melbourne University. The *Newcastle Sun* gleefully recorded that, in one fortnight in January 1919, Strong had screened and vetted an estimated 137 films.[16]

Unlike some state boards, the Commonwealth Film Censorship Board was not a voluntary, unpaid position. In 1918, Wollaston and his senior member Strong were each paid an honorarium of £100 on top of other honorariums that they received from other government boards. By 1925, the chairman, Walter Cresswell O'Reilly, was earning £600 per year, an incredible amount for the time.

The job was just as lucrative at state level. New South Wales censors each received £300 per year in 1918, an amount almost double the average annual for the time.[17]

The Face at the Window

The Face at the Window was another film that, although containing some moments of genuine horror, ended up more a comedy than anything else. The stage play had long been a popular melodrama on the British and Australian stage and at least three British film versions were made during the silent era. The Australian version found itself in competition with a British version, resulting in confusion and threats of legal action by the British distributor, with claims that the producer of a 1920 British version was the rightful copyright owner.

The plot was as follows: In the criminal underworld and the Apache dens of Paris, a battle of wits rages between the police and Le Loup, a cunning thief and murderer who hides his identity behind a hideous mask and announces himself to each victim with a frightening wolf-like howl. When he murders an important banker, de Brison, his exploits become a sensation in Parisian society. Next, detective Paul Gouffet is murdered, but with the aid of an electrical device invented by a mad doctor, he is temporarily revived from the dead and prints the name of Le Loup's real identity. The police promptly challenge Le Loup, and he is shot while trying to escape.

The movie was made at Rushcutters Bay, where a film studio had been established on the spot where, on Boxing Day 1908, American boxer Jack Johnson made history by being the first black man to win the world heavyweight championship. Directed by actor Charles Villiers, *The Face at the Window* featured David B. O'Connor as Le Loup, Agnes Dobson as Marie deBrison and Claude Turton as Gouffet. O'Connor also produced the film.

As the movie was a silent, it did not have the same effect as the stage production, in that Le Loup's howls had to be imagined rather than heard. The lack of sound was made up for in sheer action, and it was this that caused the movie to be targeted by the New South Wales censor. The censor condemned the scene where the detective is stabbed twice by Le Loup and demanded changes, or the film would be banned. After the two offending blows were edited out, the film was promptly passed for public screening.

Although the movie was labeled as horror, contemporary reports detailed how roars of laughter were heard at every screening. Part of this hilarity was directed at the comical mask worn by Le Loup—the Face at the Window. Grotesque, without the accompanying screams that had defined the stage version, the effect caused mirth. The actors that O'Connor assembled were stage veterans who performed their roles with a prominent level of professionalism and ability.

O'Connor had made his name as an operatic actor on the Australian stage before moving into production and film acting, debuting with *The Face at the Window*. His performance and the movie's production values showed that he had learned his lessons on the stage well, and early reviews were liberal with praise, stating that it was first class and could hold its own with anything in the world at the time. Opening in November 1919, the film enjoyed a healthy run throughout New South Wales, after which it toured Australia for the bulk of 1920 and well into 1923. It is believed to be a lost film.

The mask of Le Loup resurfaced three years later as part of another, more obscure but far more interesting, horror film, *The Guyra Ghost Mystery*. In that film, the mask was used not as a face at a window, but the face of the Guyra ghost itself. More people saw the mask of Le Loup in *Face at the Window* than in *The Guyra Ghost Mystery*.

Nightmares and Bigamy: *The Hordern Mystery*

The Hordern Mystery was a book and then a play before it was filmed in mid–1920. As a horror film, it is a minor entry, and only included for the sake of completeness. Written by Edward Finn and produced by Harry Southwell (his second outing as a producer), it had a plot that was simple enough, yet the film managed to mangle and dilute the impact with poor direction and even worse acting.

Described at the time as being a Jekyll and Hyde–type film, the story concerned a money-hungry man, Gilbert Hordern. To commit bigamy with a millionaire's daughter, he impersonates his evil twin brother. Succeeding in his plot, he marries the daughter, evades his wife but is wracked by his fraudulent ways. He finds himself about to be arrested for bigamy after confessing to all the evil he has done; but then he wakes up and realizes it was all one long nightmare. He then vows to change his ways, leaves his young wife and returns to his first wife, to live out his days in poverty.

The plot was hackneyed, even by 1920 standards, leaving more questions than answers. Why is the twin evil? How good was Holdern considering his actions? What happened to the wealthy wife? The only horror in the film is in the nightmare sequence, where Hordern is menaced by his friends, the police and the ruin of his first wife.

The film was released to little fanfare and was panned by all who saw it. Even *Picture Show,* an early Australian fan-based magazine, which would praise even the worst movies if they were Australian-made, gave the film the thumbs down, emphasizing the poor acting and the convoluted plot.[18]

The Hordern Mystery is now a lost film. It is doubtful that, if a copy were to become known, it would be hailed as anything other than what the contemporary reviewers called it: weak, overly complicated, poorly performed. The aesthetic value of the film cannot be underestimated. With its use of wealthy Sydney suburbs and opulent properties as shooting locations, this film would give an excellent look at Australia's upper classes of the early 1920s.

The Guyra Ghost Mystery

Out of the handful of Australia's silent horror films, *The Guyra Ghost Mystery* (1921) is the most fascinating. Despite the movie not being seen since 1921, the story of its conception, making and aftermath are the subject of myth and mystery. It may be the only commercial movie ever made based upon a real-life haunting that utilized both the actual location and the subjects of the haunting, playing themselves on the big screen. No movie before then had attempted to capture a ghost on camera and no movie since has used actual locations and people in such a manner.

From Guyra, New South Wales, in April-May 1921, came a tale of either textbook poltergeist activity or outright fraud, depending on who, or what, you believe.[19] The haunting itself lasted only a few weeks and is still shrouded in mystery. There were witnesses who steadfastly insisted that a poltergeist terrorized those in the Bowen household, while others took the contrary view, that it was nothing more than Minnie Bowen, conspiring with others, drawing attention to themselves. Either way, the events captivated the country, became front page news, and a part of popular culture.

The Guyra Ghost made its first stage appearance in early May 1921: A visiting troupe of minstrels, described as "Sixteen of the Finest Looking Niggers in the Country," sang and danced their way through a routine featuring the ghost at the Inverall Soldiers Club.[20] Henry Clay's Bargain Vaudeville Show, on the other side of Sydney,[21] offered a one-act comedy called *The Guyra Ghosts*, in which a bunch of people ran around the stage wearing sheets (with eyeholes cut in them), screaming "Boo!" and bumping into each other before falling to the floor and vanishing. Reviews weren't kind, and it was soon squeezed between Frank Moron and the singer Bessie Lester as comedy relief and ran for most of May 1921 before being retired.

Also in May, the Great Theodore, Master Hypnotist, offered his own take.[22] Like many others on the vaudeville circuit at the time, he was dedicated to exposing fake hauntings and spiritualists, advertising how he would expose the Guyra Ghost as a fake by inviting locals on stage where he was giving readings and making ghosts appear.

Another magician, the brilliantly named the Incomparable Sloggett,[23] was also dedicated to exposing the Guyra Ghost as a fake.[24] Sloggett had worked the vaudeville circuit for decades, made his name by going from town to town performing the latest attractions of the day. He specialized in the Indian Rope Trick and liked to show how he could not be hanged, live on stage. He then presented both the Human Hen (years before Tod Browning's *Freaks*) and how the knocking of the Guyra Ghost was really done. He added ectoplasm, a ghost appearing from a box of matches and objects vanishing and reappearing, none of which were reported as happening at Guyra. Sloggett turned the Guyra Ghost into a comedy act which he toured up and down the eastern coast of Australia for the bulk of 1922 through 1925.

In Sydney, a roofer, James Muir, placed a long-running ad in *The Sun* to point out that his brand of roof tiles would have resisted the Guyra Ghost with ease.[25]

John Cosgrove was a self-described impresario, actor and Shakespearean tragedian who had been on the stage in Australia since the 1880s. Cosgrove was larger than life, a con artist, producer, director, writer, comedian, actor and most certainly a bohemian, living big and for the moment. He was a large man, tipping the scales at between 17 to 19 stone (238 to 266 pounds) and his appetites ensured that he did everything to the fullest. By doing so, he was always broke. He was well-known for borrowing money for ambitious stage productions and never being able to pay it back, including for the film *The Guyra Ghost Mystery*, which left him with the nickname "The Great Australian Bite." Cosgrove did not care, his overall happy attitude was too infectious for anyone to get upset, stay mad, or resist him for long. Even people he ripped off liked him and eventually forgave him his debts.

Cosgrove had been working in New Zealand with film producer-director Frank Beaumont "One Shot Beau" Smith, writing comedies, and was keen to make his own mark in Australian cinema. Upon his return to Australia in 1921, Cosgrove found himself enthralled by the reportage of the Guyra Ghost and saw an opportunity to create something unique and profitable.

He spent an entire afternoon whipping up a scenario for the *Guyra Ghost Mystery* from newspaper reports, including a role for himself as the fictional Sherlock Doyle, an homage to Arthur Conan Doyle, creator of Sherlock Holmes and a parody of the hapless Harry Jay Moor who had visited Guyra and claimed the haunting was genuine.

With script in hand, he rounded up a camera and camera operator and made his way to Guyra. When he reached nearby Armidale, he realized that he needed money with which to pay people, so he disembarked the train and approached a local film distributor, Mr. Regan, who was suffering a loss of business due to the hauntings. Cosgrove talked up his project, promising riches and notoriety, stating he had obtained permission to film at the Bowen house, and adding that other parties were interested in investing. Regan promised Cosgrove the finances he needed but only if Regan's daughter, Nellie, could appear in the movie. Cosgrove readily agreed.

Cosgrove was keen to get a young female involved in the film because newspaper reports had Minnie Bowen living in Glen Innes, making her unavailable for the film. By casting a girl of roughly the same age, Cosgrove knew he could promote the film as having all the Bowens in it, as aside from two photos published in *The Sun* nobody outside of Guyra and Glen Innes knew what Minnie looked like. Regan assisted him, gathering several locals to reprise their roles protecting the house while fighting the ghost. Money in hand, Cosgrove and his ad hoc company caught the train to Guyra and walked to the Bowen house.[26]

As he approached the house, Cosgrove picked up a large rock and threw it onto its galvanized iron roof just to hear the noise.[27] As the rock bounced off the roof, he knocked on the door, ready to introduce himself and announce his intentions to come inside and make a movie.

Bill Hodder, the stepbrother of Minnie Bowen, answered the door armed with a rifle that he kept handy "just in case of a ghost." Hodder was confused at the sight of the massive, smiling figure of Cosgrove, complete with a camera operator, Nellie Regan and a host of locals.[28] His confusion turned to anger when Cosgrove admitted to throwing the stone onto the roof.

Cosgrove turned on the charm, detailing his travels all the way from Sydney, at great personal expense with a camera operator and camera, insisting he would not leave the house until he had spoken to the entire family. Bill, both anxious and nervous, told Cosgrove where he could go and what he could do with himself, his camera and camera operator, and then shut the door. Cosgrove simply waited and knocked again. After a few minutes, Minnie Bowen's stepfather William and her mother Catherine led everyone out onto the porch where Cosgrove waited. Cosgrove must have felt a sense of utter delight when Minnie herself came out of the house. She had arrived from Glen Innes that morning. He then pitched the film to them, in full Cosgrove fashion, and after much persuasion and money changing hands, the Bowens not only allowed him to use the house but also to star and recreate the scenes.

Cosgrove reached out to his professional contacts and arranged for the theft of the Le Loup mask from the *Face in the Window* stage play then being performed in New South Wales. Cosgrove eventually gave the mask back and called it "borrowing." There is no record of what happened to the play's performances without the mask.

Upon the arrival of the mask, at the hands of an actor who was generously described as "three pints" drunk,[29] Cosgrove quickly slapped it onto the actor's head and completed the costume with a long, white sheet and started filming.

The drunken ghost staggered and ran around the house waving his arms, peered through windows at the family, moaned frequently and yelled "Woooooo" and "Boo!" at people both inside and outside the house, as Cosgrove tried to convince the family to recoil in fright. The locals laughed and began to disband. A local policeman, Sgt. Ridge, rounded up the townsfolk and returned them to the Bowen house. (Cosgrove admired Ridge's striking white charger and worked it into the film.) Cosgrove used trick photography to capture William Bowen rushing out of the house and shooting the ghost with his shotgun, a risky proposition as Bowen insisted on using live ammunition.

Cosgrove then turned his attention to filming at night with the aid of torches, flashlights and a car's headlamps. He stood behind the lights, out of sight of the camera, and threw rocks at the roof of the house, which created an effect as if the stones were appearing from nowhere. Cosgrove wanted a shot of William throwing a stone at the house, but he refused: "No, I'm not having it. They'd blame me for the whole thing."[30]

Cosgrove shot interiors and exteriors of the house and surroundings, and got some footage of Nellie Regan holding flowers. After three days and two nights, Cosgrove paid people off and left with his camera operator, camera and drunken ghost as quickly as he had arrived. It was crude but important, as it captured the site, surroundings and, more importantly, the Bowen family, especially Minnie, on film.

Cosgrove shot an estimated 8000 feet of film at a total cost of £100, a considerable sum for the day. The film was edited down to 4000 feet for release. Cosgrove also bought the 1915 American film *The House of Fear* (dir. Arnold Daly and Ashley Miller)[31] and hired Wirth's Hippodrome in Sydney with the view of showing them both as a double feature.

He advertised the film with little fanfare, relying on word of mouth and the public's interest in the Guyra Ghost, as being based on the real events and featuring Minnie Bowen as herself, and being filmed at the actual location, strongly suggesting that the real Guyra ghost was captured on film. A poster proudly proclaimed, "Taken at Guyra on the spot showing the home of the Bowen family showing the actual stone-throwing caught by the camera. Most sensational scenes. Flashlight photographs taken revealing most remarkable results at night. The camera was especially designed for night work by Mr. A. Moolian and after developing the film it showed unexpected results [sic]."

Cosgrove then sat back and waited for the profits to roll in.

The few who bothered to see the film realized that it was a quickie with exceptionally low production values and a plot that was as simple as it gets: The Bowen family is haunted by a ghost who keeps throwing rocks at the roof and appearing at windows. The ghost comes inside and scares Catherine and Minnie. William chases the ghost outside and shoots at it, only to find that his bullet goes through it, leaving it unscathed. The ghost continues popping up at windows. William enlists the assistance of the townsfolk to fight the ghost. Police Sgt. Ridge rides up on his magnificent white charger. Nellie Regan appears from nowhere with some flowers for no apparent reason. Psychic detective Sherlock Doyle arrives and takes charge, sees the ghost appearing at windows and convinces Minnie to tell the ghost to leave. It promptly runs away into the night. Roll the credits—Starring John Cosgrove, Nellie

Regan and the Bowen Family, scenario by John Cosgrove, produced by John Cosgrove, costumes by John Cosgrove, etc.

Despite the promises, there were no "unexpected results" when the film was developed, just the simple effect of stones appearing from nowhere.

The huge crowds and profits, much like the Guyra Ghost itself, never materialized as public sentiment had turned. Most now believed the affair was a hoax, evidenced by Minnie's widely reported "confession." And, far from being the horror that it should have been, it was a limp comedy. The first screening was a matinee on Saturday, June 25,[32] and it took only £5 at the box office. Cosgrove knew the movie was a dud as he looked out at the mostly empty theater that he had hired.

It ran for a further three days, Sunday and Monday, after which time Cosgrove claimed to have cut his losses and sold it to an unknown distributor. It is also possible that Regan, who had financed the film, staked a claim on it and simply began screening the film in lieu of repayment of Cosgrove's loan. Another theory, which comes from Cosgrove himself, is that the only copy of the movie and its rights were sold to get Regan off his back. The real fate of the movie is now, much like the film itself, lost in time.

No matter if the film did or did not change hands, Cosgrove later claimed to have regretted the movie when the film's new owner told him how he had made over £300 showing it in Guyra alone. Cosgrove had thought people would not see a film of events through which they had lived. While it is true that the film was shown in Guyra, it screened for one night only, and is unlikely to have made that much there. Rather, the £300 figure came from the total profit of touring the movie around country New South Wales from July through September 1925. Screenings are known to have occurred at Bathurst (July 15),[33] Lithgow (July 26),[34] Guyra (July 30),[35] Penrith (August 16)[36] and Port Macquarie (September 10).[37] It is possible that the movie was shown in more rural towns than can be verified as it was common for ad hoc screenings to occur throughout this era, with only a poster or handbill placed on the window of the cinema or town hall and word of mouth.

Those who saw the Port Macquarie screening at Ochs' Pictures described it as five reels of laughter, and the film served as the opening attraction for Charlie Chaplin's *The Gang Leader*.

The Guyra Ghost Mystery was Cosgrove's only film as producer. He returned to acting and writing for both film and the stage. He wrote the silent *Silks and Saddles* (1921) and *Sunshine Sally* (1922) and acted in these and many other films. He passed away, weighing 18 stone (114 kilograms) and incredibly happy with it, after a run with illness in Sydney on the 11th of August 1925, at the age of 58.

Vampires as Farce-Melodrama: *The Twins*

Out of the five Australian silent movies classed as horror, the least is known about *The Twins*. Although it is continually listed in books and articles as a horror film, *The Twins* is, in fact, a comedy-melodrama with not a single trace of horror.

Made in Melbourne, *The Twins* was only screened in its entirety at a charity fundraising event, and no proper reviews were ever published. The film was produced by the Charity Moving Picture Society under the direction of Melbourne cinematographer Leslie McCallum, using amateur actors and crew.

The fragments of information that remain about the plot show that it consisted of a series of vignettes revolving around the contrast of Melbourne's back blocks with the social whirl of the city. Described as a "farce-melodrama," the movie is included on horror movie lists due to the female vampire, played by Doreen Gamp, who kills herself after "a life of intrigue, wickedness, and cigarettes." Gamp's appearance would mark the first time a vampire of any sort had appeared in an Australian movie, and the only time such a description would be afforded to a character in locally produced films until the 1970s.

The vampire was not the standard blood-sucking night dweller. The use of the word "vampire" in this film is more in line with the term "vamp." Gamp's character was more Clara Bow than Bela Lugosi and her character was more intent on leaching money, grog and drugs from her victims as opposed to blood.

As a fundraising exercise, the movie was successful. Portions of the movie were screened at a special ball held at Carlyon's Ballroom in St. Kilda, and the entire movie screened on June 19, 1923, after which it premiered at the Melbourne Town Hall on June 28. There is no contemporary record to show if it was screened after this date. The movie has been lost and is so obscure that only a few accounts of Australian cinema reference it.

The Movie That Never Was: *The Golem*

In Australia, one of the great mysteries of the silent film era is the absence of Weimar era horror films. Films such as *M, Nosferatu, The Cabinet of Doctor Caligari* and *The Last Laugh* never saw general release in Australia for reasons now lost to time. *Metropolis* was released in 1928 to great critical acclaim, but that is an oddity.

Australia was not as tolerant towards German cinema. The early 1920s saw anti–German sentiments rise across the country, fueled by the United Kingdom's attitude towards Germany in the post–World War I era. The main way German movies were imported into Australia was via American giant Paramount, who had signed a distribution deal with UFA, a German production company. The existing quota deal between Australia, England and Germany allowed for films to be exchanged on a reciprocal basis. This meant that for every German film shown in Australia, an Australian film was required to be exported and screened in Germany.

UFA, via Paramount, was able to get their films released in Australia by claiming they were American Paramount films and thus free them from the quota system. In this way, the 1921 film *The Golem* was announced for forthcoming release in the annual Christmas edition of the film industry newspaper *Everyone's*.[38] At no point was the film marked as being anything but another Paramount. Come January and the film was given a release date of August 25, 1923.[39]

Word soon got out about how Paramount was behaving dishonestly and releasing German films. According to the editors of *Everyone's*,

> The matter of Australian and British films is likely to have considerable attention before this year closes. Various patriotic bodies have had it under discussion from time to time, and definite proposals for legislation have been brought forward. It has been stated that some German films have been released here as American, and that the explanation was that American films were not accepted in Germany unless the producing firms reciprocated by purchasing German films for showing abroad.[40]

As Germany was refusing to accept any Australia films, restrictions were then placed on the amount of film that could be imported from Germany. *The Golem* was blocked from importation at some point in the early months of 1923.

Intermission 1: Cinema Has Always Been a Small World

Cinema has always been a small world when it comes to production with the same names appearing repeatedly, threading their way through a decade or two before being replaced by the next names. Two such names are Tod Browning and Lon Chaney.

Tod Browning was prolific in early film, appearing in more than 50 films and directing over 30 films, with *Dracula* (1931) and *Freaks* (1932) being the two best-remembered. His life was a storied one. One such story involved his tour of Australia in 1912 as part of a vaudeville double act called the World of Mirth, the Whirl of Mirth or the Wheel of Mirth, of which no records can be found, nor is there any mention of the American in any Australian records or newspaper reports. In the early years of the 20th century, foreign acts, or just foreign actors, touring Australia were given a lot of media exposure. An American vaudeville act in 1912 would have been spotlighted in advertisements and newspaper features, such as those including W.C. Fields (1903), Houdini (1910), Mark Twain (1895) or Arthur Conan Doyle (1920). It did not matter how obscure the cast or production, its foreignness and novelty guaranteed publicity and, generally, crowds.

According to historian-author David J. Skal[41] in *The Secret World of Tod Browning*, the information about the Australian tour came from Browning himself, who was prone to embellish stories about his early career.

The Whirl of Mirth did tour Australia in October 1911 but there is no mention of an American cast. Contemporary advertisements show that the production was a supporting act to comedians Jordan and Harvey.[42] It is inconceivable that an American vaudeville act could tour Australia in 1912 and receive no mention in any newspaper in the country.

It is also worth mentioning that Browning was in Hollywood working with film pioneer D.W. Griffith in early 1913, which would indicate that a long Australian tour would have been impossible, due to the time it took to travel to and from America.

Therefore, this is one of the myths of Tod Browning, who like many other aspiring creatives padded his résumé by claiming tours of faraway countries. Unlike today, such a claim in 1912 could not be easily checked, many people went on the person's word, so if Browning told D.W. Griffith that he had just returned from Australia, then he would have expected to be believed. If Griffith, or anyone else, had decided to check on this, it would have taken time and, by the time the results were in, Browning would have been entrenched in the business.

History tells us that it is highly likely Griffith did not believe Browning, nor did he care. He was concerned only with ability and enthusiasm, and Browning had both. Browning could consider himself lucky that Griffith did not take to calling him Tod "Aussie" Browning, as there was a tendency for Griffith's nicknames to stick. Henry Lehrman joined the Griffith company at Biograph in 1909 claiming to have been sent there by the Pathé Freres[43] studios in France. Griffith saw through Lehrman but still hired him, giving him the nickname "Pathé" Lehrman that followed him until his death.

Browning became one of Chaney's best-known and most sympathetic collaborators after *The Wicked Darling* (1919). From there on, they continued to work at a rapid pace, producing a further nine movies in ten years; seven of them came in a four-year period. Out of these, *London After Midnight* and *The Big City* are lost, while *Wicked Darling*, *The Blackbird*, the 1925 *The Unholy Three*, *Where East Is East*, *The Unknown* and *West of Zanzibar* are considered Chaney classics. Only an incomplete copy of *The Road to Mandalay* remains.

These films raised Browning's profile in the motion picture world and established him as a specialist in horror, thriller and suspense, with a penchant for more esoteric subject matter. That Browning would make *London After Midnight* as a vampire film with Chaney was a given and when it came time for Universal to make *Dracula,* they looked no further than Chaney and Browning. Unfortunately, Chaney passed away before filming began, leaving a Hungarian stage actor, Bela Lugosi,[44] to fill the role. It has long been debated how a Chaney *Dracula* would have looked and it's easy to speculate that his *Dracula* might have been like his *faux* vampire in *London*.

Lon Chaney is a true legend of the silent era, making an estimated 155 films over 17 years, of which 109 are lost. Of the 46 remaining films, some are incomplete or mere fragments of footage. The bulk, if not all, of Chaney's pre–1920 films were released in Australia. Advertisements exist for his early films *Damon and Pythias*, *The Grip of Jealousy* and *The Gilded Spider*. It was not his acting or skill with makeup that first brought him to the attention of Australian audiences. Rather, it was his association with the Australian actor Louise Lovely.

Born in Sydney in 1895,[45] Nellie Louise Carbasse began acting and touring with dramatic companies at an early age under the name Louise Carbasse.[46] A precocious child, she later claimed that at age seven she did the rounds of various businesses paying her mother's accounts. She had played in every theater in Australia, often alongside Nellie Stewart, before appearing in six films between 1911 and 1913. She looked older than she was and could be cast in adult roles.

In 1914, Lovely decided to take a chance and move to Hollywood. She arrived in America at 18 and married. Louise Welch, as she was then known, was given a screen test at Universal and offered a contract. She dyed her hair blonde the same day. Studio head Carl Laemmle also gave her a new name: Louise Lovely.

With her blonde curls and cute name, she was placed into films as Universal's answer to Mary Pickford, much to her annoyance. Lovely's co-star in her early films was a young Lon Chaney and her Australian heritage ensured that her films were rushed into cinemas across Australia, with her name being the only one mentioned. Louise Lovely's popularity as a "local made good" ensured that Chaney's early feature-length efforts were seen by many Australians. It also meant that all the press attention, review-wise, was focused on Lovely without any mention of her co-stars. It mattered not: Louise Lovely's films were popular and, by virtue of association, Chaney built a following.

Chaney's name first appeared in print in Australia in 1915 when *The Grind* was released. Ads for 1916's *The Trust* noted that Chaney both starred in and produced that short. But it was the films he made with Lovely that increased his prominence Down Under.

All the Lovely-Chaney films were directed by Joseph DeGrasse. Seven were released in Australia, but not in order of filming or American release. These films were *Tangled Hearts, The Grip of Jealousy, The Gilded Spider, Dolly's Scoop, Bobbie of the Ballet, Stronger Than Death* and *The Grasp of Greed*. The first movie that the team made, *Father and the Boys* (Lovely's Hollywood debut), debuted in America on December 20, 1915, but appears not to have been released in Australia.

In six of the films, Lovely received top billing; Chaney was usually second or third. For *Dolly's Scoop* (released February 20, 1916, in America, September 30, 1916, in Australia), Lovely was billed as Louise Welch. *Father and the Boys* saw her third-billed to Chaney's seventh, and their last film, *The Grasp of Greed,* saw Lovely third billed, Chaney fifth. The first Lovely-Chaney collaboration released in Australia was *Tangled Hearts* on August 6, 1916, and the last, *The Grasp of Greed*, appeared four months later, on November 8.

Louise Lovely was dropped by Universal in 1918 after a contract dispute—and after she angered the Laemmles by taking part in an actors' strike. She was picked up by Fox, where she made a series of westerns, all now lost films. On one such film, her blonde curls caught fire during filming. Although the fire was quickly doused and no injuries were sustained, Lovely decided the Pickford curls were finished and cut her hair into a bob that she maintained for the remainder of her Hollywood career.

Chaney's first known biography[47] appeared in newspapers in 1922, to coincide with the release of *The Trap*; it made no mention of Lovely. A year later, while Lovely became disillusioned with Hollywood, glorious full-page advertisements, with Chaney's name in bold type, heralded *The Hunchback of Notre Dame*, a cinematic masterpiece, and the film that made Chaney a household name worldwide.

"From the very first day I started producing motion pictures, I had but one desire, and that to give the industry a work of art that would stand as the cornerstone for better and greater motion picture movement," Carl Laemmle was quoted in the Australian press as saying. "The selection of *The Hunchback of Notre Dame* is the production to fulfill that dream."[48]

Advertisement for *The Hunchback of Notre Dame* (1923).

The movie was well-received in Australia, appearing on three screens simultaneously in Sydney.

In Melbourne, local makeup artist Grafton Williams created his own version of the Hunchback, based on Chaney's. Incredibly effective, this Hunchback popped up in the streets of Melbourne's Central Business District, tying up traffic wherever he went. The actor portraying the Hunchback repeated his march for a week during August 1925, with people both thrilled and horrified by the display[49] and wanting to touch his hunch for "good luck." The day before the film opened, the Hunchback was arrested and led through the streets in handcuffs by a police officer.

The Tivoli in Brisbane trumpeted the fact that their tickets would remain at their standard price, and even included a very welcome new feature: an early form of cinema air-conditioning. As *Hunchback* was released in the summer of 1924, a hot time of the year, most cinemas proudly announced that, for longer feature films, oscillating fans would be installed to ensure the comfort of patrons.

Shortly after the film's October 1925 release in Melbourne, Victoria, 11-year-old Donald McConnell was found dead in a house on Kooyong Road, Caulfield. He had been taken to see *Hunchback* and was enthralled by the film, in particular the scene where Chaney slides down a rope. The Victorian State Coroner found that McConnell was trying to emulate Chaney when he entered a house under construction with other boys, found a rope tied to the roof and tried to slide down it only to have the rope twist around his neck several times. By the time he was found two hours later, McConnell was dead. His father later stated that young McConnell was a bright, happy boy who had no reason to commit suicide.

The Hunchback of Notre Dame was quietly removed from Victorian cinemas for a period.

Hunchback was also known as *The Monk and the Woman*, which caused issues. A movie with the same title had once been banned from exhibition and when *Hunchback* began its rural run with the alternate title, complaints were made and questions asked. The title was rapidly changed back.

Chaney's magnum opus came when the 1925 *The Phantom of the Opera* was released. In the title role, Chaney created a character that is still capable of creating shock, a century later. With this film, Chaney's billing in ads was prominent, larger than anyone else's, which was fitting as he was not only the star, but also co-directed the film, uncredited.

Hunchback was still in theaters when the *Phantom* ad campaign commenced. In Melbourne, Grafton Williams once again created an effective Phantom, based on Chaney's makeup. The same unnamed person who played the Hunchback, repeated his earlier actions of appearing in the streets at random, around lunch time, and snarling traffic, but this time he was not arrested.

Phantom was banned by certain cinemas in Tasmania for being too horrific. It made little difference to the movie's popularity, but the more prominent Chaney got, the more attention his films received from state and federal censors. The results were that both *Hunchback* and *Phantom* were censored for Australian release. As these censored prints have yet to be rediscovered, it is unknown how extensive the cuts were.

Chaney's *The Unholy Three, The Tower of Lies, The Black Bird, Road to Mandalay, The Unknown* (and others) were given wide release and received complimentary reviews and publicity. He was a name actor, and one that MGM Ltd. (Sydney), Universal and cinema chains knew that people wanted to see. As such, his movies were constantly re-released, with his most popular films, such as *Hunchback* and *Phantom* being shown on an almost continuous basis. When *London After Midnight* was due for release, it was given good advance notices, along with Chaney's *Laugh, Clown, Laugh*. Director Tod Browning was also highlighted in newspapers on the strength of his Chaney collaborations.

London After Midnight, the most successful of the Chaney-Browning collaborations, was released in Australia in April 1928, four months after release in the U.S., and quickly traveled from state to state. Much was made of its detective story, with reviews making almost no mention of the film's vampire aspect. Chaney, billed as "The Screen's Greatest Character Star" and "The Prince of Actors," was praised for his performance, and Browning's direction was cited for its atmospheric overtones. On an amusing note, one regional New South Wales newspaper made mention of the moving starring "Lawrence Chaney."[50] By the end of 1928, the film was being shown on a double bill with Charlie Chaplin's *The Circus*, thus ensuring that the movie would be one of Chaney's most profitable Down Under.

In 1929, Chaney was linked to a tragic death. Twenty-eight-year-old Robert Williams was arrested, tried and convicted of cutting the throat of a servant in Hyde Park. At his trial Williams claimed that he saw the face of Lon Chaney as Quasimodo from *Hunchback of Notre Dame*, resulting in a blackout. If Williams did indeed hallucinate, then there would be two deaths that could be attributed to *Hunchback*. In 1933, the mentally disturbed Williams piled up mattresses in his padded cell and leapt to the floor, fracturing his skull. The verdict was that he had committed suicide out of guilt. This came after two previous attempts.

The news of the Hyde Park murder did not dilute Chaney's popularity, and his subsequent films, such as *The Big City* and *Laugh, Clown, Laugh* were released to much fanfare and excellent reviews. *London After Midnight* proved to be so popular that it was still screening well into the 1930s, long after Chaney passed away in August 1930.

Chaney made six silent features after *London* and one talkie, an *Unholy Three* remake which was released posthumously. The cause of death: a throat hemorrhage, brought on by a secondary infection after a bout of pneumonia. His only talkie, *The Unholy Three*, was a *tour de force* in speech, with Chaney providing the voice for five separate characters, including a parrot and an old woman.

Browning went on to make the all-time classic horror film *Dracula*, a movie that, it could be said, launched the Golden Age of horrors, and certainly the Universal Horror period. After making *Iron Man*, a potboiler with Lew Ayres and Jean Harlow, Browning made one of the most sensational movies ever, 1932's *Freaks*. Notable for using real-life freaks, the film was so horrific that it was banned in Australia until the 1980s.

In 1935, Browning made one last return to the vampire-horror genre, a thinly disguised *London After Midnight* remake titled *Mark of the Vampire* starring Bela "Dracula" Lugosi as the vampire alongside Lionel Barrymore and Lionel Atwill. A gothic masterpiece, *Mark* surpassed *Dracula* in many aspects, but it was somewhat of a swan song for Browning: He made just two more movies before turning his back on Hollywood. He retired from the business because he was fed up with studio interference on his 1939 movie *Miracles for Sale*. He passed away in 1962.

Today Browning is known primarily for *Dracula* and the landmark *Freaks*. Like Chaney, he lives on. His influence can be felt in modern gothic horror films.

The Legend of *Fisher's Ghost* and the Demise of Australian Horror Movies

For the 1924 silent *Fisher's Ghost,* Raymond Longford and Lottie Lyell took a well-known Australian ghost yarn and, with a professional production team, cast and crew, crafted the finest of all Australian silent horrors. It marked the last Australian-produced horror movie until 1973.

The legend of *Fisher's Ghost* originated in Campbell Town, NSW, in 1826 when a settler named Farley was walking home in his cups and spotted an apparition sitting on a bridge railing. The ghost claimed to be the spirit of Frederick Fisher,[51] a prospector who recently went missing after striking it rich with another man, George Worrall.[52] Worrall claimed that Fisher, after making his fortune, left in search of other adventures.

The ghost pointed to the creek and led Farley to the spot where Fisher's body was found. Farley took this in, contemplating aloud what should be done, upon which the ghost screamed bloody vengeance for his murder at the hands of Worrall. Farley took off down the dirt road, back into town like a scalded cat, and blew into the pub babbling about ghosts and murder most foul. The locals took little notice of Farley's drunken ramblings, but at his insistence decided to humor him. The group of men marched to the bridge where he had encountered the ghost, then down to the creek and the submerged body of Fisher. The group's humor faded and they turned from happy drunks to a lynch mob. They hunted down Worrall and accused him of murder, which he denied. But under the weight of Farley's drunken testimony and the word of a ghost, Worrall broke down, confessed, was arrested, placed on trial and executed.

The legend had everything nineteenth-century audiences wanted: drama, murder, theft, ghosts, revenge and justice in the form of an execution. It was one of the first mythological stories to enter white Australian folklore. The story was so ridiculous that it could made to match any place, and before long had become the template for "Dead Man's Creek" tales across the country.

Fred Fisher was robbed and murdered by George Worrall, his body dumped into a creek, and Worrall twisted in the wind for his crimes, but that is where the stories part. On the front page of the September 22, 1826, *Sydney Gazette,* a substantial reward of £20 was offered for information leading to the discovery of Fisher's body[53] and thus prove that he had met with foul play. All anyone knew was Fisher had vanished after leaving the pub with a bottle of rum, intending to walk home. A further amount, £5, was offered to anyone who could provide proof that Fisher had left Campbell Town (as Campbelltown was then called).

Worrall was the prime suspect, being the last person to see him alive and having shared a hut with Fisher and four other men. Worrall had also been seen selling off some of Fisher's property and splashing about a pile of cash. He had provided a statement saying that Fisher had left the colony on the *Lord Saint Vincent*, a ship that had never visited the harbor. He also said Fisher owed him for various debts. What led to his apprehension was a crude forgery of a receipt for a horse.

The reward, a small fortune in colonial days, saw a frantic search for the body, led by Aboriginal trackers. One tracker, Gilbert, walked along a wooden fence on the Worrall (formerly Fisher) property and, noticing either a tooth or a bone fragment and blood, stopped at a watering hole. The water was discolored with a greasy film on the surface. Gilbert waded in and, using a leaf, scraped the film up and tasted it. He turned to the people with him and simply stated, "This is the fat of a white fellow."[54]

The watering hole was connected by a small creek to a swamp. Gilbert announced that the body was in the swamp, so everybody started digging and searching until Fisher's body was recovered. A Dr. Hill, examined the body and discovered that the skull had several fractures consistent with being bashed with a blunt object. Worrall, already in custody on suspicion of foul play, was charged with the murder on June 17, 1826. He entered a plea of not guilty.

A jury found him guilty on Friday, February 2, 1827, and sentenced him to hang the following Tuesday. He continued to maintain his innocence, but at 5 a.m. on the morning the sixth, he confessed while talking to a reverend.[55] According to Worrall, he had met Fisher on his way home. The men were drinking from a bottle of rum and passed a paddock where a horse was resting. Worrall and Fisher took offense at the horse and decided to teach it a lesson. Both men jumped the fence and Worrall picked up a fence post, intending to bash the horse. Instead he "accidentally" bashed Fisher. Knowing the penalty would be the gallows, he panicked and hid the body. Two other men, suspected in the crime, were in custody; they were exonerated and set free.

The "confession," such as it was, was likely another lie, as Worrall was as much a drunkard as Fisher and, accident or otherwise, Worrall had admitted to killing Fisher. His last moments were described as "manly and becoming," meaning he did not embarrass himself by weeping, fainting or soiling himself. He approached the gallows steadily, without hesitation, and was observed to be absorbed in contemplation of his fate.[56] Minutes later, Worrall was dead.

In 1836, ten years later, the *Sydney Gazette* published an account of the Fisher case with the addition of the ghost.[57] In this account, the ghost was encountered by a friend of Fisher's, one Mr. John Hurley. The report stated that Hurley had affirmed to the court the existence of the ghost. Five years later, Hurley wrote to the editor of the *Sydney Herald* denying any such affirmation; although he knew Fisher, Hurley claimed to have been over 200 miles from Campbell Town when the body was discovered.[58]

It made no difference. Hurley's name was changed to Farley, Worrall's to Wurrell and Fisher became Fredro when a poem, written by "Felix,"[59] was published in *Bell's Life,* a literary newspaper. Titled "The Sprite of the Creek," the poem bore a disclaimer that it was based on the murder of "poor F***** at Campbelltown."[60]

From that point on, the legend of Fisher's Ghost overtook the facts, and the ghost on the fence has always been part of it ever since. The city of Campbell Town seized upon the legend to promote the town and still holds celebrations to commemorate the myth. Although it is debunked every generation, it holds a special place in Australian folklore.

The entertainment potential for the Fisher's Ghost story were plentiful. A play was touring as early as 1879. In the 1920s, it came to the screen.

Raymond Longford[61] was a prolific Australian film director, writer, producer and actor of both the silent and sound eras. He started out on the stage at the beginning of the century and then moved into cinema. While he was on stage, he met Lottie Lyell and they formed a partnership that lasted for the next decade and a half.

Lyell[62] is often called Australia's first real film star. She gained popularity as an actress and often did her own stunts, some of them breathtaking. She first met Longford at age 19, when Edwin Geach cast her as Maggie Brown in a stage adaptation of *An Englishman's Home* (Longford played Mr. Brown). Experienced and capable, Lyell had studied Shakespeare with the eminent actor Harry Weston and her career flourished with tours across Australia and New Zealand.

In 1910, Longford was put in charge of production for film pioneer Charles Cozens Spencer. He brought Lyell to the screen, where they acted together[63] before Longford moved into directing. On the surface, Longford directed and Lyell acted, but their partnership was more complex as they lived openly as a couple but were never able to marry.

That Longford and Lyell deeply loved each other has never been in dispute. Longford had been married since 1900 to Melena, a strict Catholic. Melena, who knew of the relationship between Longford and Lyell, would not agree to a divorce on religious grounds. Longford and Lyell were discreet with their relationship but after Lyell's father passed away in 1910, Longford moved into the Lyell family home and the two were inseparable.

Theirs was a true partnership in life and in work, and when he asked her opinion of adapting C.J. Dennis' Australian classic *A Sentimental Bloke,* "[s]he had nothing but praise for the contents, and was positively certain it would prove a great success on the screen." Lyell was right. Costing £2000 to make, the movie, released in 1919, was a roaring success. It's considered Longford's best film and an Australian silent classic. By 1922 it had grossed an estimated £33,000.[64]

After that success, whatever one of them did, the other was deeply involved. They quickly followed *A Sentimental Bloke* with another C.J. Dennis property, *Ginger Mick* (1920), then *On Our Selection* (1920), *Rudd's New Selection* (1921) and *The Blue Mountains Mystery* (1921), each making healthy profits.

With *Fisher's Ghost,* Lyell became one of the early woman filmmakers to co-write, produce and direct a horror film (all without credit).[65] She also worked on costume designs and, just to complete the picture, handled the pair's financial business.

Marjorie Osborne, the principal of *The Blue Mountains Mystery*, talked of Lyell in an interview at the time of the film's release: "I like brains in a woman, and she has them. She assists Mr. Longford, and the two of them have plenty of healthy arguments when their ideas about a scene are different."

In 1920, Lyell had a bout with tuberculosis which took her off the screen. She recovered sufficiently to appear in *Ginger Mick,* but the strain was too much. By 1922, she had all but retired from acting, preferring to work behind the scenes.

In 1922, Longford and Lyell formed a production company named Longford-Lyell. They raised £50,000 by public subscription and looked set for remarkable success. Within a year, the company was faltering. The first Longford-Lyell production, *The Dinkum Bloke* (1923), cost £4846 and grossed only £5831 after 16 months, a disaster. Longford quickly found work directing three films, *Australia Calls, An Australian by Marriage* and *Australia, Land of Sunshine* (all 1923) for the Australian government. Behind the scenes, Lyell attempted to save the company: While dealing with her declining health, she wrote *Fisher's Ghost, The Bushwhackers, The Pioneers* and *Peter Vernon's Silence* before Longford-Lyell Australian Picture Productions Ltd. ceased operations on May 26, 1924. Longford blamed exhibitors for the collapse of the business, often alluding to money being taken off the books where *The Dinkum Bloke* was shown.

Longford later claimed to have spent a substantial amount of time studying papers relating to the Farley murder case at Sydney's Mitchell Library; the papers dated back to 1826 when the library was founded. Longford wanted to make the legend rather than a factual retelling, but base it on the true historic record. "I took my facts from the Mitchell Library," Longford told the Royal Commission in 1927, "and upon them I made the picture although I do not believe they are accurate."[66]

Fisher's Ghost was filed for copyright on June 4, 1924, and shooting began shortly after. Longford-Lyell raised the capital by joining forces with exhibitor Charles Perry, who shared production credit. They raised a modest sum of £1000, all of which was spent on the 55-minute film. Longford kept the plot simple but added some extra details and a love story for dramatic effect, further muddying the legend. The movie is set in Penrith, a town approximately 50 kilometers from Campbell Town. The reason for the change is unknown, but it is more than likely because they could film there. Fred Fisher became John Fisher, George Worrall became Edward Smith and Farley became two people, John and Jim Weir.

The following is the plot, as detailed in the original shooting synopsis used by Longford-Lyell:[67]

> The film opens with a shot of Longford himself, visiting the Mitchell Library in Sydney, whereupon he opens a book upon which the words, "In the year 18— there lived in the little town of Penrith, a farmer by the name of John Fisher." Fisher is then shown on his farm, working with Edward Smith. The next scene shows the pair at Dean's Country Pub, sharing a drink and talking about England. Smith suggests that Fisher should go back to the mother country to visit his family. Fisher isn't so sure and recounts the tale of why he was transported in the first place—he killed a man with a stone by accident. As such he believes his family would be ashamed to see him, even if he is a rich man with £100,000 in cash stashed at his farm. Smith then tells the landlord of the pub, Dean, that Fisher is intending to visit England. Fisher agrees and the pair head off into the night.
>
> Six weeks later Smith visits the pub and tells Dean that Fisher has indeed gone back to

England. Dean is surprised as Fisher never said farewell to him, odd, considering they were close friends. Smith then tells Dean that Fisher left abruptly due to problems with a woman. Dean understands. Smith returns to the Fisher farm and tells all the workers about Fisher's leaving and him taking over. He promotes the head hand, Mr. Thompson, and tells him that he, Smith, will be moving into the main house and that Thompson can move into Smith's old house on the farm, with a raise in pay. This delights Thompson who runs home to tell his family, including his daughter, Nell Thompson. This news causes dismay for Nell as she is in love with her neighbor, Jim Weir. She tells the news to Weir who is just as disappointed as she is.

Jim has a vision of him and Nell raising children, but, although they love each other, they are poor folk who cannot afford to marry. That's not the only hurdle they face, Mr. Thompson can't stand the urchin Weir. It matters not, they duly move onto the farm.

One evening Smith makes a move on Nell, only to be interrupted by Thompson. Thompson notices Smith's interest in his daughter and encourages it. Smith is a man of wealth, so it'd be good for the entire family if Nell would just give in. Nell refuses and tells her parents she doesn't like Smith; she wants to marry Jim Weir. They refuse to give their consent, with Mr. Thompson banging the table for emphasis.

A year after Fisher's disappearance, a local asked after him. Smith produces a letter supposedly written by Fisher in which he asks Smith to sell all his property, pay off any debts and send the rest over to England. He then tells Nell he has done all of this and wants to sail to England with her as his bride. Nell tells him she has no love to give him and refuses.

Smith tells Mr. Thompson that Nell has turned him down. This now means that Thompson is out of a job, he has one week to get his family and leave the farm and the well-paying job. The family holds a crisis meeting and pressures Nell into accepting the proposal, which she does, the following morning. She then travels to the Weir farm to tell Jim the news. He isn't there, so she leaves a letter with the youngest Weir, Fred.

Weir rushes to the Fisher farm when he reads the note, but, alas, although they love each other, they can never be together. They cry.

A week later, John Weir comes home from the pub. "Well, Mother," he tells his wife, "a strange thing happened coming home tonight; I've either seen Mr. Fisher or his Ghost." Mrs. Weir puts this down to the grog as everyone knows Fisher is in England. In a flashback we see Weir riding home and seeing Fisher on a fence post. He greets him but gets no reply. He tells the story to Jim who tells him to lay off the booze.

A week later and John Weir is again in Dean's pub. This time he refuses a drink, prompting jokes about Weir taking the Pledge. Weir laughs, but says he's not drinking, but won't say why. He leaves the pub and gives a lift to two men, Bob Hamilton and Ted Williams. They drive along and come to the bridge by Fisher's farm, whereupon all three see Fisher's Ghost, sitting on the bridge. They notice that the moonlight is shining through Fisher's body. Weir stops his horses and approaches Fisher, greeting him. Fisher does not reply. He touches Fisher on the shoulder and announces that foul play has happened, so all three men head towards the house of Mr. Cox, the Magistrate.

Cox listens to Weir and speaks to Hamilton and Williams. The next morning Cox, Weir, Williams, Hamilton and three black trackers visit the bridge and are excited when one tracker discovers what he calls "White man's blood." They then track through the creek and discover the remains of Fisher's body on a waterhole behind Fisher's farm. The body, although it is now just bones, is identified as Fisher via a buck knife in the pocket with the initials "J.F." carved into it. Cox tells the trackers to gather the body up in bark and all then ride to Fisher's farm.

Smith is surprised to see the men and even more surprised to see the remains of Fisher. Upon being accused by Cox, Smith maintains his innocence. Old man Weir talks about seeing the ghost; Smith gives a knowing wink at Cox signaling that Weir is well known as the town drunk. Weir is indignant, he wasn't drunk. Smith produces the letter from Fisher and hands it to Cox. Cox reads it and places Smith under arrest for the crime of murder.

A month later all are in court. Smith is on trial but the captain of the ship that Fisher supposedly sailed to England on gives evidence saying that Fisher indeed did travel to England.

Fisher's solicitor also backs Smith's story. The evidence against Smith is the three men who saw the ghost. The jury retires to consider their verdict. Smith is guilty and sentenced to hang.

Despite petitions calling for Smith's release, the day of his execution is upon him. He writes a letter, hands it to the Reverend who is giving him comfort and heads to the gallows. Hours after he is dead, the editors of the local newspaper are readying to publish Smith's letter—it was a confession of guilt. He murdered Fisher. He arranged for a double to sail to England in Fisher's place. It's all true.

Six months later, Nell and Jim are married and live happily ever after.

Fade out.

The film starred Robert Purdie as Edward Smith, Fred Twitcham as John Fisher and Lorraine Esmond as the tragic Nell, the girl whom Smith is about to marry when he meets his fate. The film featured a special effect of the ghost on the fence, requiring a double exposure and a dust storm which Longford later claimed had used two tons of Fuller's earth to produce.[68]

Filming finished by August 1924, and it was slated for release in October; 98 years after the original events. It was then that Longford-Lyell ran into difficulties. They were stymied by Stuart Doyle, then in charge of Union Theatres,[69] the main cinema chain. He refused to screen *Fisher's Ghost* because he considered it too gruesome for public consumption, even though it had passed the NSW State Censor. Watching the film made him physically ill, and he knew people would get up and walk out in disgust if he dared show it.

The real reason was that Longford and Doyle hated each other with a passion. Longford had long railed against Doyle and his theatre chain, accusing them of collusion with other theaters, namely Hoyts, to run independent Australian producers out of the business. Doyle, and Union Theatres, had a large interest in Australasian Films Ltd. and any film produced by that company got an instant release. Longford further accused Doyle of running what he called "The Combine" which he claimed had secured control of the local markets and made it impossible for producers and backers to get full value for their movies when released.

Furthermore, Doyle had screened *Fisher's Ghost* and made Longford-Lyell wait two weeks before giving a reply through a company secretary. Incensed by the lack of respect, Longford and Perry insisted upon a meeting. At the meeting, Doyle told them that Union Theatres would not release *Fisher's Ghost*.

Doyle denied all of this. In his eyes, if Longford-Lyell films made little money, it was because they were simply not up to par with American or British films.

This animosity went back over a decade. The "Combine" was born out of a series of mergers resulting in the formation of Union Theatres and Australasian Films on January 6, 1913. The Combine's initial move was to merge Johnson & Gibson and J. & N. Tait into Amalgamated Pictures. Then in September 1912, the directors of Wests Pictures, Spencer's Pictures and Amalgamated Pictures voted to merge under the banner of the General Film Company of Australasia. The addition of Greater J.D. Williams Amusement Co. brought the centralizing of four partners under Union Theatres and Australasian Films, creating a film production and distribution monopoly.

Spencer was out of the country on holiday when the board voted to merge in his absence, as he opposed the merger. The Combine were now assured of a supply of imported film and felt that there was no longer a need for Australasian Film or Spencer's Pictures to make films other than the Australasian Gazette and Spencer's Gazette and refused to invest in any of the productions. Longford, in his role as head of production at Spencer's, was privy to the machinations of the Combine firsthand. Spencer, now out of the company that bore his name, left for Canada in late 1914[70] and never made another film. Longford never forgot.

Longford faced issues with obtaining financing for his own films, and the Combine often refused his requests to use the film studio at Rushcutters Bay, ironically funded and built by Spencer. Union Theatres refused to release *The Sentimental Bloke*, on top of the Combine refusing permission for Longford and Lyell to film at their studios. Over the years there were more slights and insults, none forgotten by Longford. Doyle also had a long memory, and he was not above using his power to make lives difficult.

The dispute between Doyle, as head of the Combine, and Longford, long kept behind closed doors, erupted at the 1927 Royal Commission on the Moving Picture Industry of Australia. Desperate to get *Fisher's Ghost* released, Longford-Lyell accepted a highly unfavorable deal from Hoyts. The managers of Hoyts informed Longford that they knew that the Combine had refused to take the film on, and the reasons why.[71] If Hoyts took the film, they argued, Hoyts would have to pay Paramount, as per their contract, for the film that *Fisher's Ghost* would be replace. Hoyts offered to take the film, for one week, at a flat cost of £30, paid in full at the end of the week, and that Hoyts would keep any profits. Longford-Lyell would also lose control of distribution and exhibition, as well as being responsible for paying Hoyts £10 for newspaper advertising for each week Hoyts had it on show.[72]

Longford was apoplectic but without options. His investors and company board were braying for money and blood. Also, Lottie's health was declining and she needed care. He agreed. The film premiered at the Theatre De Luxe, Sydney, on October 4, 1924, and arrived in New Zealand in February 1925. It was praised by critics and public alike, vindicating Longford-Lyell's judgment. At the end of the first week in Sydney, *Fisher's Ghost* grossed £1200, of which £1170 went to Hoyts. Hoyts was keen to release to the film in England and offered Longford £500 for the rights. Disillusioned, he took it.

The film was shown at a trade show in London in late February 1925, but it failed to impress. "Since the film was an attempt to boost Australian-made films, it was a pity that the picture was not more free [sic] of experiment," wrote the London representative of the Melbourne newspaper, *The Herald*. "It lacked vitality and the actors were unconvincing. It would have been an immense success, if taken in England, as an Englishman's idea of outback life, the alleged cocky's [sic] temperament and the personality being more reminiscent of a Devonshire farmer."[73]

Despite this negative review, the film received a general release and did reasonable business. But a comment by the critic for *The Bioscope* raised the ire of Longford and his fellow Australian moviemakers: "Considering that the film was made in Australia, the technical standard of the production as a whole is surprisingly high."[74] *Everyone's* immediately went on the defensive, slamming the review as being condescending and, in the process, openly attacking Australia House (located in London) for not leaping to the defense of the film when the review appeared and pointing out that the Australian film industry was not the backwater that the English might think it was.

Even though Fisher's Ghost drew large audiences and record profits for Hoyts, and excellent coverage in *Everyone's*, other cities refused to show it on the same grounds as Doyle. Not until 1926 was the movie screened in Perth, where it did a roaring trade. It continued to do so wherever it toured. The film was shown at His Majesty's Theatre, Hobart, in 1926. According to theater manager Cecil Shannon, "We exploited it in a rather novel fashion. It lent itself to exploitation. Outside the theatre we erected a fence with a mark on it showing where the ghost stood. Many people had heard of *Fisher's Ghost*, and that assisted us to put it over."[75]

Many theaters in New Zealand used a similar set of fence posts out front or in a neighboring window, most purporting to be the actual fence where the ghost perched in 1826. These posts were generic wooden posts, sourced by promoters wherever the film went.

Despite being a silent movie, *Fisher's Ghost* was still being screened in rural locations as late as 1931. But all copies of the film disappeared in the mid-1930s, probably to extract the silver nitrate from the film stock. *Fisher's Ghost* is now on the Lost Films register. Lottie Lyell did not live to see the film's success. She passed away on December 21, 1925, succumbing to tuberculosis at the age of 35. *Everyone's* referred to her death as "a distinct blow to the motion picture industry of this country, and the loss of one who has left the mark of her genius on Australian progress."[76] Although she was not fully credited for her work, it is accepted that Lottie Lyell was an equal partner with Raymond Longford. In her will, written in the mid-1920s, Lyell gave her professional occupation as "Motion Picture Producer." In 1958, Longford wrote an unpublished memoir about *The Sentimental Bloke* and confirmed, "The scenario, preparation, exteriors and interiors of the film were carried out in its entirety by Longford Lyell Film Productions—Lottie Lyell was my partner in all our film activities."[77] As Longford said to the 1927 Royal Commission about Lyell editing *Mutiny*, and his insistent claims that she was his equal partner from the moment she recommended *The Sentimental Bloke* to him in 1915, it can be assumed that she was co-directing from that *Sentimental Bloke* through to *Fisher's Ghost*. Jack Moller, an extra on *Bounty*, recalled in 1985 how he observed Lyell directing scenes for that film.[78]

A *Blue Mountains Mystery* publicity photo shows Lyell on set standing between cinematographer Arthur Higgins and Longford, her hands on the script as she looks intently at the action being filmed. A newspaper report[79] describes in detail Lyell directing scenes with Longford on the streets of Sydney for *The Dinkum Bloke*.

Sadder than the loss of the first Australian female movie star, and a pioneer of filmmaking, she was never able to marry Longford, even though Melena had finally given in to Longford's requests for a divorce in August 1925 on the grounds of desertion. The magistrate had issued the standard decree that Longford would be free to remarry six months later.

Longford was heartbroken but continued to make films including *The Bushwhackers, The Pioneers* and *Peter Vernon's Silence*, all co-written by Lyell. None of his films ever reached the heights of their work. After filing for bankruptcy in 1929, he quietly left the country and spent the next 18 months traveling Europe. Upon his return, he went to work for Frank Thring's Eftee Films, both credited and uncredited. His heart wasn't in it any more and his last film as a director was 1934's *The Man They Could Not Hang*. He married Emilie Anschutz in 1933 and returned to acting; his last role came in *The Power and the Glory* (1941).

In 1957, Longford was asked, if he could make a film, any film, what it would be. He did not hesitate, hurrying to another room in the house and returning with a new synopsis for *Fisher's Ghost*.[80] Longford had revised and registered the script in 1934, keen to make a new version of the classic tale. Funding was not forthcoming, and his vision was never to be realized. He spent his last years working as a night security guard on Sydney's wharves. Longford slipped away in his sleep on April 2, 1959, at the age of 80.

Knowing the story of *Fisher's Ghost*, one may wonder if it was a truly gruesome movie. The NSW State censor had no issue with it and cleared it, uncut. Stuart Doyle told the 1927 Royal Commission, "I admit that I said the picture was too gruesome. I still say it is." Longford, also speaking to the Royal Commission, was adamant: "There was nothing gruesome in the picture; unless a ghost on a fence is gruesome," then adding, "I was very careful about that."

The synopsis of the film correlates with contemporary reviews. It suggests that, apart from the ghost and a shot of some bones in torn clothing, there is nothing untoward in the film. Longford and Lyell would have known the limits of what could be shown and ensured that Fisher's murder happens off screen, with only a bloody knife and a body appearing.

As the film is lost, it is hard to judge who was right and who was wrong. The loathing between Doyle and Longford would have seen them disagree on anything. It can be expected that Longford downplayed the supernatural themes in the film; it can also be equally expected that Doyle would overplay them as an excuse to block its release. From the 1927 Royal Commission transcript, it becomes clear that Doyle was careful not to display his personal dislike for Longford, but his testimony, littered with short, non-committal answers, betrayed him. On the other hand, Longford was open about his contempt for Doyle and the Combine.

Doyle's co-directors and those involved with the Combine agreed with Doyle and ran the film down. Speaking before the Royal Commission, William Gibson, the general manager of Australasian Films Ltd., said:

> Quite a number of good Australian productions have cost less than £1000 to produce, pictures such as *The Man They Could Not Hang, Should a Doctor Tell, Fisher's Ghost* and others.
> I should not say they were good productions, although they might have caught the public fancy.[81]

Fisher's Ghost and *The Man They Could Not Hang* were Longford-Lyell films. George Griffith, managing director of Hoyts, the cinema chain that bought *Fisher's Ghost* for £30 and then made £1200 in a week from it, described the film as being "fair" when asked what sort of a picture it was.[82] Cecil Shannon testifyied that *Fisher's Ghost* was "not a bad picture."[83] Herbert Finlay, a producer associated with Australian Films, had been a touring exhibitor since 1898; he told the Royal Commission, "Only 18 months ago, I traveled through the Riverina with the film *Fisher's Ghost* and got ever so much better figures with it than with a double feature of *Rin-Tin-Tin* and Harold Lloyd in *Girl Shy*."[84]

Reviewers praised the film, with its uses of location shots being one of the main appeals. Not one review called it overly gruesome, nor are there any reports about patrons becoming ill. One writer called *Fisher's Ghost* "[a] splendid example of what can be done in Australia by Australians."[85]

> On the whole, the acting was very pleasing, and some good comedy included. The photography of the Australian landscape and farms was a feature of the production.[86]
>
> This production not only proves that there are actors in Australia capable of appearing in the most pretentious film creations, but also that there are unlimited possibilities for really beautiful and artistic outdoor settings in the wild bush countries.[87]
>
> It is in no way morbid but is relieved by an elevating love theme which runs the length of the film.[88]
>
> A most interesting picture, which contains many humorous incidents....[89]

It is hard to know, without seeing the film, if it was as gruesome as Doyle maintained, but no evidence points in that direction. It can, therefore, be deduced that Longford was right; Doyle rejected the film on personal, not professional, grounds.

Taxation of Cinema and Universal

The original agreement between Universal Pictures Corporation (U.S.) and Universal Film Manufacturing Co. (Australia) was signed on August 23, 1923. The deal was extended, and adjusted, in 1924 and 1925, but the terms remained the same.

Under the deal, Universal (Australia) would accept any film Universal (U.S.) sent over, at a cost set by the Americans. Universal (America) was also obligated to send over as much advertising matter as possible, at a minimum cost. Universal (America) took a cut of all the profits generated, at 65 percent, leaving 35 percent for the Australian company.

This deal operated until the tax man came calling in 1926. An audit of Universal (Australia) found that no tax was being paid on the 65 percent sent to the U.S. According to the tax man, in 1926 Universal (Australia) had sent £37,387[90] to the American company without paying tax assessed at £9346.[91]

The Commissioner of Taxation, William Henry Widdon, slapped the bill on Herc McIntyre, who promptly refused to pay. The defense was that income from Universal's films constituted a trust fund and as the Australian company was liable for all the importation and distribution costs, it should not be liable to pay the American tax. Neither Universal Australia nor the American parent company was willing to pay the fines, so the case went to court in Sydney.

Universal (Australia) lost the case and the subsequent appeal, leaving it to pay

Double-page trade magazine spread for *The Phantom of the Opera* (1925).

the tax bill, penalties and legal costs of the taxation department. McIntyre made sure that all monies came from the head office in America and not from the Australian branch.

Universal (U.S.) was sufficiently impressed by McIntyre to offer him a senior management role at the head office in America in 1929. To the amazement of the Laemmles, McIntyre turned the job down, preferring to remain in Australia where he

The Path of Censorship

Movies imported into the country had to comply with five basic rules. A film would not be cleared if the censor believed that it

is blasphemous, indecent or obscene;
is likely to be injurious to morality, or to encourage or incite to crime;
is likely to be offensive to the people of any friendly nation;
is likely to be offensive to the people of the British Empire; or
depicts any matter the exhibition of which is undesirable in the public interest.

A distributor could appeal a decision, but it would cost them, up front, and the appeal might not be successful. The censor would give the reasons why the film had been rejected, resulting in cuts being made and the film being passed on appeal.

In 1922, Robert Wallace, a Scottish-born professor of English at Melbourne University, replaced Archibald Strong as the Commonwealth's chief film censor. He was faced with the enormous task of censoring films *and* keeping everyone, if not happy, then satisfied. Upon his appointment, he was instructed that there should be "a strong moral censorship," which everyone interpreted differently.

Described as tall and spare, with an Aberdonian accent, a soft and hearty chuckle and a dry sense of humor, Wallace continued the liberal period in the history of film censorship.

In 1925, Cresswell O'Reilly was appointed as the Sydney censor and his effectiveness in the role saw him replace Wallace as chief censor in 1928. O'Reilly brought with him a stern approach to the guardianship of Australian morals. The chief censor's office went from checking the occasional film on morals grounds to checking every imported feature film. By 1925, more films had been censored or returned to their country of origin than ever before.[92]

Questions were being raised in Federal parliament as constituents were petitioning their elected members about censorship and film. To help keep the legislators on the side of the straighteners, O'Reilly arranged for a special show of "highlights" from censored films for federal parliamentarians in June 1926. Senators recoiled at the sights. A typical response came from Labor MP James Fenton, who stated that films "will have a damaging effect upon the eyesight of the people, more especially half a generation hence."

The screening had the desired effect. One parliamentarian was the right-wing Senator Guthrie, a well-connected grazier from Victoria who had lost a leg to anthrax and was a self-professed hater of profiteers and Bolsheviks and a strong supporter of British cultural standards. He argued, "[P]ictures should be produced in the British Empire to depict the traditions of our race and Empire and to advertise the great advantages for settlement offered by our far-flung dominions."

The Victorian Censorship of Films Act was established and provided for Victorian censorship of all films entering the state and permitting the censor to order the cutting or banning of a film, or to conditionally approve films for exhibition to all but those aged between six and 16. All conditional approval had to be clearly shown on advertisements and on the screen before exhibition. All the powers were then vested, under agreement with the Commonwealth, on the Commonwealth Censor, who was chosen to act on behalf of the Victorian State government.

Censorship and importation came to a head when a Royal Commission into the film industry was announced in 1927.

The Royal Commission on the Moving Picture Industry in Australia

By the mid-1920s, an estimated 110 million tickets were sold annually at Australian movie houses, an incredible figure considering the country's population was just over six million. It was becoming obvious that the film industry and cinema in Australia was in danger of being overwhelmed by the flood of movies coming from overseas, in particular, America.

An earlier move to establish tariffs had done little to slow the influx of foreign films and there was a legitimate fear that more money was leaving Australia and not coming back. To this end, the Royal Commission on the Moving Picture Industry of Australia was convened. It held its first sitting on June 2, 1927, and finally wrapped up on February 16, 1928.

The Commission had four terms of reference:

(a) the importation, production, distribution and exhibition of moving picture films;
(b) the incidence and effect of the Customs Tariff upon the importation of such films and the sufficiency or otherwise of existing duties of Customs;
(c) the sufficiency or otherwise of the existing income tax law of the Commonwealth in relation to persons, firms and companies engaged in the industry; and
(d) in connection with any or all the foregoing matters, the income, profits, expenditure and losses of such persons, firms and companies derived from, or incurred in connection with, the industry, and the amount of capital invested in the industry.

The Commission heard its first witness on June 2, 1927, and the last on February 16, 1928. In its 147 sitting days, the Commission also visited studios, laboratories, film sets, movie houses and theaters, sat through dozens of films and heard from 253 witnesses consisting of distributors, actors,[93] producers,[94] exhibitors, government officials, community groups, religious bodies and other interested parties.

Some, like Raymond Longford, took the opportunity to air their grievances. Others expressed a concern that the Australian film industry was failing, and yet others, such as Stuart Doyle and the Combine, attempted to convince the Commission that nothing was wrong and business as usual would be the best way to go.

Herc McIntyre took a broader view of censorship. He told the Commission that Universal had submitted 584 films to the censor from January 1926 to September 1927. Five hundred twenty-two were passed without cuts, 59 approved conditionally, two set aside for reconstruction and one rejected. When asked if Universal ever pressed for reviews, McIntyre was adamant that it was not worth the bother of asking for a review, nor was it worth the expense. It was cheaper, and simpler, to merely change the subtitles and make the small cuts asked.[95] Having said all of that, McIntyre was in favor of a full appeals board.

The following studios, although not all were making movies locally, but were distributing them, each sent a representative:

> Australasian Films Ltd.[96]
> British Dominions Films Proprietary Ltd.[97]
> Cinema Art Films Ltd.[98]
> Famous Lasky Film Service Ltd.[99]
> First National Pictures (Australasia) Ltd.[100]
> Fox Film Corporation (Australasia) Ltd.[101]
> Metro-Goldwyn-Mayer Ltd.[102]
> Mutual Film Exchange Proprietary Ltd.[103]
> United Artists (Australasia) Ltd.[104]
> Universal Film Manufacturing Company (Australasia) Ltd.[105]

Called before the commission on June 16, 1927, Longford claimed that he had been subject to many attacks by Australasian Films Ltd. and that the Combine was doing its best to crush the Australian film industry. The Combine had taken over the major filming studios located in Sydney and had flatly refused all of Longford's requests to film there, meaning he had to film in backyards and fields. He then outlined the failure of Longford-Lyell:

> My next effort was to float a public company termed the Longford-Lyell Australian Picture Productions Ltd. with a capitol of £50,000. The promoters (Miss Lottie Lyell, Raymond Longford and Stephen Perry) received 6000 fully paid shares—2000 each. The first year's schedule contemplated four pictures at a total cost of £20,000. The first production was *The Dinkum Bloke*, made at a cost of £4846. The picture was completed in November 1922. Of the total cost of production, the sum of £2147 was paid to the Combine for film, cameraman and studio. Despite this, the Combine refused to release the picture.[106]

Longford then related how it took seven months before *Dinkum Bloke* was released, through Hoyts, and how it grossed just over £300 in three days before being sold to the British market. The total profit to Longford-Lyell was £5831. The relative failure of the film prompted the Motion Picture Distributors Association to declare that it would not book any more Longford-Lyell films.

"The Longford-Lyell Company had apparently no desire to continue production," said Longford. "Their threat to close down meant a lot to my reputation and I was induced to surrender over 3000 fully paid-up shares without any payment or compensation of any kind. To further save the company's liquidation, I offered to produce a picture for the company at a cost of £2400."[107]

That picture was *Fisher's Ghost*. which Longford brought in well under budget and took it to Doyle to obtain a release in the Combine's theaters. Longford came up against Doyle, who was still smarting over Longford's public and private attacks. "After viewing the picture several times," Longford continued, "Mr. Doyle informed us that if he screened this picture in any of his theatres the public would walk out. His reason was that the picture was too gruesome, this even though the picture had been passed with any trouble or cutting by the State Censor."[108]

Doyle gave testimony on July 1, 1927, and flatly denied Longford's charges. When handed a list of Longford-Lyell films, Doyle stated that most were mediocre, and some he had never even heard of. As for *Fisher's Ghost,* Doyle, under oath, labeled Longford a liar. "We showed it everywhere except where Hoyts or other opposition showed it."[109]

Doyle didn't deny all the charges; instead he kept his answers non-committal. "I saw the picture, [and] I spoke with Mr. Longford.... I admit I said the picture was gruesome. I still say it is. I do not admit that I refused to release it. As a matter of fact, I released it in many theatres throughout Australia."[110] The Commission asked if Doyle booked the film for cities such as Melbourne and Adelaide due to its success in Sydney. Doyle refused to give a straight answer, instead sticking to his mantra: "The picture was booked for several theatres around Australia."

Doyle's evidence regarding *Fisher's Ghost* was full of contradictions, which angered Longford further. He appeared before the Royal Commission again on November 28 and stuck to his line: The Combine had refused to show *Fisher's Ghost* and Doyle was a liar. The film, even with its distribution issues, had been a success around the country. It was not gruesome, nor was it mediocre.

Although the Commission was established to look into the workings of the industry and the effects of importation, tariffs and control, censorship rapidly raised its head. It came as no surprise that horror films and their effect featured. Dr. Gertrude Halley's[111] professional opinion: "Night terrors are often the result of these children witnessing horror."

Other witnesses made a persuasive case for censorship and the need to prevent young people from seeing movies that might adversely affect them later in life. A clause, "six to 16," was subsequently adopted, which denoted that a film was unsuitable for audiences of that age. The age of six had been adopted to allow mothers to attend the cinema during the day without the need to arrange someone to look after their pre–school-age children. Other recommendations adopted included the mandatory appointment of a woman censor to each state censorship board and a classification of films deemed to be "Not Suitable for Children" which would cover the ages of ten to 14.

The Commission broke the report down into the following categories: Importation of Cinematograph Films, Film Censorship, Distribution of Films, Exhibitors and the Exhibition of Films, Film Production in Australia, The Quota System, The Cinema and the Community, The Film and Native Races, Children, Educational

Films, Financial Aspects, Taxation, British Films, Customs Duty, "Know Your Own Country" Series and Commonwealth and State Legislation.

Investigations led to some action being taken while sittings were happening, notably the Tax Office chasing Universal for unpaid taxes. But the real changes were to come.

The role of the censor, and the inherent flaws in the process, were singled out as being redundant. "Your commissioners consider that with the elimination of certain weaknesses which now exist in the censorship system, the necessity for the continuance of State Censorship Boards will pass away," the report said. To that end, 12 recommendations were made.

(1) That a Board of Film Censors be established, consisting of three persons, one of whom shall be a woman.

(2) That each Member of the Censorship Board view films independently, and that when in doubt, the particular film be referred to the full Board for inspection.

(3) That the remuneration to be paid to Members of the Censorship Board be such as will adequately cover the heavy responsibility which they will be called upon to bear.

(4) That the Members of the Censorship Board accept full responsibility for the censorship of all films.

(5) That the Censorship Board be invested with power to deal with the importation, production, exhibition and exportation of all motion picture films, and also all illustrated and advertising matter made without and within Australia which is to be used in connection with motion picture films.

(6) That more commodious accommodation be provided for the censorship office in Sydney, including at least three projection rooms and a room suitably fitted for the viewing of posters and advertising matter.

(7) That a Censorship Board of Appeal be created, consisting of five Members, one of whom shall be a woman; three to form a quorum.

(8) That, as it is desirable that changing and progressive opinion be adequately represented on the Appeal Board, the Chairman shall be appointed for five years, and the other Members for a period not exceeding three years.

(9) That the motion picture industry shall not have representation on the Appeal Board.

(10) That the Appeal Board be constituted:—

(a) To decide appeals made by importers, distributors or producers against rejections or cuts made by the censorship;

(b) To deal with requests for reviews from State Ministers;

(c) To grant relief from quota requirements;

(d) To make recommendations for awards of merit in connection with Australian film productions and scenarios;

(e) To carry out such other duties as may be prescribed.

(11) That the country of origin shall be marked and exhibited on all films.

(12) That, whilst your Commissioners recognize that the local distributing

companies representing the American producers have repeatedly made representations to America regarding the unsuitable nature of some of the films exported to Australia from that country, the practice, as revealed by the Censor's reports, nevertheless continues. Your Commissioners recommend, therefore, that it be enforced that any distributing firm which, during the course of one year, has 25 percent of its importations banned, shall be warned for the first offence, and for any subsequent offence may have its registration cancelled for such period as may be determined. Your Commissioners realize that the action which they propose is an indirect method of securing the object desired, viz., the prevention of the exportation to Australia of films of an objectionable or undesirable nature, but something drastic must be done to put an end to such practices. The producing exporters in the country of origin must be brought to realize that Australia will not permit the moral tone of its community to be in any way undermined by these low type films. They are sent here because it is profitable for the exporting companies to do so. To effectively end the practice, it must be made unprofitable. Your Commissioners cannot conceive of any more effective way than the method suggested. If these companies will not conform to our Australian standards, then they must be prevented from forcing upon the Australian public films which from any aspect are undesirable.

These recommendations were adopted and put into practice. They came into effect in January 1929 and remained the standard for 40 years.

A Silent Epilogue

The Royal Commission changed the cinema landscape of Australia, and the subsequent decades saw numerous changes, contradictions and business struggles for most who took part.

Although the Federal Censor oversaw what was coming in and made recommendations, cutting and banning films as required, the states kept their autonomy to cut and ban. This meant that a film that had been released for exhibition by the Federal Censor could be, and in some cases was, banned or cut by a state. This duplicity continued for the next decade, creating confusion when movies were banned from one state but on show in another.

Cresswell O'Reilly, the son of an American doctor, had risen through the ranks of the attorney general's department while maintaining a devout attendance at his local Methodist church where he was choirmaster, superintendent of the Sunday school and a lay preacher. It was this devotion, as much as his civil service, which saw the Methodist Church and the Young Men's Christian Association back O'Reilly in 1925 for the position of senior Commonwealth film censor. Most films entered Customs through the port of Sydney, and O'Reilly handled the bulk of the censoring work. He was unremitting, and even a little creative, in his moralizing zeal, immediately increasing the number of films being cut or banned. In one case, where a film depicted a couple living together before finally marrying, O'Reilly made it morally correct by shifting the marriage scene to the beginning. His de facto control of censorship was acknowledged in November 1928 when he took over from Wallace as chief Commonwealth censor.

Much to the disgust of the likes of Guthrie, O'Reilly was not going to play favorites when it came to British vs. American films. O'Reilly complained in 1929 of British films tending to depict "a particularly undesirable type of incident, namely, the hero and heroine spending the night together, sometimes after only a few hours acquaintance."

Despite his promotion, O'Reilly had come under fire from the Royal Commission itself: They claimed that a few undesirable films had managed to escape his critical scissors. The uncharacteristic laxity was attributed to the fact that O'Reilly was watching an average of 14 films a week, suggesting that this would make his sense of judgment less keen. Reminding O'Reilly that there were an estimated 1250 picture theaters in Australia with an annual audience of 110 million, many of them children, the commission claimed that the censor played a key role in molding the national character. It urged that he not allow "misspellings, Americanized spellings, or words offensive to Australians" in the subtitles of silent films, as well as enforce an even stricter regime for native races, whose imagination was capable of being "riotously aroused" by films which could "instill into their minds dangerous and sinister motives." The message for O'Reilly was clear: The moral guardians were intent on nurturing a pure, white society capable of holding the continent for posterity and standing in stark contrast to the decadence of Europe and the perceived mixed-race degeneracy of the United States.

In 1928, no less than 65 percent of all films imported into Australia were censored, or cut, by O'Reilly. Annoying him was the fact that the appeals board, led by Wallace, upheld 59 of the 114 appeals made against his cuts. Adding to his frustration, he was also hamstrung by legal limits on his power. He could not censor Australian-produced films nor could he, except in Victoria, classify films to prevent children seeing adult films. This left him in the position of censoring adult films in the knowledge that "a very large proportion of picture audiences are young people," explaining his vigor when cutting depictions of "crime and the more sordid phases of life," particularly the "frequent exhibition of certain phases of marriage, sex desire and passion."

O'Reilly's standards had their contradictions, as one angry film importer pointed out in May 1930 with the banning of the early British talkie *White Cargo* on grounds of its immoral script. He refused to lift the ban in mid–1930, despite a stage production of *White Cargo* featuring the same dialogue, running in Sydney. It would not be the last time that one of O'Reilly's bans would vex and confuse the public and exhibitors alike.

Another question one might ask is, why did Australia stop making horror films?

It was not as if horror in Australia was a massive genre to begin with. Australian-made movies were mostly about Australian tales, both fact and fiction. Bushrangers, classic stories such as *For the Term of His Natural Life* and *On Our Selection* were known to every Australian in the early part of the 20th century. There simply were not any horror stories, other than *Fisher's Ghost*, to speak of. When such a story arose, as with the Guyra haunting in 1921, it was either dismissed as a hoax or quickly made into a movie.[112] Even legends that could have been considered horror, Min-Min lights or Bunyips, to use two Australian examples, were ignored. Australians just did not have the capacity to make a decent horror film, nor did they have the desire. Even when they tried, the addition of comedy (*Guyra Ghost*, 1921), romance (*Fisher's Ghost*), guilt and redemption (*The Hordern Mystery*, 1920), crime (*The Face at the Window*, 1919) or the classic damsel in distress (*The Strangler's Grip*, 1912) were seen as essential elements to keep audiences interested. As was pointed out at the time, even the great horrors, such as *The Phantom of the Opera* and *The Hunchback of Notre Dame*, had romantic overtones.

When it came to literature, true horror came via works published by Europeans and Britons such as Mary Shelley, John Polidori, H.G. Wells, Robert Louis Stevenson, Oscar Wilde, Bram Stoker and Victor Hugo, or the Americans Ambrose Bierce, Edgar Allan Poe, Henry James, Washington Irving and their contemporaries. Australian authors, again, chose to write about Australian life, injustice and the ruggedness and harshness of the land, and not horror. It would not be until well into the 20th century before horror became a valid genre for Australian novelists.

But Australians loved a good horror movie, and a scary film was always guaranteed to do good business, even if only for a week or so before it made the rounds in the country. Imported horror was far more accessible than domestically made horror and after the Longford-Lyell experience with the Combine, producers turned away from the genre, and the flood of American- and British-made movies, often with better production values, and the overall decline of the Australian film industry, meant that movies made locally would be more Australian in tone, in safer genres. Action, romance and drama became the norm and, outside of one pseudo horror in the form of *The Haunted Barn* (1931), no true horror would be made until *Night of Fear* in 1973.

Advertising also played a large part in the demise of Australian horror films. The producers of Australian content simply could not compete with the large budgets of the American companies. A film such as *Fisher's Ghost* was promoted with simplistic advertisements, as opposed to *Hunchback of Notre Dame* (in cinemas at the same time), which was promoted with full-page color advertisements, breathless text, photos and testimonials from famous people. At a time when studios were fighting for public money and attendance, promotion was the key. Many fine movies slipped through the cracks due to limited cinema runs or poor promotion.

Star power and distribution also ranked high. As Louise Lovely discovered when she returned to Australia to find that Lon Chaney now outstripped her in popularity, the biggest names at the cinemas were American, or Britons based in America. A movie starring Chaney or Charlie Chaplin could make more in a week than most Australian movies could make in a year. Exhibitors and theater managers, when faced with taking on an American production or an Australian one, would take the former.

The Combine also played their part in the downfall of horror. Seeing the issues that Longford-Lyell had with *Fisher's Ghost* would have been enough to cause any

The Lost World. Detail image of the cover for *Everyone's*, August 12, 1925.

filmmaker to pause and consider their subject matter. The Depression was beginning as the 1930s came around, and losing money needlessly was something to be avoided. It simply was not worth the trouble to attempt to fight the Combine.

In 1929, Doyle formed the Australian Broadcasting Company, which was later taken over by the Australian government and re-titled the Australian Broadcasting Commission (it's still active today). Doyle flaunted his wealth often. In 1925, he bought a custom 44-foot luxury yacht, *Mirimar*, which caught fire at its moorings at Rose Bay and sank. Doyle collected £5000 for the loss and quickly purchased a new 75-foot yacht, also christened the *Mirimar*, in 1929.

Union Theatres, faced with massive debts to producers and the government, was forced into liquidation in 1931. A simple thing like bankruptcy did not stop Doyle; he simply formed a new company, called Greater Union Theatres Ltd., and bought up all the Union Theatres assets as soon as the liquidator offered them for tender paying £400,000, which just happened to be the amount of the new company's overdraft. Greater Union then dumped Australasian Films and moved into radio, newspaper and direct importation of films. After two years of competing, Hoyts gave up and were forced into a merger with Greater Union. The Royal Commission had been bent on cutting back the power over Australian cinema, but within five years, Stuart Doyle and Greater Union had more of a stranglehold than ever.

In 1936, under increasing pressure from the board of Greater Union, Doyle traveled overseas in search of capital. Upon his return, in 1937, Doyle was voted out of his empire, replaced by Sir Norman Rydge. The Royal Australian Navy even took the *Mirimar* from him and pressed it into service during World War II.

Doyle suffered a heart attack at his home on October 20, 1945. He died, a rich man, but not as wealthy as people thought. His estate was valued at £69,002.[113] All his fights had left their mark.

The end of the silent era marked a fundamental change: Drama, comedy and romance were what Australians wanted from their local industry, along with relevance. Horror was done better by foreign studios that had access to better-known source material and there were plenty more to come. None of them was filmed in Australia, but some had a definite Australian flavor and connection to them.

3

The Golden Age: 1930–1948

The 1930s started what is widely regarded as the Golden Age of Hollywood and a large part of it was the introduction of sound.

Filmmakers had been experimenting with sound since the 1890s but it was not until the 1920s that technology advanced to include "sound on disc." This was followed by "sound-on-film" which allowed for true synchronized soundtracks. By 1929, sound systems were being deployed in cinemas. The first talkie released to the Australian public was *The Jazz Singer* (U.S., 1927). It premiered in mid–December 1929 at the Lyceum in Sydney and faced competition from *The Red Dance* (U.S., 1928), another early talkie, showing at the nearby Regent. Both films became success stories, taking in a record-breaking £8500 in a single week, on an average ticket price of three shillings.[1] Not since the introduction of cinema in theaters in 1897 had so much money been taken at the box office of only two cinemas, and only two films.

In the capital cities, the profits more than justified the expense of installing sound equipment, but in the suburbs and rural areas, it was a different story. Exhibitors faced the considerable expense of having to wire every theater and, in rural areas, town halls and community halls, to accommodate sound that would not necessarily increase profits, no matter what they showed.

In 1930, Jim Scullin became the first Australian prime minister to record a speech on film. An Australian company, Standardtone, developed a sound-on-film system good enough to make a movie with; *Showgirls Luck* (1932. Dir. Norman Dawn). Arthur Smith at Cinesound, Sydney, developed a rival system based on the theory that sound could be recorded onto the film itself, as would become the norm. The first Cinesound film, *On Our Selection,* was released in 1932.

Other companies, such as Raycophone, Markophone, Auditone and Australtone, vied for contracts to make sound film and to wire theaters, resulting in what became known as the Talkie Wars. The expense in wiring a theater was anywhere from £600 to £2500, and the equipment, once installed, was provided on a hire basis. The expense did not deter most cinema chains and quickly became the norm, although silent films were still screened at cinemas well into the 1930s.

Sound appeared in the wake of the 1927 Royal Commission and created new difficulties alongside the stricter censorship regulations. In 1929 alone, the chief censor estimated that over 100,000 separate pieces of posters, lobby cards, stills and press sheets had been seen by their office.

Cresswell O'Reilly's first saw, and heard, a "talkie" on Christmas Eve 1928, sitting in a commercial cinema borrowed for the purpose due to the lack of sound facilities at his Bligh Street office. He was not impressed. In his report to the Customs minister in 1929, he bemoaned the loss of the desirable characteristics of the silent picture with its eloquent and vital silence. Worse than that, sound made the American culture of crime and vice, complete with American accent, "excruciating to an English ear."[2] There was also the belief that Australians would not understand Americans and vice versa, whereas pantomime was universal.

The 1930s also saw more censorship power delegated to the states, increasing confusion, and the introduction of a new classification system. Locally produced and printed advertising did not fall under Commonwealth regulations, and if a distributor thought an advertisement might fall prey to censorship, they would have a local artist redraw it for the state in question and use it there alone. It was a practice that did not always work but proved simpler than one product for all of Australia.

The new rules of classification called for the term, "Suitable for General Exhibition," to be added to any and all advertisements for movies passed by the censor. A film classified as "Restricted" (later to be abbreviated to an "R" rating) could not be shown under any circumstances to children. The classifications had to be made clear in all forms of film advertising, and penalties could be handed down for breaches. These changes came into effect on June 1, 1930.

Archibald Wallace resigned as the appeal censor in January 1930, and the Labor government appointed a new appeal board headed by English literature professor and poet, John Le Gay Brereton. Also on the board was Mary Gilmore, the renowned writer and social reformer. O'Reilly was apoplectic, as the new appeal board passed many of the films that he wanted banned. The states would often reinstate those bans, rendering the new appeal board toothless. The appeal board was disbanded in December 1931, replaced by a single appeal censor, Brigadier-General Ivor Mackay. Mackay was appointed by the new conservative prime minister, "Honest" Joe Lyons, and was expected to share and enforce O'Reilly's conservative, often right-wing social propriety. Unfortunately for O'Reilly, the number of appeals upheld remained high.

Cinema in the 1930s had a number of obstacles such as the Great Depression. At its peak, the country experienced 30 percent unemployment rate, the highest in the world other than Germany, generating poverty on a massive scale. Cinema suffered, experiencing a drop of 40 percent of patrons in 1932. Costs were cut and jobs were slashed, except for one company: Universal.

Under Herc McIntyre's management, and often against the direct orders of the Laemmle family, McIntyre not only refused to lay people off, but increased wages where he could. He invested in local films, often arranging financing and distribution out of his own pocket. And, in a move that went against most practices as the Depression heightened, he directed a significant percentage of his own commission back to his employees to establish a provident fund to assist them when they left the company. Within ten years, the fund held more than £200,000 for use for retiring staff. He also established financial incentives for hard-working employees.

The Golden Age of cinema in Australia established, under the guidance of Herb McIntyre, spectacle marketing as a mainstay in the industry for the following decades. It was this and McIntyre's investment in people, which would see Universal not only survive the Great Depression in Australia but thrive.

Commonplace since 1914 (*Lucille Love, Girl of Mystery*), movie serials were western, mystery, or military shorts with cliffhangers. The serial concept was to take a narrative and break it down to ten- to 15-minute episodes, with each having its own ending showing the hero or heroine facing death or in an impossible situation. The opening of the following week's episode would show them extracting themselves from certain death or injury with ease, and then on with the story. Wash, spin, rinse and repeat until the end of the series where the hero gets the girl and the villain is either dead, defeated or vanquished, never to be seen again … until the next series.

Serials were aimed at children, as nobody expected a child to sit through a dramatic movie that ran for 90 minutes, or even an hour, let alone some of the epics that were being made as the 1920s rolled on. The serial filled that gap, and several serials could be packaged together or with cartoons to make a full program—if it kept the children's attention. Popular serials were also re-edited and repackaged for adults providing further box office receipts. This was an inventive way of double-dipping that served the studios well.

None of the many hundreds of serials from *Arsène Lupin Contra Sherlock Holmes* (Deutsche Vitaskop GmbH, 1910) to *Blazing the Overland Trail* (Columbia, 1956) were horrors. In the 1930s and '40s, Universal released crossovers in casts, usage of stock footage from "proper" horror films, equipment, concepts and even music. Over time, the concepts evolved, production values increased, and the actors often gave better performances than the earlier, moustache-twirling villains. Some serials are now considered superior to most B movies produced during the period and their popularity, especially the science fiction entries such as *Flash Gordon*, influenced generations of young people, including George Lucas and Steven Spielberg, who became filmmakers.

The Ace of Scotland Yard (1929) was initially a silent project but as sound became the norm in Australia, Universal recognized it would be obsolete by the time the physical copies arrived there. A sound version, prepared at the same time, arrived in Australia in early 1930. Much amusement was made of the perception that Americans had no idea about England, let alone Scotland. Although the serial clearly stated that the Ace was from Scotland Yard, the hero was actually "Scotland's master detective." This was a howler for reporters, who were extremely keen to point out that Scotland Yard was, in fact, in England and not in Scotland. Further amusement arose at Craufurd Kent, the lead actor, with more than one newspaper asking why his name was misspelled.

Many cinemas ran competitions and giveaways to entice children to see it. One of the best: In the Victorian town of Traralgon, the manager of the one and only cinema cooked up the idea of giving a season pass to the first boy and girl who could identify the "Ace" of Scotland Yard and the "Queen of Diamonds," informing the children that two people would be walking down the main street, at random, on a certain day.

Bedlam ensued. Traralgon's main street was nearly shut down as children took it over and asked everyone they saw the required questions. Most people had no idea what was going on and either denied the charge or in deciding to play along. They were further puzzled when the children demanded movie tickets. Eventually the "Ace" and "Diamond" were found, and two lucky children had their prized passes.[3]

The reviews were positive and the serial remained in circulation until late 1933. This serial also went by the title *Blake, the Ace of Scotland Yard* in Australia. Also released in 1930 were *Tarzan the Tiger* (1929), released in October, and *The Jade Box* (1930) in November 1930.

In New South Wales, a promotion for *Tarzan* offered a deluxe trip to Hobart, Tasmania. The Civic chain issued a card for each of the 15 episodes with a letter of the alphabet to everyone who bought a ticket. At the end of the promotion, the first person able to make the title of a movie out of their letters won the following (complete with original spelling and grammar): "The successful competitor will be given a free trip to Tasmania, first class. In the T.S.A. Zealandia, a week in Hobart with all expenses paid, and £5 pocket money. Also, the winner can take a parent or chaperon with him or her, whose expenses will also be paid for the trip and the week in Hobart. There will also be 60 consolation prizes."[4] The Regent chain offered free sweets and "pocket money" prizes for children and put on a show that appealed to all, with *Tarzan* being supported by a live revue, comedies and cartoons.

In Melbourne and Adelaide, competition prizes were watches and *Tarzan the Tiger* badges, leaflets and sweets. To get the watch, a person needed to attend every serial episode, collect all the badges, and exchange them for the watch. In Queensland the children who assembled all the badges were then allowed to watch the last episode of the serial free of charge.

For *The Jade Box,* Melbourne cinemas gave each child a small jade box bearing a letter. Every session had an associated box and the person who managed to get the full set, which spelled "The Jade Box," won a prize.

All these promotions meant that the serials did a roaring trade. Reviews confirmed packed houses; *Tarzan* proved extremely popular. Both serials ran well into 1933.

Another factor in the rise of popularity in Australia was when the audience had an Australian to follow such as John P. McGowan in *A Lass of the Lumberlands* (1916), his wife Helen Holmes in *The Hazards of Helen* (1914–15) and Jack Lloyd in *Detective Lloyd* (1932).

Ingagi and Casey the Chimp

Australia had a fascination for simians, in part due to their relative newness to the country, having been first imported in the mid–1800s. For years leading up to, and into the early part of, the 20th century, the only way a lot of the population would have been able to see a monkey would be via illustrations in books and, if they were lucky, seeing captive spider-monkeys and small apes in zoos. The first chimpanzee displayed in Australia was Casey, exhibited in 1909 as living proof of Darwin's theory of evolution. Casey, and his antics, drew huge crowds wherever he appeared.

Casey had an interesting life. His owner toured him around Australia attempting to sell him, to no avail. Contemporary advertisements promoted Casey as being the Missing Link, which no doubt excited many people, as did the claim by his owner, Ellis Joseph, that Casey was as educated as the average human. Casey was billed as being able to play piano, shake hands, play with children, wind a watch, sign his name, smoke and drink alcohol.

In 1914, Casey attempted to escape his handler in what could have easily been the plot of a gorilla movie. He broke away, climbed to the roof of a house and waited for people to arrive. He then leapt down into the crowd (causing one woman to die of fright) before running and leaping over fences and through trees, evading the public and police until he was shot and wounded. Even then he mauled his captors, causing serious wounds. Casey was taken to America and sold to the Sells-Floto Circus. He passed away from appendicitis in May 1922.

Films such as *Tarzan* were exotic, showing apes, gorillas and big cats, all to audiences that were used to kangaroos, emus, dingoes and kolas. Pre–*King Kong* movies such as *Lorraine of the Lions*, *The Escape of the Ape*, *The Gorilla*, *The Gorilla Hunt* and the various Tarzan movies capitalized on this interest to remarkable success in Australia.

One notable exception was the precursor to *King Kong*, 1930's *Ingagi*. Presented as an "authentic incontestable celluloid document," the film strongly hinted at interspecies sex, showing a gorilla carrying off a woman to be his mate. Considered shocking, the film was exposed as being a fraud.[5] Arriving in Australia in 1931, it was banned by the censor, more due to the fraud than the content.

In December 1931, the title appeared on a list of movies slated for release in Western Australia (billed as *Ingagi the Gorilla*), but this list was assembled before the censor had screened it. Another reference to *Ingagi* can be found on the register of films deemed Unsuitable for Native Races published in the last quarter of 1931.

Dracula

Dracula was the movie that began the Golden Age of horror film. It was the first major horror talkie released by a studio, even if it did have lengthy periods of silence. The movie made an international star out of its lead, Bela Lugosi, and it became director Tod Browning's most viewed and best-known film (although not his best film) in a career that spanned both the silent and sound era.

By 1931, Australians were primed for a movie version of *Dracula*, coming on the back of a 1929 tour of the stage play. (That play's biggest drawcard, actor Nat

Madison, bolted for America as soon as the *Dracula* run ended, ensuring that it never played New Zealand or returned to Australia for an encore season.) Lon Chaney's *London After Midnight* was still in cinemas well into the 1930s, and the Bram Stoker novel *Dracula* had become a perennial best seller. All of this built anticipation for new versions of Australia's favorite spooks.

The most famous of the silent vampire films, *Nosferatu,* was not officially released in Australia until the 1970s. The movie, a thinly disguised adaptation of *Dracula,* was subject to a legal injunction for copyright infringement by Stoker's widow, which restricted the importation into Australia. Pirate copies were screened, but not widely advertised.

In December 1930, news of Browning's selection as *Dracula*'s director had been published but it took four more months for the casting of "The Distinguished Hungarian Actor" Bela Lugosi to be announced. Lugosi had been garnering positive notices and reviews as early as 1923 when he appeared in *The Silent Command* and was already known for his Broadway stage role as Dracula. While not exactly a household name in Australia, he was hardly an unknown.

There was concern regarding how the film would be received, as a few weeks earlier, the mystery film *Murder by the Clock* failed dismally, being removed from all advertising after a day due to bad reviews and adverse publicity. For *Dracula* to succeed, it would need to go beyond the usual print ads, posters and general stunts to entice the public. Universal was widely regarded as a producer of B-features, and the industry magazine *Everyone's* ranked them seventh regarding quality, far behind United Artists, M.G., Greater Australia, MGM, Paramount, Warners and Fox. The ratings were graded by performance at the Australian box office for 1930. No Universal film was rated as "Big," and only two features reached "Excellent." Knowing that *Dracula* had done so well in America, Herc McIntyre pulled out all stops to promote the film in Australia.

Dracula premiered in late June 1931, paired with a documentary about Native Americans called *The Silent Enemy.* Amazingly, the censors, both Federal and State, left the movie alone, content with the cuts that Universal had already made in America. Although the film contained some moments of genuine suspense, it was less horrific than its stage counterpart, which, in Australia at least, featured an inhuman-looking Dracula and used volume, lighting and special effects to crude but powerful effect.

Reviews of the movie were positive, with one surprising exception. Dwight Frye, playing the madman Renfield, got rave reviews in other parts of the world, but in Australia, he was often compared, unfavorably, to Nat Madison, his counterpart from the 1929 stage tour. The tone of those comparisons was that while Frye was good in the role, Madison, whom Australian audiences still loved dearly, happened to be great. It mattered not what the reviewers said of this performance, the advertising and publicity was strong enough to ensure people flocked to the cinemas.

Window displays, giant posters, larger-than-life cardboard cut-outs of Lugosi about to bite Helen Chandler, rubber bats and paper spiders hanging from fake spiderwebs were all utilized in cinema foyers. A 60-foot sign was posted at the

Melbourne Treasury Building and trams were plastered. These and many other inspired marketing tactics ensured that the public knew Dracula was coming.

Many print ads focused on Lugosi's smoldering looks and the gothic romantic overtones of the movie. The taglines "The Kiss No Woman Could Resist," "He Lived on the Kisses of Youth" and "The Strangest Passion Ever Known," helped along by images of Lugosi in profile hovering over a sleeping Helen Chandler, about to ravish her, had young women lining up in droves.

In South Australia, West's Olympia cinema took publicity one step further, taking out a £1000 insurance policy, payable to the next of kin, for anyone proven to have died of heart failure because of seeing the move, reminiscent of the 1929 stage tour. This was one of the first times such a ploy was used for a film in Australia, but it would not be the last. There is no account of anyone claiming the money. On opening night, a coffin, with the name "Dracula" painted on its side, was carried through the streets of Adelaide, making its way to Wests where it was laid in the foyer. Sadly, nobody got out.

Other promotions included the issuing of an envelope at Victorian Football League games in Melbourne containing a sprig of herb labeled "Wolfsbane." This trick was also used in Adelaide, only at the Fourth Test (cricket) between Australia and England at Adelaide Oval. Inside each envelope was a note inviting people to bring the herbs with them when they saw the film, to keep the vampires at bay.

By February 1932, in the middle of a heat wave, the film did a roaring business in Sydney. A man dressed in a cape and top

Advertisement for Bela Lugosi's *Dracula* (1931).

hat, with the name "Dracula" printed on the cape, climbed onto the roof of the Capitol cinema and remained there until removed by the police. Their most spectacular device was placing an image of Lugosi's face onto a spotlight and projecting it, which meant for a brief time the face of Lugosi was visible to anyone in Sydney as his visage floated on the clouds. The film outperformed everything else in its first week at the box office, grossing an incredible £3350. Next-best ticket-wise that week was a double bill of Ruth Chatterton's *Once a Lady* and the Richard Arlen football film *Touchdown,* which brought in £1900.

McIntyre's gamble paid off handsomely as *Dracula* was labeled a "Big" film by *Everyone's*,[6] proving to him, and Universal, that Australia was more than ready for horror films. The issues surrounding *Murder by the Clock* were forgotten, and in April 1932, McIntyre began to build hype for the forthcoming *Frankenstein*.

Dracula had an exceptionally long life in Australia, being shown at cinemas (city *and* rural) and drive-ins well into the 1980s. It also a resurgence of popularity when it became the first of the Universal Horrors to be screen on television in Australia in 1973. The popularity of the movie, and the vampire films that came after it, proved to be the death knell of the stage production. Film could show more of the story of *Dracula* than the stage could, and it would take decades before the public could accept anyone other than Lugosi as the King of Vampires.

Films Unsuitable for Native Races

In October 1931, a new form of censorship was advocated, "Cinematograph Films unsuitable & suitable for exhibition to Native Races," to protect native races from seeing any form of cinema that might lead them towards violence or having adverse feelings towards whites. These controls on what Aboriginal people could and couldn't see were recommend by the 1927 Royal Commission, which stated, "[N]o moving picture film shall be screened before audiences of aboriginals or natives of the Mandated Territories unless such film has been passed by the Censorship Board as suitable for such exhibition." Policing came directly from the Office of the Chief Protector of Aboriginals in the Northern Territory and South Australia, Cecil Evelyn Aufrere Cook. Although Cook argued to allow Aboriginals to be treated in mainstream hospitals and protected full-blood Aboriginals where possible, he was also a white supremacist who passionately believed in the White Australia policy and often argued for breeding the Aboriginal race out.

The classification was intended to "ensure a stricter classification of films portraying conflict between white and colored races," and would be controlled by a quarterly list of films that were unsuitable to be shown to Aboriginals in the Northern Territory only. The result saw a high number of Universal films banned in Darwin under the guise of containing stories or scenes "likely to influence the Aboriginal towards conflict with the white race."[7] Amongst the Universal films were several classic horror movies, including *Frankenstein, Murders in the Rue Morgue, The Old Dark House, The Mummy, Bride of Frankenstein* and *The Invisible Ray*. From other companies came *Dr. Jekyll and Mr. Hyde* (which won Fredric March an Oscar), *Angels with Dirty Faces* (Cagney and Bogart), *Strange Cargo, Invisible Ghost, Tobacco Road* and *The Lost Patrol* (featuring one of Karloff's best performances) and more. It would take decades before those films, and hundreds more, could be shown before Aboriginal people in Darwin cinemas. Oddly, despite the banning of *The Mummy*, the Chief Censor allowed the Karloff movie *The Ghoul*, made in Britain yet a virtual carbon copy of *The Mummy*, to be passed through unscathed. So did Karloff's RKO film *Bedlam*, which attracted the attention of censors in both England and America.

This new form of censorship was limited to the open-air cinemas in Darwin, as Aboriginals were rarely allowed into cinemas in the more "civilized" capital cities of Sydney, Melbourne, Brisbane and so forth, even if they wanted to attend. Leading into 1931, Darwin theaters showed silent pictures only. When the cinema owners moved to exhibit sound film, along came a new set of issues.

Cinema in Darwin was unusual to say the least due to the climate and isolation, and the diversity of the audience raised its own unique set of issues. Most were outdoor, open-air theaters, and all were strictly and unashamedly segregated. As a rule, the best seats, in the dress circle, were white only. The downstairs section was then split into two with the front section for Aboriginal people and native races while the rear was reserved for Asian races.[8] In the few cinemas with no dress circle, a section was set apart for the exclusive use of whites. Issues had been identified as far back as the late 1920s, and complaints had grown through the 1930s. Initially some station owners prevented their staff of Aboriginals and Asians from attending the cinema due to the adverse effects that movies such as Valentino's *The Sheik* had upon them.[9] The introduction of sound into these cinemas saw an upsurge of Aboriginals and Asians coming to the cinema. Keeping with the White Australia policy, the Federal government decided that action needed to be taken to protect all cinema-goers from any issue that might arise.

F.W. Thring and the Ersatz Horror Film: *The Haunted Barn*

Frank Thring, better known as F.W. Thring, was a former boot maker turned magician. Thring is believed to have entered the film industry in 1911 when he formed Biograph Pictures (no relation or attachment with the American company) in Tasmania; it promptly went broke. Thring gained employment as a projectionist and moved up the ladder until he was a managing director at J.C. Williamsons, the country's biggest entertainment company. He then became a partner in the Hoyts chain, before selling out to Fox and forming his own company in 1931, Efftee Films.

Efftee was based in Melbourne and Thring promised that he would make movies in Australia, using Australian talent and for Australians. The first two movies were announced while they were in production: *The Haunted Barn* and a potboiler called *Diggers* (Australia's first talking picture). Both were to be made at the same time with Thring overseeing them, often running from set to set. *The Haunted Barn* was always intended to be a short, running under 45 minutes, and it would serve as the opener for *Diggers*.

Thring hired His Majesty's Theatre, located on Exhibition Street, Melbourne, and filmed all of *The Haunted Barn* on one set, giving it the appearance of being a filmed play. Directing the movie was one E.A. Diettrich-Derrick, a European who claimed to have Hollywood credits. He was so inept, and so unpopular with the cast and crew, that the overall direction was taken over Australian stage veteran Gregan McMahon. McMahon was the opposite of Diettrich-Derrick when it came to directing, preferring to delve into the intellectual side of the script and coaxing the best performance possible from his actors. Diettrich-Derrick kept his focus on the action and on trying to get the women as naked as he could get them.

Actors on the set remembered Diettrich-Derrick well, with Patricia Minchin later telling Thring biographer Peter Fitzpatrick,

> Derrick Dietrich or Dietrich Derrick or whatever his wretched name was—he was a silly little fellow. He ran about like a little mouse, you know, or a little person flipping and flopping about, and all the time we thought he did not know what he was doing. We did not like him because he used to keep approaching us. He was the naughty one who kept asking us to get undressed! I have no idea where he came from, Dietrich-Derrick sounds like a very got-up name to my mind, it doesn't sound real, and I think he was posing, I always did think so.[10]

Thring soon realized that he had been duped, often getting agitated while watching the movie being made. Retakes were carried out as Thring ordered them. With two directors, an unhappy producer and actors worried about the legitimacy of the main director's qualifications (and his habit of wanting them undressed), the fact that the movie was finished is amazing.

Film historian Ina Bertram later summarized the film:

> Mr. Moon intends to spend the night in a barn hoping to see the ghost of the bushranger Sturdy who died there when betrayed to the police by his friend Rogan. Already in the barn are two tramps, one of whom is dumb, who have sheltered from the rain, and a strange wild-looking man who repeatedly threatens their lives. They are joined by Ralph and Joan, a young couple eloping and fearful of reprisals from Joan's father. Rose enters with a gun and then leaves after demanding that no-one leaves till dawn, and later a man burst [sic] in with the news that lunatics have escaped from the local asylum and ten pounds per head is offered for their capture. While all are asleep, a body appears on the floor which all (particularly Mr. Moon) are convinced is Sturdy's ghost when it mysteriously disappears again. In the morning, Rose, Sturdy and Rogan confront each other, and Sturdy explains he was not seeking to kill Rogan but to get his permission to marry Rose (who is Sturdy's sister) and thereby end the family feud. Rogan admits to being the body, having fallen from the loft while hiding from Sturdy. Dr. Glass arrives to claim Ralph and Joan are the lunatics, and Mr. Moon's two friends arrive and explain that they hired an actor to act wildly and provide the exciting ghost that Moon had hoped to find. The two tramps are left by themselves with momentary dreams of wealth till they open Ralph's wallet and find it is stuffed with newspaper.[11]

All the action happens on a single stage set, a barn, and it is all over in 40 minutes. If it sounds like a stage play that was filmed, that is because, for all intents and purposes, it was just that. As a horror film it is not scary and as a comedy it's just not funny. It is a film that doesn't know what it wants to be, so it ended up being nothing.

The movie was as finished as it would ever be and ready for release when, on September 24, 1931, the State Censor for Victoria stepped in and slapped a ban on it. The reasons were simple: A classification had been placed upon the movie preventing any child between the ages of six and 16 from seeing it—not for content as much as an unacceptable title and the fact that the sound of wind that relentlessly ran through the film would frighten children.

Thring, a student of literature, readily subscribed to Oscar Wilde's theory; "There is only one thing in life worse than being talked about, and that is not being talked about," and he set about creating his very own storm in a teacup. He went on the offensive on the 25th in newspapers and industry magazines, screaming unfairness and wailing at the lack of natural justice, all the time knowing that he could, and indeed had already, appealed the rating. The Censor was bemused and insisted that it was not unfair. When this was pointed out to Thring, he upped the stakes, cried foul and insisted that unless his movie was unbanned, he would cease making films and move his operations to London.

The media had barely enough time to report this before the ban was lifted on the 26th. The campaign was a success and *The Haunted Barn* made back its production costs upon release. As a true horror film, it was as tame as it gets, and marked the last film made in Australia classified as a horror until the 1970s. As far as Australian filmmakers were concerned, English and American product were far superior to what could be made locally and, as bans were coming into effect, it was easier to avoid the problems.

Frankenstein

The Haunted Barn amused people, but *Frankenstein* terrified its audiences.

The first mention of the film version of *Frankenstein* came via a two-line notice that appeared in various *Literary Notes* sections of newspapers in April 1930. The notice simple read, "A talking film is being made of Mrs. Mary Shelley's gruesome story, *Frankenstein*."[12] This announcement is important as it came a full year prior to Universal Studios purchasing the rights to the novel in April 1931.

Late in 1931, another story appeared in newspapers across the country stating that Bela Lugosi had been cast in the movie *and* was in the process of shooting it. The movie promised that Lugosi, hot off the success of *Dracula,* was the logical successor to the late Lon Chaney, and that Lugosi would appear on screen as an "eight-foot monster without sentiment": "[O]nly his chin and eyebrows are to show on the screen."[13] History now tells us that this announcement appeared when filming on the movie had almost finished with Boris Karloff in the role of the Monster.

Karloff was known as a supporting actor and had gained publicity in the same manner as many English and Australian actors in Hollywood had, his Anglo heritage singling him out. Amusingly, his first recorded credit in *Everyone's* saw him referred to "Karloff Boris."[14]

Fresh off the successful campaign for *Dracula*, McIntyre went all in for *Frankenstein*. Even after *Dracula*'s box office success, Universal was still rated below other studios, again finishing seventh in *Everyone's* ratings for 1931. McIntyre was determined to improve this standing, earmarking Frankenstein as the film that would do it, and had his publicity team think up some bold new stunts.

Frankenstein opened at the Mayfair Theatre in New York on December 4, 1931, and trade advertisements announcing its impending release began to appear across Australia in February 1932.[15] It had its Australasian premiere on April 9 at the Prince of Wales Theatre, Hobart, Tasmania, an apt location as it was the city where the first *Frankenstein* play premiered in Australia.

Tickets went on sale at ten a.m. Saturday morning and completely sold out by noon. Large lines formed around the cinema in the evening as people gathered in the hope that others would fail to collect their tickets and they would be put back on general sale. When it became obvious that this was not going to happen, people stormed the theater lobby and waited there for cancellations. Police had to step in to clear the theater and move people down the streets.

The next day saw more frantic scenes as the theater geared up for *Frankenstein*'s first midday screening. An estimated 500 people were turned away and police again called to disperse the crowds.[16] Similar scenes happened when the film opened at the Princess Theatre in Launceston, Tasmania, where a riot almost broke out in the rush for tickets.

In the two weeks that the film was screening in Tasmania, it become Universal's highest grossing movie for the year.[17]

As was the way in the early part of the 1930s, the movie slowly made its way across the country, playing to packed houses as it went. It arrived in Sydney on Friday the 13th of May 1932 to much fanfare. A team of 15 men brandishing notices advertising the film and walking dogs on chains were set loose through Sydney on the pretense of hunting the Monster.

A fake newspaper was prepared and given away on the streets, with a headline claiming the Monster was on the loose and being sought. Giant posters and cut-outs of Karloff were everywhere. Tall men dressed as the Monster walked the streets and menaced anyone that came near them.

For a moment it was thought that the film would be banned by the NSW censor, but an unlikely savior emerged in the form of Reverend N. Goss. He applied for, and was granted, a license to show the movie at the Croydon Congregational Church for its parishioners., coinciding with a sermon delivered by Goss, the details of which were widely covered by the press.

"*Frankenstein* is a gruesome picture," he said. "Henry Frankenstein, dissatisfied with conventional science, sets out to build a man with his own hands and endow with life. He stole bodies from graves and gallows." The Reverend then confirmed, in his statements, that the movie was indeed being shown in Australia uncut. "At length the thrilling moment arrives when his handmade man, lives. 'It's alive,' he shrieks. 'Now I know what it feels like to be God.' The Monster does the most inhuman things but is utterly unconscious that they are fearful. He kills, and yet is not cruel—to kill is the natural expression of his nature. He throws daisies into water, and because he has no more to throw, he throws an innocent and lovely child into the lake to drown."[18]

The sermon was an illustration of what a man without God would be like.

Playing under the Restricted classification (with all advertisements clearly stating it was suitable for adults only), the version that toured Australia was the uncut original and included scenes and dialogue that had been previously excised in other countries, including America. Trade ads made mention of the fact that the first person to "die during a screening of *Frankenstein*" was insured by Lloyds of London for £1000, payable to the next of kin.

Not every idea for promotion was accepted. Frank Thatcher, who oversaw exploitation for Universal, tried his best to get the Sydney morgue interested in a "Monster Frankenstein Day." His idea was to pose dead bodies, with a local made up as the Monster looming over them complete with a Frankenstein poster. Citing privacy reasons and general good taste, the morgue turned him down. Not to be deterred, Thatcher then approached several crematoriums and abattoirs, with the same results.[19]

In clashes that had never been seen before for a horror film, moviegoers fought with each other for the right to see the movie as early as possible. Police were called in to control the crowds when they threatened to surge forward and break the windows at the Capitol.[20]

In a unique, and stunningly effective stunt, the film opened in Sydney with a live prologue. A graveyard was set up and two gnomes danced out onto the stage and lifted the lid of a coffin as two magnesium bursts temporarily blinded the audience. By the time audience members' sight returned, two demons had joined the scene and a wraith was rising from the coffin. All five actors danced in silent pantomime, and then the gnomes and demons disappeared into the wings and the wraith returned to the coffin, revealing that she was, in fact, an attractive young lady. The gnomes returned and replaced the lid before the lights dimmed and the movie began.

The pre-show presentation was a smash and ensured that the film was talked about not as just another movie, but an experience. In its first two days, over 15,000 Sydneysiders saw the film, with just as many turned away at the box office.

Frankenstein was a smash. In its first week, it took an estimated £3600, making it the highest grossing film in Sydney at the time.[21] This amount was taken against ticket prices ranging from one shilling to 3/5 for the dress circle seats. The second week saw the film bring in £1950 alone, outperforming entire cinemas showing multiple films in the same city.

Frankenstein quickly became the highest grossing film, not just for Universal, but for the entire country. To celebrate, Universal paid for a special section of *Everyone's*, devoted to the film and its success.[22] The extra expense paid off as *Frankenstein* was officially labeled "Big," making it the first horror movie, and the first Universal movie, to achieve this.

From there, the movie began to appear in other states. On June 10, it was released in Queensland, where one Lance Robertson, standing 6'11" ("in his socks"), made personal appearances as the Monster, and on July 1 it came to Victoria. McIntyre created a *Frankenstein* float which was sent to cities to roam the streets. The float contained a mixture of giant monsters, coffins and an operating theater where doctors "created" life. The public lapped it all up and wanted more. The Melbourne city council informed McIntyre that no in-street advertising would be allowed due to new regulations and banned the float. Not to be deterred, McIntyre merged the float, guerrilla style, in a student parade down Swanston Street.[23] The float completed the entire route and then vanished at the end, before officials could locate it.

In Western Australia, *Frankenstein* premiered on April 18, preceded by an advertising campaign to find the biggest man in that part of the country to appear at cinemas dressed as the Monster. The Western Australian government, using the Indecent Publications Act, decreed that no image of Karloff as the Monster could be used in trade advertisements, forcing a change to the advertising strategy. Stills from the movie of Karloff as the Monster, menacing, could be, and were, widely used in articles to promote the film, but the ads themselves were made up of text only, adding to the appeal and making it the highest grossing movie that Universal had ever released in Australia before the run was finished.

Frankenstein was due to premiere in Adelaide, South Australia, on June 17. It was one of the few states that had a state-appointed censorship board that could, if necessary, rule against the Federal Board. To this point, no State Board had overturned its federal counterparts, but on June 6, 1932, the Advisory Board of Film Censors for South Australian did just that, announcing that *Frankenstein* would not be screened anywhere in the state on the grounds that it was "too gruesome."[24] The objectionable material in the film included scenes that had already been removed from prints around the world, yet remained intact in Australia, including a scene where Colin Clive yells, "Now I know what it feels like to be God," and the infamous scenes where the Monster throws a young girl into a lake and watches her drown. This ban made Adelaide the second major city in the world to ban the movie (Belfast being the first). The fallout was immediate and very public.

Publicly McIntyre was seething and was full of bluster, but privately he was now over the moon. By banning *Frankenstein* in South Australia, its further success was all but guaranteed and the losses incurred in Adelaide would be more than made up elsewhere with the resulting debate keeping it in the public eye for longer than expected.

Universal's Australian arm, Universal Film Exchange, lodged an appeal against the ban with the Chief Secretary of the Advisory Board, Mr. Whitford, but it was upheld. The Board announced its reasons in the media on June 8, stating that, other than the charge of being gruesome, *Frankenstein* was "impairing to the public morality." The president of the Motion Pictures Distributor's Association, Sir Victor Wilson, made it clear that nothing could be done to remove the ban. "Every picture must have the approval of the Commonwealth Board," he said. "In the case of a dispute with the Commonwealth censors, Gen. Mackay, of Sydney, has the final say. A State board can override this decision at present."[25] Once the Advisory Board had banned a film, they stuck with the ban and no number of cuts would appease them.

Following the lead of the Reverend Goss in Sydney, and encouraged by McIntyre, church groups across Adelaide applied for limited licenses to screen the movie to their congregations. The licenses were refused outright. This prompted incited several editorials, impassioned letters and pleas to allow the movie to be screened and calling for a centralized censorship system, as opposed to federal and state censors. Questions were asked as to how such films as *Dracula* and those with "lewd language" could be shown but not Frankenstein. The crime films *The Big House*

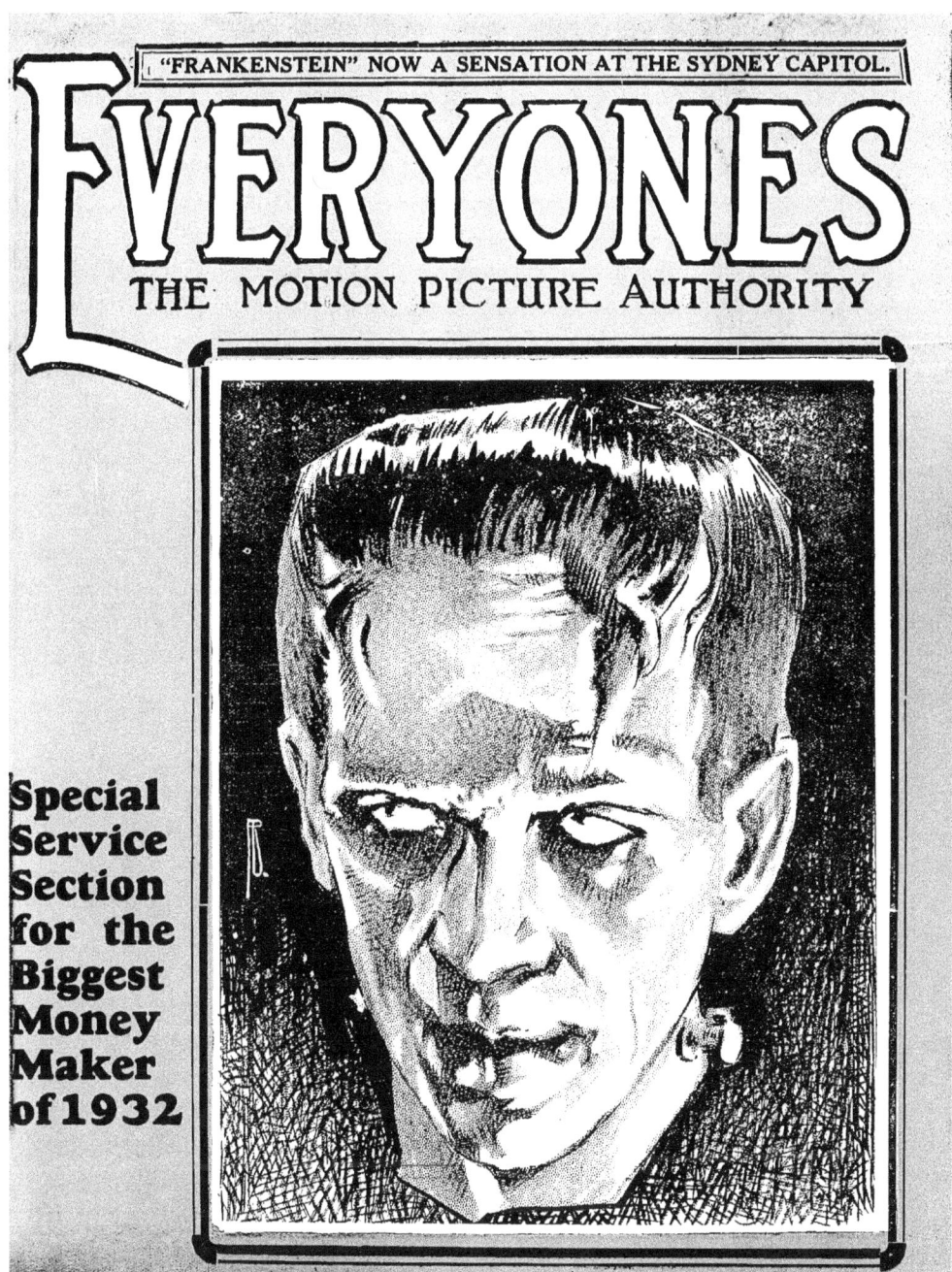

Cover of the all-Frankenstein supplement to *Everyone's*, December 24, 1932. Art by Fred Broderick.

and *Strictly Dishonorable* were two titles also being mentioned for banning on moral grounds. One of the major broadsheets of the time, *The News*, published a large photo of Karloff as the Monster on the front page of its July 15, 1932, edition, thus showing the bulk of Adelaide people what the fuss was all about and making mention of the ban. It took over two decades for the movie to be screened in South Australia.

Despite the avenue of appeals once a state board banned a film, it was unlikely to be overturned at the federal level. Further appeals were lodged in 1935, when *Bride of Frankenstein* was released, and again in 1939 (*Son of Frankenstein*). Despite the Advisory Board being wound up in 1938, every appeal was rejected and the ban upheld, although the resultant sequels were allowed release with minor cuts. Each time the answer was the same: The original *Frankenstein* was more horrific than the many sequels.

Frankenstein made its Monster, Boris Karloff, a major star in Australia and the days when he would be referred to as "Karloff Boris" were gone. In Australia, as with the rest of the world, the name "Karloff" was all that was needed to announce him.

The Box Office Value of "Horror"

"A question difficult to answer concerns the current vogue of 'horror pictures'—not as to how long it will last, but why a large selection of the public has suddenly demanded shocks."[26]

With that opening statement, Gayne Dexter, journalist and 1932 editor-in-chief for *Everyone's*, launched into an attack upon the now growing genre of horror.

Dexter was no stranger to the film industry. He had gotten his start as head of publicity at Union Theatres and later worked with Ken G. Hall at Australasian Films, the same distributors that handled Australian Reginald "Snowy" Baker's films and was responsible for handing the publicity on Karloff's first recorded credit in Australia, along with a photo, for the 1924 film, *The White Panther*.[27] By the time he began work at *Everyone's*, he had built a reputation for writing overly dramatic pieces complete with shocked, and deathless, prose.

Dexter blamed the usual suspect—the Depression—concluding that films such as *Dracula*, *Frankenstein* and *Dr. Jekyll and Mr. Hyde* should not be termed horror, but "supernatural." A true horror film, he argued, was a movie such as *Murder by the Clock*, which had "graveyards, groans, blood-chilling scenes," and was the worst horror film Dexter had seen to that point. He took delight in pointing out that the audience reaction was so adverse that the film was dropped from all advertising the day after its premiere.

Dexter claimed that the difference between *Murder by the Clock* and *Dracula* was that the latter gave the audience something to ponder after they went home: the Beyond. He wrote of the genre, "It will bring strong box office returns. It will be short (career-wise) because people's emotions in today's world crisis are as changeable as they were during the war. If the producers are studying those emotions, it might be well for them to consider religious themes as the next turn of public demand."

Herc McIntyre must surely have laughed aloud reading Dexter's words, with photos of Karloff, both in normal garb and as the Monster. If Dexter thought he would get a fight from McIntyre, he was wrong. The two men knew each other well, as seasoned veterans of the industry, 1910 for Dexter, 1912 for McIntyre, they had thought they'd seen it all.

In a letter addressing the article, McIntyre wrote, "People want to be thrilled, and if you have the right kind of medium, as we (Universal) have, the job is to go out and sell it lock, stock and barrel to the public."[28] He went on to blame the press for all of the adverse publicity, it was out of his hands, or so he claimed. Yes, he said, films such as *Frankenstein* should be called "supernatural," but until they were labeled as such, horror it was.

McIntyre closed his letter out thanking Dexter for his views, barely able to conceal the sheer joy he must have felt at the free publicity *Frankenstein* was now gaining.

Dracula and *Frankenstein* had convinced McIntyre and Universal that horror was here to stay, and they would do their best to exploit the genre if the public wanted it.

Dexter eventually stepped down from *Everyone's* and headed overseas. He worked for Warner Brothers and handled publicity.

James Whale, a Most Censored Director

James Whale is remembered as one of the finest directors of the 1930s, holding a vision that carried across all his films, standing for quality and excellence. His *Frankenstein* and the sequel *Bride of Frankenstein* are amongst the finest horror movies ever made, combining a sense of pathos and outright terror with storytelling and stunning performances. Whale was not one to shirk from controversy, be it allowing Colin Clive to evoke the Lord's name, thus being accused of blasphemy, to the overly camp gay person overtones of *Bride*'s Dr. Pretorius. But Whale also holds another, more dubious, title that he more than likely never knew of: He was more than likely the most censored Hollywood director in Australia.

Beginning in 1930 and his directorial debut with the seminal *Journey's End*, Whale is credited with making 20 movies. A total of eight were either banned outright (*Frankenstein* was banned in South Australia), cut by the censor or deemed Unsuitable for Native Races. While *The Invisible Man* (1933) passed uncut, his films cut by the censor included *Frankenstein*, *The Old Dark House* (1932), *The Kiss Before the Mirror* (1933), *Bride of Frankenstein* (1935), *Remember Last Night?* (1935), *The Road Back* (1937) and *Green Hell* (1940). Even *One More River* (1934), which had been heavily censored before arriving in Australia, was subject to more cuts before domestic release.

It is worth noting that, although his films were censored and in one case banned in one state for 21 years, he never had a film banned outright from distribution and exhibition across the country.

Freaks

"The most repulsive picture screened before this Board."[29]

Freaks was to be Tod Browning's ultimate horror film; instead it became the first

Magazine advertisement for James Whale's *The Invisible Man* (1933).

horror film to be banned outright, due to content,[30] without a single screening. The movie's selling point was the use of actual people with various disabilities who were making a living working in various circuses. It remains one of the most genuinely terrifying films of the classic horror age and its power to shock and create unease has not diminished over the decades. Australians had to wait over 40 years to officially see the movie in the cinemas, at which time, it still shocked those who dared watch it.

Australians became aware of *Freaks* in 1931 when newspapers and magazines such as *Everyone's* and *Film Weekly* began to print reports from their American counterparts. At first, they were positive, remarking that the movie would be a thriller using real-life circus freaks, but not hinting as to what was to come. Photos from the set were impossible to come by and the descriptions came from MGM's publicity machine. But anyone who might have been keen to see the movie were going to be sorely disappointed.

Freaks never made it past the censor. Its only screening in Australia was before the censor board. Even though the version they watched had already been cut to shreds by censors in America (removing 40 minutes), they walked out. The Board, expressing both disgust and horror, quickly slapped a ban on it, using the rationale of England and Ireland's ban to justify their actions.

MGM Australia questioned the ban and indicated that they were considering an appeal. The Board was emphatic: *Freaks* would not be considered for release, even if cut further, and no appeal would be considered, telling MGM not to waste their time or money. When asked by the media (and MGM) why the film was banned, the official reply was simple and to the point: "This is the most repulsive picture screened before this Board."

The reason *Freaks* was banned, while other horrors such as *Frankenstein* which contained grotesque figures were cleared, was due to Browning using real people in his film as opposed to actors donning makeup. The realism and authenticity that Browning sought to enhance his story was also its downfall. The censor would (reluctantly) rule that a fake monstrosity was acceptable to the public because no reasonable person was expected to believe in vampires, werewolves and monsters made up of dead men; whereas real monstrosities that could be found in a community's circuses and fairs was a step too far. Australia was a very conservative country, and those unfortunates who were born with such disabilities were handed over to institutions and hospitals that specialized in caring for them—and they were then forgotten. The lucky few who could manage, found gainful employment with the traveling shows who would exploit their disabilities. *Freaks* would have brought to the screen a group of people that the general population would rather believe simply didn't exist and would terrify them with their on-screen activities.

Another reason for the ban was the film's set piece, Browning's best celluloid effort. Browning created a truly horrific sequence in which the freaks attack the main characters, a strongman named Hercules and a beautiful woman named Cleopatra, at the height of a storm at night. The censors recoiled with fear and horror at the sight of Prince Randian, the Living Torso, born without arms and legs, slithering through mud with a knife firmly clasped in his mouth, along with the freaks dragging Hercules away through the roar of thunder and flashes of lightning to an unknown fate. They were stunned by the sight of Cleopatra disfigured at the end of the film. The sequence left nothing to the imagination as the freaks dispatched their enemies. It was Browning's *tour de force* as he milked it for all its worth.

Freaks was originally due for release in early 1933 in Perth, but the ban was so complete that the movie was not even mentioned in the mainstream media, as if the movie had never existed. *Freaks* remained banned in Australia until well into the 1970s, although there is evidence that a pirate copy was screened for a short season in Sydney in 1966.

Banned in Tasmania: *White Zombie*

> The Board passed *Frankenstein*, *Dracula*, *Possessed* (banned in England) and *Tomorrow and Tomorrow*; yet it banned *White Zombie*, *Murder in the Rue Morgue* and *Left Over Ladies*. Two were "horror" pictures, while *Left Over Ladies* was a tale in which inebriation and divorce played a prominent part. *White Zombie* was not witnessed by the writer, but to compare *Murders in the Rue Morgue* with *Dracula* or *Frankenstein*, even in conception or realism, is ridiculous.
>
> —editorial in the *Voice* (Hobart), November 26, 1932

White Zombie was unlike any other movie that had appeared in Australia at the time and, as such, it was hard for censors and reviewers to get a handle on it. Most reviewers felt that its star Bela Lugosi was wasted in his role as Murder, with others remarking that the emphasis on his hypnotic eyes was very reminiscent of *Dracula.*

The film was banned in Tasmania, despite it being cleared (with cuts) by the Federal censor. At the same time, another horror, *Murders in the Rue Morgue*, was also banned, both due to excessive horror.

With *White Zombie*, or *White Zombi* as it was initially known, the ban might have been justified. The subject matter disturbed those who saw it, and the use of what was labeled "Negroid customs" was at odds with the then White Australia policy.

Despite the mixed reviews, low budget and some over-the-top acting, the film was a surprise hit in Australia, until it came into direct competition with Karloff's *The Mummy*, after which its popularity began to wane. Despite the better production values and acting of the latest Karloff offering, *White Zombie* spent the better part of 1933 doing the usual circuit around the country's capital cities, before being farmed out to regional and remote country areas where it took on a life of its own, spending another five years in cinemas and town halls.

These would be amongst the last movies banned in Tasmania. In 1934, the Tasmanian state government abolished censorship at a state level, instead electing to reply upon the Commonwealth.

The Mummy Rises Amidst the Film Wars

In 1932, Universal knew they were on a winning streak with horror films. Both *Dracula* and *Frankenstein* had been incredible successes, making household names out of Bela Lugosi and Boris Karloff. Egypt, and the concept of reincarnation and mummies were fresh in the public mind, buoyed by the discovery (and plunder) of the tomb of the boy king Tutankhamen and the curse that had been placed upon it. Carl Laemmle Jr. commissioned a script exploiting those themes.

Universal saw only one choice to play the title role: Karloff.[31] Unlike European Bela Lugosi,[32] Karloff already looked Egyptian, his Middle Eastern hue coming from his naturally dark skin, attributed to his Indian heritage[33] that Karloff never officially confirmed or denied, in his lifetime, instead referring to his skin tones as his "tan."

Karloff had been born in England, but his mother Eliza was born in Mumbai (Bombay), India, to an Indian mother. A popular theory of the time, later proven true, was that Karloff was the illegitimate offspring of Eliza and an unknown Indigenous sailor and adopted into the Pratt family as their own.

It is worth noting that, over the years, much debate has been made about which man, Karloff and Lugosi, was the better actor, and why Karloff thrived in motion pictures where Lugosi suffered. Putting aside the argument over ability, it becomes clear why Karloff's star continued to rise while Lugosi's stagnated: language.

No matter how good an actor, how versatile and attractive he might have been, Lugosi never quite mastered the English language, nor could he lose his accent. Nor did he desire to do so. The British private school–educated Karloff[34] could slip into accents with ease and, despite a slight lisp, was as articulate as anyone in the industry, granting Karloff the ability to pass as Egyptian, or any Asian race for that matter, with a minimum of makeup due to his skin tone and linguistic skills. Lugosi would have struggled.

In summary, Karloff was believable in his versatility. Lugosi was not.

This is not to say that Karloff could have acted in every role that Lugosi took, or vice versa, or that either man was a better technician. It's hard to imagine *Dracula*, the story of an Eastern European count, with Karloff in the title role. We do know that when Lugosi acted as Frankenstein's Monster, one of the few, if only, times that the two men acted the same character, Lugosi's portrayal was nowhere near as effective as that of Karloff.

Directing *The Mummy* was the renowned cinematographer Karl Freund. Freund had made his name in Weimar Germany, working on classics such as *Der Golem*, *Metropolis* and *Varieté*. He moved to America in 1930 and worked on *Dracula*, contributing much to the overall mood of the film. He ended his career as cinematographer on the TV series *I Love Lucy*.

Others in the cast included two players from *Dracula*: Edward Van Sloan, who had brought Van Helsing to life, and David Manners, the perfect Jonathan Harker. Joining the trio in the lead female role was a relative newcomer to film, Zita Johann.[35] The movie was made with relative ease, void of serious issues, other than the usual discomfort to Karloff, this time when he was fully made up as the mummy.[36] The film was ready to be released in America in 1932 and an Australian premiere was planned for early 1933. It was then that the film hit a snag, being used as a bargaining chip in a long-running dispute between American film studios and Australian exhibitors.

Australian exhibitors had long been rallying against a practice known as block booking by American studios. In 1931, the Fox Film Corporation acquired a controlling share in the largest cinema chain in Australia, Hoyts, and were putting their films into circulation at the cost of everyone else's. Other studios, including

Magazine advertisement for Boris Karloff's *The Mummy* (1932).

Universal, were adhering to what was known as the contract system, aka block booking. The contract system "encouraged" exhibitors to book all of a studio's output over a given period in order to be given access to films featuring popular stars or subjects. These bookings included films not yet seen and, in some cases, yet to be made. While this practice guaranteed an exhibitor of box-office hits, they also had to take on poorer product which would not normally have been imported, let alone screened. The success of a hit movie was supposed to offset the dross, but that wasn't always the case.

By 1932, Australian film studios began to complain that block booking was squeezing out Australian- and English-produced films from cinemas. Exhibitors joined forces with Australian studios to form a new company, General Theatres Corporation, to first protest, and then fight, the American studios by refusing block bookings.

By January 1933, the "Film Wars" began to take scalps as major chain cinemas began to close their doors to the public due to the lack of new product. The Mayfair and, ironically, smaller, mostly independent cinemas were the exception as they weren't beholden to the block booking system. Fighting against these moves were the independent cinemas, located in suburban and country locations, aligned with the Motion Pictures Exhibitors Association; they weren't tied into block bookings and were screaming for a resolution. Knowing that such a resolution was in everybody's best interests, American studios began to agree to terms with the notable exception of MGM, which had struck a deal with the Fuller's Theatre chain and saw no reason to renege.

In the second week of the new year, Universal tried to break the deadlock using its Australian representative to contact independent theater owners via the MPEA (Motion Pictures Exhibitors Association) and offer to deal with them directly. In this way, suburban and country cinemas would get the latest movies before the capital cities. Two of the movies offered were *The Mummy* and the eagerly anticipated Karloff suspense-horror film *The Old Dark House*.

Universal knew it held the high cards. *The Mummy* had opened in America in December 1932 and, by the third week of January 1933, it was showing all over the country to good houses with excellent reviews.

One new Karloff film was great but two was something to be grabbed immediately. Independent theaters, claimed the MPEA, were outside any conflict between the studios and the General Theatres Corporation and, furthermore, the MPEA had long been disgruntled with the terms parceled out to non-city cinemas. The MPEA accepted Universal's offer.

But what Universal knew, and had not passed on to the MPEA, was that *The Mummy* wasn't doing the same business in America as other, similar horror movies, such as *Dracula*, with ticket sales dropping down markedly in some cities, but holding steady in others.

Universal's offer couldn't have come at a worse time for the General Theatres Corporation. Their negotiations with MGM collapsed as they continued to argue strength through unity. The MPEA didn't see things that way and made moves to accept the Universal offer, thus bypassing the usual chain of command. In doing so, and responding to threats from the General Theatres Corporation, the MPEA also contacted Prime Minister Joseph Lyons to ask for him to intervene in the dispute. Three days after the MPEA informed Universal that it wanted their films, the Film War fizzled out.

While both sides made concessions, neither side really won. Block booking continued, but the difference was that no longer did a studio's entire output *have* to be accepted. The General Theatres Corporation also called for an official government inquiry into the practice of block bookings, but that would take months, if not years, to happen. Until such a time as the rules were changed, it would be business as usual.

Advance screenings of *The Mummy* were held in all major cities in late February, and photos of Karloff in his Imhotep makeup began to appear in newspapers. "If you want to look interesting when you grow older, make more faces now," Karloff was quoted as saying.[37] The same newspapers reported that Karloff's ghoulish appearance wasn't all due to good makeup. "Karloff can distort the muscles of his face in any manner and control them in any particular position for a reasonable length of time," reported the *Sun*, "and in his *Mummy* makeup he divided his face, not according to its exterior appearance, but according to the muscles, into segments and 'columns,' accentuating the effect with greasepaint and color."[38]

The first reviews were positive. "This mummy, which is supposed to waken back to modern life, is magnificently played by BORIS KARLOFF," wrote a *Smith's Weekly* critic. "He makes his part the most shuddersome we have seen outside the fields of nightmare, and completely dominates the film."[39] Also appearing in newspapers were photos of Zita Johann. Her stunning beauty was fodder for gossip and film pages, and she was often described as being "strangely fascinating." The cinematography was also highlighted, with praise for its use of shadows and darkness to convey a suitable mood.

The Mummy was released, nationally, on March 16, 1933. Unusually for an American film of the period, it hit city cinemas in all states on the same weekend, which had been Universal Australia's plan all along. It was accompanied by *The Cohens and Kellys in Trouble* and a Slim Summerville-Zasu Pitts comedy, *What a Life*.

The Mummy's posters and advertising differed from their American counterparts, with emphasis on Johann as she stood in a seductive pose, and Karloff's head loomed behind her. David Manners was in both advertisements as well. In one he is seen in a passionate kiss with Johann; the other has him looking up at her. A third, and rarely seen, advertisement used a still of Johann from the movie, with Karloff nowhere to be seen.

Not one advertisement, or poster, had Karloff in full mummy makeup as Universal was saving that reveal for the film proper. The usual lobby displays were out in full force, but the Lyceum in Melbourne took the cake. They mocked up the inside of a crypt in their foyer, with several sarcophagi. The main sarcophagus, left open, contained a sign reading, "It's alive!" A light display was set off and, slowly, the mummy inside would begin to move and come to life. The display was so effective that people came to the Lyceum just to see it in action.

Universal had struck box office gold again, proving that horror movies were now a viable source of income. If *Frankenstein* marked the "arrival" of Karloff as a box office draw, *The Mummy* cemented this position. Reviews heaped praise on Karloff, with many claiming that his Imhotep portrayal was better than his star turn in

Frankenstein. Johann was labeled "exotic" and big things were predicted for her. The film was eerie and the acting excellent.[40] The critics' responses to the movie were summarized by a two-line review in *Table Talk*: "Karloff's best. The weird story of an Egyptian high priest, who comes back to life, has some truly thrilling moments."[41]

The Mummy proved to be incredibly popular with public and was showing throughout the decade and into the 1940s. It would have appeared that, at this stage, neither Karloff, nor Universal, could put a foot wrong and the public eagerly awaited the inevitable sequel to arrive, starring the magnificent Karloff.

They would be waiting a long time.

King Kong

King Kong remains one of the most visually inventive and powerful films of the immediate post–silent era. Its concept, scope and execution made it an instant classic, loved by filmgoers worldwide, and giving life to the giant animal-giant monster genre that filmmakers would forever after exploit, especially in Japanese cinema with their *Godzilla* series.

Kong was released in America in early April 1933 and copies were rushed around the world, finding their way to Australia in time for a late 1933 release. The prints arrived in Sydney from RKO in late June and were screened for the Commonwealth Censor, Walter Cresswell O'Reilly. There was little O'Reilly could do to the film as it had already been cut prior to shipping but the Commonwealth Film Censorship Board were still able to remove just under a minute of footage, thus managing to bring the running time down to 99 minutes.

The film remained cut in Australia until the video release in the mid–1980s when the standard RKO cut was used. It was further noted by the censors that while *King Kong*'s stop motion animation in a jungle setting would be acceptable to adults, the sight of a giant gorilla running amok in downtown New York, treading on people, creating mayhem and kidnapping a scantily clad woman, could easily scare or upset children, women and those with a "nervous disposition." To that end, O'Reilly slapped a restricted rating on the film and then took it one step further by insisting that the following text be added to all publicity items, from advertisements to posters and even as a spoken warning before the film itself:

> "Censorship Warning: Persons of nervous temperaments are warned of the intense excitement in *King Kong*."[42]

RKO's Australian representative and the owners of cinemas showing the movie couldn't have been happier with the official disclaimer. When asked for comment, the proprietor of the Aberdare Star Theatre, Mr. Lowe, implored people of a nervous temperament not to see the film as it would be likely to remain "on their minds for months." In the same article, Lowe stated that he considered the film one of the greatest productions of all time, serving only to ensure that his cinema had a booming business. Warnings of possible fainting fits, collapse and even potential fatalities makes moviegoers want to see what the commotion is all about. Furthering the mystique, ladies were advised to see only day sessions so that they could leave the theater in daylight.

Kong was heavily publicized in newspapers, with considerable column space dedicated to the film's technical aspects and its overall impact on overseas audiences. Its advertising campaign resembled that of an adventure-romance movie targeted at women, much in the way that *Dracula* had been two years earlier. Where *Dracula* hinted at a love between the dead and the living (necrophilia), *Kong* suggested a love between a woman and an ape (bestiality).

Initial ads focused on Fay Wray only, with no images of Kong at all. Copy for the ads included these bits of text: "Ninety-nine women out of a hundred will surrender to the thrill of new sensations when they sit beneath the spell of *King Kong*!,"[43] "Made for women who desire a NEW EMOTIONAL EXPERIENCE—and are brave enough to seek it!"[44] and "Every woman's heart will flutter strangely with new and overpowering sensations under the amazing and exciting influence of King Kong."[45]

A poster of Wray looking upwards in a torn dress barely covering her body, along with an insert of Bruce Cabot and Wray locked in a romantic embrace about to kiss, could easily lead to mistaking *Kong* for a romantic film rather than the monster movie it was.

The film had its Australian premiere in Melbourne at the Capitol on July 15, 1933. It opened in Sydney at the Civic on August 19, Adelaide at the Rex on September 9, Brisbane and Hobart at their respective Hoyts Regent theaters on October 7 and Perth at the Grand on January 19, 1934. For the movie's Australian run, *Kong* was paired with a throwaway short feature, *So This Is Harris*, starring comedian Phil Harris in his debut film, along with a Pathe news review and a cartoon of the cinema's choice.

Another gimmick used to promote the movie Australia-wide: a radio serial adapted from the script. It ran for five consecutive nights leading up to the film's premiere in that city. On the sixth night, the broadcast would cut to the theater that was holding the state premiere, and 15 minutes of the movie was broadcast. Exactly which 15 minutes is unknown. This sixth night was promoted as being the "Prologue to *King Kong*" and it was streamed to stations around the relevant state. In this way, the broadcast gave listeners at home the ability to listen to dialogue from the actual movie.[46]

The first proper Australian review of *Kong* wasn't a good one. While praising the special effects and commenting on the uniqueness of the creatures, the reviewer took the filmmakers to task for what was perceived as an utterly tepid opening, designed only to establish a love interest for the female audience. Once Kong appeared, the reviewer was over the moon.[47] Other reviewers noticed the similarities between *Kong* and *The Lost World* (1925), unaware that Willis O'Brien, the animator of *Kong*, had worked on the earlier movie and co-writer-producer-director Merian C. Cooper had used the Conan Doyle story as his template.

From its Melbourne debut, *Kong* traveled quickly, gaining complimentary reviews for its technical scope and fast-paced storyline (the first section notwithstanding). One sour note was hit when an unnamed reviewer penned the following:

> *King Kong*, the advertisements for which were typical Yankee Bally-hoo, proved the greatest comedy success of the year at the Kinema [*sic*] this week. The part that raised the greatest laugh was the censor's warning to nervous people. If the censor was serious in issuing this warning, then we advise the general public not to say boo in his presence in case they scare him to death. The picture from start to finish was a joke, and the worst of bad entertainment.[48]

By the time the movie reached Perth, Western Australia, all pretense of romance was gone, with the advertisement focused on *Kong* with emphasis on the giant ape running riot in Manhattan. The movie made another round of the country before being placed into storage.

The Ghoul

Boris Karloff, unhappy with Universal's contract offerings, declined their offers and instead returned to England in triumph in 1933. He was now a major, established film star, known worldwide and well off financially. He was lauded and feted everywhere he went.

In England, producer Michael Balcon approached Karloff with the view of having him feature in films made in the U.K. Karloff, always the proud Englishman, and always up for making some quick money, couldn't accept fast enough.

The result was *The Ghoul*, a thinly disguised remake of *The Mummy* which did take some small inspiration from the 1929 novel of the same name. The collaboration allowed Karloff to work with actors Cedric Hardwicke and Ralph Richardson, who were at the beginnings of their film careers, and would become two of the finest stage and screen actors of the 20th century, receiving knighthoods for their services towards acting. Also in the cast, one of James Whale's friends, Ernest Thesiger, already known to Karloff from *The Old Dark House*. An English horror film with top billing to Karloff was a coup to be exploited to the fullest, even with his limited participation.

The Ghoul premiered at the Strand, Hobart, on March 7, 1934, albeit in an abbreviated state, when selections were shown prior to the midnight premiere of *The Invisible Man*.

Ghoul advertisements presented an image of Karloff looking all the world like a toned-down version of Frankenstein's Monster. His versatility was noted in many reviews, and although the role was like *The Mummy,* the makeup was, at least, different. The movie proved popular with audiences and remained in circulation into 1935 when it became a second feature, usually to a John Wayne western or a comedy. It also enjoyed a second life in rural Australia where it was in circulation well into 1939.

For decades, *The Ghoul* was considered a lost film until a damaged, incomplete version of the film was discovered in the Czech Republic. The ABC broadcast this copy in the mid–1990s. A near pristine copy of the complete film, now available on DVD, was later uncovered at Shepperton Studios in England.

The Son of Kong

King Kong was still screening in regional centers when the sequel, *The Son of Kong* was released in Australia in April 1934. As with *Kong*, the advertising emphasized forbidden romance, showing a woman imprisoned in the cargo hold of a ship being taken to the island of Kong. The censor left *Son* intact: no cuts of note were made to the running time. Reviews were kind to *Son*, recognizing it as an adventure film with hints of comedy and more romance, for the ladies. *Son* received better reviews than *Kong* overall, in part due to the reviewers already knowing what the special effect was to be (gigantic ape plus prehistoric creatures) and a familiarity with both the actors and the story overall. The romance angle placated the reviewers, making it an easier film to recommend.

Even though both movies were screening at the same time, it appears that no cinema in Australia put them on as a double bill.

The Son of Kong had a good run, with its season extending well into 1935, before being shelved and not screened again until it appeared on Australian television in the late 1970s. At that time, networks were cashing in on the *Planet of the Apes* series and screening anything that featured a gorilla.

Son was cleared for release on videotape in early 1984, 50 years after it first screened, when a series of RKO films were rushed out to capitalize on the new medium. Although the movie was submitted, cleared and classified in 1984, this doesn't mean it was released on videotape at that point. RKO, along with other production houses, would routinely submit many titles at once for classification and then release them when they saw fit, or as demand called for it. Interestingly, *King Kong* wasn't submitted for official classification in Australia until 1988, four years after *Son of Kong*. But the overall lack of revival, and indeed interest, ensured that *Son* became a forgotten entry in the Giant Ape series in Australia until the advent of television.

Bride of Frankenstein

The longer he was chief censor, the more rigorous was O'Reilly in imposing his moral standards on a public unaware of what it was being denied. Among the few critics was *Film Weekly* who described the censor as a "misfit" whose "cramped, restricted standpoint" as a preacher could not be sensitive to the views of his fellow citizens. O'Reilly was buoyed by support for his efforts when the activities of the American Decency League led to Hollywood studios accepting strict moral guidelines for their films. Whereas 52 percent of imported feature films were cut or banned by O'Reilly during the first nine months of 1934, only 25 percent were so treated during the last three months of that year.

One film that O'Reilly hated, and wanted banned, was the sequel to *Frankenstein*.

Midway through 1935, the first trade ads began to appear promoting the sequel to *Frankenstein*. The ads promised a stranger, more horrific picture, with posters appearing bearing Karloff's Monster to full effect. O'Reilly passed the film, with cuts, on June 6, 1935, and rated it "suitable only for adults." O'Reilly was quite clear that all advertising had to bear that legend, and the film could not be shown on a double bill where children might access it. All the state censors fell into line, including the Advisory Board of Film Censors for South Australia. Lines stretched long down the road upon its release in Sydney, with promotion including an actual wedding couple (in ghoulish makeup). The bride and groom were paraded around Sydney in a garish-looking Pontiac.

The reviews were positive, with the bulk highlighting James Whale's inventive direction, the gothic architecture and, of course, Karloff's stellar turn as the Monster.

All was running smoothly until O'Reilly noticed potentially misleading advertisements in violation of the strict advertising guidelines appearing in Sydney newspapers. A letter explaining the issue was duly sent off to Universal's Australian arm,[49] who promptly replied that this mistake was not theirs as advertising was the responsibility of the General Theatres publicity department.[50] It should have ended there, but it didn't.

In late August 1935, O'Reilly saw an ad for *Bride*, again in the *Sydney Morning Herald*, which drove him to write Edwin Abbott, then the Comptroller-General of Customs, to point out that it was stated that children were able to see *Bride* at a reduced cost, except on Saturday nights.[51] Universal was contacted again with the breach pointed out and again they handed the complaint to the Motion Pictures Distributors Association. As was the practice at the time, a bond of £500 had been paid as surety against any such breaches and the MPDA were now being asked to explain why they should have that bond refunded in full.[52] The head of the MPDA, Sir Victor Wilson, acted promptly and in doing so illustrated the flaws with censorship within Australia.

Sir Victor wrote to each studio head in Australia to point out that each studio was responsible to apply the Commonwealth guidelines for advertising for their films, making it clear that any loss of the bond would be coming from the studio responsible. Also made clear was the right of the Commonwealth to withdraw a picture from exhibition that it felt breached the guidelines, and this would result in the film being withdrawn nationally. The MPDA would be asking for the film to be withdrawn on a state level.[53] Sir Victor followed this up with another letter, this time to Edwin Abbott, explaining the situation and drawing attention to his recent discussion with O'Reilly. Sir Victor outlined his plan and assured the Department of Trade and Customs that he'd sort the problem out.[54] Each studio head responded to Sir Victor, with some drawing attention to previous breaches of the guidelines. Others made it clear that they had never gone outside of the rules. One studio did not respond: the General Manager of Universal was in Melbourne at the time of Sir Victor's letter and out of reach. Sir Victor again wrote to Abbott pleading for more time.

Once back in Sydney, Vic Heslop, the assistant general manager of Universal in Australia, contacted Sir Victor. Heslop correctly pointed out that while the bulk of their films were passed by the Commonwealth and the advertising guidelines adhered to, each state acted differently, especially Victoria. Thus, argued Heslop, it was hardly fair to hold the studio accountable for a lack of uniformity in censorship laws.[55] It was an argument that couldn't be debated, so Sir Victor again met with Cresswell O'Reilly and gave assurances that the guidelines would be policed more stringently in the future. It was also pointed out that, by this stage, the first run of *Bride* was all but over; any future runs wouldn't bring as much attention nor have such prominent advertising. This meeting was enough for Abbott and O'Reilly to close the file and write to Sir Victor of their decision to allow *Bride* to continue.

Although the letter to Sir Victor was positive, the copy retained for the Commonwealth files made things clear. "The Chief Censor," reads a handwritten note by Edwin Abbott, "To note the action take and to promptly bring under notice any further breach." Cresswell O'Reilly added his own notation, "Noted and returned. Any further breach will be promptly brought under notice." By drawing out their response, Universal had dodged a bullet but had also managed to draw far more attention to themselves than previously.[56]

Bride of Frankenstein was as successful as *Frankenstein* at the Australian box office, outperforming all other films for three weeks before it branched out into regional centers where it continued its success.

WereWolf of London

"Wanted—a GIRL—with COURAGE"[57]

Buoyed by the success of their horror movies, Universal decided to tap another mine, werewolves. Although people now associate Universal's werewolf with Lon Chaney Jr., the studio's first entry into the genre came with the 1935 movie *WereWolf of London*, starring Henry Hull.

To promote the film, cinemas were encouraged to advertise for a girl, over the age of 21 of course, who would be willing to sit through the entire film, alone, after midnight. If the girl was able to carry out this feat of pure courage, she would be rewarded with a "crisp £1 note," which was not an inconsiderable sum at the time.

Perth attempted the campaign and at the stroke of midnight on September 7, 1935, one E. Ross sat alone (barring camera operators) in the Grand Theatre and watched the movie.[58] Unfortunately for the Royal, Ms. Ross watched the movie alone and calmly walked out. The plan of her being photographed running in horror from the cinema had failed. She duly collected her £1 note and was dropped off at her home. Similar campaigns were run in all major cities, with the same result: The girls engaged to see the film failed to be suitably terrified.

This was the latest attempt of these promotions to fail in achieving the desired effect of a terrified patron making a screaming exit from a horror movie. Some cinemas tried to tip the scales in their favor by only offering the promotion to young girls or sending in someone covered in a sheet, making moaning noises. Others left it open to all, even going as far as to offer dinner during the screening. Whatever they tried, from *Dracula* to *The Mummy*, *The Ghoul* to *WereWolf of London*, Australian audiences simply refused to be scared stupid by watching a film alone, especially in Depression and post–Depression times when a pound note went a long way indeed.

The industry changed tactics and focused upon the werewolf itself. Previously, studios rarely revealed the monster before a film's release, but Universal had noticed that the reveal gimmick was wearing thin.

In New South Wales, a promotion was run whereby any child attending an early screening of the movie was presented with a comic book, showing that horror movies were being aimed at all ages, and forever cementing the link between horror and comic books. Other promotions included the use of a stereoscope in theater foyers. The idea was that a person would look through the scope, close their right eye and see Henry Hull. Upon opening their right eye, Hull would "magically transform" into a werewolf. This promotion was a hit with the public, although it was noted that, with both eyes open, a person tended to go cross-eyed.

The film was initially paired with a Warren William light comedy, *Don't Bet on Blondes*, and the combination did excellent business. Reviews praised the film and singled out Hull's performance and the effective use of makeup.

Newspaper advertisement for *Bride of Frankenstein* (1935). Art by Fred Broderick.

Poverty Row Enters Australia

There was a pecking order amongst studios in Hollywood right from the start. This pecking order became more defined as time went on and some studios became more profitable. At the top of the tier were the likes of MGM, Warner Brothers, Paramount, RKO and 20th Century–Fox. These studios tended to spend money to make quality films, had a roster of talent under contract and won Academy Awards as well as gaining praise for intelligent, well-constructed films. It was considered a badge of honor to obtain a long-term contract with one of the Big Five, especially MGM. Against this was the fact that many contracts amounted to indentured slavery, with provisions for extensions, unpaid suspensions and the forcing of talent to accept any job offered. Only the biggest of stars were able to occasionally buck this trend.

The second tier contained the likes of Universal, United Artists and Columbia. These studios employed talent that, although household names, weren't the kind that won awards. Their movies were straightforward and made with a minimum of fuss. The studio heads could be just as tyrannical as the Big Five, but they were there to make money. Everything else was secondary.

The second-tier studios were where the Big Five often sent their talent to work when punished. At times this backfired, most notably when, according to urban legend, MGM and Paramount sent Clark Gable and Claudette Colbert, respectively, to Columbia to work on a Frank Capra film as "punishment." The resulting film, *It Happened One Night* (1934), swept the Academy Awards, earning Oscars for Gable, Colbert and Capra, as well as Best Picture and Best Adaptation.

Below these tiers were the rest, studios that worked quick and cheap and were lumped together as Poverty Row. With budgets typically of five figures, they would engage the services of household names who were almost famous or hasbeens and pay them as little as possible while shooting over a matter of days. Republic, Monogram, PRC, Grand National Films and Mascot Productions were the most notable Poverty Row studios, but there were others.

The name Poverty Row doesn't come from a physical location, but the low budgets and production values. Fading stars and out-of-work actors such as Buster "Flash Gordon" Crabbe, George Zucco, Dwight Frye, J. Carrol Naish, Ralph Morgan, Lionel Atwill, John Carradine, Erich von Stroheim, Patsy Kelly and more were sought by Poverty Row studios, along with the two big names of horror, Bela Lugosi and Boris Karloff. These actors, some of whom were once considered to amongst the top of their craft and retained "name" value, were paired up with the likes of the East Side Kids, along with comedian Ole Olsen, boxer Max "Slapsie Maxie" Rosenbloom, Willie Best,[59] Shemp Howard[60] and Ace the Wonder Dog to churn out as many B-grade movies as humanly possible, often recycling plots from other studios' movies.

With the Poverty Row studios entering the marketplace, more horror films were produced, not always to the benefit of the genre. Amongst the dross, some gems can be found, in the same way the Big Five often produced expensive flops. They didn't purposely make bad films but tight budgets, poor sets and the cheapness of the studios all but ensured it. Still, the cannier writers, directors, producers and actors persisted, resulting in a film that was generally either unbelievably bad or good, and often still had entertainment value.

Poverty Row films were subjected to the same standards from the censors as any other studio, the difference being that the larger studios could question or appeal censorship. Poverty Row films, once banned or cut, remained that way.

The first major Poverty Row studio to gain a foothold in Australia was Monogram Pictures, which sealed an international distribution deal with British Empire Films in February 1935. Within Australia, Max Ehrenreich's distribution company, Films Distributors Ltd., quickly snapped up the distribution rights to both British Empire and Monogram.[61]

As a company, Films Distributors Ltd. had some muscle behind them, boasting the likes of A.F. Albert from J. Albert and Sons,[62] Harry Ward, a noted Sydney-based accountant and director of Waddington's Theatres, and noted Sydney solicitor J.J. Mulligan. They quickly released several movies into the marketplace, including *Jane Eyre, A Girl of the Limberlost, Oliver Twist, The Moonstone, Mystery Liner, Shock, Head, The River, Broken Dreams* and *Woman's Man*. While not box office smashes, they did establish Monogram and British Empire in Australia and opened the door for other independent studios and producers, chipping away at the monopoly of the major Hollywood studios.

The main era of Poverty Row horrors ran from 1940 to 1949, albeit a shorter time in Australia: They became a casualty of the horror ban of 1946 with only a few thrillers later slipping past the censor.

Dozens of Poverty Row horrors saw general release in Australia, but a few were banned outright or refused classification: *The Corpse Vanishes* (Monogram, 1942), *The Mad Monster* (PRC, 1942), *The Ape Man* (Monogram, 1943), *Return of the Ape Man* (Monogram 1944), *The Monster Maker* (PRC, 1944), *The Vampire's Ghost* (Republic, 1945), *Strangler of the Swamp* (PRC, 1945), *White Pongo* (Sigmund Neufield, 1945), *Spook Busters* (Monogram, 1946), *The Catman of Paris* (Republic, 1946), *Devil Bat's Daughter* (PRC, 1946), *The Face of Marble* (Monogram, 1946), *The Flying Serpent* (PRC, 1946) and *Valley of the Zombies* (Republic, 1946).

Overall, Poverty Row horrors were accepted by audiences as being harmless entertainment.

Universal Stumbles

When asked about horror films in mid–1936, Universal president Carl Laemmle went on the record as saying, "That cycle is quiet at present. *Frankenstein* began it and it was successful. So many tried to follow the formula that it is too worn out."[63] Before his comments were published, the reign of Carl Laemmle and his family at Universal had ended.

The studio had fallen foul of the Depression in America and borrowed beyond its means. Once it was clear the loans couldn't be repaid, the studio was taken over by Standard Capitol Corporation, in conjunction with Associated Talking Pictures, headed by C.M. Woolfe, himself formerly aligned with the British studio Gaumont.

Telegrams were instantly sent to the Australian arm of Universal, assuring them that it would be business as usual. Universal movies were being distributed by General Film Distributers in both Australia and New Zealand, and with product already in the works for release, and more to come, Herc McIntyre, the long-serving managing director of Universal Films (Australia), told the press that Woolfe had told *him*, "As far as Australia is concerned, we will continue doing business as the same old stand with the same staff."[64]

Despite Woolfe's reassurance, McIntyre was still concerned about the financial state of Universal America. Spurred by rumors of mass layoff after the company changed hands, McIntyre decided to take steps to protect his staff. Instead of obeying the edict from America to cut staff and save money, he increased and expanded financial incentives for employees. This saw his staff working longer and harder, but they were rewarded better than they would have been at other companies of the time. Such financial generosity was not the norm for an industry, and indeed world, coming out the Great Depression.

There was no mention of where horror would feature in the new Universal's regime (if at all). *The Invisible Ray* and *Dracula's Daughter*, produced and completed under the reign of the Laemmles, were slated for release. No new Universal horrors were produced for the remainder of 1936 and many in America believed the studio had all but finished with the genre.

Son of Frankenstein

Universal, the main horror film–producing studio, stopped making horror movies in 1936. RKO, after the *Kong* series, closed up shop for horrors, offering *The Monkey's Paw* (1933) as its last major entry. Warner Brothers had delivered the amazing *The Walking Dead* in 1936 and then began putting its star Karloff in more mundane productions. MGM, hurt by the failure of *Freaks* to raise a profit, or to be even released in some parts of the world, kept busy with *Kongo* (1932), *The Mask of Fu Manchu* (1932), *Mad Love* (1935), *The Devil-Doll* (1936) and *Mark of the Vampire* (1935)—the latter a reunion of Bela Lugosi and Tod Browning for a remake of *London After Midnight*. Then MGM, too, deserted the genre.

'In Herc McIntyre's keynote speech before delegates and employees attending the 1937 New Universal convention, the word horror wasn't mentioned. McIntyre, freshly back in Australia from a meeting with Universal's new bosses in America, sang the praises of Danielle Darrieux, Deanna Durbin, Irene Dunn, Claudette Colbert and the Ritz Brothers. The focus would now be on light comedy, musicals and romance, with an emphasis on youth.

Not everybody bought what McIntyre was selling with enthusiasm. Although the American studios had deserted horror and England had banned them, Australian audiences continued to embrace such fare. All the major horror movies, a sizable percentage of which were Universal's, were all in active circulation. *Frankenstein, Bride of Frankenstein, Dracula, The Invisible Man, King Kong, The Black Cat, The Raven, Mad Love, White Zombie, The Mummy, The Ghoul* and *Mystery of the*

Wax Museum still made for solid box-office. Even silent horrors, such as Chaney's *Hunchback of Notre Dame, London After Midnight, The Unknown* and *The Unholy Three*, were still being shown in regional and country theaters. In Australia, Karloff and Lugosi were as popular as they'd ever been.

What Australian distributors, and the public, had been calling for were newer, fresher movies, but with the same old faces. In the late '30s, the announcement of a new Frankenstein movie was greeted with joy, and that joy turned to sheer elation when the cast of Karloff, Lugosi and Basil Rathbone was announced. Audiences were familiar with all three actors: Rathbone was known as Tasmanian Errol Flynn's main rival in *The Adventures of Robin Hood* and *Captain Blood*. Censorship was always going to be an issue, but there was no way that this movie wouldn't be released, and the forecast was for a hit.

But as the 1930s ended, a strong move to take powers of censorship away from the states and place it back into the hands of the federal government was growing. At a meeting of the Racial Hygiene Association, the minister for customs, Thomas White, made an argument for uniformity of laws between all the states which would see federal powers applied on a state level, but with no ambiguity.[65] This would lead to less confusion and, the hope *was*, end the banning of films on a state level. Unfortunately, Australia was experiencing an unprecedented amount of political upheaval in the months leading to its eventual entry into World War II: Between the time of the announcement in August 1938 and the release of *Son of Frankenstein* in March–April 1939, two prime ministers and another minister for customs had come and gone.

In the middle of this political confusion, the last Frankenstein movie to feature Boris Karloff as the Monster, *Son of Frankenstein*, was released. It opened in Sydney on March 17, 1939, and slowly made its way around the country, opening on Good Friday in Perth and Brisbane, then in mid–June for Tasmania and Victoria before finally being given the green light for release in Adelaide on August 23. Again, Universal's Australian arm petitioned for the release of 1931's *Frankenstein*, and were again refused.

Son was preceded by the re-release of other Universal horror films, namely *Frankenstein* (which was still uncensored), *Bride of Frankenstein* and *Dracula*, the latter to cash in on the appearance of Bela Lugosi. *Son* was also the subject of two major ad campaigns. The first campaign consisted of various warnings, imploring people to lock their doors and bolt the windows as the "Son of Frankenstein" was coming.[66] The second campaign promised that all filmgoers were insured by Lloyds of London, who would pay the now standard amount of £1000, "to the next of kin of any patron dying in any theatre in Australia from heart failure directly caused by and during the screening of *Son of Frankenstein*." The money was safe as nobody was reported as dying during, or as a direct result of, any screenings of the movie.[67] Reviews were positive with most singling out Rathbone and Lugosi as being the standout performers, and it enjoyed a lengthy run before being replaced with a double bill of *Bride of Frankenstein* and *Dracula's Daughter*.

Australia formally entered the European conflict on September 3, 1939, and World

War II was now officially underway. Closer to home, the situation was just as uncertain. Japan had invaded China in 1937 and was now beginning its expansion through Asia and the Pacific. Nineteen forty dawned with rumors of an impending invasion of Australia and newspapers were filled by the losses being suffered by Australians fighting in Europe. The escape that cinema offered was needed more than ever but with the violence of war a daily reality, Australia's hunger for horror began to abate.

Tensions continued to build and, after two more prime ministers, erupted with the bombing of Darwin by the Japanese. The war increased the audience appetite for horror by the boat load and left a populace conserved for the survival of their sons and themselves. In such a world, what good does a man in monster makeup do?

Where ten years earlier a Frankenstein movie was almost guaranteed to have a premiere and a long run, *Frankenstein Meets the Wolf Man* (1943) was quickly relegated to opening for the latest Dr. Kildare film and fodder such as the unmemorable *Atlantic Convoy*.

House of Frankenstein (1944) and *House of Dracula* (1945) opened and closed quickly in capital cities, vanishing into double and, in some places, triple "horror" bills. The former featured Boris Karloff's return to the Frankenstein series (albeit as a mad doctor) and both featured the "unholy trio" of Frankenstein's Monster, the Wolf Man and Dracula

As the '40s rolled on, large premieres, midnight screenings, gimmicks, insurance policies and lines around the block became distant memories. And with each subsequent Frankenstein release, the Adelaide censor was petitioned to lift the ban on the original *Frankenstein* and each time was refused.

Lon Chaney Jr. Banned

Lon Chaney's only child, Creighton, didn't have the easiest life. Although he was doted on by his parents, his desire to become an actor went against his famous father's wishes. The old man more than likely passed away quite happy and secure in the knowledge that Creighton was intending on earning an honest living as a plumber.

Creighton waited until after his dad's passing to take his shot and became a full-time, professional actor. For all his achievements, Chaney Jr. was never able to escape the shadow of his father—although he did manage to star in a banned film which his father never achieved.

Creighton resisted calls to change his stage name to Lon Chaney Jr. throughout his early career, preferring to be billed by his birth name,[68] under which he made an estimated 13 films and some serials. He saw himself as a light romantic lead but due to his sheer size and weight, and the legacy of his father, the studios and public saw him as a heavy in drama or horror roles. He was soon typecast as the villain in films, mainly westerns.

This changed when he was cast as Lennie in the film adaptation of John Steinbeck's *Of Mice and Men* (1939). It was a challenging role: Chaney had to find the right level of pathos to play the simpleton unable to control his strength, who inadvertently kills small animals, such as rabbits, by petting them to death. This trait culminates in the accidental killing of a young woman.

Of Mice and Men was Chaney's first major film for a studio, having only featured in B-movies to that point. It had a well-known director in Lewis Milestone, an excellent cast led by Burgess Meredith, Betty Field and Noah Beery Jr., and the Hal Roach Studio should have been the platform to propel Chaney Jr. to the A-list.

The film was a critical and financial success, being nominated for four Academy Awards in 1940, including Best Picture. It wasn't released in Australia until 1955 due to Cresswell O'Reilly slapping a ban on it: "I don't give any information on individual films. Every distributor has the right of appeal, but whether the distributor in this case has exercised his right I am not going to tell you."[69] O'Reilly also banned *Each Dawn I Die*, *A Child Is Born* and *Hell's Kitchen* around that same time.

United Artists, the film's distributor in Australia and worldwide, appealed the ban, claiming that it would cost them more than £30,000 in lost revenue; they pointed out that the film was currently screening, uncut, in New Zealand. O'Reilly would not be moved. In the face of calls for an explanation, O'Reilly acquiesced, listing: the murder of Mae by Lennie, the mercy killing of Lennie by George, and: "Morbid exploitation of an imbecile."

The media pointed out that more than 260,000 copies of the novel had been sold and the stage play had run for over six months to rave reviews. Gregan McMahon saw an opportunity and staged the play in place of the film. The stage version, which ran for eight nights in Sydney to packed houses, was the same as the film, complete with the murders, but as O'Reilly had no power to censor the theater, he could do nothing about it. McMahon was "magnificent" and insisted that he could not recall a single complaint about the play in all the times that he, and J.C. Williamson, had presented it.[70]

When the ban was rescinded in early 1955, *Of Mice and Men* was exhibited to rave reviews.

As for Chaney, the film was a millstone around his neck and rather than launch his career, he became typecast, which led him to horror films and down the road of depression and alcoholism. Of all the horror films that Chaney made in the 1940s, none was banned.

The Mummy's Hand

The next Mummy series installment was released in Australia, after a hiatus of eight years, by which time Karloff had moved on. His replacement was a B-western actor, Tom Tyler.

As Karloff had been replaced, so had the Mummy: Imhotep was "out," Kharis,[71] brought to life by the application of tana fluid, was "in."[72] The movie was promoted with the following phrase, "*Frankenstein* was a sissy compared with *The Mummy's Hand*!"

The *Sun*, in its review, stated, "Best that *The Mummy's Hand* has to offer is tipsy act by Cecil Kellaway."[73]

The South African–born Kellaway[74] was an object of interest for Australian audiences because he had moved to Australia in 1921 and acted on the stage for the J.C. Williamson firm. He transitioned to film while in Australia and left for Hollywood in the late 1930s. Down Under, he was still remembered fondly as an Australian Actor, if not by birth, then by adoption. Advertising for *The Mummy's Hand* placed Kellaway's name above the title, giving him fourth billing.[75]

Critics savaged *The Mummy's Hand*, offering up reviews which praised the overall feel of the film as "eerie"[76] while tearing it apart, mainly because it wasn't as good as its predecessor. *The Sunday Sun* found the whole film amusing:

> When Princess Ananka was buried, Karis [sic], her Egyptian adorer (played by Tom Tyler), was buried with her—alive. Sorcery by the high priests of Ananka's tomb prevented death from claiming him. So, Karis had insomnia per the thousand years, ready to become a monster of revenge should the tomb be desecrated. That's why Prof. Petrie (Charles Trowbridge), bone-hunter Banning (Dick Foran) and his sweetheart Marta (Peggy Moran) stir up a little hell of horror when they do ravage the tomb. Karis, a dreadful sight in his clammy wrappings, gets up from his sarcophagus (scream here, girls), proceeds to strangle members of the party and finally carries Marta off to his Master, the High Priest of the Tomb (Eduardo Ciannelli).
>
> Verdict: Don't be mum. Yell your loudest.[77]

Smith's Weekly had two separate reviews of the film. Their first impression of the movie was scathing: "Muddled in writing and clumsy in production. Altogether an inferior chiller and will not appeal to average adult."[78]

A few months later, and now that the movie had done good business, *Smith's Weekly* changed its mind, but only to a point. Their hypocrisy went as far to praise local actor Cecil Kellaway. "Best performance is given by Australian Cecil Kellaway. Why hasn't Hollywood yet woken up to this actor's ability? He makes this film something more than a mere midnight thriller. For the rest, the cast is able, the thrills laid on with a trowel, the result satisfactory."[79]

The Mummy's Hand proved popular enough with audiences for an extended run in most cities, beginning in New South Wales in January 1941. Then it moved around the country, ending in South Australia in October 1941. After that point it was given a second life in suburban and country cities where the local newspaper critics were kinder.

The Ghost of Frankenstein

At 9:58 a.m. on February 19, 1942, Japanese forces' raid on Darwin eclipsed Pearl Harbor. Another wave of bombers attacked at midday, destroying the port. The city was in ruins with hundreds dead and more wounded, the port littered with damaged and sunken ships (over 20), from Australia, American and England. The RAAF base had been damaged and over 30 aircraft damaged beyond repair. Australia's Top End was now open and vulnerable to invasion.

Civilians were rapidly evacuated[80] and the Menzies government drafted plans (the Brisbane Line) which would see the northern parts of Australia abandoned and handed over to invading forces should they arrive. Menzies also capitulated to Winston Churchill and ordered two boatloads of Australian troops to be sent to Myanmar to defend the English positions there. Despite more air raids, Japanese forces never landed in Australia.

The incoming government, led by John Curtin, rejected the Brisbane Line defense and called upon all Australians to take up arms and fight, as opposed to defending England in Europe, India or Africa. He also recalled the troops from Myanmar. Churchill, irate, promptly withdrew England's support for Australia. Australia then turned to America for assistance, and an alliance was formed. The young country was at war, both with a foreign agent and, at times, with itself as American troops were brought in to help hold the line, causing friction. This friction culminated with the infamous Battle of Brisbane which saw Australian civilians and armed forces engaged in a running riot with American armed forces, resulting in one death and several injuries. Despite the censor's best effort to keeping these events quiet, news spread.

American soldier Eddie Leonski landed in Melbourne on February 2, 1942. In his brief time in the country, he murdered three women. He was known as the Brownout Strangler, due to his tendency to strangle his victims during night-time periods when the lighting was low. Leonski was caught and handed over to the U.S. Army. He was court martialed and then executed on November 9.[81]

Into this mix of confusion, fear and upheaval, horror films kept coming, but they paled in comparison to the newsreels highlighting the true horrors of the war on the Australian doorstep. As each new horror film was released, it was paired up with another horror film such as *Bride of Frankenstein,* which was still running a decade after its original release.

The Ghost of Frankenstein, with Lon Chaney Jr. stepping into Karloff's shoes, was launched like *Bride* and there was a midnight screening competition akin to *WereWolf of London.* An ad was placed in the classifieds in the major newspapers calling for people willing to attend a screening of the new movie, in the presence of a ghost, at midnight. The winner of the competition was treated to a supper, catered by the "ghost" (a cinema employee draped in a giant white sheet), after which the cinema was darkened, all lights turned off and the movie screened. Once the movie started, the "ghost" leapt out and screamed "Boo!" at random moments, scaring the poor person senseless.[82]

The movie premiered on July 24, 1942, in Tasmania. The successful applicant, brilliantly photographed looking nonplussed as the "ghost" loomed over him, was Leslie Owen, who stated that he had seen all the Frankenstein pictures, "but this one caps them all."[83] The effect in Adelaide was the same, although the winner, Mrs. Polson, posed for a photo in which she attempted to appear terrified.[84] It didn't work.

With few notable exceptions, this was one of the last successful launches of horror against the backdrop of World War .

The Mummy's Tomb

If the selling point in Australia for *The Mummy* had been Boris Karloff and *The Mummy's Hand,* Cecil Kellaway, then *The Mummy's Tomb* was Lon Chaney Jr., fresh from his turn as the title character in *The Wolf Man*. "[Chaney], now quite renowned for his blood-chilling roles, appears at the Grand tonight in *The Mummy's Tomb,* probably the most awesome of his pictures."[85]

The Mummy's Hand was still in cinemas when *Tomb* premiered but, unlike the previous entries in the series, it was paired with other films, usually a popular western or war film. Its running time was one hour, 13 minutes shorter than *The Mummy*, too short to be billed on its own. From now on, every Mummy movie released in Australia would be the bottom end of a double bill.

The film received excellent reviews with Chaney and makeup artist Jack Pierce being singled out for praise. For Pierce, praise was long overdue, as reviewers made mention of his skills in making up Karloff ten years previously, while revealing that Chaney's mask was rubber. Rubber mask or not, Chaney's performance was hailed as being his best yet in a horror film, even if the plot was recycled. "The vogue of the horror film," wrote the critic in the *Voice*, "although somewhat diminished, still continues to hold its own. *The Mummy's Tomb* is the latest creation to enter the field of entertainment. The idea of an ancient Egyptian mummy, kept alive for thousands of years, is certainly a fantastic one."[86]

The film had a staggered release around Australia, supported by the usual western. It began its run in Western Australia in December 1942, then around the country, ending in South Australia in July 1944

The Catholic Weekly Grades Your Films

In early March 1942, *The Catholic Weekly*, a widely distributed broadsheet published out of Sydney, entered the game of film censorship by publishing a weekly list of all films currently at the cinemas, with the editors informing their readerships as to which movies were decent enough to see. These grades were broken down into four categories: Suitable for All, For Adults Only, Not Yet Graded and Unsuitable.

Sex, immorality and the erosion of Catholic values were the underlying themes of the editorials, with the low moral standards of film being the chief source of audiences falling, neatly bypassing the fact that a world at war isn't going to see as many movies as a world at peace. There was a major flaw in their assessments, though, as a study of trading results from various cinemas showed that the number of people attending the movies had increased from 1939 to 1943. In some cases, these numbers had doubled. Just where *The Catholic Weekly* was getting its information from, was never detailed.

Most of the films recommended for all (read: good, church-going children) were harmless fare such as the Andy Hardy series, westerns and the occasional war film but the movies cleared were tame and innocuous.

Despite *The Catholic Weekly*'s fire and brimstone editorials warning people away from horror films and comic books (the latter was a constant source of delinquency for the *Weekly*), the only film in the entire two years of the column named as Unsuitable for viewing by all audiences was the non-horror film *Life on the Dole*, a social comedy.

By 1947, the newspaper had moved onto other forms of media to attack (comic books!) but their parting shot at horror films was just as impressive as anything they'd published to date.[87]

At the beginning of school holidays, 1947, horror films were most popular with children, causing "dangerous emotional stimulation" which would lead to delinquency and interaction between boys and girls that the *Weekly* believed could only mean one thing: sex. Children's behavior was due to the negligence of the parents, cried the *Weekly*, and if the parents wouldn't act to prevent their children from seeing horrors such as *Son of Dracula* and *The Ghost of Frankenstein*, then surely the state must. The solution: Round the kids up and put them into homes to save them from themselves, or arrest the exhibitor for allowing children into the cinemas.

The horror films rated AO by the *Catholic Weekly*, denounced as having no value for anyone, were a rather small and select list that made no real sense: *The Invisible Man* (1933), *The Gorilla* (1939), *The Ape* (1940), *The Ghost Breakers* (1940), *The Mummy's Hand* (1940), *Dr. Jekyll and Mr. Hyde* (1941), *The Wolf Man* (1941), *Cat People* (1942), *The Ghost of Frankenstein* (1942), *I Walked with a Zombie* (1943), *Phantom of the Opera* (1943), *Son of Dracula* (1943), *The Mad Ghoul* (1943) and *Frankenstein Meets the Wolf Man* (1943). Other movies in the same series, such as *The Invisible Man Returns* and *The Invisible Woman*, were fine, as were other *Frankenstein* movies.

At the very least, the *Weekly* argued, stronger censorship was needed, and this demand was going to be heeded before the decade was out.

Rape, Murder and *The Mummy's Ghost*

Two years after *Tomb*, *The Mummy's Ghost* hit cinemas. By now, audiences were used to the sight of Kharis on the screen, and the thrills weren't as vivid as they once were. The short running time meant that it couldn't be released as a stand-alone feature, and was paired with a Charles Starrett western, *Riding West*. The lack of previews saw critics write the barest of reviews based on the publicity material that Universal had sent them and, in some cases, the plots of the previous two movies. It was business as usual for the franchise—grave robbers steal a mummy; Kharis comes back to life, kills people, then is destroyed. Wash, rinse, and repeat. *Ghost* saw Chaney return as Kharis, and his performance received glowing reviews, despite the limited acting required for the role.

The Mummy's Ghost would become the horror movie that caused a murder.

On October 4, 1944, Ronald Morgan, a 24-year-old returned soldier with an intellectual disability, hopped on the tram to see *The Mummy's Ghost*, just one of a few dozen people who would see it on a typical spring day in Melbourne.

Morgan emerged from the movie and caught the tram back to Moonee Ponds, where he lived. Passing by Janice Baul, a bright seven-year-old girl on her way home from school, he kidnapped her. He dragged her into his house and bashed her head in with the jagged end of an exploded mortar shell that he'd souvenired from the army. He removed her clothing and sexually assaulted her, then dragged her body into a nearby alleyway, assaulted her again and left her for dead.

Baul was found, barely alive, and rushed to the Children's Hospital. Without regaining consciousness, she died two days later.

As Morgan had been seen talking to Baul, police quickly arrested him. While in custody he made a full confession, stating that he had been strongly affected by the movie and had left in a daze, remembering nothing until his arrival at home, whereupon he read a newspaper and blacked out. The next thing he knew, Baul was in his lounge room, so he hit her in the head. He then panicked and dumped both her and her clothing. He didn't admit to the sexual assaults but didn't deny them either. The charge of carnal knowledge and abuse was quietly withdrawn, and the murder charge pursued.

Morgan's history was a sad one, having suffered from an undiagnosed and unrecognized intellectual disability from birth; he had been described as a lunatic. As a child in South Australia, he tended to wander away from home, leading his parents to institutionalize him in a Salvation Army receiving home. When his family moved to Melbourne, they took him with them but promptly placed him in another receiving home. Morgan was tired of being locked up and escaped. He was captured, sent back and officially certified as insane.

He escaped again in 1940 and joined the AIF (Australian Imperial Force). It didn't take long for the army to realize he had problems: It discharged him and again officially certified him as insane, sending him to yet another receiving home. He escaped and enlisted again, although it is unknown if he enlisted under his own name or a pseudonym. It didn't matter; the army promptly sent him into battle, although he was woefully inadequate for this situation. By 1943 he had been found out, was certified insane for the third time, and discharged, before finding himself in Moonee Ponds, unemployed, unsupported and alone.

The jury was faced with a difficult decision: Was Morgan responsible for his actions? Doctors testified that while Morgan knew what he had done was wrong from a legal standpoint, he had no idea what he had done wrong morally. The jury had no choice but to find him guilty and despite its pleas for mercy, Morgan was sentenced to death. With the war in full force, and the Eddie Leonski murders still fresh in people's minds, the death sentence was welcomed.

The connection between the murder and the horror movie was reported in the newspapers, but not to the extent that it could have been. Universal Australia was very keen to keep the connection out of the media, to avoid having one of their horror films connected with a very real horror.

Morgan was quickly forgotten as the war entered its last months. *The Mummy's Ghost* was eventually paired with other horror films and released in the "Horror Show" series, the tragedy forgotten by all, barring the family of Janice Baul and the police who worked on the case.

Morgan's sentence was commuted to life without parole upon appeal, and he remained in jail until his release in 1969. Once released, he couldn't control his urges and was arrested, charged and convicted for 15 sexual offenses upon girls under the age of ten. He was given a further ten-year sentence, to be served on top of the 17 years he now owed the parole board for his initial release. In 1976, he was jailed for another 36 years. He won the right to appeal his sentence in 1989, but remained incarcerated, earning the dubious distinction of becoming Victoria's longest serving prisoner.

The Censors' Decade

The 1940s saw the Censor Board busier dealing with horror films than any other decade, resulting in the 1948 ban of horror films. Frustratingly, the complete scope of the number of cuts, and exactly what was removed, is difficult to trace due to poor records.

In 1942, Cresswell O'Reilly was replaced by J.O. Alexander. Alexander wasted no time banning *The Man with Two Lives*. This was followed by cuts on another high-profile film, the Spencer Tracy *Dr. Jekyll and Mr. Hyde* (1941)—a loss of 13 minutes of footage. *The Mad Doctor of Market Street* starring Lionel Atwill was cut. *The Mad Ghoul*, released in October 1944, was also reduced. *House of Horrors* was cut and retitled *The Sinister Shadow*. Most of the cuts in that film were to excise the image of Rondo Hatton, whose character was renamed "The Shadow."

Some films had the reverse applied to them. *Dr. Cyclops*, released in Australia in April 1941, was advertised as having a running time of 77 minutes. The standard American version has a running time of 75 minutes, which indicates that an extra two minutes of footage was inserted into the Australian release. Just what that footage was, and indeed if it existed, is unknown. It is more likely that the extra two minutes never existed, and that the running time was recorded incorrectly.

As the number of imported films returned to pre-war levels, straining the Sydney accommodation of the censors, there was an increase in the number of films being banned or cut. No films were rejected in 1944, but ten were banned in 1946 with two subsequently passed on appeal. The number of films being cut by the censors also increased from three percent to 7.3 percent. While Alexander took satisfaction from the fact that the films banned in 1946 had all been American, he was dismayed the following year to report that more than twice as many British as American films had been cut by his censorial scissors. This was even though 85.7 percent of feature films in 1947 were American.

The Mummy's Curse

The last entry in the Mummy series hit Australian cinemas in April 1945 to a disinterested audience. Running for an hour, the movie was never considered to be a stand-alone feature and was paired up with comedies, musicals and the ever-popular westerns.

Unlike the earlier installments, the reviews were harsh, reflecting the recycled plot from the 1932 *The Mummy*. The *Voice* in Tasmania gave the film two stars out of five, rated the actors' performances, including Chaney, as "fair" and gave the impression that, if one had seen the Karloff original, then there was no real need to see this one. The *Western Herald* (New South Wales) critic was crueler, claiming that the lead canine in the supporting feature, *Sergeant Mike*, was better than the *Mummy* cast.

In Adelaide, a Charles Starrett western was placed with the movie and the reviews were good, with the film's scarier moments being described as genuinely chilling.

It had all been seen and done before, better, and the public knew it. Each capital city ran the film for a week, after which time it was parceled out to the suburbs and country. In most country areas, the film was chosen as the supporting feature for the likes of *The Ghost of Frankenstein, The Spider Woman* and *House of Frankenstein*, the latter feature illustrating that a movie with a lot of monsters was more entertainment than one with a single monster. *House* also proved that, when it came to monsters, Universal was pinning their hopes on the Big Three, Frankenstein's Monster, Dracula and the Wolf Man. The Mummy was no longer a factor.

Curse began its run in Sydney in April 1945 and a week later was quietly sent around the country, for one-week runs, finishing in Adelaide in March 1946. New life was breathed into the movie, and a few others, when horror films were mass-released in August 1947. *Curse* and *Tomb* were two of the films selected, along with *The Wolf Man, Frankenstein Meets the Wolf Man, Son of Dracula, The Ghost of Frankenstein* and *Revenge of the Zombies*. The movies were then placed into theaters with advertising targeted at children on school holidays. As the children entered the cinemas, they were given headache powders and told that their lives were now insured for £1000—facts that the kids loved hearing.[88] Parents and the media were horrified at the thought of children as young as 12 being able to walk in and see such films, but this was proof that what was horrific in the 1930s was now tame entertainment for kids.

The Real Horror Movie: Atrocity Films

People entering cinemas in May 1945[89] were horrified by what they saw on the screen and virtually nobody was prepared for it. The Nazi film showed Germans, civilians and SS officers alike, healthy and smiling, and often mugging for the camera. Countering this were images of emaciated Jews, Gypsies, gay people, Englishmen, Americans—anyone that had fallen foul of the Nazi regime—standing stunned and shocked behind barbed wire fences and gates.

Bodies of the dead were shown being bulldozed into ditches and buried, or set alight, by the same soldiers that had liberated the camps. Films taken of death camps such as Belsen, Dachau, Auschwitz, Majdanek and Mauthausen were particularly horrifying, showing partially burnt bodies still smoldering in crematoriums along with images of bones, skulls, mountains of teeth, luggage and other personal items.

Audiences in Australia didn't quite know what to make of it. There had been word about the camps, via newspapers, radio reports and letters from soldiers based in Europe but, due to wartime censorship, these accounts were watered down. To finally see the reality of these atrocities was nothing short of shocking.

The call immediately went up for all German POWs in Australia, held in camps such as Murchison in Victoria, Loveday in South Australia and Hay in New South Wales particularly, to be forced to view the films before being repatriated back home. This didn't always happen as the emphasis was now on getting prisoners of war from Germany and other parts of Europe home as quickly as possible.

Screenings were arranged in some locations for the POWs, with limited success. Some prisoners were shocked by what they saw, some had full or partial knowledge of what had been happening and weren't surprised, and there were those who were delighted to see the fate of their enemies. Later reports suggested that most Germans felt that the films were Allied propaganda and the victims shown were from the Allied raid on Dresden.[90] Ironically, a lot of the German POWs interred in Australia ended up emigrating back to Australia, often applying for refugee status before being shipped back to Europe, once they realized that any property and family they had in Germany were now long gone.[91]

The films, as important as they might have been, were rated as being suitable for adults only, yet, as they were newsreels, they were often shown as the preview for films and serials available for anyone, including children. This sent mothers and parents groups into overdrive, calling for the films to be banned. Children began coming home and recounting what they'd seen at the cinema.

> "It is a serious crime against children to allow them, to see these horror films," stated the vice-president of the New South Wales Teachers Federation, one Lucy Woodcock. "I saw the atrocity films at a newsreel theatre last Saturday. I was deeply affected by the stark bestiality of the films. I hate to think what effect it had on the child. Police should see that no children enter theatres where these films are being shown."[92]

Yet the Government was insisting that everyone, including children, should watch them and there were those who fully agreed. "Children should see the films, so they will never forget what the Nazis did to men and women," said Tony Wood, a salesgirl. "My ten-year-old sister saw the film and was horrified." She said she was determined that there would never be another war if she can help it. "Letting children see the pictures will have a better effect than if they were prevented from seeing them."[93]

Cinema managers were in a quandary. By refusing entry to children, they ran the risk of being abused by angry parents who had brought their families to see innocuous fare during school holidays. By allowing parents to take their children into the cinemas, managers then faced the risk of being abused for screening the atrocity films.

A compromise was reached. Lights would go up before the atrocity newsreels, thus allowing parents to remove their children to the foyer for the duration. Once

Advertisement for *The Beast with Five Fingers* (1947) from *The Film Weekly*, July 31, 1947.

the newsreel was finished, children would be allowed back in. Advertising was also altered to read, "Not Entirely Suitable for Children. This is a Horror Film."

This worked as a stopgap.

The concentration camp movies were labeled "Atrocity Films," but they were also identified as horror films. They were being shown in cinemas at the same time as *House of Frankenstein* and *The Mummy's Curse* and often on the same bill, resulting in parents' groups escalating their battle against the genre, unable to differentiate between the real horrors of the war and the filmed horrors of Universal Studios. They took the calls for the banning of horror films moved up to a new level.

The calls for atrocity films to be banned failed. Amazingly the Chief Censor, J.O. Alexander, not only refused to ban the films, but he also refused to censor them and came out in favor of the movies. Speaking about one film, showing the hanging death of a German, he commented, "It is only fair to show what is happening to those people who inflicted untold misery and suffering on millions of people."[94]

Alexander further justified his stance: "I believe that the Nazi who was executed had murdered two British soldiers," he told the press. "I feel sure that the wives or families of the two men would be glad to see the newsreel."[95]

By the end of 1945, the Australian public had grown weary of atrocity films, and they slowly faded from the screens.

Horror Movies Banned

"No cultural or entertainment value."

After the war concluded, the government and censors renewed their attack on horror films using the fatigue of war as a reason that the public were turning away from the genre.

At a meeting of State Premiers in 1946, it was decided that all states, barring one, would enact uniform film censorship. The dissenting state was South Australia, ironic because South Australia had banned more films than any other. Each state then proceeded to pass their own bills in their relevant legislative councils.

The first real step came with the passing of the Film Censorship Bill in Queensland.[96] It allowed for a government-appointed censor in the state of Queensland to ban any movie they saw fit with the right of appeal lying with the relevant Minister. The reasons for potential banning were given in Section 17, part (2):

> The Censor shall not approve a film which is, in his opinion—
> (a) Indecent or obscene, or likely to be injurious to morality; or
> (b) Likely to encourage public disorder or crime; or
> (c) Undesirable in the public interest.

The similarities with the federal standards were remarkable, but the application of these standards would be vastly different.

Once the Queensland bill had been passed, J.O. Alexander announced a decision to ban horror films entirely at a federal level, effective April 1948. In his letter to the Motion Picture Distributors Association of Australia, he made his case clear:

> For some considerable time, past consideration has been given to the doubtful value of "Horror" stories on the entertainment screen, this type of film has no cultural or entertainment value and its appeal extends [sic] only to a very limited section of the community, a section whose mental outlook should not be fed with films of this nature. In addition, such films are a source of potential danger to women in a delicate state of health.[97]

The letter went on to say that all horror films would be refused registration by the Censorship Board; thus any film made after 1948 would not be shown at Australian cinemas. Films that had been passed prior to 1948 would be exempt from this policy and could still be shown. Two states refused to take part in the uniform legislation, South Australia and New South Wales,[98] although both came into line in 1972. But as any movie had to be passed by the Commonwealth censor, and all films were coming into Sydney first through customs, all states and territories were part of the ban by proxy.

Privately, Alexander admitted to the Comptroller-General that no horror films had been imported into Australia in 1947, so the ban had already been in *de facto* effect for 12 months. Alexander had been prompted to formally ban horror anyway because of verbal observations by the former Customs Minister Keane and by public pressure.

The horror ban was reported immediately by the newspapers,[99] and the film industry magazine *Film Weekly* put the ban onto its cover. In a strong editorial, *Film Weekly* quoted A.R. Payne, president of the NSW Exhibitors' Association, as being "not surprised" at the Chief Censor's decision to refuse registration to all future films which might normally receive horror classification. *Film Weekly* also reported how Payne had been confronted with numerous complaints from various Parents and Citizen's Associations who wanted horror films banned. The editorial then damned the decision by the Chief Censor directly:

> The Censor, then, will not be damming the flood of undesirable film: there isn't any flood. He will not be preventing exhibitors from feeding horror to children: they don't.... What the Censor will do is silence the amateur censors, officials of women's organizations and parents' associations, who have constantly exaggerated the number and influence of horror films in Australia. The decision is a safeguard, too; by eliminating the possibility of any future horror film coming into an exhibitor's booking calculations, it will prevent his standard of showmanship from slipping. The elimination of the horror film will therefore ensure a better type of programme being maintained; it will reduce causes for complaint against the industry, thereby serving as a valuable piece of public relations. Also, it will ensure that no hard-spared dollars will leave this country to pay for a type of film which, in the words of the Chief Censor, "has no cultural or entertainment value" and whose appeal "extends only to a very limited section of the community." No longer will Australians be able to see films wherein any of the cast sucks blood, turns into a wolf, or lies in a coffin with a stake through his heart.[100]

Film Weekly was right, and yet wrong at the same time. While it was true that no new horrors would be allowed into the country, the loophole that was inserted into the legislation allowed for the continued exhibition of any and every movie that had been cleared by the censor, prior to the 1948 cut-off date. This loophole covered the classic Universal Monsters period.

Publicly the exhibitors expressed their dismay at the ban and the lost revenue; privately they were relieved as the ban would now see fewer complaints against their products. The industry saw the move as a positive one and placed its own unique spin on the ban by pointing out that film standards would now improve. The ban would also serve to silence the many groups that had attempted to censor films on an amateur basis, such as the *Catholic Weekly* and the various community groups around the country.

If Alexander believed that such a ban would lessen his workload, he was mistaken. The emphasis on banning and censorship now moved to home movies and independent shorts that were being brought into the country, every single one of which Alexander was forced to watch. It was gleefully reported, within Customs, that Alexander was found asleep on more than one occasion during such screenings.

In a subtle move, exhibitors were now bringing back the Universal Horrors for another run at cinemas while the ban was being reported. F. Keith Manzie, writing for *The Argus*, pointed out that mainstream movies such as *Great Expectations* often featured moments of true horror in them, but they would not be banned in the future.[101] Ross Campbell of the *Sydney Morning Herald* noted that Universal would be the hardest hit and pondered the fate of the forthcoming *Abbott and Costello Meet Frankenstein*.[102]

Meet the Ghosts. Abbott and Costello Renamed

A major loophole in the newly minted horror ban was exposed almost immediately. Despite a cast of horror stalwarts in the form of Bela Lugosi, Lon Chaney Jr. and Glenn Strange and the subject matter, *Abbott and Costello Meet Frankenstein* was classified as a comedy and allowed release in Australia. The larges of the censor only went so far. No mention of the words "Frankenstein," "Dracula" or "Wolf Man" in advertisements would be permitted, so Universal simply fell into line with U.K. standards. *Abbott and Costello Meet Frankenstein* was subsequently renamed *Meet the Ghosts.* Interestingly, there was no mention of Bud and Lou in the official title—the movie was not *Abbott and Costello Meet the Ghosts*, it was, simply, *Meet the Ghosts.* The movie was released in late November 1948.

The film was cleared for release in late September 1948, but not without 20 minutes being cut, leaving it at just over an hour. These cuts were carried out despite the movie already being cut by four minutes in the U.K.

The Australian censor cuts meant the movie made little sense and gave it a disjointed feel; scenes ended suddenly without resolution, the action jumped from location to location and at times scenes ended mid-sentence. This 63-minute version of the film was later shown on Australian television, with the only redeeming feature being the restoration of the original title. The first time Australians were able to see the film in its uncut state was when it was released on home video, then DVD and Blu-Ray. Even today, television stations keep with the butchered version.

Trade ads made no mention of who the "ghosts" might be, but there was an expectation in newspapers that every Universal Monster would appear: Dracula, Frankenstein's Monster, the Wolf Man, the Mummy, the Invisible Man, various mad doctors, hunchbacks and other sinister people. Again, newspaper advertisements were not allowed to mention the names of the monsters, but articles in the same papers could.

Eventually reviewers gave away the plot[103] and pointed out that Dracula, the Wolf Man and Frankenstein's Monster were present and accounted for, the others were absent, and that genuine horrors did exist in the film. After the first run, restrictions on the print advertisements for the film were relaxed, and all the monsters were named—along with a few who were not in the film.

The fate of other Abbott and Costello films varied. *Abbott and Costello Meet the Killer, Boris Karloff* had at least three titles in Australia. The first was the standard film title,[104] the second simplified it to *Meet the Killer* (advertisements for this title mentioned the presence of Karloff[105]) and the third labeled the movie *Meet the Killers*. The latter sported an advertisement boasting the presence of not only Karloff but also Lon Chaney Jr. as the Wolf Man; Chaney being listed separately.[106] One could only guess the puzzlement of anyone seeing the movie from the advertisements and wondering when the Wolf Man and Chaney were going to pop up. He would not have been able to save the film. Reviews were not kind and the movie soon slipped off the screens.

The Strange Case of the Schizophrenic *Smith's Weekly*

Rarely has there been a broadsheet as influential, literate and bohemian as the late *Smith's Weekly*. The newspaper, founded by Clyde Packer, Claude Smith and Sir James Joyton, began life in 1919 and ended in 1950. At its best, its importance and influence cannot be overstated, at its worse it was still widely read and believed. It was patriotic, stood up for soldiers and claimed to represent the average person.

Smith's Weekly was run by a mixture of rascals, intellectuals and some of the finest journalistic minds, writers, artists and cartoonists of the era. This was reflected in its content. The likes of cartoonists Stan Cross, Jim and Dan Russell, George Finlay, Eric Joliffe and Syd Miller rubbed shoulders with writers Vince Kelly, George Blaikie, Henry Lawson, Lennie Lower, Errol Knox and more. In a Golden Age of Australian newspapers, *Smith's Weekly* was a diamond, and its influence was still being felt, both directly and indirectly, across Australian newspapers decades after its closure.

The newspaper's staff often took it upon themselves to promote a cause, sometimes just to amuse themselves. In the teens they promoted the cause of the Australian soldier, the "Digger," and promised to hold politicians accountable for promises made. They often went after dodgy politicians and businesspeople. Censorship was a big issue for the staff at *Smith's* and they would often take both sides of that debate.

Smith's Weekly staff had their finger on the pulse of the Australian public. They knew what fights would be popular and, more importantly, what sides to take. One such cause was the calls to ban all horror movies, beginning in the early 1940s, but in their calling for bans, the staff of *Smith's Weekly* revealed a certain degree of deliberate hypocrisy: They would often give rave reviews to the very same movies they wanted banned.*Smith's Weekly*'s reviewers used their own scale to rate films. Called "the Smith's Barometer," the ratings were as follows:

AAA: The Gold Cup. "*Smith's*" highest award.
AA: The Bouquet. For outstanding excellence.
A: Handclaps. Good.

B: The Bee. Average.
BB: The Raspberry. Inferior.
BBB: The Fair Cow. Don't say we didn't warn you.

Frankenstein, Bride of Frankenstein, Dracula's Daughter and *The Mummy* all rated A+. *Dracula, The Ghoul, The Black Cat, The Raven, The Walking Dead, The Invisible Ray, Son of Frankenstein, WereWolf of London* and *The Gorilla* all rated an A. In fact, the only 1930s–40s horror movie that received a B was *Black Friday*.[107]

At the same time, *Smith's Weekly* was advising people to go out and see horror films (with reviews such as "A picture worth seeing,"[108] "*The Mummy* is just about as hair-raising as it sets out to be,"[109] "The whole film is a piece of good entertainment and well directed,"[110] "It's worth seeing"[111]), it was also editorializing, often on the very same pages as the reviews, against the entire horror genre. The first real attack came in 1932 in an editorial calling Carl Laemmle to account for creating the genre. Ken Sessor wrote,

> It is not news that there are vogues and fashions in films. But it serves as an introduction to a discussion of the current cycle of horror films. One explanation of how these swings to one type commence is anything but flattering to moviedom. If a single producer is credited with getting a full house at the opening morning session with a new class of story, by the evening-session the remainder of the producing-companies are bound to have a similar story on location. Something of that nature occurred to bring about the current hair-raising cycle, embracing *Frankenstein, Dr. Jekyll and Mr. Hyde, Dracula,* etc., etc., with knobs on.
>
> Carl Laemmle is credited with having started the blood-freezers with *Dracula*. He is understood to have discovered that there is no provision in the American censorship laws, or the Hays production code, to limit the extent of gruesomeness in a film. When, on top of this, Hollywood found that people were glad to pay good money to be horrified, morbidness came into its own.

Sessor continued, "The appeal of *Frankenstein* is candidly one of blood-and-thunder. Universal seems to have accepted it as a foregone conclusion that feminine picturegoers are bound to get some emotional thrill out of this sublimation of the bedtime ghost story, done with all the literal accuracy of the camera. *Dracula*'s business gives them good ground for the belief."[112]

This attack came shortly before Sessors reviewed *Frankenstein*. Giving the movie an A+ grading, Sessor wrote,

> [T]he film is remarkable for its lighting and photographic effects, and, strangely enough, for a certain restraint. But it is obvious that any audience must watch it merely as a series of preludes to murder. Coffins, gibbets, skeletons, graves and other accessories are sprinkled throughout, and there has been a careful and systematic distribution of sudden death, so that the lingering expectations of the audience may be revived. The slaughter of a cripple and a child has been represented with a restraint which adds to the horror. These scenes are indicated by suggestion, not by direct narration; similarly,[113] the dazed villager who bears the corpse of his maimed child through the streets makes a scene which really horrifies by its reticence.

Other than confirming that the Australian print of *Frankenstein* showed the murder of little Maria, the review made it clear that this was a movie not to be missed. More positive reviews followed for other horror movies, all intermixed with a series of short editorials, poems and letters attacking the same films.

Things remained calm for several years until religious groups began to call for an end to horror films being shown at children's matinees. In 1944, this resulted in a brilliant, and biting, article in which Lennie Lower took on the guise of a reformer who was shocked that children were using their imaginations and pointing out that more of them played war and cops-and-robbers than anything from a horror film.[114]

The satire was short-lived as the following year saw editorials blasting the decision to show such movies to kids. *Smith's* began to give protest groups more column space and tended to agree with them as the tide of public opinion turned. By 1948, the newspaper, entering its last years, was actively calling for bans on horror films, Australia wide. When the word came that horror films were to be banned from children's matinees in Victoria, *Smith's* celebrated a victory. Their ultimate victory came when the horror ban came into effect. Taking credit for the ban, *Smith's* wrote,

SMITH'S GETS THINGS DONE! HORROR FILMS BANNED! LONG CAMPAIGN ENDS!

Chief Commonwealth Film Censor (Mr. J. O. Alexander) has decided at last to ban all horror films from Australia. That's the climax to a long campaign by *Smith's*.

Mr. Alexander says that for some time he has been considering the doubtful value of horror stories on the screen. There was no need for him to so waste his time. For years now Smith's has been stressing the extremely "doubtful" value of these films.

Had Mr. Alexander followed the advice tendered by highly qualified child-welfare officers and the Parents and Citizens' Association in this paper, he would have banned horror films long ago. A few weeks back (*Smith's*, 10/4/48), we quoted welfare workers who claimed that when "suitable only for adults" horror films are advertised, juvenile attendances increase by more than 25 percent.

These same welfare workers claimed that these films are an important spur to child delinquency. The week Mr. Alexander announced his decision, one Sydney theatre headed its advertisement: "Ugh! Horror on Friday!"

The programme was then proudly announced as *Frankenstein Meets Wolfman*, plus *Night Monster* which were described as "dripping with bloodcurdling horror!"

Mr. Alexander's action now marks the end of these senseless shockers.[115]

With that win, *Smith's* was vindicated. And now that horror was banned, the newspaper looked elsewhere for its next battle. *Smith's* folded less than 18 months later.

Intermission: The Fall of the Cinema, the Rise of the Drive-In

By the end of the 1940s, cinema was firmly entrenched in Australia. More people were attending the movies on a weekly basis than ever before. Even when the rising population was considered, the numbers were impressive. The 1927 Royal Commission stated that 110,000,000 admissions had been recorded across the country, with a total population of a mere 6,182,488. In 1953, the population had increased to 8,795,778 and the admissions had also risen to 133,959,000 tickets sold. In the first half of the twentieth century, Australians loved cinema and the studios loved Australia. Things changed, radically, as the second half of the 20th century kicked in; by 1976, a mere 604 cinemas were in operation.

Cinema had been in the country for ten years before T.J. West built a movie house in Sydney in 1906. Films had been shown in town halls, institute halls, outdoors and in theaters as part of vaudeville shows or on their own, but West saw the need for a purpose-built cinema, with permanent screens in place. He started the first in an extensive line of cinemas across the country, known as Wests. By 1909, there were 20 cinemas in Sydney alone, and more were coming. In 1919, there were 750 cinemas; by 1927, at the time of the Royal Commission, the number had exploded to a total of 1250.

The 1930s saw more cinemas built, all of them wired for sound. The 1940s saw a slight downturn in admissions, understandable as the world war saw the population drop slightly. Also, there were restrictions placed on when movies could be shown; the bombing of Darwin closed that city's cinemas for the duration, and the fear of invasion in Queensland, coupled with submarines in Sydney Harbor, meant that most cinemas went into lockdown and only operated in daylight hours.

Once the war was over, the explosion began anew. The peak for cinemas and attendances came in the early to mid–1950s when 1730 cinemas were recorded in the country.

The first drive-in cinema opened at Burwood, a suburb of Melbourne, in 1954. The next was at West Beach, Adelaide. Other states quickly followed and by 1956, 23 drive-ins were recorded in the country, with more *ad hoc* drive-ins operating in various areas. Adding to the woes of cinema was the introduction of television in 1956. Television kept an older audience home, in the same way that drive-ins became hugely popular with young people who could load a car, pay the one admission price and have a good night out. Most drive-ins also had seated areas which catered to people without cars: They could merely walk up, pay and go inside, sitting under the stars on a warm night and watch two films and cartoons.

The decline was gradual. By 1965, TV and drive-ins had taken a firm hold, and the number of cinemas began to drop. By 1965, 1000 cinemas were left. Drive-ins became increasingly popular once the owners realized that their patrons were not interested in serious drama or romance, they wanted thrills and spills. The old horror movies were dusted off and alternated on drive-in screen with the new science fiction, Atom Age monsters. These movies became major hits on weekends, as people could go to the drive-in, remain until the wee hours and not have to worry about school or work the next day.

The drive-in became a cultural phenomenon in Australia as it added benefits that a cinema couldn't compete with. The appeal of going to the drive-in was not just limited to seeing a movie. For many, the movie was just an added extra. The thrill of loading up as many people as could fit into the boot of a car, and the challenge of smuggling them into the drive-in, often became the most important aspect of a Friday or Saturday night (especially for those drive-ins who charged per person) once it became obvious that charging per car wasn't working. Charging per car would see dozens of people sitting on the back of a Ute, or crammed into a station wagon, resulting in potentially lost sales. At drive-ins where the cost was per person, cars with large boots, such as Leyland P76s or muscle cars by Holden and Ford, became the norm. It was perfectly natural to see a car pull up to a fence, the boot pop and several people spilling onto the gravel, laughing at the deception.

The drive-in also flourished because it was a safe environment for young people to have sex. This was enabled by the advent of two movies being shown at a single session. One movie was a hugely popular film; the other was of moderate interest, thus giving people plenty of time and opportunity to engage in whatever behaviors they wanted to. Panel vans and station wagons became the preferred vehicles for this activity, but people would often take any opportunity to copulate in any car they could commandeer, even if it were a Volkswagen or a Mini. Again, it was common to walk past a car and see the occupants either kissing or engaging in full-blown intercourse. The unwritten rule was that such activities were ignored, unless the couple could be sufficiently embarrassed by their drunken friends. This leads to another appeal of the drive-in—alcohol.

Alcohol was banned from cinemas, but at the drive-in, alcohol could be, and often was, smuggled in. The rule was that drive-ins were a dry area, with all food and drink to be bought on site. But the reality was that this rule could not be policed, other than a token walk around by staff and the ejection of drunken, disruptive patrons. Fights would often break out. On the rare occasion that a riot loomed, police would intervene.

Despite their growing popularity, the number of drive-ins never surpassed the number of cinemas. By 1976, the year after the introduction of color TV in Australia, there were 280 drive-ins and 604 cinemas across the country.

The introduction of video helped bring down the drive-in phenomena. By the early 1980s, drive-ins were starting to screen softcore pornography, and more drive-ins began to close as young people found a new medium. Despite the high prices, video recorders were becoming standard in households. Rental stores began to pop up, offering movies for less than the average drive-in admission price. The thrill of the drive-in diminished as films could be sourced and parties given at houses, which reduced the costs of going out for the evening.

Cinema began to feel the pinch, and by the time DVD was introduced, along with the Internet, drive-ins were all but finished and the number of cinemas had plunged to a mere 475 (1991 screens) Australia-wide in 2011. By 2015, there were 12 functioning drive-ins left in Australia; in Tasmania, the ACT and Western Australia, *none*. The number of cinemas had increased, barely, to 493 (2804 screens), but the introduction of streaming services will see that number again begin to fall. The once proud cinema is becoming a novelty, multiplexes are the way of the future and the concept of a single- (or even double-) screen cinema is now a thing of the distant past.

4

The Ban Years: 1949–1969

Even though horror films were banned from entering the country, a new genre began to appear: science fiction. Distributors soon found the major loophole in the legislation: a movie could be imported and exhibited, so long as it was not labeled horror. To this end, movies were defined as thrillers, science fiction or strong drama, with many movies being allowed through that should have fallen foul of the censor. Dozens of atomic age monster movies came into the country to feed the public's desire for horror, albeit in a roundabout way.

Classifying a movie as thriller or science fiction did not exclude the film from the censors, who would take out anything they deemed unsuitable. This allowed movies such as *Them!*, *The Blob*, *Conquest of Space*, *Mark of the Gorilla*, *The Black Castle*, *The Strange Door*, *The Day the Earth Stood Still*, *The Man from Planet X*, *Destination Moon*, *The Flying Saucer*, *Rocketship X-M*, *Two Lost Worlds*, *Captive Women*, *Red Planet Mars*, *It Came from Outer Space*, *The Son of Dr. Jekyll* and *Creature from the Black Lagoon* and its sequels to be screened nationally. Even a movie such as Vincent Price's *House on Haunted Hill* was classified as a thriller and screened.

Cinemas were able to offer a variety of new films, including some horror, via the loophole, although movies starring Karloff, Lugosi and Chaney were instantly dismissed as having no cultural value, with *The Strange Door* and *The Black Castle* notable exceptions. The reclassification loophole was not perfect, and films like *Abbott and Costello Meet Frankenstein* had to renamed entirely as no titles with horror connotations could enter Australia.

To meet demand for horror films, exhibitors routinely dipped back into their stock of pre–1948 films and re-released them at certain times of the year, usually around October 31 for Halloween and in December, coinciding with school holidays. Thus, *Frankenstein* and its sequels were given new leases on life every year. In this regard, even though new horror films were treated with dismay, Karloff classics were always readily available and were still popular. Once the horror ban was public knowledge, the estimated 25 known "true" horror films left in the country[1] were dusted off and instantly put back into circulation.

The Bela Lugosi Tour That Wasn't

The announcements were too good to be true. Once *Meet the Ghosts* came out, Universal wanted Lugosi to push the film wherever he could, including Australia. Lugosi was asked to fly Down Under and plug the movie for a week or two, first class, all expenses paid, for himself and his wife Lillian in January 1949. It appeared to be a given, as Hollywood actors leapt at the chance to travel to Australia and, as Lugosi was always cash poor, the money would come in handy. There was only one flaw: Lugosi had a lifelong fear of flying and flatly refused the offer. It did not matter how much money was put before him, or how desperately he needed it. "I have never flown in my life," he told reporters, "and I don't intend to start now."[2] The alternative was a boat trip, which could take up to four months in total. Lugosi could not afford to be at sea, both literally and figuratively, for that amount of time.

By this point in Lugosi's life, he was hopelessly addicted to morphine, methadone and other prescription and non-prescription drugs. A boat trip for that length of time would have required a lot of drugs to be both bought and smuggled on board. If that could not happen, then the trip might very possibly have killed him. Lugosi could not, and would not, take the risk.

This wasn't the only time that Lugosi fielded an offer from Australia. In 1951, while undertaking a successful *Dracula* revival on the English stage (a quicker boat trip), Lugosi was offered the opportunity to revive the play in Australia. The initial offer would see Lugosi spend six months of 1952 Down Under, staging the play across the country, beginning in Sydney in late January.[3] With the estimated three months of travel time to and from Australia, this would see Lugosi tied up for all of 1952. Again, citing his fear of flying, Lugosi passed.

The offer was then reduced to a four- and then two-week run, in Sydney, all for the same guarantee. As tempting as it was, it was conditional on Lugosi flying to Australia as he would not have time to sail. Faced with this dilemma, and as much as it would have pained him to turn down much-needed money, Lugosi again passed on the offer. He passed away in August 1956.

Mighty Joe Young and the Troubles of the Gorilla Suit

The horror ban did not stop RKO from bringing in the recently completed *Mighty Joe Young* as a "jungle adventure" film. Re-titled *Mr. Joseph Young of Africa*, the movie was released in late 1949 and people flocked to see it, keeping it in steady circulation well into 1951. Many gimmicks were used to promote the movie with one common aspect being a man dressed up in a gorilla suit, visiting cinemas where the movie was showing.

The "man in the gorilla suit" gimmick reached its zenith in October 1949, when "Mighty Joe Young" and his handler appeared on a quiet but sweltering day in Newcastle. The day was tame until Mighty Joe Young was led near a primary school where schoolchildren mobbed him. The children clawed at the monkey suit and one latched onto the zipper on its back. Joe twisted and leaned toward the child, hissing to leave him be, but to no avail. The children poked his groin with sticks, belted his stomach and kicked his shins and rear end. Mighty Joe Young snapped, his hissing erupting into snarls and swearing blue murder to all and sundry, instructing the children what they could do to themselves and where. The rage became fury. His handler, sensing potential violence, gained control and led him away from the screaming kids.

A brief time later, after Joe had been calmed, they walked up Main Street. "Where's Tarzan?" came a cry, to which Joe replied with a growl. A crowd began to form, with children not in school climbing the local tram for a better view and men emerging from the pub to ogle and heckle. It was not a good day.

When lunchtime arrived, Joe went into the nearby pub to "rehydrate," not bothering to remove the costume or headpiece. He sat at the bar drinking heavily through a straw. His liquid lunch finished, and his resolve restored through beer, Joe made his way to the beach thinking it would be cooler and quieter. The October heat radiated from the sand, broiling Joe in the unventilated costume. Sweating profusely, filled with amber courage, and a little sun-touched, Joe tried to carry away a young lady, to the irritation of her boyfriend: He ran at full speed, tackling Joe to the sand.

Joe's keeper stepped in and removed the 20-pound head from the suit, giving the man inside some fresh air. Joe let forth a litany of obscenities directed at the keeper, the suit, the movie, Newcastle and its inhabitants. The keeper, considering Joe to be refreshed, put the head back on him and led him to the next location, a community hall.

By now, Joe was all over the place, still drunk and concussed, and dehydrated. He eyed two women and pounced upon them, dragging them into a wild rumba. Joe's handler interceded, reminding him that he still had to go to the cinema where his movie was playing. Joe, dragged up the road to the theater, ran screaming into the building.

The ushers were startled at this man-ape, hooting and hollering and leaping about. The handler tried to control Joe and drag him away with moderate success before Joe was given a given a beer. The handler tried harder to control him, but Joe would have none of it and grabbed the heavy chain yoke that had bound him all day, reared up and swung, splitting his handler's skull.

Mighty Joe Young stood triumphant a moment before collapsing and soiling his suit.

It was an eventful day, which ended with one man bleeding from the scalp needing stitches at the local hospital, terrorized locals and a dazed, drunken "gorilla" passed out on the floor in his own vomit and urine. It would also mark the last time that Mighty Joe Young was unleashed for such an extended period. Henceforth, he was seen for an hour at most, inside the cinema.

"Soldier Affected by Horror Films"

On November 28, 1950, anti-horror advocates and the press secured the evidence they needed to support their position for the banning of horror films.

Marion May Megson received a call at work, telling her she was needed at home immediately. She hurried to her home in Redfern, a Sydney suburb, where she was greeted with a blow to the head, fracturing her skull. As she collapsed to the floor, her assailant stood over her.

"I had intentions of killing her. And I wanted to get her on her own,"[4] 19-year-old John Eric Cunningham told police. "…I hit her a number of times with the iron until she fell on the floor. I knelt beside her and tried to strangle her with my hands. The girl was still breathing, and I pulled my knife out of my pocket and held it for a minute over her heart. Something stopped me and I just could not do it."[5]

Cunningham then called for an ambulance and fled the scene. He later visited St. Vincent's Hospital and verified that Megson was alive. With that, he walked to a nearby police station and turned himself in.[6]

The court case caused a stir. Megson testified that she had rejected Cunningham three days earlier after he had suddenly broken off conversation and stared at her intensely. "How would you like your arms pulled from their sockets?" he hissed.[7] Megson told the court that Cunningham mentioned that he had just watched a horror movie where ants ate a man's eyes after he was strung up alive. That was enough for Megson to tell Cunningham to go away and never contact her again.[8]

Cunningham, who gave his occupation as "soldier," was raised an orphan in the notorious Westmead Boys Home[9] from the age of five. He was described to the court as being disturbed, unbalanced and delusional.[10] He had no family, no concept of family life, and very few social skills.

Amidst headlines such as "Soldier Affected by Horror Movies" and "Soldier Talked of Horror," the trial raised a number of issues. According to the media, it was the horror movie that led him to assault Marion, a positive link between on-screen horror and real-life horror. No other details mattered. Not Cunningham's history nor Marion's rejection, or any other factor that drove him over the edge.

Cunningham received five years on jail and Megson made a full recovery.

Frankenstein Returns

In May 1952, four years into the horror ban, an amazing thing happened in South Australia. The chief censor attended a private viewing of *Frankenstein* (1931) and promptly lifted the ban, ending two decades of appeals. The film could finally be screened, as it fell under the umbrella of being a horror film already in the country and one already exhibited (albeit in other states) pre–1948. Thus, *Frankenstein* gained a new first run in South Australian cinemas 21 years (and six sequels) after initial release. "The grunting, gangling monster by Boris Karloff seems scarcely able to excite a tingle to a generation which has lived through war with Nazis and Japanese and the peacetime fear of atom bombs," wrote one reviewer.[11]

Those who believed the lifting of this ban meant that the 1948 ban would soon be overturned were very wrong. This was a single movie in a single state, and an old movie at that. The horror ban, still in effect, would prevent the release of Hammer films and delay the horror revival for over a decade to come.

This was not the final fight for *Frankenstein* in Australia, just one more episode in the long tale of horror and censorship.

Lon Chaney Jr., (Not) Down Under

It was strange and highly unusual when, in July 1952, news broke about a potential visit to Australia by none other than Lon Chaney Jr. Just what Chaney was going to do when he visited the country is unknown, but the idea floated was to perform on stage, reprising many of his classic monsters. Each night Chaney would appear out on stage, made up as the Wolf Man, Frankenstein's Monster, the Mummy and the son of Dracula. The money offered was not the greatest, but as Chaney was in a career slump, due to the wind-up of horror in America, any money would be welcomed.

What was a factor was the length of the contract, in this case, a three-year deal. The confusion, for Chaney, was that he believed that the deal meant he would have to stay in Australia for three years straight rather than the more likely three-year commitment to tour, with the winter months free for Chaney to travel back to America. By the time he worked out the deal, it was too late, he had already rejected it, giving his ailing film career as the excuse; he did not want to be away from Hollywood for that length of time. Movies were hard enough to come by without vanishing to the other side of the world for an extended period.

Thus, Chaney joined Lugosi in rejecting Australia, albeit for entirely different reasons.

The Birth of 3-D

By 1952, "horror" movies became taboo in Australia. Universal, once the king of horror, shied away from the word, dumping any mention of it as soon as the ban came into effect. In the 1953 *Film Weekly Annual Directory,* Universal made mention of all the genres that they were now filming. Action, adventure, comedy, drama, music and romance were all listed, as was an emphasis on showmanship, top stars and best-selling stories, but nothing about horror or even thrillers.

The ban did not stop all horror movies from coming into the country. While any movie with the mention of "monster," "vampire," "Dracula," "werewolf" or "Frankenstein" in the title was likely to be rejected without question, the studios knew there were ways around the censor, such as labeling the film with a different title or genre. And if a gimmick could be attached to a film, even better. One such horror film was not only admitted to the country on full release, it was heralded as being one of the top-grossing, most successful films in Australia for 1953: the 3-D thriller *House of Wax*.

Cinemas began to prepare for the introduction of 3-D and widescreen in late 1952. Three-D kicked off with *Bwana Devil*, but it was not as successful as the build-up had promised, which made cinema operators nervous about the added expense of 3-D. They needed not have worried.

The first hit 3-D movie shown in Australia on general release was the magnificent *House of Wax*, starring Vincent Price. The film was a huge hit, partly assisted by the horror aspects of the storyline. *Wax* exceeded expectations and more than made up for the failure of *Bwana Devil*. It also had a shelf life of over a decade, although subsequent releases were in the standard 2D format. The movie's success was recognized by critics, who confessed to enjoying the spectacle at the same time as ridiculing the movie's plot, direction and acting (Price aside). Out of all the reviews, only the *Catholic Weekly* denounced the film entirely, calling it poor and questioning why anyone in their right mind would want to see it.

With the success of *House of Wax*, due to the marriage of horror, color and 3-D, RKO threw its support behind 3-D, announcing in trade ads that every single RKO film from 1953 onwards would be available in both 3-D 35mm, although this pledge never eventuated.

King Kong Redux

"The Highest Grossing Movie of 1953"

Out of all the films released in Australia in 1953, including the Oscar-winning *From Here to Eternity, Hondo, Julius Caesar* and *The Moon Is Blue*, one movie easily outgrossed them all. What made this feat even more remarkable is that the movie was now 20 years old and black and white.

RKO Australia, hurting from the success of *House of Wax,* decided to take a punt and tackle it head on with a tried-and-true monster from a generation before. They ordered a fresh set of prints from America and unleashed the great ape once more, in the process scoring the top-grossing film of the year.

The idea of reissuing *King Kong* came from the success of *Mighty Joe Young.* Reviews of that movie drew strong comparisons, due to the involvement of Merian Cooper, and this did not go unnoticed by the Hoyts chain of cinemas and RKO.

In January 1953, as soon as *Joe Young*'s season had finished, *Kong* returned to cinema screens after an absence of 19 years and provided fresh scares and thrills for a new generation of filmgoers who had wondered what all the fuss was about. *Kong* exceeded all expectations when it broke the box office record in Sydney over the Australia Day long-weekend. This record was assisted by a strong promotion of print and publicity, the latter seeing three live monkeys being brought into the Hoyts Palace in Sydney, a trapeze artist in a gorilla suit doing backflips on the cinema awning and skywriting over the beaches.

This was not the same performer who had disgraced himself as *Mighty Joe Young* a few years earlier in Newcastle. "Kong" gave the performance of a lifetime, climbing walls and yelling at pedestrians when he was told to stop and get down by police as his antics were blocking traffic on Pitt Street. "Kong" reluctantly climbed down, after pitching a few empty beer cans in the general direction of the police (he was cleaning debris off the awning), resulting in many boos from the crowd.

Once the police left, "Kong" re-emerged, gave the "V" sign to the departing police and, accompanied by cheers from the crowd, climbed back up onto the awning and continued his display, thus blocking Pitt Street once more. The man in the ape costume made appearances in other cities, usually pictured climbing the walls of the cinemas involved, albeit with the aid of a strategically placed ladder.

Kong made more money during this run than it did 20 years previously: To the amazement of both Hoyts and RKO, there were lines around the block to see the film. *Kong*'s success caught people by surprise, and it did not go unnoticed that the public were keener than ever to see horror movies.

After its incredible Sydney run, *Kong* was shuttled off to the other capital cities and into the country where, again, it managed to set new records.

By moving *Kong* from city to city, RKO and Hoyts were able to drag another two years out of the movie, with screenings going well into 1954. The reviews show that the movie had lost none of its impact, with the special effects holding up well. Reviewers were also quick to point out that the film was a thriller, not a horror; RKO and Hoyts insisted on referring to the movie as an "exploitation film," thus erasing any stigma that might be attached to it. The cut used for the re-issue was the same one used for the original release, just over 99 minutes.

Kong held a special spot in the hearts of Australians since it was released. At Sydney's famous Taronga Zoo, the first gorilla to be displayed in the country was named King Kong. Newspapers reported with delight how the large ape tended to lure people near him before roaring loudly and belting his chest before flinging feces and sawdust at his unwitting victims. The beast was gifted to the zoo by Sir Edward Hallstrom in 1959. The zoo built him a special enclosure, described as a luxury apartment at a cost of £4000[12]; it featured a kitchen, bedroom, day bed, open play area and more, Kong settled in and those who saw him still recall him with delight and joy. Efforts to find a mate for Kong failed and he passed away from old age in 1968.[13]

Creature from the Black Lagoon

In amongst all the banning and censorship, Universal had one last hurrah for its Monster series: the Gill Man featured in *Creature from the Black Lagoon* and its sequels. Despite the ban on anything remotely horror-related, which included a large number of Universal films, the *Creature* series was released, with minor censor cuts, in Australia.

The industry had been caught by surprise regarding the success of *Kong* and Universal Australia was now also raking in the money from their repackaging of the *Frankenstein* series, along with their many other vintage, pre–World War II horrors. As popular as the old movies were with new audiences, there was now a push to get fresh content into the marketplace. Thus Universal Australia was keen to get

Creature to the public, but still had to find a way to slip it past the censor and not have it classified as a horror film. Despite *Creature* being another Universal Monster and, as such, part of the horror genre, fortune was on Universal's side. *Creature* was classified as a thriller and, after the obligatory private screening for the censors, released uncut.

Universal's representative in Australia instantly placed promotional pieces[14] on the makeup tricks used to create the Gill Man in Australian newspapers and magazines. The film, rated "A" for Adults, was well received, with reviews making special mention of the underwater photography, praising the Gill Man's overall look and highlighting that there wasn't enough terror in the movie for it be classified as a proper horror film.

As with all of Universal's horrors, it did not matter what the critics thought, the public flocked to see the film, resulting in excellent business. Once the city runs had finished, the movie was shipped out to regional cinemas, where it continued its life well into the 1960s, becoming a mainstay at drive-ins and midnight screenings.

Atomic Age Monsters at the Drive-In

As the 1930s and 1940s were defined by traditional Universal horror films, the 1950s brought new horrors reflecting the new atom age. Restricted to adults only, films such as *The Incredible Shrinking Man, Them!, Behemoth the Sea Monster* and *Godzilla, King of the Monsters!* thrilled audiences who had now become both used to, and jaded by, the likes of Dracula.

Exhibitors quickly found that such movies had a limited life in traditional cinemas after the initial rush for something new. Where a film such as *On the Waterfront* had prestige, either via awards or by its cast, *Godzilla* was assumed to be disposable trash and as such hold no allure for a return screening. The rating also helped keep the atomic age monsters out of the cinemas, but they quickly found another life at drive-ins.

The drive-in was quickly embraced in Australian society, combining the rising ownership of cars with the ability to see movies without having to get dressed up or being concerned with the propriety of being sat next to someone. In their cars, you could eat noisily and talk to your date without being shushed. Drive-in owners ealized that the people flocking to the Friday and Saturday night films were not interested in seeing Oscar-worthy material; they wanted entertainment. In short, they wanted the atomic age monsters.

Every so often, drive-in managers booked an old horror to reasonable business, but plot driven black-and-white could not compete with the flashy, action-packed Technicolor films the 1950s were providing. Giant ants eating people were far more appealing to audiences at Australian drive-ins than the sight of Boris Karloff lumbering around in his giant boots.

The other benefit for drive-ins was that a film could be alternated with others and thus be shown indefinitely. It was common to find a film such as *Creature from the Black Lagoon* or *Godzilla* still at the drive-in, usually in regional areas, well into the 1970s.[15]

Magazine advertisement for *Forbidden Planet* (1956) from *The Film Weekly*, October 18, 1956.

Magazine advertisement for *The Time Machine* (1960).

The Death of 3-D

Barely a year old, 3-D movies were in trouble by mid–1954. After the initial excitement of the "deepies" (as they were called) wore off, audiences began to look for more serious entertainment and content within the films on offer, but the studios were coming up short.

20th Century–Fox attempted to go one better than RKO's reissue of *King Kong* by releasing the Technicolor 3-D *Gorilla at Large*, starring a young Anne Bancroft, who went on to win an Oscar for her performance in *The Miracle Worker* (1962) and be forever imprinted into people's minds as Mrs. Robinson in 1967's *The Graduate*. Joining Bancroft in the cast were Lee J. Cobb, Raymond Burr and Lee Marvin in a bit role as a police officer who falls asleep while guarding the gorilla. As films went, it was entertaining enough, and the image of Bancroft screaming on the poster with the gorilla behind her, while effective, just was not anywhere near as powerful an image as the original *King Kong* posters.

Where *King Kong* could still draw crowds and make new record profits, *Gorilla at Large* failed. Few were interested in seeing the gorilla running about, and the selling point of the film—it being 3-D—failed to entice.

The reasons for its demise were many. There was a shortage of films, and less quality ones. *House of Wax* aside, the rest of the fare offered to Australian audiences was like *Bwana Devil* and *Gorilla at Large*. Neither film was fine art, nor would either film entice viewers back for return screenings. The experiment was failing and even the news that Sir Robert Helpmann was intent on filming a Shakespeare play in 3-D could not help the cause.[16] Some chains spending as much as £6000 to upgrade their facilities,[17] solely for showing 3-D films, were never going to recoup that money in a short length of time.

Medical factors came into play. It did not take long before rumors began that 3-D glasses were often filthy, and eye diseases were being spread.[18] This caused exhibitors and cinema chains to issue statements claiming that after each showing, the glasses were disinfected for up to five minutes in a solution which was the equal of carbolic acid, at great cost to the cinema. The denials made no difference to the public. Once it was out there, urban legend or otherwise, people believed it.

It was also an effort for cinemas to get the glasses back. The specially made glasses did not come cheap, costing on average £1 each. Most major cinemas, clearly expecting a roaring trade, ordered big, with some ordering 4000 pairs at a single time. At each screening, the audience members were told, before, during and after the film, to hand them back to the ushers upon their exit. The interruptions became a source of annoyance for patrons and resulted in people keeping glasses as a souvenir out of spite. This practice, exhibitors claimed, was foolish as the glasses, with their special lenses, were useless for use as sunglasses. Warnings aside, the glasses were, at times, damaged or simply stolen, either by design or accident.

Australians never took to the 3-D craze like Americans did. The wearing of glasses was a pain for some, and the films themselves often made people dizzy to the point of being physically sick. Whatever the excuses, by June 1954, 3-D was all but finished in Australia.

Abbott and Costello Meet the Mummy

By the mid–1950s, the Mummy, like all of Universal's classic monsters, was totally played out, and the Abbott and Costello formula was not that far behind. The Universal horrors were now dusted off each school holiday season for runs at the cinemas and were squarely targeted at children. In just over 20 years, what had once been objects of sheer terror for adults were now comedy for children.

As for the Mummy, he was now just a boob, a foil, a plaything for Bud Abbott and Lou Costello. What once captivated, terrified and fascinated audiences with concepts of reincarnation and Egyptology, had become a joke, and a poor one at that. Veteran stuntman Eddie Parker, who had doubled for Chaney in the earlier Mummy movies as well as doing the bulk of the work for Chaney in *Frankenstein Meets the Wolf Man,* played the renamed mummy. Nobody ever saw his face through the rubber mask and body suit as he went through the paces striking the now-clichéd mummy poses and grunting when required. It was quite different from the heady days of Karloff, Freund, Johann and Manners, and it showed.

The film was one of the last movies the duo made. Their routine was becoming tired and old hat, but the kids still lapped it up. Bud and Lou started in film in 1940 with *One Night in the Tropics* and, before the decade was out, they made 25 films, all with the same formula. Lou would mess things up, Bud would bash and browbeat him, things would get better, and Lou would end up on top, much to the amusement of Bud. Wash, rinse and repeat.

Meet the Mummy was the fifth "Meet" film the pair made in the 1950s and they were coming to their end. Reviews of the movie were as tepid as the film itself. "You can imagine the mirth-making scrapes A and C get themselves into when they slip into the crypt of old King Tut."[19] "Much the slapstick as before."[20] And those were two of the better ones. The film quickly fell to the bottom of the bill, supporting the likes of *Foxfire*, a Jeff Chandler-Jane Russell potboiler. But, popular with children, the film remained in cinemas, as a support to other films, until the end of the decade. Eventually it popped up on television and became a regular Saturday afternoon feature.

Imhotep or Kharis or Klaris, whatever people wanted to call him, had suffered the same fate. As a screen character, he was 23 years old, and his glory days were already ten years past when Bud and Lou terrorized him. It was a sad and ignoble way to put him and the rest of the Universal Monsters to rest.

The casts of the various films had found different fates over the decades and were scattered all over the planet.

Boris Karloff was busy, as always, taking on almost every job he was offered, working on television and films, and doing voiceovers for children's records.

Bela Lugosi, the first real horror star of the talkie era, was still making films although fewer every year. He passed away on August 16, 1956. His body, ravaged by decades of drug abuse, simply gave out on him, and he died in his sleep.

Zita Johann, the mysterious beauty of *The Mummy*, had retired from stage and screen and was teaching acting to people with learning difficulties. She was lured out of retirement to appear in a truly forgettable horror film, the straight-to-video *Raiders of the Living Dead,* in 1986.

Karl Freund was working as a d.p. on *I Love Lucy.* Having conquered cinema as a medium, and having introduced such innovations as the tracking shot, Freund went into television for, he said, the challenge. The steady paycheck was also a bonus.

David Manners, who had played Jonathan Harker in Lugosi's *Dracula,* as well as the main lead in *The Mummy,* had retired from the screen in 1936 and went to live the quiet life with his partner, Bill Mercer. He authored novels and painted.

Edward Van Sloan, who appeared in *Dracula* (as Van Helsing), *Frankenstein* and *The Mummy,* had also retired from the screen and stage. At the age of 73, he felt he deserved the rest.

Carl Laemmle, founder of Universal, suffered a fatal heart attack in 1939.

His son Carl Jr. was retired, but not voluntarily. Leaving Universal after a takeover in 1936, he retired to his mansion in Beverly Hills where he lived his life as a recluse, surrounded by the ghosts of his past. He was washed up before he had reached 30 and now, not yet 50, his best days were behind him.

Others who had also died included Colin Clive, who succumbed to tuberculosis in 1937, and Lionel Atwill, who died in 1946. Dwight Frye, who had played Renfield against Lugosi's Dracula so brilliantly, collapsed on a bus with a heart attack in 1943. At the time he was struggling to find work and was employed as a tool designer for Lockheed at nights while working on stage during the day.

Director James Whale drowned in May 1957. There is still conjecture as to if he committed suicide or was bashed and thrown into his pool by a gay lover. A suicide note, withheld for decades, would have put an end to the salacious rumors. As it stands, there are still those who believe he was murdered.

Even Bud and Lou did not last for long after *Meet the Mummy,* their penultimate film. Their final film *Dance with Me, Henry* bombed at the box office. Lou, tired of Bud's drinking,[21] dumped him and went out on his own.

Costello[22] would make one solo film before he died of a heart attack in 1959. Bud Abbott hung on long enough to see their films enjoy a revival, before passing away in 1974.

The Black Sleep and *The Creeping Unknown*

On Halloween 1956, any hope that Bela Lugosi's last film *The Black Sleep* would be cleared for exhibition was dashed when newspapers reported "Boy Dies of Fright in Theatre."[23]

The day before, a young boy named Stewart Cohan had an apparent heart attack while viewing a double bill of *The Creeping Unknown* and *The Black Sleep* at a cinema in Chicago.

Cohan had just settled into his seat when *The Creeping Unknown* began. As the opening scene, of a spaceship crash, played out, Cohan turned to his friends, murmured some words and fell to the floor, dead.

The pathologist who conducted the autopsy, Albert Baugher, told the coroner that Cohan had a smaller heart than what was usual. "In layman's terms," Baugher said, "the boy died of a heart collapse after extraordinary tension while watching a film."[24] Coroner Walter McCarron went on record with a recommendation: that all double-feature horror films in America be stopped immediately.[25]

The cinema owner in Chicago, William Cole, did himself no favors by claiming that the movie could not be to blame as it wasn't as horrific as others that he'd screened. He followed that up with a media statement: "It never occurred to me the program was unsuitable for children. My ten-year-old daughter saw it and liked it. Kids eat up shows like that."[26] With those words, the damage was done.

This was just the latest fatality to occur in a cinema. Three years earlier, during a screening of the 3-D film *The Maze* in Philadelphia, Albert Orsini collapsed and succumbed to a heart attack, dying in the cinema.[27] The death of Orsini was rarely mentioned again.

The Creeping Unknown (aka *The Quatermass Xperiment*) had long been earmarked as a true horror film, and should have been banned just by classification, but the sheer Englishness of the production ensured its release, albeit with censor cuts. Under the *Creeping Unknown* moniker, it hit Sydney cinemas in early November 1956, and, unusual for the time, was readily described as a horror film.

The day after the news of Stewart Cohan's death, *The Creeping Unknown* began its run. "Here is a British-made science fiction-cum-horror film that knocks-spots off most of the juvenilities produced in this vein by Hollywood," read the *Sydney Morning Herald* review. "Even though dialogue and characterization still never get beyond the pulp magazine level, the story of a rocket pilot who comes back to Earth possessed by a strange new force provides some deliciously grisly excitements, helped along by ingenious management of atmospheric detail."[28]

At the next sitting of the Senate, Senator Ivy Wedgewood (the first woman appointed to the Australian Senate) posed a series of questions to the minister for Customs and Excise. "Has the Minister seen a report from the United States of America that a nine-year-old boy died of fright whilst watching a double feature horror film programme?"

Without waiting for an answer, Senator Wedgewood followed up. "In view of the fact that leading child educationists are alarmed at the horror scenes contained in the picture *The Black Sleep*, will the Minister inform the Senate whether this film will be allowed to enter Australia? If entry is permitted, will the government take action to ensure that the film is not shown at sessions where children are present?"

With that statement, Wedgewood condemned *The Black Sleep* and all but cleared *The Creeping Unknown*, which was the film showing when Cohan suffered his heart attack. This was despite the newspapers naming *The Creeping Unknown* as the film responsible, and that the unfortunate Cohan had already sat through a screening of *The Black Sleep* without any adverse reaction. *The Creeping Unknown* was never once mentioned in the Senate.

With *The Creeping Unknown* already in cinemas, *The Black Sleep* may have been the easier target as it had yet to be cleared. No investigations have been made to properly explain the choice. The concept of pulling a film from the public *after* its release was not unprecedented, and it would have held more appeal than banning a film that was unlikely to be cleared in any regard.

The Creeping Unknown should have been banned for the very reason that saw *The Black Sleep* prohibited from release, but *The Black Sleep* was an American film, and even worse, starred at least three easily recognizable horror stars in the form of Bela Lugosi, Lon Chaney Jr. and John Carradine.

American-made films were always targeted over their British counterparts, barring the most extreme of the Hammer Horrors. This patriotism also explains why *The Maze* was released. Michael Pate, the Australian actor, was a featured player in that film and Australian audiences were always going to see it, if only to cheer Pate.

The Senator being challenged, Norman Henty, did not waste time with his answers. After stating that he had seen the newspaper article in question, he explained what was to happen.

> The film *The Black Sleep*, on arrival in Australia, will be censored in accordance with the terms of the Customs (Cinematograph Films) Regulations, These regulations provide that no film shall be registered which, in the opinion of the Censorship Board, or on appeal, in the opinion of the Appeal Censor, is blasphemous, indecent or obscene; is likely to be injurious to morality, or to encourage or incite to crime; or depicts any matter the exhibition of which is undesirable in the public interest. If released, the film will be appropriately classified by the Commonwealth Film Censor as "G—General Exhibition," "A—Not Suitable for Children" or "A.O.—Suitable for Adults Only," as the case may be. These classifications are not a requirement of Commonwealth law but were adopted as an aide to State authorities, parents and other interested persons or organizations. The Commonwealth Government has no authority to enforce classifications by requiring exhibitors to prevent the entry of children to cinemas showing films unsuitable for children, that is, films classified as "A" or "AO." Any such restriction is entirely a matter for action under State law.[29]

Like Senator Wedgewood, Senator Henty never once mentioned *The Creeping Unknown*. His statements sealed the fate of *The Black Sleep*. It was not cleared for exhibition in Australia and remained banned until well into the 1970s when television found it suitable for midnight screenings.

The Creeping Unknown was classified as "A"—Not Suitable for Children, meaning children could still see the film, if accompanied by an adult.

Part of *The Creeping Unknown*'s moderate box office success can be put down to the sensationalist reporting of the unfortunate Stewart Cohan. While politicians were debating *Black Sleep*e's merits and insisting that it never be released in Australia, the film that had been playing when Cohan suffered his heart attack was being screened in cinemas. People knew this and went to see it, with a morbid curiosity to find out what the fuss was about.

It was the last anybody would see of Prof. Quatermass until the 1970s as the official sequels *Quatermass 2* (1957) and *Quatermass and the Pit* (1967) were banned. The unofficial sequel *X the Unknown* (1956), starring Dean Jagger, was given a general release in 1959, again with censor cuts.

Lord of the Flies

"Makes Dracula Look Cuddly"

Even with the bans in place, horror and non-horror alike from overseas was still being attacked. In late 1957, questions were being asked in Parliament about advertisements placed in Australian newspapers asking for 30 Australian boys to appear in the Ealing Studios film *Lord of the Flies*. William Golding's 1954 novel was, and still is, an essential study if the breakdown of society and good vs. evil. Even before it was made, the film was being described as following the novel, in both tone and subject, as closely as possible.

The ad asked that the boys be able to "behave like savages" and to "look and act depraved." It was Ealing's intent to make the film in Australia, which would see money pumped into the economy, but Federal Senator Sandford sought to prevent this "horror" movie, which had already been described as a "bloodcurdling masterpiece," from being made in Australia. At the least, he wanted to prevent all Australian boys from appearing in it.

Sandford need not have bothered. Ealing eventually passed on making the film and the official reply to Sandford was that the federal government could not, and would not, prevent anyone from obtaining gainful employment on any motion picture filmed in Australia. The film, made by director Peter Brook in 1962 and released worldwide in 1963, was filmed just off Puerto Rico and used a cast of non-professionals who, in the absence of a script, ad libbed after scenes were explained to them. It remains one of the most powerful movies of its genre, and even though it has been remade more than once, it is still a disturbing movie. It was released in Australia in 1967 to rave reviews—and classified as being unsuitable for children

Midnight Horror Show Riots

"[T]he most alarming feature about the audience was that most were teenagers of the most extreme type..."

Midnight movies were not new, having been around since the 1920s. The novelty wore off quickly. Where a midnight screening might be reserved for a one-off to promote a horror film, as was done for 1942's *The Ghost of Frankenstein*, or as a New Year's Eve promotion, the new generation of the 1950s wanted to party. So midnight screenings became commonplace again, and with them came trouble.

In Melbourne, the Lyceum Theatre on Burke Street began to run Festivals of Fear. These Friday evening events featured many pre-ban horror movies. *Man Made Monster, The Ghost of Frankenstein, Dracula's Daughter, House of Frankenstein* and *The Mummy's Curse* were all given a run, resulting in full houses and a windfall for the cinema. Other cinemas saw what was happening and began to book the same movies and screen them at midnight, generally on Fridays or Saturday and, although more rarely, Sundays. The early screenings attracted as many critics as they did paying customers.

A letter published in *The Argus* gives a great insight into the kinds of people who attended these midnight screenings in the early 1950s.

> On Friday night, out of curiosity, I entered a city picture house for an early morning picture screening. I was late and was given a front seat. Near me sat a bored little boy of 12, with a cigarette butt dangling from his lips. Farther away were children of about ten, highly excited by the lack of restraint in other adolescents. Soldiers, sailors and toughs were present, with language that matched their attitudes. Here and there were couples, and a sprinkling of the ageless weather-beaten men seldom seen in the daylight. In this atmosphere of emotional instability there must have been several wealthy and/or responsible people, to judge by the taxi afterwards employed. After the show, at 2:30 a.m., noisy groups departed homewards while little boys scurried through them home to their beds.
>
> From my car I watched a lad of nine hurrying along whistling nervously frightened by his own footsteps. A nearly deserted city at early morning is a terrifying place, the father of that child a scoundrel.[30]

The practice of midnight horror movies soon spread across the country, but the main problems occurred in Victoria and its capital, Melbourne.

The first reported brawl occurred in Ballarat, a country town outside of Melbourne, in April 1952. *The Argus* noted how midnight horror movies were now banned in that city due to weeks of regular fighting and vandalism.

The 1950s saw the rise of the teenager, complete with rebellion, alcohol, sex, rock'n'roll, fast cars and motorbikes. The Bodgie (an equivalent of the greaser) and his female counterpart, the Widgie, would fight with anyone, especially authority figures.

It did not matter who was with what gang: By midnight, the teenagers were half-drunk and ready for anything. Once seated, they continued to drink and in the wee hours they would pour out onto the street where any slight, real or imagined, would trigger an all-in brawl. The screening of old Universal horror films was not the trigger, it just provided the location.

Things came to head in Thornbury, an outer suburb of Melbourne, on March 10, 1958, when a riot broke out, resulting in heavy damage to the theater and injuries to police. The blame was placed squarely at the feet of young people and horror films. According to eyewitness John Brideson,

> To see this programme 1700 arrived, some two hours before midnight, but the most alarming feature about the audience was that most were teenagers of the most extreme type—in clothes, language and attitude. They were so rough that a plate glass screen was broken, a side door was surreptitiously opened, and the crowds swamped the theatre. The crew of a police patrol car and local police were required to maintain order during the show, which lasted till 3:45 a.m.[31]

The cinema was not even playing horror films that night, but due to a card placed out in front of the theater ("The whole theatre will quiver; you will shiver; but please don't faint"), it received the blame.

Solutions to the problem came thick and fast. An influential minister and liberal theologian, Sir Irving Benson, proposed a simple solution: Sunday school. Benson told a gathering at Wesley College in outer Melbourne,

> You probably have read that, when three lads were before the court for trying to overturn a motor car after they had left one of these so-called midnight entertainments, their solicitor

said, "The people who should be in this court are the people who run the theatre." We want, in this country, freedom of expression and thought, but such freedom does not entitle picture shows to provide for these midnight parties films [sic] which could only disturb and unbalance and give a wrong sense or values to the young people who see them. One of the best things that could happen in Australia would be a great national resurgence of Sunday school.[32]

Benson's call was for all young people (under 21) to mandatorily attend Sunday school, either for Bible studies or for work training.

The Victorian State Government replied with a tried-and-true solution: parents. "If we could only persuade parents to go out more with their children, we would have a far less serious problem of juvenile delinquency and hooliganism on our hands," Chief Secretary Arthur Rylah said. "It would be unwise to rush in and take hasty action."[33] Rylah claimed that the bulk of the damage at theaters came about when some lads were refused entry or when boys and girls could sit next to each other. Segregating the audience had seen a reduction in the damage done.

The opposition party did not agree. "We want the Government to do something about these shows, and not adopt a 'wait and see' attitude," said the Leader of the Labor Party, Ernie Shepherd. "We can't take the risk of allowing this to grow. Only this morning I received a telegram from the Mother's Club Federation of Victoria, representing 55,000 mothers, expressing concern on the matter."[34]

Faced with growing attacks by the Church and Opposition, Rylah ordered an immediate investigation and report. The report revealed that gangster movies, not horror, were shown on the evening in question. "They were, in fact, some that could have been described as rather poor melodrama and detective stories," claimed Rylah.[35] All were approved by the censor and were American in origin. The showing of films, in particular horror, had contributed to vandalism at both Ascot Vale and Thornbury. Even as the report laid blame, it continued to defend horror films by deflecting some of the blame for "larrikinism" onto "objectionable" literature, recordings, television and newspapers. Rylah again called for parents to take a more active role in their children's education and supervision.

Thirteen "objectionable" films were named in the report, and the media focused on the obvious horrors: *Donovan's Brain, The Creeper, The Black Castle, The Creeping Unknown, The Strange Door* and *The Creature Walks Among Us*. Gangster films were not mentioned by title.

To bring an end to the riots, the Victorian Government called in the heads of Hoyts Theatres and negotiated a deal which would see a reduced number of midnight screenings with greater supervision. This placated the public. Brawls and riots became less frequent as the 1950s ended. As the 1960s began, midnight screenings moved to drive-ins, which provided new locations for fights.

Before the Rylah-commissioned report was tabled, more problems arose, this time in Brunswick, another outer suburb of Melbourne. The Hoyts Padua Theater hosted a midnight screening of two movies, described as being horror, a year to the day after the 1958 Thornbury incident. Despite opening the doors at 10:30, people flooded the theater and police were summoned to restore peace. Government minister William Slater told the Victorian parliament,

The show started shortly after midnight, and among the audience was a considerable number of teenage boys and girls and some children aged from eight to ten years. They had displayed to them in an abominable fashion, according to my informant, these "horror" films depicting such scenes as a surgeon from Mars performing an operation on the brains of persons destroyed by a monster. I think it is time a strong protest was registered, in the name of youth, against the sordid commercialism of certain interests which are prepared, for the sake of money, to display these extraordinary and horrible films to that section of the community.[36]

This time the principal of the nearby Brunswick Technical School was the complainant, with support from the State Labor party in the form of stalwart Slater (then in the last year of his life). Slater read letters that had been sent to him and thundered his opposition about horror films and midnight screenings.[37]

As Slater's health declined, his colleague, Campbell Turner, took up the gauntlet. "Our chaplain attended a midnight 'horror' session at a Sydney-road picture theatre during the early hours of Monday, March 9," wrote the principal of the Brunswick Technical School.

The films screened were of a particularly morbid type, and the large audience included children and adolescents from the age of eight or nine upwards. It may be argued that what occurs outside school hours is not the business of the school, but teachers have a moral responsibility toward their students, and I know that some of our boys attend such "horror" screenings. From the standpoints of morality, health and plain common sense, these shows appear to be highly undesirable, and I would urge that the Government be encouraged to bring down legislation to at least curb this social evil.

Australian daybill for a 1960s reissue of *Son of Frankenstein* (1939).

Faced with yet more attacks, the government opted not to legislate, but handball to the local councils. When Rylah's report was tabled in the Victorian Parliament, he included this statement: "In districts where midnight performances are held from time to time, the remedy seems to be for those who oppose such entertainments to make their representations to the local municipal councils and urge that a bylaw be made and enforced regarding the times at which picture theatres may be open to the public."[38] This ensured that all complaints about Thornbury, Ballarat, Brunswick or anywhere else would now not be the State Government's problem.

Hammer Films Banned ... Almost

The late 1950s saw Hammer Horrors rise, presenting a new wave of horror cinema. None reached Australian cinemas upon initial release. Their existence was noted, though, through articles[39] and reviews from overseas; but if anyone wanted to see *The Curse of Frankenstein* with Christopher Lee taking on the mantle of the Monster and Peter Cushing as the doctor, they would have to travel to another country to do so.[40]

In 1957, the new Chief Censor, Colin Campbell, reminded distributors that horror films had been banned for nine years and would be restricted accordingly as more began to encroach on Australian shores.

Hammer had dabbled with a few genres including science fiction (*The Quatermass Xperiment*), action, light comedy and drama, but it was at horror that they truly excelled, starting with *The Curse of Frankenstein* (1957) and *Dracula* (1958), the latter renamed *Horror of Dracula* in Australia upon its eventually released in the early 1970s. Both movies featured Lee and Cushing, but it was the role of Dracula that would see Lee typecast much the same manner that Lugosi was 27 years previously. But Lee would eventually break free of the Lord of Vampires by the sheer volume and diversity of his output and his refusal to perform the role past the 1970s.

The problem with Hammer films was addressed in Federal Parliament in August 1958: Asked about a newspaper article detailing the rise of British horror films, Senator Henty was again in the thick of things, telling the House:

> Since 1948, the importation of horror films into Australia has been banned. ...The board defines a horror film as one which portrays characters of a monstrous or abnormal type, shows episodes of a hideous, revolting or gruesome nature tending to terrify or shock sensitive persons, irrespective of age, the main theme of which may be classed as horrific and is portrayed in a manner tending to appear abnormal. That is the interpretation of Regulation 13 (d) of the Customs (Cinematograph Films) Regulations upon which the board relies in respect of films considered to be not in the public interest. The number of such films imported has recently increased. More have been rejected in the last six weeks than during the whole of 1957. The board is watching this type of film very closely.[41]

Henty had been discussing the issue with Campbell after the Australian Broadcasting Commission's chairman, Sir Richard Boyer, argued that the censor should no longer have the power to ban films on the basis of their being likely to be offensive to the people of a friendly nation or to the people of a part of the Queen's dominions, or undesirable in the public interest, since these blanket provisions would severely restrict television news services and discussion shows. Campbell protested that, if Boyer's suggestion were accepted, the censors would be unable to control films "showing horror of the Frankenstein type, violence, brutality, antisocial behavior, excessive use of alcohol, drugs or narcotics, scenes affecting or likely to affect public morale or confidence in the law and public institutions, ridicule of the sanctity of marriage and the importance of the home." Armed with Campbell's objections, Henty rejected Boyer's appeal.

The number of movies rejected by the censor was misleading, at best. The Board constantly pointed at a small number of films outright rejected (usually one or two) but this number did not take into consideration the fact that any movie classified as horror was automatically banned. While it was true that the number the Board gave applied to films that they had viewed and rejected personally, and that horror films no longer required such vetting, unless the film was classified as thriller, science fiction or any other label, the Board never viewed it. In this way, they could always point at a dwindling number and show that they were not being over-the-top. The reality was that the Board, by virtue of its actions and rules, was rejecting films, automatically, on an almost weekly basis.

Hammer did not bother appealing *Dracula* but 20th Century–Fox did protest the ban on *The Fly*, insisting that Henty and Campbell watch the movie before deciding its fate. Fox pointed out that the movie was being screened, uncut, in Britain, New Zealand and Hong Kong, and there had been no uproar in any of those Commonwealth areas. Henty backed both Campbell and the ban but did arrange for a private screening for his fellow senators. In a cunning move, Henty asked that only certain scenes be shown. These scenes were those containing true moments of horror, resulting in his fellow senators backing the calls for the horror ban to remain in place.

The Mummy: How Hammer Avoided the Ban

Despite the ban on horror films, a true horror film managed to get past the censor: Hammer's *The Mummy* (1959). It featured Christopher Lee (in the title role) and Peter Cushing,

Hammer Films were everything that Universal and the other Hollywood studios were never able to be, due to the restrictions placed upon them by American censors. Hammer horrors were colorful, packed with sex, blood and gore. It was not unusual to see just as many bare female breasts in a Hammer film as it was to see graphic blood and guts.

Since one mention of the words *Dracula*, *Frankenstein* or *Werewolf* in a Hammer movie's title was enough for the Chief Censor to issue a ban without screening the film, just how *The Mummy* got past him remains a mystery. The film is a genuine horror and, unlike *Creature from the Black Lagoon*, displayed no traces of science fiction. Nor could it be classified as a thriller. Its classification was that of a mystery-suspense film, and it was given an "A" (For Adults Only) rating. Advertising made it clear that the movie was not suitable for children.

Critics savaged the film and did not shy away from labeling it as horror:

Advertisement for *Village of the Damned* (1960).

This Technicolor piece has all the familiar ingredients of mummyism; archaeologists in cotton suits; a mysterious Egyptologist in a red fez who spends most of the time chanting to a hawk-beaked God; an intrepid young man (capably played by Peter Cushing); the young man's beautiful wife, who at the climax is conveniently left unattended so that the mummy can march away with her; and, of course, the mummy itself, a fabulous creation in tattered grey bandages. It is quite necessary, too, to have a quota of skeptical detectives, as well as some gibbering pubfolk. Theoretically this adds to the drama of the final hunt, even though it's really Christopher Lee under the bandages. It is, to coin a phrase, mummybo-jumbo.[42]

The Mummy was the first genuine Hammer Horror to be released in Australia featuring one of the classic monsters from the Universal period—and the public ate it up. It quickly settled into the drive-in circuit and became an annual feature for New Year's Eve horror movie marathons and Midnight Horror shows. In cinemas it was often paired with a classic Universal (for some reason *House of Frankenstein* was selected) and it ran at suburban and art house cinemas throughout the 1960s.

Despite Hammer's success in getting *The Mummy* released in Australia, none of the sequels were shown until long after the ban was lifted in 1969. *The Curse of the Mummy's Tomb*, produced in 1964, was not released in Australia until 1973, when it became an instant drive-in hit. If it reached cinema screens, it was

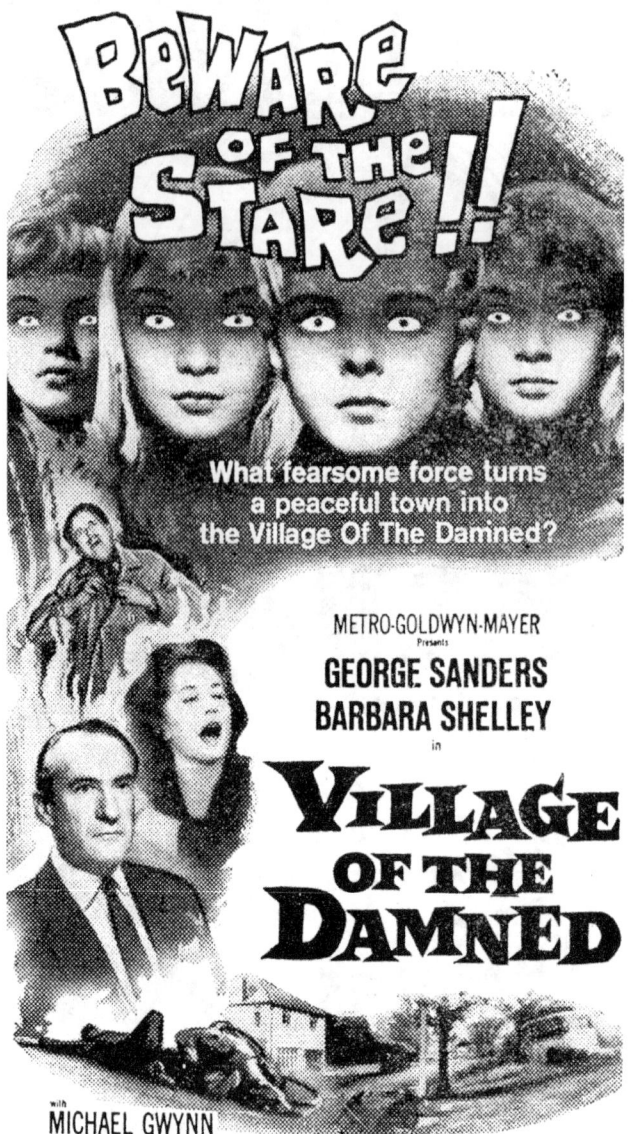

Advertisement for *Village of the Damned* (1960).

as an art-house film or part of a horror movie marathon. *The Mummy's Shroud*, released worldwide in 1967, was the second Hammer *Mummy* movie to be released in Australia, appearing in cinemas in November 1970. Their fourth and last *Mummy* movie, *Blood from the Mummy's Tomb*, was released in 1972 and, as with most of Hammer's 1970s releases, went straight to small cinemas and drive-ins. At one point, it was possible to see Hammer's *Mummy* movies on television while they were at the cinema.

Even worse was that all the *Mummy* movies suffered at the hands of the censors.

An Australian daybill for 1963's *The Haunted and the Hunted* (better known as *Dementia 13*).

The films were brutally cut, and it would not be until the rise of video in the early 1980s that Australians got to see these movies full and uncut.

Faces on the Cutting Room Floor

One of the biggest blows to the censorship regime came when Charles Higham wrote a blistering six-page article on what he termed "the unnecessary secrets" of film censorship in Australia, published in the respected weekly magazine *The Bulletin*.[43] Higham had researched his topic very well, he had spoken to the Chief Censor along with the Board, he had researched the reasons behind the 1928 Royal Commission and the establishment of the Board, and he asked for, and amazingly received, a list of films banned and censored and the reasons why.

It is entirely possible that the Board agreed to assist Higham thinking that he would be writing about the benefits of censorship. If this was the case, they were bitterly disappointed. Higham took the Chief Censor to task, systematically taking his arguments apart one by one and showing the inadequacies of a system that, although adequate in the 1940s, was now antiquated. He accused both the censorship board and the government of being out of touch, unqualified to sit in judgment of films, short-sighted, secretive and dishonest in the way that a film could be rejected with no reason given as to why, nor any idea as to what could be cut to save it.

Although the Chief Censor's annual report listed the number of films that had been cut and banned, at no point did it list the titles of the films or the reasons. This is what made Higham's list important: He listed the titles of films banned since 1929 and, naturally, horror took the bulk of the space. For the first time, Australians could see the titles of movies they had been denied.

It did not take long for people to react. John Baxter, writing in his newsletter *Film Digest*,[44] listed over 50 more films that had been banned or cut since Higham's list appeared. David Stratton, then a young film journalist, published reviews of some of the banned films to illustrate that the reasons given for censorship were no more valid in 1966 as they had been in a year earlier when Higham published his piece.

Pirate *Freaks*

Tod Browning's 1932 masterpiece *Freaks* had been banned since 1932. In countries where it had been released, it was cut beyond recognition. It appears that a pirate copy had an extremely limited run in Australia in mid–1966, reviewed by Stratton in *Film Digest*.[45]

Stratton had deliberately not mentioned where he saw the film, but he did make mention of the U.K. ban. At the time, Stratton was based in Sydney and ran the Sydney Film Festival, so the movie must have been screened there. Stratton was actively questioning film censorship and banning and would have known that the movie was not subject to the 1948 horror ban but had been banned in Australia since 1932. Even the mere act of reviewing it placed people at risk as such a public exhibition of the movie could have led to arrests.

The activities of the likes of Stratton, Higham, John Baxter, Bruce Chandler, Bruce Hodsdon, Ian Klava, Barrie Pattison and Ken Quinnell (plus contributors to *Film Digest* and similar publications) helped raise awareness of the outdated censorship standards of the era. Gradually the public became acutely aware of the movies they were denied, due to legislation regarding moral concerns a generation removed from 1968.

Horror Ban Lifted

As the '60s ended, new attitudes were coming to the fore. The Vietnam War was being screened into households in full, graphic color on television news. Australians had been jolted by the footage of Gen. Nguyen Ngoc Loan, chief of the national police, firing his pistol into the head of suspected Viet Cong officer Nguyen Van Lem on a Saigon street, early in the Tet Offensive. Reportage from Australian journalists such as Neil Davis painted a horrific picture of the war, instantaneous, bloody and graphic, the likes of which had not happened before.

Suddenly a horror movie made over 30 years before, in black and white, did not appear to be as much a threat. The ban on horror films was officially lifted in 1969, with no fanfare, when the censor began to allow Hammer films such as *Frankenstein Must Be Destroyed*,[46] *Horror of Dracula* and *Dracula Has Risen from the Grave*, the latter advertised at cinemas as the first original Dracula movie cleared by the censor since 1946. All the Hammers were slapped with "H" (for Horror) classifications and heavily censored to remove the gorier sequences.

Hot on the heels of the lifting of the ban came yet another re-release of Karloff's *Frankenstein*, first at the Capitol in Sydney[47] and the second teamed with *House of Dracula* and the first official Australian release of F.W. Murnau's *Nosferatu* (1922).[48]

The July 24, 1969, *Film Weekly* announces the return of Dracula to Australian screens in *Dracula Has Risen from the Grave*. The horror ban had finally been lifted.

Australian advertisement for *The Valley of Gwangi* (1969).

As the 1970s began, the advertisements for horror—for example, this one for 1971's *Count Yorga, Vampire*—took on a more sexualized feel.

Hammer Horrors, including 1970's *Frankenstein Must Be Destroyed*, began flooding the country.

This loosening of restrictions trickled down to TV with Karloff, Chaney and Lugosi's monsters all finally being seen on the small screen, albeit in the form of an episode ("Monsters We've Known and Loved") of the documentary series *Hollywood and the Stars*.[49]

The Minister for Customs in 1970, Don Chipp, began to implement reforms around censorship in general,[50] with the traditional cinema ratings dropped and new ratings introduced. From 1972 onwards, horror films were rated "R" (restricted to adults). Other ratings included "M" (for mature audiences, over the age of 17), "NRC" (not recommended for children) and "G" (general). Introduced in late 1971, these classifications paved the way for horror to once more be shown freely at cinemas and drive-ins. The use of state censors was also eliminated and a central, federally appointed censor was appointed. This censor would also cut film, issue bans and write weekly reports as to which films were prohibited and which were allowed. The results saw viewing brought into line with the then-current, more liberal and permissive views of society. Every horror movie was judged upon its own merits, and virtually every horror movie was either cut, censored or banned outright for local release.

These reforms also applied to television but in different degrees and began to highlight some fundamental flaws in the censorship system in Australia.

5

Television: 1956–1973

"Good evening, and welcome to television."

With those six words, Bruce Gyngell introduced television[1] to Australia on September 16, 1952.

Early Days

The first shows broadcast in Australia were a mix of variety programs hosted by Graham Kennedy (*In Melbourne Tonight*), Bert Newton, Bob Dwyer and Barry Humphries, along with news, drama and sports shows. Plays were also performed, as were burlesque, vaudeville and musicals. Records of what was performed are now long lost, and nowhere in newspaper or television guides are there any hints that horror was screened as a live production.

From the start, Australian TV looked to the U.S. of A. to fill the gaps. Among the first were the American staples *I Love Lucy, Dragnet, Father Knows Best, The Bob Cummings Show, Long John Silver, The Life of Riley, The Mickey Mouse Club, Perry Mason* and *Hopalong Cassidy,* along with shows hosted by George Burns, Ronald Colman and Red Skelton The main selling point, for many Australians, was the TV coverage of the 1956 Olympic Games, held in Melbourne.

Television was mostly for affluent Australians. In 1956, the average cost of a set was £200,[2] against the average weekly wage of £12.6. A television set cost slightly less than a new car and was considered a luxury item. Adding to the cost was the need for a viewer's license, which added another £5 to the cost (1957), and which rose, annually. The license remained until the early 1970s. People went to great lengths to hide their roof antennas behind chimneys and roofs and their TVs in cupboards to avoid detection and the resulting £50 fine that came with watching TV (and listening to the radio) without a license.

One of the packages selected for the newly minted medium was the American series *Science Fiction Theatre*. ABN-2 was started by the Australian Broadcasting Commission (ABC) and went live in Sydney on November 5, 1956. The first week went off without a hitch and the second week saw the debut of *Science Fiction Theatre*, beginning with the series' first episode "Beyond" (dir. Herbert L Strock, 1955). The series went on air in Melbourne as well, on the ABC-run ABV-2.

The series suffered at the hands of censors but did well for ABC and ran steadily until 1960, with selected repeats extending its life until late 1961. In Sydney it started on Tuesday evenings, moved to Sunday, then Thursday in 1957 and Wednesday and Friday in 1958, and back to Thursday in 1959. Melbourne, Adelaide and Brisbane followed suit.

By moving the days, but not the timeslot (6:30 p.m. each week), the series could be, and was, repeated. Another ploy was to give new titles to episodes. For example, in Melbourne the first run of "Y.O.R.D." (dir. Leon Benson, 1955) was billed with the just-as-unwieldy title "The Pretty Young Secretary and the SOS."

Alfred Hitchcock Presents debuted less than a month after *Science Fiction Theatre*. While it was technically not a horror series, some episodes did contain elements of horror, and complaint letters often mentioned murders and other violent crimes. *Hitchcock* remained a mainstay until the late 1960s. *The Twilight Zone* made its debut in 1960, and much like *Science Fiction Theatre*, suffered the censor's wrath. Debuting in 1964, *The Outer Limits* also ran afoul of the censor. It appeared first in May throughout regional Victoria; Sydney aired it in June, followed by Melbourne in August and Adelaide in September.

The censors rejected half of the episodes of *The Outer Limits* and heavily cut what was left. The Nine network, which had the rights to the series (and then licensed those rights to the Ten network in Melbourne), appealed, but to no avail. It took a decade for the "lost" episodes to be seen on Australian TV.

As television grew in popularity and more content was required, it was only logical that old movies could fill the time. Television stations bought movies from the American film studios, with the cheaper studios selling their films for a modest price. These would be submitted to the Chief Censor who, without fail, instantly banned anything horror-related.

The First Television Horrors

On March 14, 1957, the first movie that could be considered a horror was screened. *The Monkey's Paw* (dir. Norman Lee, Butcher's Empire Films, 1948) aired on ABV-2 as part of its *Saturday Screenplay* series. ABV-2, which had recently (January 19, 1957) begun transmitting, was the Australian Government–owned network, which made the screening even more significant, as the censor had cleared it[3]; it had been banned from a cinematic release in 1948.

The reasons why the film could be televised while still banned at the cinema are unknown, but it would become common as years passed. Of interest to Australians was the fact that the *Monkey's Paw* script was co-written by Barbara Toy,[4] who hailed from Sydney. After moving to England in 1935 after a failed marriage, Toy had made her name as a playwright and theatrical director. *The Monkey's Paw* was the second screenplay that she co-wrote with director Lee.

The Monkey's Paw was repeated in May and September of the same year and became a staple of Sydney and Melbourne television. The film would hit other cities in due course.

Horror movies appeared elsewhere, slowly and innocuously. HSV-7 (Melbourne) screened *The Woman Who Came Back* (dir. Walter Colmes, Republic, 1945) in late December 1957, with Sydney following suit in February 1958. Unlike *The Monkey's Paw*, this movie had been given a cinematic release in Australia. Nineteen fifty-eight also saw the TV release of *The Return of Doctor X* (dir. Vincent Sherman, Warner Brothers, 1939), *The Girl Who Dared* (dir. Howard Bretherton, Republic, 1944) and *The Phantom Speaks* (dir. John English, Republic, 1945).

In 1959, Australian TV watchers saw *Bedlam* (dir. Mark Robson, RKO, 1946) starring Boris Karloff with Anna Lee. *Bedlam* contains one of Karloff's finest performances as Master George Sims, who runs the St. Mary's of Bethlehem Asylum, a fictionalized version of Bethlem Royal Hospital (Bedlam). Next came *The Catman of Paris* (dir. Lesley Selander, Republic, 1946), which also had not been cleared for cinematic release.

Despite this promising start, no horror films were released to television in 1960. But TV programming could, and did, change at the last minute, so it is possible that films could have been screened with no records kept.

The introduction of video recorders to television stations in 1960, replacing kinescope, saw more American movies, cartoons, serials and television performances on the small screen. As the broadcast industry evolved, regulators were once more playing catch-up. Parliament drew up, debated and passed legislation only to see the industry powering ahead of them.

In 1956, the Broadcasting and Television Act (itself an amendment to the old Broadcasting Act) included categories which covered licenses, content criteria, broadcasting times and, most importantly, classifications. These standards took a lot from the Film Censorship Board and, as TV required more scrutiny, more censors were added to cope with the increased workload. As with cinema, before any film could be screened it had to pass the Film Censorship Board, no matter if it had been passed for exhibition previously.

The Board made it clear that no horror movie would be passed for classification for television. The process of reclassification for films was arduous, with the censors devoting an estimated 1985 hours to the viewing of films for television as opposed to 800 hours to the viewing of films for the cinema in 1957. At that stage, television was being broadcast in Sydney and Melbourne only.[5] As broadcasting spread nationally, the hours required to censor or ban increased with it. Even with this workload, not a single horror film was considered without heavy censorship. The censor had a special clause to ban horror on television; it stated, "[T]he deliberate use of horror for its own sake should not be permitted." The clause was broad and was applied liberally.

HSV-7 (Melbourne) decided to test the waters, so to speak, by running a short-lived series titled *Adult Theatre*. Across a two-month period beginning in October-November 1958, late on a Monday night, the station screened *The Man with Nine Lives*, *The Face Behind the Mask*, *The Devil's Mask*, *The Amazing Mr. X*, *The Dark Past*, *The Black Room*, *The Devil-Doll*, *The Lady and the Monster*, *Scared to Death*, *The Beast from 20,000 Fathoms*, *House of Wax* and *Phantom of the Rue Morgue*. The series proved to be popular enough to be revived in later years and extended to other states.

The 1960s saw the growing TV audience begin to change, become more sophisticated, with a desire for more content later in the evening. The horror films of the 1930s and 1940s were perfectly suited the medium of late-night television: filmed in black and white with stories that were now considered tame by anyone's standards but still held in high regard. The ban on horror films for television was total and could not include the pre–1948 films.

Slowly, as the decade progressed, standards began to relax. Science fiction films started appearing on Australian TV in the early 1960s and as the decade progressed, program directors began to push against the ban, both privately and in public, by exposing the ban and its hypocrisy. The attacks on the ban were helped by a shift of focus from horror films to semi-pornographic and outright pornographic "stag" films. These films, usually 8mm loops, were easily ordered from overseas sellers and could be brought into the country in small packages, with the hopes that Customs would overlook them. This was not always the case as the censors were still insistent on viewing every film bought into the country. By this diversion, censors began to slowly overlook films that would otherwise have been rejected.

Prelude to a Storm: Horror Creeps In

From 1960, ABV-2 in Sydney began to screen silent movies under the series title *Silents Please*.

Silents Please was an American-produced series highlighting heavily cut versions of classic silents. Unlike the American version, which included *Nosferatu*, *Dr. Jekyll and Mr. Hyde* and *The Phantom of the Opera*, the Australian series focused on classics, westerns and comedies. As the horror ban was still in effect, any episode known to be horror was pulled by the censor. Still, the series was considered an easy decision, programming-wise, as there were still plenty of people who had grown up seeing these films at the cinemas and longed for that era.

By purchasing *Silents Please*, the ABC was able to cheaply obtain classic movies by Douglas Fairbanks, Charlie Chaplin, Mary Pickford, Harold Lloyd and William S. Hart. The films were screened with a piano accompaniment. As the decade rolled on, the series spread to all the capital cities and be repeated each year.

One film did slip by the censor, in what appears to be the only Australian television screening of (a truncated version of) Lon Chaney's classic *The Hunchback of Notre Dame* (dir. Wallace Worsley, Universal, 1923), airing on January 11, 1961. This is certainly the oldest horror movie, the first Universal horror and only Lon Chaney film screened on Australian TV that was not part of a clip show.

Although many Boris Karloff movies were banned from TV, Karloff himself was not and on April 5, 1961, Boris Karloff's *Thriller* debuted, albeit with cuts. Karloff noted this hypocrisy at the time: "Terror is much better done nowadays," he said, "because it's handled gently—and that adds to the fear the viewer feels. We injected more ghastliness into an hour of my *Thriller* series than you'd see in 60 reels of the old shockers."[6] Horror cartoons, such as the Disney reference to Poe's "The

Premature Burial" in *The Haunted Mansion,* were also allowed, this time by children, as were other cartoons.

Old movies were shown on *Science Fiction Thriller* which made its bow in 1963 in Sydney and Adelaide, and the continuation of *Adult Theatre* in Melbourne. *Science Fiction Thriller* was a cover-all package to allow films such as *The Monster That Challenged the World* and *Forbidden Planet* to be shown, late on Friday or Saturday nights. Even though Hammer's movies were heavily censored and even banned, some were beginning to be screened in the form of *The Abominable Snowman* and *Enemy from Space.*

In September through to October 1964, ATN-7 Sydney took a leaf from their Melbourne counterparts and began to screen vintage horror under the *Theatre of Thrills* banner. Among the films shown were *The Invisible Ray, The Captive, This Island Earth, It Came from Outer Space, The Man in Half Moon Street* and *Fingers at the Window.* Other capital cities followed Sydney's lead and more Universal films began to appear on the small screen. *Abbott and Costello Meet Frankenstein* (December 22, 1964, HSV-7, Melbourne), *Black Friday* (November 13, 1964, ADS-7, Adelaide), *Tarantula* (October 23, 1964, ADS-7, Adelaide), *The Frozen Ghost* (March 9, 1965, TEN-10, Sydney) and *Dead Man's Eyes* (January 26, 1965, HSV-7, Melbourne) all had their first run, as did the classic *Them!* (December 18, 1964, HSV-7 Melbourne).

July 1965 saw ATN-7 Sydney again begin to raid the horror vaults. *The Mummy, The Cat Creeps, The Black Cat* and *Murders in the Rue Morgue* were rolled out under the *Theatre of Thrills* banner. More horror and science fiction were being shown to the delight of late-night television viewers. There were still those movies that were considered too horrific for TV, *Frankenstein, Dracula* and *The Wolf Man* were, unofficially, banned from the small screen, as were the recent Hammer Horrors.

What was also being noticed was the spike in ratings each time anything related to horror was shown, especially late at night on weekends. At times, episodes of Karloff's *Thriller* were beating out more popular family fare. Networks began to take notice.

Horror as Comedy: *The Munsters*

In America and other parts of the world, TV stations continued to look to old feature films to meet quotas and to attract people to buy sets and watch them. Popular movies, such as John Wayne or Gary Cooper westerns, Clark Gable dramas, Humphrey Bogart gangster films, Bing Crosby musicals, Bob Hope comedies and anything with Bette Davis or Joan Crawford meant money for a channel as advertisers knew people would tune in.

The National Censor took to issuing what was commonly called *The Blue Book,*[7] which detailed what films could and could not be screened. At the top of the "Not Suitable for Screening" list were 35 horror movies, led by Boris Karloff's *Frankenstein* and Tod Browning's *Freaks.* If the standards were not adhered to, a station

5. Television: 1956–1973

Horror as TV comedy: a 1964 ad for *The Munsters*.

would face serious sanctions, including heavy fines; it even stood to lose its license. It would take decades for the power to shift away from the censor and into the hands of the license holders but, until then, there would be no *Frankenstein*.

The Munsters, a parody of the Universal monsters, debuted in Australia on, appropriately enough, October 31, 1964 (ATN-7) in Sydney. The series became a hit and was shipped around Australia, quickly gathering more popularity for its comedic value. By mid–1965, *The Munsters* was being shown in all states of Australia.

The Munsters was based upon the classic Universal Horrors, with Herman Munster's makeup based upon Karloff's Frankenstein Monster. *The Munsters* was cleared by the censor as it was a comedy, but the irony of the censor allowing this show to screen and the original source material to be banned was not lost upon people.[8]

King Kong on the Small Screen

On June 14, 1965, Melbourne TV station ATV-0 announced that it would screen the RKO classic *King Kong* for the first time at 8:30 p.m. In doing so, they caused one of the biggest horror-related controversies for television to date. What should have been the first full-blooded horror movie seen on Australian TV was cancelled at the last minute.

According to ATV, the movie had been submitted to the censor for clearing a week previously. The board replied that the movie could be screened, but first it had to be cut so deeply that it would no longer make any sense to the viewer. ATV-0 declined to make the cuts but scheduled the film anyway.

Just hours before the scheduled showing, Commonwealth Censor R.J. Prowse insisted that the movie could not be aired, pending an official decision. After stating that *Kong* could be regarded as a classic, Prowse added, "I realize this film has possibly been a favorite at children's matinees, but standards for TV films are much higher than normal theatres." This claim was rebutted by the Head of Philosophy at Sydney University, Dr. A. Stout, who posed a rhetorical question: "Has it been suggested that any child has been frightened out of his wits in the past years by this rather ridiculous monster?"

ATV-0 station manager Norman Carlyon was outraged. "It would appear that after 32 years, the Censorship Board has discovered a monster," he told the media. "If this film is banned, I will launch an immediate appeal. This is a valuable film from the point of view of being somewhat of a classic and one I believe should be screened. It is not just another thriller."[9]

Two days later, June 18, the film was formally banned from television. True to his word, Carlyon appealed the decision and invited members of the media to a private screening at the ATV-0 studios. In questioning the merits of the ban, *The Bulletin* drew attention to the fact that *Kong* was not only a classic but had been so successful that it had spawned a sequel. The irony and insanity of the *Kong* ban came when ATV-0 announced the screening of *The Son of Kong* for October 14, four months later. *King Kong* was banned, but *Son of Kong* had been cleared and rated "A" for Adults.

In 1969, the Saturday morning cartoon series *The King Kong Show*[10] began airing,[11] with repeats well into the 1970s and a resurgence in 1980. As usual, the comical cartoon could be shown, with the same characters, but the original, no matter how tame and dated it might now appear, was banned.

King Kong was finally telecast on ATV-0 in Sydney in November 1972, heavily cut to just under 90 minutes. From 1972 onwards, this butchered version switched from TV station to station, appearing as a triple monkey feature on Channel 7 with *Planet of the Apes* and *Beneath the Planet of the Apes*.

Awful Movies with Deadly Earnest

A change was coming to television, albeit subtly. Karloff's *Thriller* series, along with others such as *A for Andromeda*, *Andromeda Breakthrough*, *The Outer Limits*, and *Twilight Zone* had shown that Australian audiences were primed for a return of horror. But it was not all plain sailing though.

Announced, but banned outright in 1963 in Sydney, was an episode of *Science Fiction Thriller* featuring Universal's Karloff-Lugosi starrer *The Invisible Ray*. The censor quickly pulled the plug on the film, forcing Channel 7 to replace it with yet another giant bug movie. Nothing was said, though, when the film screened on Adelaide TV in late September 1964.

The constant announcements, retractions and replacements saw people asking questions as to why a ban established in 1948 was still in effect a generation later. It was beginning to be noted that what might have terrified the post–World War II children would not have the same effect upon the Baby Boomers who were roaming the streets and could just as easily see the same movies in a cinema or drive-in late at night.

When the Chief Censor, Ray Hall, announced a ban on the 1950s film *Tarantula* from being screened on television in 1964, he addressed the issue of the ban and shifted the blame back squarely onto the Federal Government: "A policy on horror films was laid down 17 years ago. Since then, there has been a number of governments, but this department has never received a directive from any of them to change the horror film policy." When asked which horror movies had been banned from TV, Hall was very evasive: "I am not at liberty to discuss this matter. I would be talking about the importer's property, and as television is a competitive industry, I could be letting the cat out of the bag. We do face problems with modern television science fiction series. We have the problem of deciding what science fiction is and what is horror; what is an acceptable subject and what is not in the interest of the public."[12]

Again, although banned, *Tarantula* was screened on Adelaide TV shortly after its ban was announced.

Something was missing from Australian television screens: hosts for horror.

In 1961, Australia took a popular idea from the U.S. and began to make its own hosted horrors. With the relaxing of censorship for movies shown after 10:00 p.m., it was decided that late Friday nights would be put aside for horror, science fiction, mystery, chillers, thrillers and strong drama.

The character Deadly Earnest had its origins in Perth in 1961, when a musical director created the character. The Perth-based Deadly Earnest sporadically presented movies on TVW-7. But other than the name and idea, it was just another local identity used for comical effect.

Channel 10 in Sydney took the idea one step further and engaged a local musician-presenter named Ian Bannerman to produce a concept like American horror hosts Zacherley and Vampira. The Ten Network then bought up dozens of horror films from various libraries around the world: Hammer, Universal, Republic, Toho, RKO, Columbia, Allied Artists, American International Pictures and dozens of sub–Poverty Row productions. In fact, the lower the budget, the better for television.

In collaboration with others whose names are now lost to time, Bannerman produced a new, and unique, look for the character Deadly Earnest. His Bannerman's Deadly Earnest would wear white corpse paint with black, almost gothic touches, along with capes and dark clothing. He would not be alone, though: Deadly Earnest had an offsider in the form of a skull named Yorick.

Yorick, it was claimed, was a real human's skull, and there is evidence to support that claim with the Adelaide Deadly Earnest, Headly Cullen, telling people, off the air, that Yorick was real. The very few Yoricks that have surfaced have proven to be fake.

Deadly Earnest presented his *Aweful Movies* from a dungeon, complete with dripping water, spiderwebs and melted candles. He would also appear during commercial breaks to remind his audience just how horridly bad the movies they were watching were, using a combination of sarcasm and high camp.

Aweful Movies with Deadly Earnest debuted in Sydney on Friday, July 22, 1966. Its first offering was the Japanese monster movie *Varan the Unbelievable* (dir. Ishirō Honda, Toho, 1958).[13]

Deadly Earnest was an instant hit. Young people and horror movie fans across New South Wales made a star out of Bannerman, and he milked his fame, appearing in advertisements and going as far as to release a record of original songs, under the Deadly Earnest persona. Ratings soared and Bannerman soon found that Deadly Earnest was in demand for public appearances. Such was his popularity that the decision was made to move the show from Friday to Saturday nights and to replicate the concept in other states.

Each state would have its own Deadly Earnest. Adelaide's was Headly Cullen, an experienced actor known for his voiceover work. He debuted on July 21 and remained on the air until well into the 1970s. In Melbourne, a floor manager, Ralph Baker, was their Deadly Earnest. Aspiring young actor Shane Porteous filled the role in Brisbane.

Each Deadly Earnest was unique to his city, but the movies were all the same, licensed by Channel 10 Australia-wide. The station was limited to what movies it could show pre–1969, but they were able to source pre-ban horrors (*The Ape*), atomic age science fiction, giant monsters and B-grade fodder. Again, showing the limitation of the movie library, movies were often repeated, sometimes up to four times a year, with *The Gorgon* being shown twice in successive weekends in 1967.

Deadly Earnest increased in popularity over the years: Friday and Saturday nights saw young people, horror buffs and university students gathering to watch their local Deadly Earnest decimate the movies that he showed, heaping scorn on the production values and acting, and discussing their merits to Yorick (who had lightbulbs, that lit up, for eyes). The surrealism, and freshness, of the concept appealed to the new youth culture.

Television has never been an industry to let another station hold a monopoly on gimmicks and variations of the Deadly Earnest model followed, with mixed success. In 1968, the Ten network, TVQ-0, in Brisbane let Professor MacCarb (John Dommett) loose onto the screens. In the early 1970s, Channel Seven in Sydney responded with an Australian version of Vampira (Jill Forster), while the same network in Perth provided Elvira the Witch.[14] Channel Nine in Adelaide took local stage actor Russell Starke and put him up against Headly Cullen, a move that did not pay off as well as they hoped, despite Starke's over-the-top, often camp mannerisms and exaggerated presentations.

Television Horror Explodes

Deadly Earnest's popularity saw an increase in the number of horror movies shown on TV. As this was still in the era where the genre was banned, films were sourced from many locations. The reliance upon the major studios and

Australian-based distributors were no longer a factor as American companies began to package up old films and sell the rights to the Australian networks. This resulted in a wide variety of films coming into the country and onto the small screen, many of which had never seen any form of release in Australia.

Often these were atomic age monster and science fiction films. A look at the initial 298 first-run films screened between 1957 and the end of 1969: Ninety-four were movies that were either banned, rejected or not given a cinema release. These films include movies from companies that had little, if any, distribution in Australia, such as American International[15] and Toho.[16] Adding the appeal was that films such as *13 Ghosts* (1960), *The Giant Gila Monster* (1959), *Blood and Roses* (1960) and a host of AIP movies were still banned from cinemas when they ran on TV.

Other films that never got a cinematic release, began appearing at drive-ins at the same time as they were appearing on TV. Poverty Row companies such as Republic[17] and Monogram[18] were well represented, as were major studios such as Universal,[19] RKO[20] and Columbia.[21]

Although the focus was on American-made horror and science fiction, Deadly Earnest and his mimics also introduced their audiences to films from Italy, Japan and the United Kingdom. Along with Hammer, television premiered the likes of *Doctor Blood's Coffin* (1961) and *The Snake Woman* (1961), both produced by Caralan, along with titles from Eros, Ealing, New Elstree, London Film Productions and more. The bulk of the films originated from the United States and the United Kingdom. The remainder of the films consisted of dubbed features that might never have made it to cinemas in Australia at the time of their original release. There were films from Japan, Italy, Germany, Mexico and Poland.[22]

Once the ban on horror films was lifted in 1969, it was left to each individual TV station to decide what was going to appear. The influx of more low-budget films from the likes of Roger Corman and AIP increased, as did the Hammer horrors. Each city then adjusted what fare their Deadly Earnest hosts showed, with comedies, westerns and even dramas appearing. Nineteen seventy-two saw the Melbourne Deadly Earnest series presenting the previously banned-from-TV *Outer Limits episodes*.

In 1973, the Nine network launched the series *The Evil Touch,* Australian-funded and -produced (albeit by American Mende Brown), and featuring American actors Leslie Nielsen, Darren McGavin, Vic Morrow, Ray Walston, Kim Hunter *et al.* to give it a polished, international flavor. In a coup for the network, Anthony Quayle presented the series. Despite the push, and the money invested into it, the series lasted just over a year.

Deadly Earnest gradually went off the air throughout Australia from the mid–1970s. Despite promises of a resurrection, it never happened. Yet more people followed in Deadly Earnest's footsteps, Peter Goers (Adelaide, 1986), Tabitha Clutterbuck (Tabitha Halley, Syndicated, Arena, 1997–1999) and Fosdyke (Robert Mascara, Melbourne, ATV-10, 2005) being the most notable. The rise of Internet streaming, such as YouTube, has seen a new rise in horror hosts, in Australia at least, and some of these hosts have lineage that can be traced directly back to the days of Deadly Earnest.

Frankenstein Premieres 40 Years Later

Fittingly, the first Universal Horror talkie screened on Australian TV was the one that started the craze: *Dracula*. It ran on a double feature with *The Mummy's Tomb* in early 1973[23]; both films had been submitted to the censor and passed, albeit with minor cuts and an Adults Only rating. Once they were cleared, the censor announced that a further 160 movies would be cleared for screening, including Karloff's *Frankenstein*.[24]

Finally, on November 5, 1973, rated Adults Only, *Frankenstein*, starring Boris Karloff, Mae Clarke and Colin Clive, premiered on Australian television, on a double bill with *WereWolf of London* starring Henry Hull.[25] It had taken 42 years but *Frankenstein*'s last Australian ban was finally lifted, this time for good.[26] The TV version was censored, removing the drowning scene and excising the reference to God,[27] but the rest was there for all to see. The ban had outlived the majority of the movie's participants, including director James Whale[28] and actors Karloff,[29] Clive,[30] Dwight Frye,[31] John Boles,[32] Frederick Kerr,[33] Lionel Belmore[34] and Edward Van Sloan.[35] Indeed, the last of the listed cast members still alive were Frankenstein's bride-to-be Elizabeth, Mae Clarke, along with Michael Mark and Marilyn Harris. (The latter played the girl thrown in the lake by Karloff's Monster.)

What had once worked in the cinema lost some power on the small screen. As a nation, Australia was beginning to enjoy the benefits of color television in the early 1980s and the sight of almost silent (*The Mummy* and *Dracula* in particular) black and white films did not hold the same power and impact as they once did. It did not help that by the time the Universal Monsters finally did appear on TV, everybody had seen the color Hammer Horrors, with their blood and gore. After seeing Christopher Lee being staked through the heart, Bela Lugosi meeting the same fate, off screen, held few thrills.

6

Rebirth:
The '70s and Beyond

The Censor Cuts Again!

The rescinding of the horror ban did not grant carte blanche to horror films as they now had to contend with a new ratings regime: the Australian Classification Board. The board replaced the previous classifications with "G"—General Audiences, "NRC"—Not Recommended for Children Under 12, "M"—Mature Audiences, "R"—Restricted Exhibition. This new system was intended to refresh the cinematic offerings available while still applying the stern hand of the censor.

The censor went after anything from Hammer vigorously, slashing entire scenes and rendering some films almost nonsensical. Even though a few Hammers had managed to get past the censor unscathed in the 1960s, including the Cushing-Lee *The Mummy,* a new regime was in power. Horror films might now be back at the cinemas and drive-ins, but it did not mean that scenes of gore, blood and violence would be on display.

The one major bonus for Australian filmgoers was the sudden flood of 20 years of horror and science fiction that now saturated the market—films such as *The Day of the Triffids, The Kiss of the Vampire* and *Curse of the Fly* were now freed from earlier rejections. Although the censor was not about to ban movies outright, unless the content and circumstances called for it,[1] they merely cut everything that came in.

This did not mean that some genuine horror films didn't sneak past the censor back in the mid– to late 1960s, albeit sometimes years after release. *Terror in the Haunted House* was cleared, with cuts, in 1967 after being released in the U.S. in 1958. Even Bette Davis was not immune with her two classics, *What Ever Happened to Baby Jane?* and *Hush...Hush, Sweet Charlotte* both having themes designated as "horror" being excised from the prints pre-release.

In the period between 1968 and 1975, Hammer horrors such as *Frankenstein Must Be Destroyed, Horror of Dracula*[2] and *Dracula Has Risen from The Grave,*G suffered the most. The general procedure followed by the Film Classification Board was to refuse horror films formal classification until the film was cut. If the film was not cut, then it would simply be banned. The Hammers *Nightmare, Maniac, The Phantom of the Opera, The Kiss of the Vampire, The Curse of the Mummy's Tomb, The Gorgon, Dracula Has Risen from the Grave, The Revenge of Frankenstein, Countess*

Dracula, Frankenstein Must Be Destroyed, Hands of the Ripper, Scars of Dracula, The Vampire Lovers, The Brides of Dracula, Dracula AD 1972, Dracula—Prince of Darkness, Horror of Dracula and *Taste the Blood of Dracula* were all chopped by the censor to remove excessive violence and/or gore. Non-Hammer films did not escape the censor: *Dracula vs. Frankenstein, The Fear Chamber, Night of the Living Dead, Black Sunday, House of Dark Shadows, Pit and the Pendulum, Scream and Scream Again* and *Lady Frankenstein* were also cut.

Even films such as *Billy the Kid versus Dracula* (with John Carradine reprising his Universal Dracula) and *Jesse James Meets Frankenstein's Daughter* were cut, as cartoonish as they were. The *Planet of the Apes* series was cut, as was *Blacula, Count Yorga, Vampire, The Abominable Dr. Phibes* and their sequels. The movies were then further cut for exhibition on television, at times rendering them unwatchable, suddenly jumping between scenes, and more often ending abruptly mid-scene with a well-timed commercial break.

Night of Fear, the First Modern Horror Film

If the last horror movie made in Australia was 1924's *Fisher's Ghost*, then it seemed apt that the first horror movie made after the bans were lifted would also be a silent(ish) film. *Night of Fear* is notable for having little, if any, dialogue. Ironically enough, even though the ban on horror movies had been lifted, *Night of Fear* received its own ban, not for horror, but for indecency.

As the 1970s began, a new wave of Australian filmmakers with state and federal government bodies began to sense the possibilities of making world-class films without having to go overseas or resorting to importing actors to ensure overseas sales and distribution. Although the practice of importing talent still happened, there was more reliance upon local talent. Films such as *The Naked Bunyip* (1970, dir. John Murray), *Stork* (1971, dir. Tim Burstall) and *Homesdale* (1971, dir. Peter Weir) showed that Australians could make films that were uniquely Australian, yet still have international appeal. Talent from other countries were still courted by Australian producers: *Wake in Fright*[3] (1971, dir. Ted Kotchoff) and *Walkabout* (1971, dir. Nicholas Roeg) used both foreign directors and actors, Donald Pleasence in the former and Jenny Agutter in the latter.

A new breed of directors, producers and actors came to the fore. Directors such as Burstall, Weir, Bruce Beresford, George Miller, Jim Sharman, Gillian Armstrong and Fred Schepisi all had full-length feature film credits by 1973. Australian actors were also in demand: Jack Thompson, Graeme Blundell, Bruce Spence, Jackie Weaver, Barry Humphries, Barry Crocker, Judy Morris, John Meillon and more.

This resurgence was due to the emergence of the National Institute of Dramatic Art. Formed in 1958, NIDA nurtured a new generation of actors, writers, producers and directors, some of whom went on to make their mark amongst the finest the world has seen.[4] Seeing the potential of the Australian scene, talent such as Chips Rafferty, Frank Thring and Michael Pate also headed back to realize projects. It was an exhilarating time to be working in the Australian film industry. Into this excitement walked one of the more controversial figures of 1970s Australian cinema, Terry Bourke.

Depending on who you speak to, Bourke[5] was either an incredibly talented visionary or a devious, hopeless, untalented con man. No matter his legacy, and how people saw him during his lifetime, the fact remains that Bourke did achieve a lot and made an impact.

Bourke wrote a lot of his own history. Some true, some embellished for effect, and some outright lies. Separating fact from fiction when it comes to Bourke can be problematic. He claimed to have been a professional boxer in his youth. He was babysitter to INXS lead singer Michael Hutchence and his brother Rhett. He was childhood friends with playwright David Williamson. He was a professional cyclist and a drummer of repute.

What *is* known is that Bourke got his start in film while working as a correspondent in Hong Kong in the mid–1960s. His entry into the film industry came when he somehow (he never said how) managed to raise a sizable amount of money[6] to fund a Hong Kong film, *Strange Portrait* (1965, dir. Jeffrey Stone). Bourke then claimed to have been employed by Robert Wise to work both as a production assistant and Steve McQueen's minder during the filming of *The Sand Pebbles*. While there is a photograph of McQueen and Bourke on the set of that film, Bourke is never mentioned in McQueen biographies, which makes his later claim that McQueen was a close friend dubious. His name is absent from the film's credits.[7]

In 1968, Bourke wrote, produced and directed his first feature film, *Sampan*, in Hong Kong. The movie attracted attention by being both the subject of censorship and, according to Bourke, being the most successful film in Hong Kong cinema for its time. Bourke moved to Guam and produced and directed another film, *Noon Sunday* (1968), and then moved back in 1971 to Australia, where he worked as a director for the television series *Spyforce*.

While in Guam, Bourke conceived the idea for a TV series which he titled *Fright*. He wrote a synopsis for a pilot episode, which he titled "Night of Fear." This pilot was designed to be a short feature, no more than an hour's running time, and with as little dialogue as possible. Stopping at Los Angeles on his way back to Australia, Bourke approached Roger Corman with his ideas of filming the series in the Philippines; Corman, sensing that Bourke was a tad reckless with other people's money, quickly turned him down. That is, if the meeting ever happened, as we only have Bourke's word that it did.

Upon his return to Australia, Bourke approached commercial television stations with the *Fright* concept, only to be rejected. At the time, Channel 0–10 was busy with the *Deadly Earnest* concept, which was now national and proving to be successful, ATN-7 had their own *Creature Feature* in place, in addition to the *Outer Limits* series, and they were looking at purchasing the rights to the American produced *Ghost Story* series. The Nine network simply played horror and science fiction when it suited them.

Bourke's contacts at the ABC proved to be his lifeline. A conversation with

Moya Iceton, then working on continuity for *Spyforce,* led Burke to pitch the series to the ABC. They tentatively accepted it and gave approval for the pilot to be filmed. This meant that Bourke now had funding and a professional crew, with a TV network behind him. There was a bit of an obstacle which was only known to Bourke at the time: He had already sold "Night of Fear."

In 1972, Bourke met film editor Roy Hay while they were working on *Spyforce*. Hay was the opposite of Bourke, quiet and reserved where Bourke was loud and boisterous. The pair joined forces and formed a company called Terryrod Productions. While Bourke was meeting with the ABC, Hay approached the Australian Film Development Corp. with the view of obtaining a grant which would see pre-production work begin on what was then being called *Fright: Night of Fear.* The AFDC gave assurances that the amount requested, $13,500, would be approved if the film were released to cinemas.

The plot of *Night of Fear* was as simple as it got. A young woman crashes her car on a lonely country road and is terrorized by a crazed hermit. It is a plot that had been used many times before, and would be used many times since, notably by *The Texas Chain Saw Massacre* and *Wolf Creek*. The film would be unique in that no dialogue would be spoken, making the quality of the actors, and the selling of their roles, extremely important. The film would not be completely silent though, with people heard talking in the background, or a radio announcer, along with sound effects, ambient noise, music, grunts and screams. According to Hay, "For an Australian horror film to get up there was really no precedent, so we were trying to play off against an American precedent over here. Our film in many ways played off *Ben* and *Willard*, which were also about rats at that stage, so we were sort of trying to capture a theme that had proved already successful."[8]

With the ABC still believing that the film was to the pilot of an ongoing series, they assigned people to the project. The agreement was for the ABC to provide below-the-line costs in the form of crew, equipment, transportation, technical facilities for post-production and stage space. Bourke and Hay's costs would include raw stock, laboratory charges, sets, props, wardrobe, makeup supplies and catering. The ABC also gave approval for the film to be shot on location, as opposed to a studio set, and the film would be shot in 35mm color—the standard for Australian television at the time was 16mm color, but one would often see 16mm black and white. Keeping an eye on their investment was ABC executive producer Charles Russell, who worked with Rod Hay. Terryrod also paid Bourke to both write and direct. Sensing an opportunity and still waiting for the money to come through from the AFDC, Bourke and Hay each pitched in $4000 and began work.

Just how Bourke raised his half is open to debate. In later years, people who knew him told of how he would never invest his own money, instead he would borrow, beg or just outright steal what he needed. In 2017, writer Richard Harris wrote an obituary of Bourke, in which director Brian Trenchard-Smith claimed, "[Bourke] still owes me $600 from *Night of Fear!*"[9] It is more than probable that Bourke never really invested in *Night of Fear*; instead he raised the money via loans, most of which were never paid back. Bourke and Hay then set about casting the film. None of the characters would have names; instead, they would be credited by the role they performed.

For the pivotal role of the Hermit, veteran stage, film and TV actor Norman Yemm was cast. An athlete[10] turned actor, Yemm was a well-known face on Australian TV, having appeared in featured roles in a few series; his most notable work came as a grizzled detective figure in both *Homicide* and *Division 4*. He took up TV work after his career as the Australian Opera Company's principal baritone ran its course in 1965. At the time of filming *Night of Fear*, Yemm was also about to appear in the classic Australian TV series *Number 96*. *Night of Fear* was not Yemm's first movie, he had appeared, albeit briefly and uncredited, as one of the submarine crew members in *On the Beach*; but *Night of Fear* was to be his first leading film role.

Yemm was a better actor than most of his roles had shown. He could project, both visually and vocally, thanks to his years with the AOC (although he was reduced to a series of grunts in *Night of Fear*) and his height, thin build and unique face (he always looked older than he really was) gave him a mysterious aura. Yemm also took his roles very seriously and was known for the diversity of his roles. Speaking ten years later, he explained why he took the role:

> I stayed with *Homicide* for three and a half years, but I left because my acting wasn't a good as I wanted it to be in certain areas. I needed to get out and work with different production companies in a variety of roles to develop myself as an actor. That led me to *Number 96* as Harry Collins, Vera's ex-husband, who came back and raped her, and in the movie *Night of Fear*, in which I played a hermit type who terrorized Carla Hoogeveen with a lot of rats. Those two roles, if they did nothing else, made sure that I wasn't going to be typecast as a policeman.[11]

As the Hermit would be surrounded by rats, Yemm brought home the four rats that were to be his companions in the film. Three rats were normal, brown rats and their leader was an albino named Pinkie, who got a credit in the film. Yemm and Pinkie became inseparable, with Pinkie being adopted by Yemm.

"We got the rats from the vivisection department of the University of Sydney," Yemm told the *Sydney Morning Herald*. "The idea was that by having them in the house, I could get used to the rats and they could get used to me."[12] It was not that simple. "The children thought it was great, but my wife wouldn't come in the door when they're around. She still won't come any closer than four feet." Mrs. Yemm's reaction aside, the rats and Yemm did bond and their familiarity with each other makes for chilling scenes. This is most notable when the rats, casually and without hesitation, join the Hermit as he eats. The rats also gleefully gnawed on cue at a severed horse head, which had been procured by the ABC props department for a sequence that would not be possible to film in this day and age of protected animals.

Mike Dorsey was cast as the Lover. An English-born veteran of TV and stage, he had appeared alongside Yemm in *Riptide* and *Homicide*. Dorsey's list of credits was longer than Yemm's, stretching back to the Gate Theatre in Dublin. While working as a publicist for the Rolling Stones, Dorsey first visited Australia, and he chose to remain behind when the Stones left.[13] Because Dorsey had the face of an innocuous man, he was perfectly cast for the role.

Briony Behets was 20 when she was cast as the Horse Girl. A graduate of

London's Guildhall School of Drama, she made her film debut in *Night of Fear*. Behets had first appeared in Australia on stage in a production of *Don's Party*. After following this up with another stage production, *Private Lives,* she was cast in the TV series *Bellbird*. Like Yemm and Dorsey, Behets also appeared in the first series of *Number 96*.

With three of the four main roles cast, Bourke was ready to begin filming. The role of the Woman would require a nude scene and those actors approached to audition balked at the idea of stripping for the camera. According to Bourke, those who did agree to strip then demanded more money than had been allocated. Three days before filming was set to begin, Bourke was faced with shutting down, paying the extra money or reworking the script to remove the nude scene. At the last minute, an agent sent in Dutch actress Carla Hoogeveen.

The attractive blonde Hoogeveen was, like the other players, at the start of her career. Her most notable credits to date had come on the comedy series *The Aunty Jack Show*. Within 24 hours, she had been fitted for her *Night of Fear* wardrobe and was ready to begin filming. She would be appearing, on screen, for the bulk of the film. The moviemakers didn't know if she could carry the movie, so her casting was a gamble. The remaining minor roles were quickly filled, with Peter Armstrong as the Truckie, James Moss as the Client and Curt Jansen as the Garage Attendant.

With promises of payments to come, Bourke and his ABC crew shot the film in 12 days. The shoot was not without problems. The first scenes to be shot (the interior of the Hermit's hut) were done at the ABC studios. Charles Russell began to object to the direction that the movie was moving into, knowing that some scenes being shot would not pass the ABC censor: a dream sequence which showed Hoogeveen bound naked to a table being approached by an equally naked Yemm holding the dripping skull of Briony Behets; a "Last Supper" sequence in which Yemm hacks the hair from Hoogeveen's skull, and a rat attack led by Pinkie. Also concerning to Russell was the fact that these scenes weren't in the original script that had been approved by the ABC; Bourke had rewritten the script to play up the gore when the Australian Film Development Corporation showed interest.

Bourke decided, before filming began, that he would not be filming a television pilot; rather he would be making a motion picture for cinema release. He maintained that this idea came to him later in the process of filming. "Halfway through the shooting," said Bourke in 1973, "both Rod Hay and I decided that the ABC, or any other network, wouldn't be supporting a horror series. *Night Gallery* was being axed in the States and William Castle's *Ghost Story* series, to fill the gap, was about to start. At buying rates, the U.S. shows were more attractive for Australian buyers. So, we went hammer and tongs at the violence and horror and sex."[14]

This claim is misleading. Bourke and Hay had clearly decided, prior to shooting, that the film would play up the violence and sex, not halfway through the shoot. Russell's observations on set led to verbal confrontations with Bourke, culminating with Russell washing his hands of the project and leaving the location. With the interior scenes completed, the crew moved to the north shore area of Sydney for the remainder of the shoot.

The location shoot of seven days and three nights ran smoothly with only two hours lost to rain. The ABC crew was highly professional and used to rapid filming for episodic television. Money was becoming an issue and it came as a relief when, with two days of filming to go, the Australian Film Development Corp. finally made contact and gave the go-ahead to release its investment funds, which amounted to $13,500. The ABC estimated that it had sunk $14,000 into the film via salaries, equipment and production costs, making the total cost of the film $35,500. Other reports put the budget at a mere $21,500 and at least one contemporary report, in *The Age,* puts the budget at $32,000, with the breakdown being $13,500 from the AFDC, $14,500 from the ABC and $4000 from Terryrod.[15] As people's memories are now clouded, the actual cost of the film might never be known.

No matter what the cost was, it eventually recouped every cent, and brought an enormous return. The Australian Film Development Corp.'s investment was fully repaid, along with Bourke and Hay getting a decent return. Going on statements made since, Bourke did not use the profits to repay the personal loans he had taken out to finance the film.

Once filming was finished, Bourke and Hay took the film back to the ABC for the final editing. This was done using the ABC's facilities, with the full knowledge that the station would not be given the final product. "The ABC offered us facilities in return for local television rights and equity in the actual theatrical release as and when it happened," Hay said. "But I don't think the ABC and their straitlaced manner of the time realized just exactly what a horror film entertained. And when they saw the finished product, they were suitably horrified and said [that they needed to distance themselves] from this film."[16]

That the ABC still believed that the film would be part of an ongoing series comes with the opening credits. A title card, bearing the word *Fright*, is shown, this then dissolves to show the film's, or rather, episode title, "Night of Fear." If the ABC had been aware that the series was not going ahead, or that the film was not intended for them, then the *Fright* title would not have been seen. It is also doubtful that they would have put any more time or money into it.

The ABC became suspicious of Bourke when he demanded that Hay be the film's sole editor. ABC policy was firm: The only people who were to edit potential ABC material were ABC staff members. As the film's director, an exception was made for Bourke to be present as an observer and advisor. Editor Ray Alchin began to chop at the footage with the aim of bringing the film in under an hour. In the process, he removed sequences involving the Truckie, much to the dismay of Peter Armstrong, and made minor cuts to scenes involving Behets and Dorsey.

The movie's first cut ran 62 minutes. For the film to be considered for television, more cuts were required and Alchin pared another eight minutes and brought the final cut in at 54 minutes. Bourke and Hay then screened the finished product for the ABC. As they had hoped, it proved too graphic for 1972 television, so the series was cancelled. The ABC then signed the film over to Hay but kept an option for any future television screenings. Bourke and Hay now owned the film outright and began the task of promoting it as a feature film.

Incidentally, the rats had become amorous during filming (Pinkie was quite the handsome fellow), and as a result, some of the rat extras left behind the fruits of their labors in the form of litters. The legend, which might be an urban one, is that the ABC studios in Sydney suffered from a rat infestation for years to come.

Night of Fear opens with the Horse Girl (Behets) riding her horse through the bush, these shots juxtaposed with shots of the Hermit. The Horse Girl is the only principal with any dialogue as she encourages the horse as she rides it. She stops, gets off and ties her horse to a tree, going for a walk. The Hermit unties the horse and takes it away with him. Horse Girl goes looking for the horse and finds the Hermit's hut. Hearing her horse in distress, she knocks on the door. Suddenly the Hermit attacks her from behind, tearing her clothes and locking her in the hut before shooting the horse.

The Girl is introduced in the shower and before dressing. Using jump cuts, Bourke shows the Girl, the Lover and the Truckie, all going about their business. The Girl, now in a tennis outfit, is shown playing tennis with the Lover. The tennis leads to sex. Next we see the Hermit feeding fresh, bloody meat to his rats in cages. This scene is ambiguous, as it is not established if the meat is from the corpse of the horse, or the Horse Girl.

The Girl is then shown driving and plows through a road sign and nearly collides with the Truckie, who stops to assist her. She frees her car from the ditch and drives off before the Truckie can reach her. Both go their separate ways. The Girl promptly drives into another ditch, this time cracking her forehead against the steering wheel, drawing blood.

The Hermit appears, with Pinkie on his shoulder and begins to terrorize the Girl but she manages to escape. She flees into the bush and hides. It is here that Bourke really creates a sense of fear as the Hermit begins to scrape a shovel on the ground, herding the Girl away from her car and towards his hut. The girl approaches the hut and sees horses' heads nailed to trees, dripping blood. Instead of obeying her instincts and running away, she enters and explores. Other than finding three stuffed rats in the bedroom, everything appears normal. The Girl then passes out and dreams of being tied to a table, naked, while the naked Hermit approaches her with the Horse Girl's severed skull in front of his groin. Meanwhile the Hermit is tucking into his dinner, at the Girl's car, with Pinkie as company.

She awakes as the Hermit nears the hut and manages to keep him out, but only long enough for the Hermit to flick a switch releasing rats inside the house. As the rats swarm toward the Girl, the Hermit watches through a window. The Girl faints and rats are seen happily chewing away at a severed arm. The Hermit then cuts the Girl's hair off and mops the blood from his floor.

The police find the Girl's car in the ditch and search the area, eventually finding the Hermit's hut. Feeding his chickens, he looks like any good person living in the bush. End of movie, roll credits.

The plot of *Night of Fear* is riddled with holes, and the lack of principal dialogue is both impressive and frustrating. One wonders if the eight minutes of cuts would have helped the film overall, but that footage is long gone. A sense of horror and fear permeates, more due to Yemm's acting than the writing or directing of Bourke. The sinister, murderous, amoral Hermit is an equal to any horror villain seen before or since. Pinkie leads his rats in scenes far more effective than those in *Willard* or its sequel *Ben*, and the shots of them eating the severed horse head are disturbing. The sex is gratuitous yet minor. The nudity is fetishistic, with photos of breasts and behinds on the wall of the hut, next to newspapers detailing missing person cases, implying that the Hermit has been murdering women for a long time.

There are a number of typical horror clichés, the sight of a doorknob turning, the Girl locked in her car while the Hermit stalks her, the Horse Girl deciding to explore the house rather than simply release her horse and ride off, the foot chase through the bush and the car crash itself. But these do not detract from the experience.

All told, the film looks a TV movie rather than a feature film but is highly effective. Seeing the Hermit killing and raping his way through the movie was a real shock for Australian audiences, who were used to Yemm portraying law-abiding figures.[17] It is also disturbing seeing the obvious affection that his character has for Pinkie the rat, and how that affection is reciprocated. Bourke's direction, combined with Peter Hendry's camerawork and tight editing by Ray Alchin, is also a highlight; the fear that the Girl experiences seems very real. It remains some of Bourke's best work as a filmmaker and is only let down by the red poster paint used as an unrealistic substitute for blood.

Bourke and Hay had no distributor, so they hired the Avalon Theatre in Sydney and arranged a special industry-only preview. According to Bourke, 746 people turned up to watch the film. "Reactions were mixed," remembered Bourke. "Technically, no one could fault the production to any real degree. Naturally, as entertainment, the reviews ranged from excellent to morbid, sick, lackluster and 'without any trace of talent.' But Rod and I knew we had a commercial prospect on our hands."

One person in attendance that night who didn't believe that Bourke and Hay had a "commercial hit on their hands" was from the Film Censorship Board. Taking exception to the scenes of Yemm approaching a tied-down Hoogeveen while carrying Behets' skull, the Board quickly slapped a total ban on *Night of Fear* on the grounds of indecency, making it the first Australian film banned since *Devil's Playground* (dir. Victor Bindley) in 1928.[18]

The Chief Censor, R.J. Prowse, wrote to Bourke and Hay informing them of the ban, causing the pair to go on the attack. They first contacted the media, announcing that they were intending on appealing the ban, pointing to the film's funding from the ABC and AFDC, and questioning the hypocrisy of the Censorship Board. Bourke and Hay also realized that this was the best publicity the film could ever get and milked it. "It is ludicrous when two Government bodies are involved in financing and making a film and a third Government body bans it," Bourke said.[19] The horror in the film was no worse than anything that had come into the country. Bourke also pointed out that the scenes of Hoogeveen being eaten by Yemm's rats contained implied violence and horror which was not actually shown. According to Hay,

> We of course went up in arms, and we approached Stanley Hawes, I think his name was, who was head of the censor board, and he said no, that film is banned for the following reasons, which included that particular scene. Which we could not even regard as being risqué, quite frankly. I mean, today you would get worse scenes in Bugs Bunny and Mickey Mouse. ... But that scene, coupled with a couple of other scenes with rats which they regarded as being confrontational and brutal, they said, sorry, that film is not going to play in an Australian cinema.[20]

The ban meant that the film could not be shown in cinemas or drive-ins, but that did not stop Bourke and Hay. Hay recalled, "I thought, well, the only way I'm going to retrieve that money is to make sure that we not only make our point, but we do actually get a release which will allow us to get funds back in the kitty for the next film we were planning. So it meant that we were part of a pioneering brigade that were out there to knock on independent doors, because we just could not get into theatre chains...."

The film screened to secondary school students (not old enough to see R-rated films) in their school auditoriums. Bourke used drive-ins and finally settled on the adult cinema, the Penthouse, in Kings Cross, Sydney, for the premiere. Bourke knew he had to get the film into as many cinemas as possible because, if the ban was upheld, both he and Hay would be responsible for the costs, which had now blown out. The film moved to Queensland, Perth and Melbourne, being shown at drive-ins and smaller, independent cinemas.

In 1972, the censorship board held a hearing on the appeal: They screened *Night of Fear* and heard a presentation from Bourke and Hay. Hay remembered:

> Let me tell you what we did when we walked through the door of the Censor Board. We concocted this idea that we'd bring in there a ... board, which was about 24 feet long, and it was about four feet high. And we had on it the prejudice that was now being made against Australian films and these other films had been allowed censorship clearance, and they had all these elements in them, and how can they allow a film, or disallow a film that has not a tenth of what these films have. By the time we got in there, we had Caroline Jones, who we demanded replaced Stanley Hawes as the Chairman of the Appeals Board, and it was almost a lay-down misère after that. They looked at it, and they said, "Oh, well, we can see the commitment you have made. We'll look at the film," and within a minute of having seen the film, they said, "Okay, film approved," and we were out and running.

The ban was formally lifted on December 4, 1972 (the film received an R rating). By that time, Bourke and Hay had negotiated the sale of overseas rights, which cleared all the debts for the film (other than those that Bourke had run up with friends and which he would never repay) and the film was being shown in London, distributed by Hammer Film Productions.

"We were never told what was indecent about the picture," Bourke said, "so we screened our film, gave some verbal information, and then showed the board four files on other pictures.[21] Our film was rated X in London—an equivalent of somewhere between the Australian M and R certificates."[22]

With the ban lifted, Bourke and Hay rushed the film onto the drive-in circuit, where it was paired with *The Thing with Two Heads* (1972, dir. Lee Frost), a low-budget Ray Milland film, the less said about the better.[23] *Night of Fear* opened the double bill, with *Two Heads* promoted as the main feature. In some cities, the film served as the opening feature to a revitalized *King Kong* (1933, dirs. Merian C. Cooper and Ernest B. Schoedsack) and was promoted as being the "controversial restricted shocker."

Without the censors or the ABC to placate, Bourke played up the horror even more, telling the *Sydney Morning Herald*, "There were times when the cameraman didn't want to watch."[24] When asked about the genre of sex-horror films, Bourke was clear: "It's the only work I'd do for nothing. All we expect is the freedom allowed overseas filmmakers. People who don't like it, should stay away."[25] Reviews were mixed, with some calling the film low-rent trash, and others praising its originality. From *The Canberra Times*:

> The subsequently rescinded banning of Terry Bourke's locally made minor opus *Night of Fear* is a classic example of censorship making itself looks ludicrous. The film contains little that is horrifying, violent or calculated to arouse prurient interest. And those of its elements that do meet these criteria are not displayed explicitly but merely suggested. It is not until the closing sequence where a rat-gnawed arm is shown that anything appears that might be close to the aesthetic knuckle. But it is not only on account of its lack of real horror quality that the film is a failure. It is so incredibly badly crafted in every department that its total effect is closer to comedy than horror. The script is minimal—and by this I do not mean to carp at the absence of dialogue but rather to comment on its illogicality even in its intended framework of fear. The camerawork is pure kitsch, and the editing looks as if it might have been done by the axe-brandishing nut (Norman Yemm), who is the film's main character.[26]

Calling the film "[a] must for those with platinum-coated nerves," the *Sydney Morning Herald* continued:

> Only an hour long, and made on a tiny budget, this is still one of the most encouraging pointers towards the future of the Australian film industry.
>
> It's a straightforward, hideous account of a modern ogre who lives in a lonely shack in the woods with an army of rats, an axe and an unpleasant interest in young blondes, the fate of two of whom is the film's subject matter. Norman Yemm is thoroughly frightening as the maniac, and the film's brutal effectiveness is enhanced by the fact that not a word of dialogue is spoken, except for his howling, mumbling and drooling, and the screams of his victims.

> There are, it must be said, certain blemishes; the claustrophobic atmosphere is endangered by the occasional shots of the outside world, and the eventual arrival of the police, looking as though they've stepped straight out of *Homicide*, and one or two of the horrors seem gratuitous. But these are minor points, and overall, this film is second among recent shockers only to *Straw Dogs* which had vastly greater resources to play with. Like *Straw Dogs* and unlike other films of the sort, it is completely plausible, a parable of extremity, Beauty and the Beast dragged out of the fairy tales and into a grim world the viewer may recognize as an extension of his own.[27]

The next day, the same newspaper tore the film apart: "It is an empty film, with nothing to generate audience interest except a few cheap and tasteless thrills. Such niceties as characterization and motivation are flagrantly ignored in favor of pure gruesomeness."[28] *The Age* chimed in with: "Sadly, it turns out to be a second-rate *Willard* with gum trees. Catering to an audience's lowest instincts, [Bourke] shows, with maximum sadistic suspense rather than horror, a crazed cousin to the Marquis De Sade who drools and gibbers and limps around a lonely forest cottage, terrorizing to death two girls in turn who venture near it. Of course, *Night of Fear* will make money."[29]

By the time the film made it to the cinemas, Bourke and Hay had moved on. The pair granted the ABC the television rights but knew full well that the film would never make it past the TV censors, and they no longer cared. They had made plenty of money, and the publicity helped them raise much needed funds for their next project, a full-length horror film set in 1890s Australia. Bourke and Hay bypassed the ABC and approached the AFDC directly and obtained an incredible $160,936. They threw in $67,064 of their earnings from *Night of Fear* and thus had $228,000 to make what Bourke predicted would be a "Hitchcock-style western, with some horror."[30]

"Basically, the story is about a lot of people who disappear at a lonely overnight inn in Gippsland in 1896," Bourke said. "We are bringing the American actor Stuart Whitman out to star in the film."

The film, *Inn of the Damned*, reached cinemas in 1975, although without Stuart Whitman.[31] But the cast was impressive. Leading the way was veteran Australian stage actress Dame Judith Anderson, who relished her role as the innkeeper's wife and chewed through the scenery reminiscent of Bette Davis at her histrionic best. American Alex Cord played the role originally slated for Whitman, and well-known Australian actors Tony Bonner and John Meillon[32] also were featured.

As with *Night of Fear*, the reviews were mixed. From the *Sydney Morning Herald*:

> *Inn of the Damned* is as unreal and as formally horrific as Grand Guignol. Loose ends of the plot need to be tied up with a hangman's knot, and the lesbian scenes seem unnecessary and distasteful. Still, the film overall is exciting and entertaining, Brian Probyn, director of photography, provides exquisite scenes of horseback chases through orange orchards, fights by waterfalls, and of lonely valleys. *Inn of the Damned* is very gruesome, of course. At one stage an axe falls and the whole screen flashes red. Flashback scenes are shown with misty formality and pretty lost children run to their doom.[33]

Inn of the Damned was Bourke's last foray into the horror field.

As a director, Bourke was not as highly regarded as his peers at the time. Writing about Bourke's 1982 feature *Brothers,* respected critic David Stratton opined, "[Bourke] is a second-rate director and *Brothers* is a second-rate film, in which the 'hero' … is so boorish and unsympathetic that the audience quickly loses any sympathy for him. Though Bourke can handle the action scenes, his big dramatic scenes are poorly written and awkwardly acted."[34]

Writing about the same movie, actor Roger Ward[35] said,

> Terry Bourke was a shifty but clever and cunning little character who did a lot of work. Some was good. The good was cancelled out by his cavalier attitude to money (always other people's), his disrespect of his peers, and an almost obsessive jealousy of anyone else in the industry. To his credit, Terry had an uncanny ability to make a tiny creek in the suburbs of Sydney look like the back blocks of Vietnam. He could also carve a piece of cardboard, put lights

behind it and shoot it with a title beneath, and those that saw it on the silver screen would swear it really was a Manhattan skyline. He could shoot beneath a doctored typewriter or through a disassembled camera or use a single house for the entire shoot of a film. He also wrote many show business articles for daily newspapers, but at best he was an egotistical arsehole who was nowhere near as talented as he imagined he was, and a terrible spendthrift of other people's money. He was also a pathological liar."[36]

Bourke could be equally as scathing in return, telling Ward that Academy Award–nominated director George Miller "can't even direct traffic,"[37] and telling Ward that a script that he (Ward) had written, which would be made into the film *Brothers*, was a "piece of shit."[38] Once Bourke made an enemy, they remained one for life.

Terry Bourke passed away on June 29, 2002.

No matter his professional and personal failings, Bourke made the first true Australian horror movie since 1924's *Fisher's Ghost,* using an all–Australian cast and crew, with funds obtained from Australian government agencies. In doing so he brought a close to almost 50 years of stigma that had surrounded horror in Australian cinema and kicked open the door. Through that door, other directors such as Peter Weir, Philippe Mora, Ken Hannam, Jim Sharman, Tim Bustall, Richard Franklin and many more followed.

Horror in Australia was now back, and vigorously.

Official *Freaks*

Freaks (1932) had been banned since 1932 in Australia, unseen aside from rumored illegals and a limited exhibition in at the Roseville Cinema on July 12 and 13, 1973. From that point on, the film remained a popular movie at art house cinemas. Advertisements talked up its banned status and director Tod Browning's use of real-life circus performers as cast members. Due to its short running time, the movie was often paired with a longer feature. Hitchcock films, such as *Psycho* and *The Birds,* and even Robert Altman's *Nashville* were then deemed to be the feature, with *Freaks* as the opener. In this way, director Tod Browning's masterpiece was finally being appreciated, by an audience made up of people who were not even alive when it was originally banned.

The censors formally cleared the film for cinematic release in 1975. Television was another matter and, due to its graphic scenes of true horror, it remained banned from TV until 1982.[39]

Bring Your Baby and see…. *The Exorcist*?

Australia's new "R" rating contained a caveat whereby children under the age of six were able to attend when accompanied by a parent, to enable and encourage young mothers to attend the cinema. Mothers were expected to take their kids to see were romantic films such as *Love Story*, or the latest offering from Elizabeth Taylor, not hard-core horrors. Politicians had once more underestimated the draw of horror films and how much they had evolved through the ban years.

The thought of children as young as five being able to view *The Exorcist* was enough to raise questions in the Australian Senate and, especially, in the country's newspapers. The movie was preceded by a fair amount of publicity as William Peter Blatty's novel was debated and denounced by the Catholic Church. The subject matter was salacious enough to generate interest and when the film finally opened in Sydney, on February 26, 1974 (in the presence of Blatty, who flew to Sydney for the premiere), it was instantly labeled a classic and made Film of the Week by the *Sydney Morning Herald*. In a brilliant display of irony, the cinema that screened *The Exorcist* was next door to the cinema screening *Jesus Christ—Superstar*.

It was in Sydney that young children were reported as being carried out screaming and crying. Another movie that affected children was the rock opera *Tommy*, which featured a truly horrific sequence featuring Tina Turner, Roger Daltrey and a silver sarcophagus with needles, which opened to reveal a skeleton with snakes slithering between its bones.

Editorials attacked the censors and the NSW Government for dragging their feet in bringing the rating system in line with other states. Pointing out that the minister responsible, Mr. Griffith, was more interested in dealing with pornography than horror, the *Sydney Morning Herald* went on the attack and demanded change. The "R" rating was eventually changed to restrict anyone under the age of 18 years from being able to see such a movie, but not before the damage had been done.

Ironically, it was a horror film that caused the system to be changed. No matter how much pornography, violence and objectionable material entered the country, it was always horror that was the breaking point.

The Exorcist proved to be extremely popular in Australia, remaining at cinemas and drive-ins for the next few years, boosted after it was nominated for ten Academy Awards, winning two. As interest in the film was still strong in mid–1974, child star Linda Blair, accompanied by her sister Debbi, was sent to Sydney and Melbourne on a three-day promotional visit. Blair surprised the media by announcing that, after five screenings of the film, it had become somewhat of a laugh for her. When asked about the more extreme scenes, she replied that a stand-in had done that work. "Too many people took the film seriously," she said in Sydney. "I can't see how anyone can get upset over the film."[40]

Friday Night Horror Films

As the 1980s began, the world was becoming increasingly desensitized to blood and violence. The Cold War was reaching a new peak, with the threat of nuclear conflict becoming all too real, and news services were broadcasting blood and gore into houses via color television. Movies were now being shown in color, which had once been a novelty. Hammer Horrors, such as the *Dracula* series, were shown, usually late at night, in full color. That combined with genuine horrors such as *Trilogy of Terror* meant that the older films no longer held their fright value and could not generate enough profits, advertising-wise, to be shown anywhere near a prime-time spot. But the movies were cheap for stations to buy and run, so the appeal was there.

The introduction and increasing availability of video cassette recorders (VCR) added to the mix. Video Nasty's were readily available in Australia with films such as *Basket Case, I Spit on Your Grave, Halloween, The Texas Chain Saw Massacre, Night of the Living Dead et al.* available for purchase or rental. There was now a delay between video release and television release which opened the window for older films to be screened once more. The Universal Monster period had a resurgence in the 1980s, usually on Fridays around midnight, in winter.

The Seven network held the license to screen the Universal Horrors and did a particularly respectable job of running them in order. While not the sensation they once were, the films proved popular enough, if only for nostalgia.

Ed Wood Hits the Film Festival Circuit

"Its awfulness has to be seen to be believed."

Amongst the atomic age monsters and low-budget thrillers entering the country, one name was surprisingly absent: infamous actor-writer-transvestite-director Edward Davis Wood Jr., or, to give him his more recognizable name, Ed Wood. Out of everything Wood wrote or directed in his lifetime, only one movie was officially released in Australia for general exhibition, albeit on TV, and just a few days before Wood's demise. Pirate copies of his films had been entering the country since the 1960s.

This does not mean that Wood was absent from Australian screens. Wood's first screen appearance was as a stuntman in *The Baron of Arizona* (Deputy Corporation, 1950). This film, a low-budget western starring Vincent Price and directed by the legendary low-budget specialist Samuel Fuller, was released to Australian cinemas in 1951. It was afforded headline status on a double bill with the equally low-budget horror film *The Creeper* (Reliance Pictures, 1948) starring Onslow Stevens.

Reviews were not kind. *The Age* headlined their entry with two words, "Bad Acting." Despite this, the movie proved popular enough, and could be bought cheaply enough, to play in small and rural cinemas for the next few years, eventually ending up on TV in 1960. The presence of Vincent Price was enough to guarantee it "Movie of the Week" status.[41]

Nobody watching the movie would have recognized Ed Wood: His one and only verified stunt came when he doubled for principal Ellen Drew as she and Price were dragged off their stagecoach by an angry mob. Wood dressed himself in Drew's finest film frocks and threw himself to the ground. That one shot marked the only time Wood was seen on the cinema screen, in Australia, during his lifetime.

Wood's films did appear on television. *The Lawless Rider* (1954), a Johnny Carpenter western that Wood may or may not have had a hand in writing, popped up on the small screen in October 1971. This was followed by another Carpenter western, the predecessor to *The Lawless Rider: Son of the Renegade* (1953), with Wood listed as co-writer, in January 1974. His horror and science fiction films began to appear in the late 1970s.

Wood's first collaboration with Bela Lugosi, *Bride of the Monster*, was seen on late night TV on October 7, 1978.[42] The irony of this comes from the knowledge that, two months later to the day, in America, the poverty-stricken Wood and his wife Kathy, both suffering from depression and alcoholism, were evicted from their apartment and became homeless. Wood died at a friend's house three days later.

The absence of Wood films on Australian screens can be easily explained. They were so low-budget that they were never screened outside of America. No mainstream distributors in Australia touched a Wood film: the genre was wrong (horror) and the films were too low-quality to be taken seriously by Australian audiences. Two decades passed before Wood and his unique films graced Australian cinemas.

Australians knew of Ed Wood through printed media. Magazines such as *Famous Monsters of Filmland* published articles about Wood, he was mentioned in books about horror films and about Bela Lugosi's career and his sad end.

Outside of *Bride of the Monster* and its television screening, the first written and directed Wood film to hit cinema screens that can be verified was *Glen or Glenda* (1953), which featured on a double bill with the all-midget film *The Terror of Tiny Town* in November 1981. Advertisements boasted that *Glen or Glenda* required a person to "see it to believe it."[43]

Shortly after, an interest in bad movies was fueled by the publication of the Medved brothers' *Golden Turkey Awards*. Harry Medved visited Australia in 1980 to promote the book, which awarded *Plan 9 from Outer Space* (1958) the dubious distinction of being the worst movie ever made, which made people keen to see it. As part of Medved's tour, he would screen a double bill of *Glen or Glenda* followed by *Robot Monster* (1953). Medved would also take the opportunity to emphasize Wood's transvestism and bad filmmaking techniques, which led the Valhalla in Sydney to secure the rights to run *Plan 9* on a double with *Robot Monster* in 1981. The Valhalla promoted them as the worst movies ever made. The *Sydney Morning Herald* called them "serious science fiction treats which are so badly produced, directed and acted that they have been acclaimed as screamingly funny comedies." The screening of *Plan 9* was a success.

Ed Wood had arrived in Australia, finally, and he was being embraced and celebrated, three years after his death.

Throughout the 1980s, *Plan 9* was seen at several art-house cinemas, usually on a double bill with films such as *Reefer Madness* or *Terror of Tiny Town*. In 1982, a series of events led to *Glen or Glenda* finally taken seriously by critics. The film was selected to lead off a season of movies under the banner of "The Celluloid Closet, or Homosexuality According to Tinsel Town." The several films, documentaries and medical shorts screened dealt with gay themes; *Glen or Glenda* was in the same company, and taken just as seriously, as *The Boys in the Band*, *Nighthawks*, *The Victim*, *Cruising* and *To an Unknown God* along with comedies such as *Pagan Rhapsody* and the British documentary *Coming Out*.

After pointing out the film's shortcomings ("It is a very bad, very funny film complete with appalling acting, cardboard sets and a truly nonsensical script"), reviewer Geraldine Brooks noted that the movie was now considered disturbing due to its content and themes. "In the 1950s, *Glen and Glenda* was a liberal film, presented as a serious analysis of transvestism, yet it is riddled with clichés, misinformation and confusion. It is also one in a long line of films that have portrayed homosexuality as a disease and a crime, to be dealt with by doctors and policemen. Homosexual characters in films are invariably neurotic, miserable, inferior individuals who almost always meet violent deaths." After this denunciation, Brooks closed out her write-up with: "*Glen or Glenda* is destined to become a cult film. Its awfulness has to be seen to be believed."[44]

It might have amused Wood to know that one of his films had been selected for a film festival and that it was now being examined in a serious light. It would not have amused Wood to be called gay. He always maintained that he was not gay, he was a transvestite.

Glen or Glenda was screened on TV in November 1989, under the title *I Led Two Lives,* being described as a "Humorous docu-drama about the troubles faced by a transvestite. With Bela Lugosi."[45]

In what must surely be its most unique screening, *Glen or Glenda* was seen on election night, 1993, when it was included in an all-night movie marathon in Sydney, taking its place with horror films such as *Amityville II, X—The Man with the X-Ray Eyes* and *The Tomb of Ligeia*. In this case, the film was titled *I Lived Two Lives: Glen or Glenda*. It is not known what people who tuned in expecting to see a Bela Lugosi horror movie made of the sight of Dolores Fuller stripping her angora sweater off and handing to the eager Edward D. Wood Jr.[46]

A Tale of Two *Kongs*

In 1980, the 1977 remake of *King Kong* was shown on television, uncut, over two nights as a special event due to both its length and the trend of the time to create TV "events."[47] The popularity of the screening of the *Kong* remake had channels scrambling to run the 1933 original. For a brief period, confusion reigned, as nobody knew who had the rights, but by mid–1984 it became clear that the ABC had purchased them, for a pittance, from RKO and were gearing up for something special.

In mid–December 1984, the ABC quietly announced that they would screening *King Kong*, the original, on Christmas night. This would not be the jerky, scratchy, censored version that Australians were used to; rather, a new print from RKO as complete as it had ever been. The intention was to screen the full 100-minute RKO cut commercial-free, the first such time that the movie had been shown in the country in such a format.

Compared to the remake, the original looked dated, but the film, in a fresh print, retained its impact. It had taken 51 years, but from that point on, *Kong* was able to be shown on television, and bought on video tape, as it was always intended to be seen.

Epilogue

Left: House of Dark Shadows (1970) was originally banned, then released, with cuts. This is the Australian daybill. *Right:* Horror as unintentional Western comedy: *Jesse James Meets Frankenstein's Daughter* (1966) was often shown on late night TV in the 1970s and early 1980s.

Left: Original Australia daybill for *The Satanic Rites of Dracula*. *Right:* Original Australia daybill for *Scars of Dracula*.

Horror had many a fascinating turn throughout the 20th century, from being embraced to vilified, watched in droves and picketed by naysayers and puritans, from being banned in one generation to liberated for another. Horror had seen it all, been it all and then—like so many of its monsters—rose again.

While horror is always in vogue, the types of horror films made in Australia continue to evolve with the times. In the '70s there was ozploitation like *Patrick* (1978), while the '80s saw Australian twists on old traditions such as *Howling III: The Marsupials* (1987), the '90s added satire as in *Body Melt* (1993), while the 2000s returned to their roots with *Wolf Creek* (2005), and the 2010s hybrid horrors such as in *Daybreakers* (2010).

Australian Horror can draw A-list talent from across the world and Australian talent is high demand as well. The first century was an adventure full of highs and lows, but it is by no means over, and the second century of horror movies in Australia promises to be just as fascinating.

Filmography, 1897–1973

Assembling a checklist of what films were and were not released in Australia, along with what was shown on television, is a thankless task. Details of screenings of silent films by Georges Méliès and other early filmmakers are notoriously hard to track down. In most cases, titles were changed, and Anglicized, and the new titles did not reflect the original title, let alone the contents. At times the content of early films was described in contemporary reports, but only titles were listed in ads.

As more people began to import films by Méliès, Edison and other filmmakers, confusion began as to what exactly was being shown. Films were run as part of traveling film shows, in town halls, mechanics halls and tents, and no records were kept. A traveling picture show man would rotate films, often showing the same film with a new title. They would also buy, sell and trade films with others, again, all without records. There is evidence of several titles existing for one film; without a synopsis, it is near-impossible to verify if a film was released.

The longest period that passed from a film's original release to when it was shown at the cinema in Australia is 48 years and four months. The film was *Nosferatu*. The film was first shown on March 4, 1922, but itwasn't screened in Australia until July 25, 1970. Following on the heels of that is *Freaks*, which was banned in Australia for just under 44 years.

When it comes to television, an amazing 64 years and four months passed from when *White Zombie* was shown at the cinema in 1932 to when it finally hit the small screen in 1996. That just beat out *Nosferatu*, which was shown on TV a full 62 years after its first cinema screening.

Nosferatu is also the oldest horror film screened on TV in the period I studied. As it was made in 1922, it just beats out the Lon Chaney *Hunchback of Notre Dame*, released in 1923, which screened as part of the *Silents Please* series in 1961.

Films Released: 1897–1973

The following is a breakdown of selected films known to have been released in Australia, in either a cinema or drive-in. These lists focus on films made between

1897 and 1973. Some films on this list were not released at the cinema until many years after their production, hence there are release dates up to 1995.

Cinema Release Date (YYYY-MM)	Year Produced	Title	Director	Country of Origin	Studio
1897–06	1896	The Vanishing Lady	Georges Méliès	France	Méliès
1897–06	1897	The Haunted Castle	George Albert Smith	U.K.	GAS Films
1897–12	1898	The Astronomer's Dream	Georges Méliès	France	Méliès
1898–12	1897	The Alchemist's Hallucination	Georges Méliès	France	Méliès
1898–12	1897	The Bewitched Inn	Georges Méliès	France	Méliès
1899–01	1898	Faust and Marguerite	Edwin S. Porter	U.S.	Edison
1899–01	1898	Photographing a Ghost	George Albert Smith	U.K.	GAS Films
1899–07	1897	The X-Rays	George Albert Smith	U.K.	GAS Films
1900–07	1896	A Terrible Night	Georges Méliès	France	Méliès
1906–10	1903	The Infernal Cake Walk	Georges Méliès	France	Méliès[1]
1907–02	1904	Dream of a Rarebit Fiend	Edwin S. Porter	U.S.	Edison
1907–10	1896	The Haunted Castle	Georges Méliès	France	Méliès
1909–09	1908	Dr. Jekyll and Mr. Hyde	Otis Turner	U.S.	Selig
1910–02	1909	Dr. Nicola in Tibet	Viggo Larsen	Norway	Nordisk Film Company
1910–06	1910	Frankenstein	J. Searle Dawley	U.S.	Edison
1911–01	1910	The Necklace of the Dead	August Blom	Norway	Nordisk Film Company
1911–02	1909	The Sealed Room	D.W. Griffith	U.S.	Biograph
1911–05	1911	Dante's Inferno	Francesco Bertolini	Italy	Milano
1911–06	1911	The Ghost in the Vaults	August Blom	Norway	Nordisk Film Company

Filmography, 1897–1973

Cinema Release Date (YYYY-MM)	Year Produced	Title	Director	Country of Origin	Studio
1912–02	1912	The Strangler's Grip	Franklin Barrett	Australia	West's Pictures
1912–04	1912	Dr. Jekyll and Mr. Hyde	Lucius Henderson	U.S.	Thanhouser
1913–01	1912	The Spider's Web	Van Dyke Brooke	U.S.	Columbia
1913–06	1913	After the Welsh Rarebit	Edwin S. Porter	U.S.	Edison
1913–10	1913	Dr. Jekyll and Mr. Hyde	Herbert Brenon	U.S.	Universal
1913–11	1913	The Vampire	Robert Vignola	U.S.	Kalem
1913–12	1913	The Student of Prague	Paul Wegener	Germany	Apex-Bioscop
1915–04	1914	The Avenging Conscience	D.W. Griffith	U.S.	Essanay
1916–03	1915	The Devil's Daughter	Frank Powell	U.S.	Fox
1916–03	1915	The Mystery of the Tapestry Room	Murdock MacQuarrie	U.S.	Universal
1916–06	1915	The House of Fear	Arnold Daly	U.S.	Pathé
1917–05	1916	The Crimson Stain Mystery	T. Hayes Hunter	U.S.	Consolidated Film Corp.
1919–11	1919	The Face at the Window	Charles Villiers	Australia	D.B. O'Connor Films
1920–08	1920	Dr. Jekyll and Mr. Hyde	J. Charles Haydon	U.S.	Paramount
1921–06	1921	The Guyra Ghost Mystery	John Cosgrove	Australia	Cosgrove and Regan
1922–03	1920	The Penalty	Wallace Worsley	U.S.	Goldwyn
1923–03	1915	A Fool There Was	Frank Powell	U.S.	Fox
1923–03	1922	The Ghost Breaker	Alfred Green	U.S.	Famous Players-Lasky

Cinema Release Date (YYYY-MM)	Year Produced	Title	Director	Country of Origin	Studio
1923-05	1922	One Exciting Night	D.W. Griffith	U.S.	D.W. Griffith Productions
1923-06	1923	The Twins	Leslie McCallum	Australia	Blue Gum Company[2]
1923-10	1922	A Blind Bargain	Wallace Worsley	U.S.	Goldwyn
1924-01	1923	The Last Moment	J. Parker Read	U.S.	J. Parker Read Jr. Productions
1924-01	1923	Waxworks	Paul Leni	Germany	Neptune-Film A.G.
1924-04	1921	The Haunted Castle	F.W. Murnau	Germany	Decla-Bioscop AG
1924-08	1924	The Wolf Man	Edmund Mortimer	U.S.	Fox Film Corporation
1924-10	1924	Fisher's Ghost	Raymond Longford	Australia	Longford-Lyell Productions
1924-12	1923	The Hunchback of Notre Dame	Wallace Worsley	U.S.	Universal[3]
1925-08	1925	The Lost World	Harry O Hoyt	U.S.	First National Pictures
1925-10	1922	The Headless Horseman	Edward D. Venturini	U.S.	Sleepy Hollow Corp.
1926-01	1925	The Phantom of The Opera	Rupert Julian	U.S.	Universal[4]
1926-04	1925	The Monster	Roland West	U.S.	MGM
1926-07	1926	The Bat	Roland West	U.S.	United Artists
1926-09	1926	Faust	F.W. Murnau	Germany	UFA
1927-02	1926	Maciste in Hell	Guido Brignone	Italy	Fert Studios[5]

Cinema Release Date (YYYY-MM)	Year Produced	Title	Director	Country of Origin	Studio
1927–06	1926	The Magician	Rex Ingram	U.S.	MGM[6]
1927–10	1927	The Cat and The Canary	Paul Leni	U.S.	Universal
1927–12	1927	The Unknown	Tod Browning	U.S.	MGM
1928–02	1927	The Gorilla	Alfred Santell	U.S.	Ascher, Small and Rogers
1928–04	1927	Metropolis	Fritz Lang	Germany	UFA
1928–04	1927	The Spider's Web	Oscar Micheaux	U.S.	Micheaux Film
1928–05	1927	London After Midnight	Tod Browning	U.S.	MGM
1928–10	1928	The Man Who Laughs	Paul Leni	U.S.	Universal[7]
1929–04	1929	The Last Warning	Paul Leni	U.S.	Universal
1929–05	1928	4 Devils	F.W. Murnau	U.S.	Fox Film Corp.
1929–06	1928	The Terror	Roy Del Ruth	U.S.	Warner Brothers
1930–03	1928	The Fall of the House of Usher	James Watson	U.S.	Epstein[8]
1930–03	1929	The Last Performance	Paul Fejos	U.S.	Universal
1931–11	1931	The Haunted Barn	Gregan McMahon	Australia	Efftee Studios
1932–02	1931	Dracula	Tod Browning	U.S.	Universal
1932–03	1931	Dr. Jekyll and Mr. Hyde	Rouben Mamoulian	U.S.	Paramount

Cinema Release Date (YYYY-MM)	Year Produced	Title	Director	Country of Origin	Studio
1932-04	1931	Frankenstein	James Whale	U.S.	Universal[9]
1932-04	1931	The Mad Genius	Michael Curtiz	U.S.	Warner Brothers
1932-08	1932	Doctor X	Michael Curtiz	U.S.	Warner Bros.
1932-11	1932	Murders in the Rue Morgue	Robert Florey	U.S.	Universal[10]
1932-11	1932	White Zombie	Victor Halperin	U.S.	United Artists
1932-12	1932	Kongo	William J. Cowen	U.S.	MGM
1933-03	1932	The Old Dark House	James Whale	U.S.	Universal
1933-03	1933	The Monkey's Paw	Wesley Ruggles	U.S.	RKO
1933-04	1932	The Most Dangerous Game	Irving Pichel, Ernest B. Schoedsack	U.S.	RKO
1933-05	1932	Island of Lost Souls	Erle C. Kenton	U.S.	Paramount
1933-05	1932	The Mummy	Karl Freund	U.S.	Universal
1933-07	1933	King Kong	Merian C. Cooper, Ernest B. Schoedsack	U.S.	RKO
1933-08	1933	Supernatural	Victor Halperin	U.S.	Paramount
1934-02	1933	Murders in the Zoo	Edward Sutherland	U.S.	Paramount
1934-02	1933	The Invisible Man	James Whale	U.S.	Universal
1934-03	1933	The Ghoul	T. Hayes Hunter	U.K.	Gaumont

Cinema Release Date (YYYY-MM)	Year Produced	Title	Director	Country of Origin	Studio
1934-04	1933	Night of Terror	Bentoloff	U.S.	Columbia
1934-04	1933	Mystery of the Wax Museum	Michael Curtiz	U.S.	Warner Brothers
1934-04	1933	The Son of Kong	Ernest B. Schoedsack	U.S.	RKO
1934-05	1933	The Lost Patrol	John Ford	U.S.	RKO
1934-07	1934	The Black Cat	Edgar G. Ulmer	U.S.	Universal
1935-07	1935	Bride of Frankenstein	James Whale	U.S.	Universal
1935-07	1935	Mark of the Vampire	Tod Browning	U.S.	MGM
1935-09	1935	The Black Room	Roy William Neill	U.S.	Columbia
1935-09	1935	WereWolf of London	Stuart Walker	U.S.	Universal
1935-11	1935	Mad Love	Karl Freund	U.S.	MGM
1935-11	1935	The Raven	Lew Landers	U.S.	Universal
1936-03	1936	The Invisible Ray	Lambert Hillyer	U.S.	Universal
1936-04	1936	The Walking Dead	Michael Curtiz	U.S.	Warner Brothers
1936-07	1936	The Man Who Changed His Mind	Robert Stevenson	U.K.	Gainsborough Pictures
1936-07	1936	Things to Come	William Cameron Menzies	U.S.	London Film Productions

Cinema Release Date (YYYY-MM)	Year Produced	Title	Director	Country of Origin	Studio
1936-08	1936	Dracula's Daughter	Lambert Hillyer	U.S.	Universal[11]
1936-11	1936	The Man Who Could Work Miracles	Lothar Mendes	U.S.	United Artists
1936-12	1936	Suicide Club	J. Walter Ruben	U.S.	MGM
1936-12	1936	The Devil-Doll	Tod Browning	U.S.	MGM
1937-03	1936	The Man Who Lived Twice	Harry Lachman	U.S.	Columbia
1937-08	1937	Night Key	Lloyd Corrigan	U.S.	Universal
1939-03	1939	Son of Frankenstein	Rowland V. Lee	U.S.	Universal
1939-06	1939	The Gorilla	Allan Dwan	U.S.	20th Century–Fox
1939-12	1939	The Cat and The Canary	Elliott Nugent	U.S.	Paramount
1939-12	1939	The Return of Doctor X	Vincent Sherman	U.S.	Warner Brothers
1940-03	1939	The Hunchback of Notre Dame	William Dieterle	U.S.	RKO
1940-03	1939	Tower of London	Rowland V. Lee	U.S.	Universal
1940-04	1939	The Man They Could Not Hang	Nick Grinde	U.S.	Columbia
1940-04	1940	The Invisible Man Returns	Joe May	U.S.	Universal
1940-05	1940	Black Friday	Arthur Lubin	U.S.	Universal
1940-08	1940	The Man with Nine Lives	Nick Grinde	U.S.	Columbia
1940-10	1940	The Ghost Breakers	George Marshall	U.S.	Paramount

Cinema Release Date (YYYY-MM)	Year Produced	Title	Director	Country of Origin	Studio
1940-11	1940	Doomed to Die	William Nigh	U.S.	Monogram
1941-01	1940	The Ape	William Nigh	U.S.	Monogram
1941-01	1940	The Mummy's Hand	Christy Cabanne	U.S.	Universal
1941-02	1940	Stranger on the Third Floor	Boris Ingster	U.S.	RKO
1941-02	1940	You'll Find Out	David Butler	U.S.	RKO
1941-04	1940	Dr. Cyclops	Ernest B. Schoedsack	U.S.	Paramount
1941-05	1940	Before I Hang	Nick Grinde	U.S.	Columbia
1941-05	1940	The Invisible Woman	A. Edward Sutherland	U.S.	Universal
1941-06	1941	Horror Island	George Waggner	U.S.	Universal
1941-06	1941	Man Made Monster	George Waggner	U.S.	Universal
1941-06	1941	The Black Cat	Albert Rogell	U.S.	Universal
1941-10	1941	King of the Zombies	Jean Yarbrough	U.S.	Monogram
1941-10	1941	The Face Behind the Mask	Robert Florey	U.S.	Columbia
1941-11	1941	The Devil Commands	Edward Dmytryk	U.S.	Columbia
1942-02	1941	Dr. Jekyll and Mr. Hyde	Victor Fleming	U.S.	MGM
1942-04	1941	Nine Lives Are Not Enough	A. Edward Sutherland	U.S.	Warner Brothers

Cinema Release Date (YYYY-MM)	Year Produced	Title	Director	Country of Origin	Studio
1942–04	1941	The Wolf Man	George Waggner	U.S.	Universal
1942–05	1942	The Mad Doctor of Market Street	Joseph H. Lewis	U.S.	Universal
1942–07	1942	Black Dragons	William Nigh	U.S.	Monogram
1942–07	1942	The Ghost of Frankenstein	Erle C. Kenton	U.S.	Universal
1942–08	1942	The Strange Case of Doctor Rx	William Nigh	U.S.	Universal
1942–09	1942	The Man Who Returned to Life	Lew Landers	U.S.	Columbia
1942–11	1942	Fingers at the Window	Charles Lederer	U.S.	MGM
1943–02	1942	Invisible Agent	Edwin L. Marin	U.S.	Universal
1943–03	1942	The Mummy's Tomb	Harold Young	U.S.	Universal
1943–04	1940	The Door with Seven Locks	Norman Lee	U.K.	Pathé Pictures[12]
1943–04	1942	Night Monster	Ford Beebe	U.S.	Universal
1943–06	1942	The Boogie Man Will Get You	Lew Landers	U.S.	Columbia
1943–06	1942	The Undying Monster	John Brahm	U.S.	20th Century–Fox
1943–07	1943	Frankenstein Meets the Wolf Man	Roy William Neill	U.S.	Universal

Filmography, 1897–1973

Cinema Release Date (YYYY-MM)	Year Produced	Title	Director	Country of Origin	Studio
1943-08	1942	The Living Ghost	William Beaudine	U.S.	Monogram
1943-09	1942	Cat People	Jacques Tourneur	U.S.	RKO
1943-09	1943	The Captive	Edward Dmytryk	U.S.	Universal
1943-09	1943	I Walked with a Zombie	Jacques Tourneur	U.S.	RKO
1943-10	1941	Spooks Run Wild	Phil Rosen	U.S.	Monogram
1943-10	1942	I Married a Witch	Rene Clair	U.S.	United Artists
1943-10	1943	Ghosts on the Loose	William Beaudine	U.S.	Monogram
1943-11	1943	Son of Dracula	Robert Siodmak	U.S.	Universal
1943-12	1943	The Seventh Victim	Mark Robson	U.S.	RKO
1944-01	1943	Revenge of the Zombies	Steve Sekely	U.S.	Monogram
1944-01	1943	The Leopard Man	Jacques Tourneur	U.S.	RKO
1944-02	1943	The Mad Ghoul	James P. Hogan	U.S.	Universal
1944-02	1943	The Return of The Vampire	Lew Landers	U.S.	Columbia
1944-07	1944	The Curse of the Cat People	Robert Wise	U.S.	RKO

Cinema Release Date (YYYY-MM)	Year Produced	Title	Director	Country of Origin	Studio
1944-07	1944	The Mummy's Ghost	Reginald LeBorg	U.S.	Universal
1944-07	1944	The Scarlet Claw	Roy William Neill	U.S.	Universal
1944-08	1944	The Invisible Man's Revenge	Ford Beebe	U.S.	Universal
1944-08	1944	The Uninvited	Lewis Allen	U.S.	Paramount
1944-08	1944	Weird Woman	Reginald LeBorg	U.S.	Universal
1944-09	1943	Phantom of the Opera	Arthur Lubin	U.S.	Universal
1944-09	1943	The Mysterious Doctor	Ben Stoloff	U.S.	Warner Brothers
1944-09	1944	Jungle Woman	Reginald LeBorg	U.S.	Universal
1944-09	1944	The Lady and the Monster	George Sherman	U.S.	Republic
1944-10	1944	Ghost Catchers	Edward F. Cline	U.S.	Universal
1944-11	1944	The Man in Half Moon Street	Ralph Murphy	U.S.	Paramount
1944-12	1944	Cry of the Werewolf	Henry Levin	U.S.	Columbia
1944-12	1944	Dead Man's Eyes	Reginald LeBorg	U.S.	Universal
1945-01	1944	Cobra Woman	Robert Siodmak	U.S.	Universal

Cinema Release Date (YYYY-MM)	Year Produced	Title	Director	Country of Origin	Studio
1945–03	1942	Dead Men Walk	Sam Newfield	U.S.	Producers Releasing Corporation
1945–03	1944	House of Frankenstein	Erle C. Kenton	U.S.	Universal
1945–04	1944	Nabonga	Sam Newfield	U.S.	Sigmund Neufield Productions
1945–04	1944	The Mummy's Curse	Leslie Goodwins	U.S.	Universal
1945–04	1945	The Frozen Ghost	Harold Young	U.S.	Universal
1945–05	1940	The Devil Bat	Jean Yarbrough	U.S.	Producers Releasing Corporation
1945–05	1944	The Climax	George Waggner	U.S.	Universal
1945–05	1944	The Mask of Dimitrios	Jean Negulesco	U.S.	Warner Brothers
1945–08	1944	Dark Waters	Andre DeToth	U.S.	United Artists
1945–08	1944	The Girl Who Dared	Howard Bretherton	U.S.	Republic
1945–08	1945	The Picture of Dorian Gray	Albert Lewin	U.S.	MGM
1945–09	1945	The Body Snatcher	Robert Wise	U.S.	RKO
1945–11	1945	Strange Confession	John Hoffman	U.S.	Universal
1945–11	1945	The Brighton Strangler	Max Nosseck	U.S.	RKO

Cinema Release Date (YYYY-MM)	Year Produced	Title	Director	Country of Origin	Studio
1945-12	1945	Pillow of Death	Wallace Fox	U.S.	Universal
1946-01	1945	The Phantom Speaks	John English	U.S.	Republic
1946-04	1945	Isle of the Dead	Mark Robson	U.S.	RKO
1946-05	1945	Dead of Night	Alberto Cavalcanti	U.K.	Ealing Studios
1946-06	1946	Bedlam	Mark Robson	U.S.	RKO
1946-07	1944	Bluebeard	Edgar G Ulmer	U.S.	Producers Releasing Corporation
1946-07	1945	Fog Island	Terry O. Morse	U.S.	Producers Releasing Corporation
1946-07	1945	House of Dracula	Erle C. Kenton	U.S.	Universal
1946-07	1945	The Strange Mr. Gregory	Phil Rosen	U.S.	Monogram
1946-07	1946	House of Horrors	Jean Yarbrough	U.S.	Universal[13]
1946-08	1942	The Night Has Eyes	Leslie Arliss	U.K.	Pathé Pictures
1946-10	1945	The Woman Who Came Back	Walter Colmes	U.S.	Republic
1946-10	1946	She-Wolf of London	Jean Yarbrough	U.S.	Universal
1946-10	1946	The Spider Woman Strikes Back	Arthur Lubin	U.S.	Universal

Filmography, 1897–1973

Cinema Release Date (YYYY-MM)	Year Produced	Title	Director	Country of Origin	Studio
1946-11	1946	The Cat Creeps	Erle C. Kenton	U.S.	Universal
1947-01	1946	The Devil's Mask	Henry Levin	U.S.	Columbia
1947-11	1946	The Beast with Five Fingers	Robert Florey	U.S.	Warner Brothers
1948-05	1947	Uncle Silas	Charles Frank	U.K.	Two Cities Films
1948-07	1920	The Cabinet of Dr. Caligari	Robert Wiene	Germany	Decla-Bioscop AG
1948-11	1948	Abbott and Costello Meet Frankenstein	Charles T. Barton	U.S.	Universal International
1949-02	1948	The Creeper	Jean Yarbrough	U.S.	Reliance Pictures
1949-07	1949	The Dark Past	Rudolph Maté	U.S.	Columbia
1949-10	1948	Corridors of Mirrors	Terence Young	U.S.	Apollo
1950-07	1949	Murder at the Windmill	Val Guest	U.S.	Monogram
1951-07	1948	Queen of Spades	Thorold Dickinson	U.K.	Associated British Picture Corp.
1951-11	1951	Abbott and Costello Meet the Invisible Man	Charles Lamont	U.S.	Universal International
1951-11	1951	The Thing from Another World	Christian Nyby	U.S.	RKO
1951-12	1950	The Flying Saucer	Mikel Conrad	U.S.	Realart Pictures

Cinema Release Date (YYYY-MM)	Year Produced	Title	Director	Country of Origin	Studio
1951-12	1951	The Man from Planet X	Edgar G. Ulmer	U.S.	United Artists
1951-12	1951	When Worlds Collide	Rudolph Maté	U.S.	Paramount
1952-02	1951	The Day the Earth Stood Still	Robert Wise	U.S.	20th Century–Fox
1952-04	1951	The Strange Door	Joseph Pevney	U.S.	Universal International
1952-06	1951	The Stolen Face	Terence Fisher	U.K.	Hammer Films
1952-10	1951	The Son of Dr. Jekyll	Seymour Friedman	U.S.	Columbia
1952-10	1952	Red Planet Mars	Harry Horner	U.S.	Melaby Pictures
1953-05	1953	City Beneath the Sea	Budd Boetticher	U.S.	Universal International
1953-07	1953	House of Wax	Andre DeToth	U.S.	Warner Brothers
1953-09	1953	The Black Castle	Nathan Juran	U.S.	Universal International
1953-10	1952	The Ringer	Guy Hamilton	U.K.	London Film Productions
1953-11	1953	Phantom from Space	W Lee Wilder	U.S.	United Artists
1953-11	1953	The Maze	William Cameron Menzies	U.S.	Allied Artists
1953-12	1953	The Magnetic Monster	Curt Siodmak	U.S.	United Artists

Filmography, 1897–1973

Cinema Release Date (YYYY-MM)	Year Produced	Title	Director	Country of Origin	Studio
1954-02	1952	The Voice of Merrill	John Gilling	U.K.	Tempean Films
1954-03	1951	Cry, the Beloved Country	Zoltán Korda	U.K.	London Film Productions
1954-03	1954	It Came from Outer Space	Jack Arnold	U.S.	Universal International[14]
1954-05	1951	Flight to Mars	Lesley Selander	U.S.	Monogram
1954-05	1953	Abbott and Costello Meet Dr. Jekyll and Mr. Hyde	Charles Lamont	U.S.	Universal International
1954-05	1953	The Beast from 20,000 Fathoms	Eugene Lourie	U.S.	Warner Brothers
1954-07	1953	The War of The Worlds	Byron Haskin	U.S.	Paramount
1954-07	1954	Killers from Space	W. Lee Wilder	U.S.	Planet Films
1954-11	1953	The Neanderthal Man	E.A. Dupont	U.S.	United Artists
1954-11	1954	Phantom of the Rue Morgue	Roy Del Ruth	U.S.	Warner Brothers
1954-11	1954	Creature from the Black Lagoon	Jack Arnold	U.S.	Universal International
1954-11	1954	Tobor the Great	Lee Sholem	U.S.	Dudley Pictures Corporation
1954-12	1954	Gorilla at Large	Harmon Jones	U.S.	Panoramic Productions
1955-02	1953	Invaders from Mars	William Cameron Menzies	U.S.	20th Century–Fox

Cinema Release Date (YYYY-MM)	Year Produced	Title	Director	Country of Origin	Studio
1955–02	1954	Devil Girl from Mars	David MacDonald	U.S.	Danziger Productions
1955–02	1954	The Mad Magician	John Brahm	U.S.	Columbia
1955–02	1954	Them!	Gordon Douglas	U.S.	Warner Brothers
1955–04	1954	An Inspector Calls	Guy Hamilton	U.K.	British Lion Film Corp
1955–06	1953	Donovan's Brain	Felix Feist	U.S.	Dowling Productions[15]
1955–06	1954	Gog	Herbert L Strock	U.S.	United Artists
1955–06	1954	Radio Cab Murder	Vernon Sewell	U.K.	Eros Films
1955–06	1955	Conquest of Space	Byron Haskin	U.S.	Paramount
1955–08	1955	This Island Earth	Joseph Newman	U.S.	Universal International
1955–10	1955	Revenge of the Creature	Jack Arnold	U.S.	Universal International
1955–11	1955	Abbott and Costello Meet the Mummy	Charles Lamont	U.S.	Universal International[16]
1955–12	1955	Moonfleet	Fritz Lang	U.S.	MGM
1956–03	1955	Cult of the Cobra	Francis D. Lyon	U.S.	Universal International
1956–05	1954	Svengali	Noel Langley	U.S.	Renown Pictures

Cinema Release Date (YYYY-MM)	Year Produced	Title	Director	Country of Origin	Studio
1956-06	1953	The Limping Man	Cy Endfield	U.K.	Eros Films
1956-07	1954	The Scarlet Web	Charles Saunders	U.K.	Fortress Film Productions
1956-07	1955	Tarantula	Jack Arnold	U.S.	Universal International
1956-08	1956	Earth vs. the Flying Saucers	Fred F. Sears	U.S.	Columbia
1956-09	1955	It Came from Beneath the Sea	Robert Gordon	U.S.	Columbia
1956-10	1956	The Creature Walks Among Us	John Sherwood	U.S.	Universal International
1956-11	1955	The Quatermass Xperiment	Val Guest	U.K.	Hammer Films
1956-12	1956	Curucu, Beast of the Amazon	Curt Siodmak	U.S.	Universal International
1957-01	1956	The Mole People	Virgil W. Vogel	U.S.	Universal International
1957-03	1957	The Night Runner	Abner Biberman	U.S.	Universal International
1957-04	1956	The Beast of Hollow Mountain	Edward Nassour	U.S.	United Artists
1957-04	1957	Pharaoh's Curse	Lee Sholem	U.S.	Schenck-Koch Productions
1957-05	1957	The Incredible Shrinking Man	Jack Arnold	U.S.	Universal International
1957-07	1956	X the Unknown	Leslie Norman	U.K.	Hammer Films

Cinema Release Date (YYYY-MM)	Year Produced	Title	Director	Country of Origin	Studio
1957-07	1957	The Deadly Mantis	Nathan Juran	U.S.	Universal International
1957-08	1957	Kronos	Kurt Neumann	U.S.	Regal Pictures
1957-08	1957	Zombies of Mora Tau	Edward L. Cahn	U.S.	Columbia
1957-09	1956	Godzilla—King of the Monsters!	Ishirō Honda	Japan	Toho
1957-09	1956	Invasion of the Body Snatchers	Don Siegel	U.S.	Allied Artists
1957-09	1957	Lure of the Swamp	Herbert Cornfield	U.S.	Regal Pictures
1957-09	1957	The Land Unknown	Virgil W. Vogel	U.S.	Universal International
1957-10	1951	Bride of the Gorilla	Curt Siodmak	U.S.	Realart Pictures
1957-10	1957	The 27th Day	William Asher	U.S.	Columbia
1957-11	1957	The Giant Claw	Fred F. Sears	U.S.	Columbia
1957-11	1957	The Monolith Monsters	John Sherwood	U.S.	Universal International
1957-12	1957	The Vampire	Paul Landres	U.S.	United Artists
1958-01	1956	Satellite in the Sky	Paul Dickson	U.K.	New Elstree
1958-01	1957	The Manbeast	Val Guest	U.K.	Hammer Films

Cinema Release Date (YYYY-MM)	Year Produced	Title	Director	Country of Origin	Studio
1958-02	1957	The Black Scorpion	Edward Ludwig	U.S.	Warner Brothers
1958-05	1957	The Invisible Boy	Herman Hoffman	U.S.	MGM
1958-05	1958	The Brain Machine	Nathan Hertz	U.S.	Howco International
1958-06	1951	Mother Riley Meets the Vampire	John Gilling	U.K.	Fernwood Productions[17]
1958-06	1954	The Snow Creature	W. Lee Wilder	U.S.	Planet Filmways Inc
1958-07	1957	Man on the Prowl	Art Napoleon	U.S.	United Artists
1958-07	1957	Curse of the Demon	Jacques Tourneur	U.S.	Columbia
1958-08	1956	The Sorceress	André Michel	Italy	Films Metzger et Woog
1958-08	1958	Screaming Mimi	Gerd Oswald	U.S.	Sage Productions
1958-08	1958	The Space Children	Jack Arnold	U.S.	Paramount
1958-10	1958	The Fiend Who Walked the West	Gordon Douglas	U.S.	20th Century-Fox
1958-11	1956	Rodan	Ishirō Honda	Japan	Toho
1958-11	1958	Spaniard's Curse	Ralph Kemplen	U.K.	Independent Film Distributors
1958-11	1958	The Camp on Blood Island	Val Guest	U.K.	Hammer Films

Cinema Release Date (YYYY-MM)	Year Produced	Title	Director	Country of Origin	Studio
1958-12	1957	The Monster that Challenged the World	Arnold Laven	U.S.	Gramercy Pictures
1958-12	1957	Voodoo Island	Reginald LeBorg	U.S.	Bel-Air
1958-12	1958	I Bury the Living	Albert Band	U.S.	United Artists
1959-01	1958	I Married a Monster from Outer Space	Gene Fowler Jr.	U.S.	Paramount
1959-01	1958	Space Master X-7	Edward Bernds	U.S.	Regal Pictures
1959-01	1958	The Mugger	William Berke	U.S.	Barbizon Productions Inc
1959-02	1958	Woman of Mystery	Ernest Morris	U.K.	Danziger Productions
1959-03	1958	It! The Terror from Beyond Space	Edward L. Cahn	U.S.	United Artists
1959-04	1958	Monster on the Campus	Jack Arnold	U.S.	Universal International
1959-05	1958	Curse of the Faceless Man	Edward L. Cahn	U.S.	United Artists
1959-07	1958	Macabre	William Castle	U.S.	Allied Artists
1959-07	1958	Machete	Kurt Neumann	U.S.	United Artists
1959-07	1958	The Flame Barrier	Paul Landres	U.S.	Gramercy Pictures
1959-08	1957	The Mysterians	Ishirō Honda	Japan	Toho

Cinema Release Date (YYYY-MM)	Year Produced	Title	Director	Country of Origin	Studio
1959-08	1958	The Lost Missile	Lester William Berke	U.S.	United Artists
1959-10	1959	The Hound of the Baskervilles	Terence Fisher	U.K.	Hammer Films
1959-11	1958	The Blob	Irvin S. Yeaworth	U.S.	Fairview Productions
1959-11	1959	The Man Who Could Cheat Death	Terence Fisher	U.K.	Hammer Films
1959-12	1959	Floods of Fear	Charles Crichton	U.K.	Universal Studios
1960-01	1959	First Man into Space	Robert Day	U.K.	Amalgamated Productions
1960-03	1958	The Long Knife	Montgomery Tully	U.K.	Merton Park Studios
1960-03	1959	Killers of Kilimanjaro	Richard Thorpe	U.S.	Columbia
1960-03	1959	The 30 Foot Bride of Candy Rock	Sidney Miller	U.S.	Columbia
1960-04	1959	The Mummy	Terence Fisher	U.K.	Hammer Films
1960-06	1959	House on Haunted Hill	William Castle	U.S.	William Castle Productions
1960-07	1959	The Tingler	William Castle	U.S.	Columbia
1960-08	1960	The Lost World	Irwin Allen	U.S.	20th Century–Fox
1960-08	1960	The Leech Woman	Edward Dein	U.S.	Universal International

Cinema Release Date (YYYY-MM)	Year Produced	Title	Director	Country of Origin	Studio
1960-08	1960	The Stranglers of Bombay	Terence Fisher	U.K.	Hammer Films
1960-09	1959	Gigantis, the Fire Monster	Motoyoshi Oda	Japan	Toho[18]
1960-09	1959	Invisible Invaders	Edward L. Cahn	U.S.	United Artists
1960-09	1960	Psycho	Alfred Hitchcock	U.K.	Paramount
1960-10	1960	Dinosaurus!	Irvin S. Yeaworth	U.S.	Fairview Productions
1960-10	1960	Village of the Damned	Wolf Rilla	U.K.	MGM
1960-12	1959	Jack the Ripper	Robert S. Baker	U.K.	Midcentury
1960-12	1960	Battle in Outer Space	Ishirō Honda	U.S.	Toho
1961-03	1960	The Hypnotic Eye	George Blair	U.S.	Allied Artists
1961-03	1960	Three Came to Kill	Edward L Cahn	U.S.	United Artists
1961-04	1960	The Two Faces of Dr. Jekyll	Terence Fisher	U.K.	Hammer Films
1961-04	1961	Gorgo	Eugene Lourie	U.S.	King Brothers Productions
1961-05	1960	13 Ghosts	William Castle	U.S.	Columbia
1961-05	1960	Circus of Horrors	Sidney Hayers	U.K.	Hammer Films[19]

Filmography, 1897–1973

Cinema Release Date (YYYY-MM)	Year Produced	Title	Director	Country of Origin	Studio
1961-08	1960	Macumba Love	Douglas Fowley	U.S.	United Artists
1961-09	1959	Behemoth the Sea Monster	Eugene Lourie	U.S.	Allied Artists[20]
1961-10	1961	The Shadow of the Cat	John Gilling	U.K.	BHP Films
1961-10	1962	Most Dangerous Man Alive	Allan Dwan	U.S.	Columbia
1961-11	1959	4D Man	Irvin Yeaworth	U.S.	Fairview Productions
1961-11	1959	Terror in the Midnight Sun	Virgil W. Vogel	Sweden	Jerry Warren Productions[21]
1961-11	1961	Homicidal	William Castle	U.S.	Columbia
1961-12	1961	Voyage to the Bottom of the Sea	Irwin Allen	U.S.	20th Century–Fox
1962-02	1957	20 Million Miles to Earth	Nathan Juran	U.S.	Morningside Productions
1962-02	1961	The Day the Earth Caught Fire	Val Guest	U.K.	Val Guest Productions
1962-03	1961	The Innocents	Jack Clayton	U.S.	Achilles Film Productions
1962-04	1960	The Hands of Orlac	Edmond T. Gréville	U.K.	Brittania Films
1962-04	1960	Warlord of Crete	Silvio Amadio	Italy	Gino Mordini
1962-04	1961	Master of the World	William Witney	U.S.	American International

Cinema Release Date (YYYY-MM)	Year Produced	Title	Director	Country of Origin	Studio
1962–05	1961	Doctor Blood's Coffin	Sidney J. Furie	U.K.	Caralan Productions
1962–08	1962	The Cabinet of Caligari	Roger Kay	U.S.	20th Century–Fox
1962–08	1962	The Magic Sword	Bert I. Gordon	U.S.	United Artists
1962–09	1960	12 to the Moon	David Bradley	U.S.	Columbia
1962–09	1961	Mothra	Ishirō Honda	Japan	Toho
1962–11	1962	The Phantom of The Opera	Terence Fisher	U.K.	Hammer Films
1962–12	1959	The Four Skulls of Jonathan Drake	Edward L. Cahn	U.S.	United Artists
1963–02	1962	Captain Clegg	Peter Graham Scott	U.K.	Hammer Films
1963–03	1961	The Flight That Disappeared	Reginald LeBorg	U.K.	Harvard Film Corp.
1963–03	1962	Journey to the Seventh Planet	Sid Pink	U.S.	American International
1963–04	1963	Night Tide	Curtis Harrigan	U.S.	Virgo Productions[22]
1963–05	1961	Flight of the Lost Balloon	Nathan Juran	U.S.	American International
1963–06	1962	Corridors of Blood	Robert Day	U.S.	Amalgamated Productions[23]
1963–06	1963	House of the Damned	Maury Dexter	U.S.	20th Century–Fox

Filmography, 1897–1973

Cinema Release Date (YYYY-MM)	Year Produced	Title	Director	Country of Origin	Studio
1963-07	1960	The Spider's Web	Godfrey Grayson	U.K.	Danziger Productions
1963-07	1962	The Day Mars Invaded Earth	Maury Dexter	U.S.	20th Century–Fox[24]
1963-08	1963	Paranoiac	Freddie Francis	U.K.	Hammer Films
1963-08	1963	The Birds	Alfred Hitchcock	U.S.	Universal
1963-09	1962	What Ever Happened to Baby Jane?	Robert Aldrich	U.S.	Warner Brothers
1963-09	1963	The Old Dark House	William Castle	U.S.	Hammer Films
1963-10	1963	The Raven	Roger Corman	U.S.	American International
1963-11	1961	Blood and Roses	Roger Vadim	U.K.	Films EGE[25]
1963-11	1961	The Devil's Messenger	Herbert L. Strock	U.S.	Herts-Lion International
1964-02	1963	The Haunting The Haunting	Roger Corman	U.S.	American International
1964-03	1961	So Evil, So Young	Godfrey Grayson	U.K.	Danziger Productions
1964-03	1964	Children of the Damned	Anton M. Leader	U.K.	MGM
1964-04	1958	From the Earth to The Moon	Byron Haskin	U.S.	RKO
1964-06	1960	The Tell-Tale Heart	Ernest Morris	U.K.	The Danzigers

Cinema Release Date (YYYY-MM)	Year Produced	Title	Director	Country of Origin	Studio
1964-06	1964	Strait-Jacket	William Castle	U.S.	William Castle Productions
1964-07	1962	Tales of Terror	Roger Corman	U.S.	American International
1964-10	1960	The Little Shop of Horrors	Roger Corman	U.S.	Filmgroup
1964-11	1962	Carnival of Souls	Herk Harvey	U.S.	Harcourt Productions[26]
1964-12	1964	Moro Witch Doctor	Eddie Romero	U.S.	Associated Producers International
1965-02	1964	The Masque of the Red Death	Roger Corman	U.S.	American International
1965-03	1964	The Gorgon	Terence Fisher	U.K.	Hammer Films
1965-04	1956	Fire Maidens from Outer Space	Cy Roth	U.K.	Criterion Films
1965-04	1962	The Phantom Planet	William Marshall	U.S.	Four Crown Productions
1965-05	1963	Diary of a Madman	Reginald LeBorg	U.S.	Robert E. Kent Productions
1965-08	1960	Battle of Blood Island	Joel Rapp	U.K.	Hammer Films
1965-08	1962	Panic in Year Zero!	Ray Milland	U.S.	American International
1965-09	1961	Reptilicus	Sidney Pink	U.S.	American International
1965-10	1965	The Night Walker	William Castle	U.S.	Universal

Filmography, 1897–1973

Cinema Release Date (YYYY-MM)	Year Produced	Title	Director	Country of Origin	Studio
1965-11	1964	The Secret of Blood Island	Quentin Lawrence	U.K.	Hammer Films
1965-12	1965	Dr. Who and the Daleks	Gordon Flemyng	U.K.	AARU
1965-12	1965	Where the Spies Are	Val Guest	U.K.	MGM
1966-03	1965	Two on a Guillotine	William Conrad	U.S.	Warner Brothers
1966-04	1963	X—The Man with the X-ray Eyes	Roger Corman	U.S.	American International
1966-05	1965	Repulsion	Roman Polanski	U.K.	Royal/ Compton/ Tekli
1966-09	1965	The Face of Fu Manchu	Don Sharp	U.K.	Anglo-Amalgamated Films
1966-12	1939	The Dark Eyes of London	Walter Summers	U.K.	Argyle Film
1967-02	1963	Dementia 13	Francis Ford Coppola	U.S.	American International[27]
1967-02	1966	Munster, Go Home!	Earl Bellamy	U.S.	Universal
1967-03	1966	Rasputin the Mad Monk	Don Sharp	U.K.	Hammer Films
1967-06	1966	The Deadly Bees	Freddie Francis	U.K.	Amicus Productions
1967-07	1966	Carry on Screaming!	Gerald Thomas	U.K.	Anglo-Amalgamated Films
1967-07	1967	Eye of the Devil	J. Lee Thompson	U.K.	Filmways Productions

Cinema Release Date (YYYY-MM)	Year Produced	Title	Director	Country of Origin	Studio
1968-03	1968	Torture Garden	Freddie Francis	U.K.	Amicus Productions
1968-04	1963	The Comedy of Terrors	Jacques Tourneur	U.S.	American International
1968-04	1967	The Fearless Vampire Killers	Roman Polanski	U.K.	MGM
1968-05	1967	Berserk!	Jim O'Connolly	U.K.	Columbia
1968-05	1967	Five Million Years to Earth	Roy Ward Baker	U.K.	Hammer Films
1958-04	1967	Rocket to the Moon	Don Sharp	U.S.	American International
1968-06	1967	The Shuttered Room	David Greene	U.K.	Troy-Schenck Productions
1968-06	1967	Theatre of Death	Samuel Gallu	U.K.	Pennea Productions
1968-09	1966	The Psychopath	Freddie Francis	U.K.	Amicus Productions
1968-10	1968	Hour of the Wolf	Ingmar Bergman	Sweden	Svensk Filmindustri
1968-11	1968	The Devil Rides Out	Terence Fisher	U.K.	Hammer Films[28]
1969-01	1967	The She-Freak	Byron Mabe	U.S.	Lion Dog
1969-01	1968	Rosemary's Baby	Roman Polanski	U.S.	Paramount
1969-03	1963	The Haunted Palace	Roger Corman	U.S.	American International

Filmography, 1897–1973

Cinema Release Date (YYYY-MM)	Year Produced	Title	Director	Country of Origin	Studio
1969-03	1964	Blood and Black Lace	Mario Bava	Italy	Emmepi Cinematografica
1969-04	1966	Sting of Death	William Grefe	U.S.	Essen Productions Inc.
1969-06	1968	Submarine X-1	William Graham	U.K.	United Artists
1969-06	1968	The Green Slime	Kinji Fukasaku	Japan	MGM
1969-08	1958	The Revenge of Frankenstein	Terence Fisher	U.K.	Hammer Films
1969-08	1964	Devil Doll	Lindsay Shonteff	U.K.	Gordon/ Associated/ Galaworld
1969-10	1968	Destroy All Monsters	Ishirō Honda	Japan	Toho
1969-10	1968	Dracula Has Risen from the Grave	Freddie Francis	U.K.	Hammer Films[29]
1969-11	1969	Eye of the Cat	David Lowell Rich	U.S.	Universal
1970-05	1954	The Tomb of Ligeia	Roger Corman	U.K.	American International
1970-06	1969	Nightmare in Wax	Bud Townsend	U.S.	Crown/ Paragon
1970-07	1922	Nosferatu	F.W. Murnau	Germany	Decla-Bioscop AG
1970-07	1970	The Dunwich Horror	Daniel Haller	U.S.	American International
1970-08	1966	Billy the Kid versus Dracula	William Beaudine	U.S.	Circle Productions

Cinema Release Date (YYYY-MM)	Year Produced	Title	Director	Country of Origin	Studio
1970-08	1966	The Ghost in the Invisible Bikini	Don Weis	U.S.	American International
1970-09	1968	Twisted Nerve	Roy Boulting	U.K.	Charter Film Productions
1971-01	1970	Count Yorga, Vampire	Bob Kelljan	U.S.	American International
1971-03	1961	Pit and the Pendulum	Roger Corman	U.S.	American International
1971-03	1969	The Haunted House of Horror	Michael Armstrong	U.K.	Tigon/ AIP
1971-04	1970	The Vampire Lovers	Roy Ward Baker	U.K.	Hammer Films
1971-06	1971	Homesdale	Peter Weir	Australia	Richard Brennan—Grahame Bond
1971-07	1970	Trog	Freddie Francis	U.K.	Herman Cohen Productions
1971-08	1968	Curse of the Crimson Altar	Vernon Sewell	U.K.	Trigon Films
1971-08	1971	The Brotherhood of Satan	Bernard McEveety	U.S.	Columbia
1971-09	1962	The Premature Burial	Roger Corman	U.S.	American International
1971-09	1969	Scream and Scream Again	Gordon Hessler	U.K.	Amicus Productions[30]
1971-09	1970	House of Dark Shadows	Dan Curtis	U.S.	MGM[31]
1971-09	1971	The Abominable Dr. Phibes	Robert Fuest	U.S.	American International

Cinema Release Date (YYYY-MM)	Year Produced	Title	Director	Country of Origin	Studio
1971-10	1969	Frankenstein Must Be Destroyed	Terence Fisher	U.K.	Hammer Films[32]
1971-10	1971	Creatures the World Forgot	Don Chaffey	U.K.	Hammer Films[33]
1971-10	1971	The Mephisto Waltz	Paul Wendkos	U.S.	20th Century-Fox
1971-10	1971	Wake in Fright	Ted Kotcheff	Australia	NTL Productions
1971-11	1970	The Horror of Frankenstein	Jimmy Sangster	U.K.	Hammer Films
1971-11	1970	The Scars of Dracula	Roy Ward Baker	U.K.	Hammer Films[34]
1971-12	1971	Murders in the Rue Morgue	Gordon Hessler	U.S.	American International
1971-12	1971	The Return of Count Yorga	Bob Kelljan	U.S.	American International
1972-02	1965	Dr. Terror's House of Horrors	Freddie Francis	U.K.	Amicus Productions[35]
1972-02	1971	I, Monster	Stephen Weeks	U.K.	Amicus Productions
1972-03	1971	Night of Dark Shadows	Dan Curtis	U.S.	MGM
1972-03	1971	Twins of Evil	John Hough	U.K.	Hammer Films
1972-04	1971	Fright	Peter Collinson	U.K.	Fantale Films
1972-05	1970	The Beast in The Cellar	James Kelly	U.K.	Tigon British Film Productions

Cinema Release Date (YYYY-MM)	Year Produced	Title	Director	Country of Origin	Studio
1972–05	1970	The Blood on Satan's Claw	Piers Haggard	U.K.	Tigon British Film Productions[36]
1972–06	1971	Blood from the Mummy's Tomb	Seth Holt	U.K.	Hammer Films
1972–06	1971	Lust for a Vampire	Jimmy Sangster	U.K.	Hammer Films
1972–08	1971	What's the Matter with Helen?	Curtis Harrington	U.S.	Filmways Pictures
1972–08	1971	Willard	Daniel Mann	U.S.	Bing Crosby Productions
1972–09	1971	The Black Belly of The Tarantula	Paolo Cavara	Italy	MGM[37]
1972–09	1971	The Nightcomers	Michael Winner	U.S.	Scimitar Productions
1972–10	1968	Night of the Living Dead	George A. Romero	U.S.	Continental
1972–10	1970	And Soon the Darkness	Robert Fuest	U.K.	Associated British
1972–10	1971	Dr. Jekyll and Sister Hyde	Roy Ward Baker	U.K.	Hammer Films
1972–10	1971	Queen Doll	Sergio Olhovich	Mexico	Cinematográfica Marco Polo S.A.
1972–10	1971	The Vampire Happening	Freddie Francis	Germany	Aquila Film Enterprises
1972–10	1971	Who Slew Auntie Roo?	Curtis Harrington	U.K.	Hemdale
1972–10	1972	Dr. Phibes Rises Again	Robert Fuest	U.K.	American International

Cinema Release Date (YYYY-MM)	Year Produced	Title	Director	Country of Origin	Studio
1972-11	1961	Mr. Sardonicus	William Castle	U.S.	Columbia
1972-11	1968	Witchfinder General	Michael Reeves	U.K.	American International
1972-11	1970	Goodbye Gemini	Alan Gibson	U.K.	Joseph Shaftel Productions
1972-11	1971	A Reflection of Fear	William A. Fraker	U.S.	Columbia
1972-11	1971	The House That Dripped Blood	Peter Duffell	U.K.	Amicus Productions
1972-12	1971	Night Digger	Alastair Reid	U.K.	MGM
1972-12	1972	Dracula AD 1972	Alan Gibson	U.K.	Hammer Films
1972-12	1972	Tales from the Crypt	Freddie Francis	U.K.	Amicus Productions
1973-01	1972	Frogs	George McCowan	U.S.	American International
1973-01	1972	Night of the Lepus	William F. Claxton	U.S.	A.C. Lyles Productions
1973-02	1961	The Curse of the Werewolf	Terence Fisher	U.K.	Hammer Films
1973-02	1971	Hands of the Ripper	Peter Sasdy	U.K.	Hammer Films
1973-03	1971	Let's Scare Jessica to Death	John D. Hancock	U.S.	Paramount
1973-03	1972	Asylum	Roy Ward Baker	U.K.	Amicus Productions

Cinema Release Date (YYYY-MM)	Year Produced	Title	Director	Country of Origin	Studio
1973-03	1972	Blacula	William Crain	U.S.	American International
1973-03	1972	Shirley Thompson versus the Aliens	Jim Sharman	Australia	Kolossal Pictures
1973-04	1964	The Curse of the Mummy's Tomb	Michael Carreras	U.K.	Hammer Films
1973-04	1967	Blood Beast Terror	Vernon Sewell	U.K.	Tigon British
1973-04	1970	Equinox	Jack Woods	U.S.	Tonylyn Productions
1973-04	1970	The Evils of Dorian Gray	Massimo Dallamano	Germany	Sargon Film
1973-04	1972	Baron Blood	Mario Bava	Italy	Euro America Produzioni
1973-05	1972	The Thing with Two Heads	Lee Frost	U.S.	American International
1973-05	1973	Night of Fear	Terry Bourke	Australia	Terryrod Productions[38]
1973-06	1972	The Possession of Joel Delaney	Waris Hussein	U.S.	Haworth Productions
1973-07	1964	Kwaidan	Masaki Kobayashi	Japan	Toho
1973-07	1966	Dracula—Prince of Darkness	Terence Fisher	U.K.	Hammer Films
1973-07	1972	Vampire Circus	Robert Young	U.K.	Hammer Films[39]
1973-07	1973	The Sabbat of the Black Cat	Ralph Lawrence Marsden	Australia	Ralph Lawrence Marsden

Cinema Release Date (YYYY-MM)	Year Produced	Title	Director	Country of Origin	Studio
1973-08	1957	The Curse of Frankenstein	Terence Fisher	U.K.	Hammer Films[40]
1973-08	1970	Cry of the Banshee	Gordon Hessler	U.K.	American International
1973-08	1971	Dracula vs. Frankenstein	Al Adamson	U.S.	Independent International
1973-09	1960	Black Sunday	Mario Bava	Italy	Galatea Film
1973-10	1964	Castle of the Living Dead	Luciano Ricci, Lorenzo Sabatini	Italy	Serena Film Filmsonor
1973-10	1969	The Oblong Box	Gordon Hessler	U.K.	American International
1973-10	1972	Fear in the Night	Jimmy Sangster	U.K.	Hammer Films
1973-11	1970	Mark of the Devil	Michael Armstrong	Germany	Hi Fi Stereo
1973-11	1971	Crucible of Terror	Ted Hooker	U.K.	Glendale Film Productions
1973-11	1972	The Deathmaster	Ray Danton	U.S.	R.F. Brown Productions
1973-11	1972	Tower of Evil	Jim O'Connolly	U.K.	Grenadier Films
1974-02	1971	Tombs of the Blind Dead	Amando de Ossorio	Spain	Hispamex
1974-04	1962	King Kong vs. Godzilla	Ishirō Honda	Japan	Toho
1974-04	1967	Frankenstein Created Woman	Terence Fisher	U.K.	Hammer Films

Cinema Release Date (YYYY-MM)	Year Produced	Title	Director	Country of Origin	Studio
1974-05	1971	Daughters of Darkness	Harry Kümel	Belgium	Showking Films
1974-07	1971	The Corpse Grinders	Ted V. Mikels	U.S.	Geneni Film Distributors
1974-09	1968	Queen of the Vampires	Jean Rollin	France	Les Films
1974-09	1972	Dracula, Prisoner of Frankenstein	Jesús Franco	Spain	
1974-10	1958	Dracula	Terence Fisher	U.K.	Hammer Films
1974-10	1966	Jesse James Meets Frankenstein's Daughter	William Beaudine	U.S.	Embassy
1974-11	1967	The X from Outer Space	Kazui Nihonmatsu	Japan	Shochiku
1974-11	1971	The Night Evelyn Came Out of The Grave	Emilio Miraglia	Italy	Phoenix Cinematografica
1974-12	1968	Goke, Body Snatcher from Hell	Hajime Sato	Japan	Shochiku
1974-12	1968	Mantis in Lace	William Rostler	U.S.	Box Office International
1974-12	1971	Countess Dracula	Peter Sasdy	U.K.	Hammer Films
1974-12	1971	Simon, King of the Witches	Bruce Kessler	U.S.	Fanfare Films Inc
1975-02	1972	Godzilla vs. Gigan	Jun Fukuda	Japan	Toho
1975-03	1968	Spirits of the Dead	Federico Fellini, Louis Malle, Roger Vadim	France	American International

Cinema Release Date (YYYY-MM)	Year Produced	Title	Director	Country of Origin	Studio
1975-07	1971	Brain of Blood	Al Adamson	U.S.	Independent International
1975-08	1972	The Creeping Flesh	Freddie Francis	U.K.	World Film Service
1975-10	1960	The Witch's Curse	Chano Urueta	Italy	Panda Cinematografica
1975-10	1971	The Incredible 2-Headed Transplant	Anthony M. Lanza	U.S.	American International
1975-11	1972	Horror Express	Eugenio Martín	Spain	Granada Films
1975-12	1971	Werewolves on Wheels	Michel Levesque	U.S.	South Street Films
1976-01	1932	Freaks	Tod Browning	U.S.	MGM[41]
1976-04	1971	Virgin Witch	Ray Austin	U.K.	Tigon British Film Productions
1976-04	1972	Horror Rises from the Tomb	Carlos Aured	Spain	Avco Embassy
1976-05	1969	The Nude Vampire	Jean Rollin	France	Les Films
1977-08	1973	Godzilla vs. Megalon	Jun Fukuda	Japan	Toho
1977-10	1965	Planet of the Vampires	Mario Bava	Italy	American International
1977-10	1972	Necromancy	Bert I. Gordon	U.S.	Compass/ Zenith International
1979-06	1972	The Flesh and Blood Show	Pete Walker	U.K.	Heritage

Cinema Release Date (YYYY-MM)	Year Produced	Title	Director	Country of Origin	Studio
1979-08	1971	Psychomania	Don Sharp	U.K.	Benmar Productions
1981-09	1959	Plan 9 from Outer Space	Edward D. Wood Jr.	U.S.	Reynolds Pictures
1981-09	1972	The Asphyx	Peter Newbrook	U.K.	Glendale Films
1981-10	1970	Bloodthirsty Butchers	Andy Milligan	U.S.	Constitution Films
1985-02	1964	Frankenstein Conquers the World	Inoshiro Honda	Japan	Toho
1985-08	1966	Curse of the Swamp Creature	Larry Buchanan	U.S.	American International [1]
1986-03	1968	The Astro-Zombies	Ted V. Mikels	U.S.	Ram
1988-09	1965	Frankenstein Meets the Spacemonster	Robert Gaffney	U.S.	Futurama Entertainment
1990-08	1968	Spider Baby	Jack Hill	U.S.	American General
1991-07	1958	The Fly	Kurt Neumann	U.S.	20th Century–Fox[42]
1991-07	1959	Return of the Fly	Edward Bernds	U.S.	20th Century–Fox[43]
1991-07	1965	Curse of the Fly	Don Sharp	U.K.	20th Century–Fox[44]
1993-02	1964	I Eat Your Skin	Del Tenney	U.S.	Cinemation[45]
1993-02	1970	I Drink Your Blood	David E. Durston	U.S.	Jerry Gross Productions[46]
1995-08	1971	The Velvet Vampire	Stephanie Rothman	U.S.	New World Pictures[47]

Films Banned or Not Given a General Cinema Release: 1897–1973

The following is a list of selected films that were either banned outright or not afforded a cinema release in Australia for their first run. In some cases, such as *Freaks*, the film was finally released when the ban was lifted.

All horror movies were banned from importation and exhibition from 1948 to 1969. This ban did not apply to movies that had already been cleared by the censor, meaning any movie, pre-1948, that was already in the country, could still be shown and new prints could be imported and exhibited. Despite this ban, some horror movies slipped through the net. Post-1948 films that were not given a release and were listed on official ban lists issued by the Censor are listed here.

Year Film Produced	Title	Director	Country of Origin	Studio
1898	The Accursed Cavern	Georges Méliès	France	Méliès
1898	The Cavalier's Dream	Edwin S. Porter	U.S.	Edison
1898	Faust and Marguerite	Edwin S. Porter	U.S.	Edison
1898	Photographing a Ghost	George Albert Smith	U.K.	GAS Films
1899	Cleopatra	Georges Méliès	France	Méliès
1899	The Devil in The Convent	Georges Méliès	France	Méliès
1899	The Infernal Palace	Edwin S. Porter	U.S.	Edison
1899	The Miser's Doom	Walter R. Booth	U.K.	R.W. Paul
1899	Raising Spirits	Georges Méliès	France	Méliès
1900	Chinese Magic (Yellow Peril)	Walter R. Booth	U.K.	R.W. Paul
1900	The Prince of Darkness		U.S.	American Mutoscope
1901	Bluebeard	Georges Méliès	France	Méliès

Year Film Produced	Title	Director	Country of Origin	Studio
1901	The Haunted Curiosity Shop	Walter R. Booth	U.K.	R.W. Paul
1902	The Devil and The Statue	Georges Méliès	France	Méliès
1902	The Devil's Kitchen	Georges Méliès	France	Méliès
1902	Les Trésors de Satan (The Treasures of Satan)	Georges Méliès	France	Méliès
1903	Beelzebub's Daughter	Georges Méliès	France	Méliès
1903	Le Chaudron Infernal (The Infernal Boiling Pot)	Georges Méliès	France	Méliès
1903	Le Monstre (The Monster)	Georges Méliès	France	Méliès
1905	Le Diable Noir (The Black Imp)	Georges Méliès	France	Méliès
1906	The Four Hundred Devil's Pranks	Georges Méliès	France	Méliès
1906	La Maison hantée (The Haunted House)	Segundo de Chomón	France	Méliès
1908	Cave of Spooks	Segundo de Chomón	France	Pathé
1908	The Changing of Souls		Norway	Nordisk Film Company
1909	The Human Ape (Darwin's Triumph)		Norway	Nordisk Film Company
1910	Dr. Jekyll and Mr. Hyde		Norway	Nordisk Film Company
1912	The Mask of Horror	Abel Gance	France	Pathé Frères
1912	The System of Dr. Tar and Professor Plume	Maurice Tourneur	France	Société Française des Films Éclair
1913	The Skull	William V. Ranous	U.S.	Vitagraph Studios

Year Film Produced	Title	Director	Country of Origin	Studio
1913	The Werewolf	Henry McRae	U.S.	Bison
1914	Vampires of Warsaw	Wiktor Biegański	Poland	Merkurfilm
1915	Der Golem	Paul Wegener	Germany	UFA
1915	The Haunting Fear	Robert Vignola	U.S.	Kalem
1915	Life Without Soul	Joseph W. Smiley	U.S.	Ocean
1916	A Night of Horror	Richard Oswald, Arthur Robison	Germany	Lu Synd-Wartan-Film
1916	Hævnens nat	Benjamin Christensen	Denmark	Dansk Biograf Compagni
1917	Der Golem und die Tänzerin	Paul Wegener	Germany	UFA
1917	Fear	Robert Wiene	Germany	UFA
1918	Alraune	Michael Curtiz, Fritz Odon	Austria	Hunnia Filmvállalat
1919	The Beetle	Alexander Butler	U.K.	Urban Trading Company
1919	Unheimliche Geschichten	Richard Oswald	Germany	Richard Oswald-Film AG
1920	Anita	Jacob Fleck, Luise Fleck	Austria	Wiener Kunstfilm
1920	Genuine	Robert Wiene	Germany	Decla-Bioscop AG
1920	The Golem: How He Came into The World	Paul Wegener, Karl Boese	Germany	PAGU[48]
1920	The Head of Janus	F. W. Murnau	Germany	Lipow Film Company
1920	The Monster of Frankenstein	Eugenio Testa	Italy	Albertini Film
1921	Der Muede Tod	Fritz Lang	Germany	Decla-Bioscop AG

Year Film Produced	Title	Director	Country of Origin	Studio
1924	The Hands of Orlac	Robert Wiene	Germany	Pan Film
1925	Wolfblood: A Tale of the Forest	George Chesebro, Bruce M. Mitchell	U.S.	Ryan Brothers Productions
1926	The Student of Prague	Henrik Galeen	Germany	Sokol-Film
1928	Alraune	Henrik Galeen	Germany	Ama-Film
1928	The Ape	Beverly C. Rule	U.S.	Milt Collins
1929	Dark Red Roses	Sinclair Hall	U.K.	British Sound Film[49]
1931	Dracula	George Melford	U.S.	Universal[50]
1931	The Phantom	Alan James	U.S.	Supreme Pictures
1932	Castle Sinister	Widgey R. Newman	U.K.	Delta Pictures
1932	Freaks	Tod Browning	U.S.	MGM[51]
1932	The Monster Walks	Frank Strayer	U.S.	Mayfair Pictures
1933	The Vampire Bat	Frank Strayer	U.S.	Majestic Pictures[52]
1933	Wasei Kingu Kongu	Torajiro Saito	Japan	Shochiku[53]
1934	Lost in the Stratosphere	Melville W. Brown	U.S.	Monogram
1934	The Ghost Walks	Frank R. Strayer	U.S.	Invincible Pictures Corp[54]
1934	Black Moon	Roy William Neill	U.S.	Columbia
1934	Chloe, Love Is Calling You	Marshall Neilan	U.S.	Pinnacle Productions
1934	House of Mystery	William Nigh	U.S.	Monogram

Filmography, 1897–1973

Year Film Produced	Title	Director	Country of Origin	Studio
1934	Maniac	Dwain Esper	U.S.	Roadshow Attractions
1934	Shock	Roy Pomeroy	U.S.	Monogram
1934	The Tell-Tale Heart	Brian Desmond Hurst	U.K.	Blattner Studios
1935	Condemned to Live	Frank Strayer	U.S.	Invincible Pictures Corp
1935	The Crime of Dr. Crespi	John H. Auer	U.S.	Liberty Pictures[55]
1935	Ouanga	George Terwilliger	U.S.	George Terwilliger Productions
1936	Revolt of the Zombies	Victor Halperin	U.S.	Victor Halperin Productions
1936	Sweeney Todd: The Demon Barber of Fleet Street	George King	U.K.	Select
1938	King Kong Appears in Edo	Sōya Kumagai	Japan	Zenshō Cinema
1939	Buried Alive	Victor Halperin	U.S.	Victor Halperin Productions
1939	The Devil's Daughter	Arthur H. Leonard	U.S.	Sack Amusement
1939	The Face at the Window	George King	U.K.	George King Productions
1939	Torture Ship	Victor Halperin	U.S.	Sigmund Neufield Productions
1940	Boys of the City	Joseph H. Lewis	U.S.	Monogram
1940	Son of Ingagi	Richard Kahn	U.S.	Sack Amusement
1941	Tower of Terror	Lawrence Huntington	U.K.	Associated British Picture Corporation
1941	The Mad Doctor	Tim Whelan	U.S.	Paramount
1941	Invisible Ghost	Joseph H. Lewis	U.S.	Monogram

Year Film Produced	Title	Director	Country of Origin	Studio
1941	The Monster and The Girl	Stuart Heisler	U.S.	Paramount
1942	The Captive	Edward Dmytryk	U.S.	Universal
1942	The Man with Two Lives	Phil Rosen	U.S.	A.W. Hackel Productions
1942	Bowery at Midnight	Wallace Fox	U.S.	Monogram
1942	The Corpse Vanishes	Wallace W. Fox	U.S.	Monogram
1942	Dr. Renault's Secret	Harry Lachman	U.S.	20th Century–Fox
1942	The Mad Monster	Sam Newfield	U.S.	Producers Releasing Corporation
1943	Calling Dr. Death	Reginald LeBorg	U.S.	Universal
1943	The Ape Man	William Beaudine	U.S.	Monogram
1944	Crazy Knights	William Beaudine	U.S.	Monogram
1944	The Monster Maker	Sam Newfield	U.S.	Producers Releasing Corporation
1944	Return of the Ape Man	Phil Rosen	U.S.	Monogram
1944	Voodoo Man	William Beaudine	U.S.	Monogram[56]
1945	Zombies on Broadway	Gordon Douglas	U.S.	RKO
1945	The Jungle Captive	Harold Young	U.S.	Universal
1945	Strangler of the Swamp	Frank Wisbar	U.S.	Producers Releasing Corporation
1945	The Vampire's Ghost	Lesley Selander	U.S.	Republic
1945	White Pongo	Sam Newfield	U.S.	Sigmund Neufield Productions

Year Film Produced	Title	Director	Country of Origin	Studio
1946	The Catman of Paris	Lesley Selander	U.S.	Republic
1946	Fear	Alfred Zeiser	U.S.	Monogram[57]
1946	The Brute Man	Jean Yarbrough	U.S.	Producers Releasing Corporation
1946	Devil Bat's Daughter	Frank Wisbar	U.S.	Producers Releasing Corporation
1946	The Face of Marble	William Beaudine	U.S.	Monogram
1946	The Flying Serpent	Sam Newfield	U.S.	Producers Releasing Corporation
1946	The Mask of Diijon	Lew Landers	U.S.	Producers Releasing Corporation
1946	Spook Busters	William Beaudine	U.S.	Monogram
1946	Valley of the Zombies	Philip Ford	U.S.	Republic
1947	Scared to Death	Christy Cabanne	U.S.	Golden Gate Pictures
1948	The Monkey's Paw	Norman Lee	U.K.	Butcher's Empire Films
1948	The Amazing Mr. X	Bernard Vorhaus	U.S.	Eagle Lion
1948	House of Darkness	Oswald Mitchell	U.K.	International Motion Pictures
1951	Lost Planet Airmen	Fred C. Brannon	U.S.	Republic
1952	Crow Hollow	Michael McCarthy	U.K.	Eros Films
1952	Ghost Ship	Vernon Sewell	U.S.	Vernon Sewell Productions
1952	Bela Lugosi Meets a Brooklyn Gorilla	William Beaudine	U.S.	Realart Pictures
1953	Port Sinister	Harold Daniels	U.S.	RKO

Year Film Produced	Title	Director	Country of Origin	Studio
1953	Nine Steps to the Gallows	John Gilling	U.K.	Eros Films
1953	Robot Monster	Phil Tucker	U.S.	Astor Pictures
1953	Project Moon Base	Richard Talmadge	U.S.	Galaxy Pictures
1953	The War of the Worlds	Byron Haskin	U.S.	Paramount
1953	Mesa of Lost Women	Herbert Tevos, Ron Ormond	U.S.	Howco Productions
1954	Monster from the Ocean Floor	Wyott Ordung	U.S.	Palo Alto
1954	Serpent Island	Tom Gries	U.S.	Z-A Productions
1954	Island Monster	Roberto Bianchi Montero	Italy	Romana Film
1954	Gojira	Ishirō Honda	Japan	Toho
1955	The Beast with a Million Eyes	David Kramarsky	U.S.	American International
1955	Dementia	John Parker	U.S.	H.K.F. Productions
1955	Half Human	Ishirō Honda	Japan	Toho
1956	Warning from Space	Koji Shima	Japan	Daiei Film
1956	The She-Creature	Edward L. Cahn	U.S.	American International
1956	The Day the Earth Froze	Aleksandr Ptushko	Russia	American International
1956	The Phantom from 10,000 Leagues	Dan Milner	U.S.	Milner Bros. Productions
1956	It Conquered the World	Roger Corman	U.S.	American International
1956	The Black Sleep	Reginald LeBorg	U.S.	United Artists[58]

Year Film Produced	Title	Director	Country of Origin	Studio
1956	Night of the Damned	Filippo Ratti	Italy	Primax
1956	Indestructible Man	Jack Pollexfen	U.S.	Allied Artists
1956	Bride of the Monster	Edward D. Wood Jr.	U.S.	Rolling M. Productions
1956	Man Beast	Jerry Warren	U.S.	Jerry Warren Productions
1956	The Werewolf	Fred F. Sears	U.S.	Columbia
1957	Enemy from Space	Val Guest	U.K.	Hammer Films
1957	The Cyclops	Bert I. Gordon	U.S.	Allied Artists
1957	Voodoo Woman	Edward L. Cahn	U.S.	American International
1957	The Amazing Colossal Man	Bert I. Gordon	U.S.	American International
1957	The Undead	Roger Corman	U.S.	American International
1957	Fiend Without a Face	Arthur Crabtree	U.K.	Amalgamated Productions
1957	The Abominable Snowman	Val Guest	U.K.	Hammer Films
1957	Attack of the Crab Monsters	Roger Corman	U.S.	Allied Artists
1957	Back from the Dead	Charles Marquis Warren	U.S.	20th Century–Fox
1957	Beginning of the End	Bert I. Gordon	U.S.	AB-PT Pictures
1957	Blood of Dracula	Herbert L. Strock	U.S.	American International
1957	Cat Girl	Alfred Shaughnessy	U.K.	Insignia Films
1957	Daughter of Dr. Jekyll	Edgar G. Ulmer	U.S.	Allied Artists

Year Film Produced	Title	Director	Country of Origin	Studio
1957	The Disembodied	Walter Grauman	U.S.	Allied Artists
1957	From Hell It Came	Dan Milner	U.S.	Allied Artists
1957	I Was a Teenage Frankenstein	Herbert L. Strock	U.S.	American International
1957	I Was a Teenage Werewolf	Gene Fowler Jr.	U.S.	American International
1957	Monster from Green Hell	Kenneth G. Crane	U.S.	DCA
1957	Night of the Demon	Jacques Tourneur	U.K.	Sabre
1957	Quatermass 2	Val Guest	U.K.	Hammer Films
1958	The Strange World of Planet X	Gilbert Gunn	U.K.	Eros Films
1958	Attack of the Puppet People	Bert I. Gordon	U.S.	American International
1958	Teenage Cave Man	Roger Corman	U.S.	American International
1958	The Day the Sky Exploded	Paolo Heusch	Italy	Lux Film
1958	Teenage Monster	Jacques R. Marquette	U.S.	Marquette Productions Limited
1958	Terror from The Year 5000	Robert J. Gurney Jr.	U.S.	American International
1958	How to Make a Monster	Herbert L. Strock	U.S.	American International
1958	Man Eater	Compton Bennett	U.S.	Beaconsfield Productions
1958	The Screaming Skull	Alex Nicol	U.S.	Madera Productions
1958	The Brain from Planet Arus	Nathan Juran	U.S.	Howco International
1958	Terror in the Haunted House	Harold Daniels	U.S.	Howco International

Filmography, 1897–1973

Year Film Produced	Title	Director	Country of Origin	Studio
1958	The Haunted Strangler	Robert Day	U.K.	Amalgamated Productions
1958	The Brain Eaters	Bruno Ve Sota	U.S.	American International
1958	Frankenstein's Daughter	Richard E. Cunha	U.S.	Astor/Layton
1958	Frankenstein 1970	Howard W. Koch	U.S.	Allied Artists
1958	The Astounding She-Monster	Ronald V. Ashcroft	U.S.	American International
1958	Blood of the Vampire	Henry Cass	U.K.	Artistes Alliance
1958	The Bride and the Beast	Adrian Weiss	U.S.	Allied Artists
1958	Night of the Blood Beast	Bernard L. Kowalski	U.S.	American International
1958	The Thing That Couldn't Die	Will Cowan	U.S.	Universal International
1959	The Cosmic Man	Herbert Greene	U.S.	Futura Productions
1959	The Man Who Liked Funerals	David Eady	U.K.	Pennington Eady
1959	The Headless Ghost	Peter Graham Scott	U.K.	Anglo-Amalgamated Films
1959	The Giant Gila Monster	Ray Kellogg	U.S.	McLendon-Radio Pictures
1959	Prince of Space	Eijirō Wakabayashi	Japan	Toei Company
1959	Missile to the Moon	Richard E. Cunha	U.S.	Layton Film Productions
1959	Giant from the Unknown	Richard E. Cunha	U.S.	Astor Pictures
1959	Ghost of Dragstrip Hollow	William J. Hole Jr.	U.S.	Alta Vista Productions
1959	Attack of the Giant Leeches	Bernard L. Kowalski	U.S.	Balboa Productions

Year Film Produced	Title	Director	Country of Origin	Studio
1959	The Wasp Woman	Roger Corman	U.S.	Allied Artists
1959	The H-Man	Ishirō Honda	Japan	Toho
1959	Fellowship of the Frog	Harold Reinl	U.S.	Rialto Film
1959	Invasion of the Animal People	Virgil W. Vogel	Sweden	Jerry Warren Productions
1959	The Alligator People	Roy Del Ruth	U.S.	20th Century–Fox
1959	A Bucket of Blood	Roger Corman	U.S.	American International
1959	Beast from Haunted Cave	Monte Hellman	U.S.	Allied Artists
1959	Caltiki—The Immortal Monster	Riccardo Freda	Italy	Allied Artists
1959	Curse of the Undead	Edward Dein	U.S.	Universal International
1959	The Ghost of Yotsuya	Nobuo Nakagawa	Japan	Shintoho
1959	The Hideous Sun Demon	Robert Clarke	U.S.	Pacific International
1959	Horrors of the Black Museum	Arthur Crabtree	U.K.	American International
1959	The Killer Shrews	Ray Kellogg	U.S.	McLendon-Radio Pictures
1959	The Monster of Piedras Blancas	Irvin Berwick	U.S.	Vanwick Productions
1959	The Manster	George Breakston	U.S.	Shaw-Breakston Enterprises
1959	Night of the Ghouls	Edward D. Wood Jr.	U.S.	Atomic Productions
1959	The Three Treasures	Hiroshi Inagaki	Japan	Toho
1960	First Spaceship on Venus	Kurt Maetzig	Germany	Roter Kreis

Year Film Produced	Title	Director	Country of Origin	Studio
1960	The Angry Red Planet	Ib Melchior	U.S.	American International
1960	The Pusher	Gene Milford	U.K.	United Artists
1960	Beyond the Time Barrier	Edgar G. Ulmer	U.S.	American International
1960	Unstoppable Man	Terry Bishop	U.K.	Anglo-Amalgamated Films
1960	Face of Terror	Isidoro M. Ferry	Italy	Documento Films
1960	The Amazing Transparent Man	Edgar G. Ulmer	U.S.	American International
1960	Secret of the Telegian	Jun Fukuda	Japan	Toho
1960	Minotaur Wild Beast of Crete	Silvio Amadio	Italy	Gino Mordini
1960	The Terrible People	Harald Reinl	Germany	Rialto Film
1960	Sweetheart of the Gods	Gottfried Reinhardt	Germany	Central Cinema Company Film
1960	The Fall of The House of Usher	Roger Corman	U.S.	American International
1960	Vampire and the Ballerina	Renato Polselli	Italy	Consorzio Italiano
1960	The Fiends	John Gilling	U.K.	Regal Film Distributors
1960	The Brides of Dracula	Terence Fisher	U.K.	Hammer Films
1960	Atom Age Vampire	Anton Giulio Majano	Italy	Lions Films
1960	The City of The Dead	John Llewellyn Moxey	U.K.	Vulcan
1960	The Ghost Cat of Otama Pond	Yoshihiro Ishikawa	Japan	Shintoho
1960	Horrors of Spider Island	Fritz Böttger	Germany	Peacemaker/Intercontinental

Year Film Produced	Title	Director	Country of Origin	Studio
1960	The Incredible Petrified World	Jerry Warren	U.S.	Governor Films
1960	Jigoku	Nobuo Nakagawa	Japan	Shintoho
1960	Mill of the Stone Women	Giorgio Ferroni	France	Paradise
1960	Peeping Tom	Michael Powell	U.K.	American International
1960	The Playgirls and the Vampire	Piero Regnoli	Italy	Fanfare Films Inc
1960	Teenage Zombies	Jerry Warren	U.S.	Governor Films
1960	Tormented	Bert I. Gordon	U.S.	Allied Artists
1960	The World of Vampires	Alfonso Corona Blake	Mexico	American International
1961	The Snake Woman	Sidney J. Furie	U.K.	Caralan Productions
1961	Invasion of the Neptune Men	Koji Ota	Japan	Toei Company
1961	Battle of the Worlds	Antonio Margheriti	Italy	Ultra Film
1961	Journey Beneath the Desert	Giuseppe Masini	Italy	Compagnia Cinematografica Mondiale
1961	The Black Abbot	F.J. Gottlieb	Germany	Central Cinema Company Film
1961	The Bacchantes	Giorgio Ferroni	Italy	Lyre Films
1961	Creature from the Haunted Sea	Roger Corman, Monte Hellman	U.S.	Roger Corman Productions
1961	The Beast of Yucca Flats	Coleman Francis	U.S.	Cinema Associates
1961	The Brainiac	Chano Urueta	Mexico	American International
1961	The Curse of the Crying Woman	Rafael Baledón	Mexico	American International

Filmography, 1897–1973

Year Film Produced	Title	Director	Country of Origin	Studio
1961	Konga	John Lemont	U.K.	Anglo-Amalgamated Films
1961	Maciste in the Land of the Cyclops	Antonio Leonviola	Italy	Medallion
1961	The Mask	Julian Roffman	Canada	Warner Brothers
1962	Varan the Unbelievable	Ishirō Honda	Japan/ U.S.	Toho
1962	Hands of a Stranger	Newton Arnold	U.S.	Allied Artists
1962	Invasion of the Star Creatures	Bruno Ve Sota	U.S.	American International
1962	The Invisible Dr. Mabuse	Harald Reinl	Germany	Central Cinema Company Film
1962	Sherlock Holmes and the Necklace of Death	Terence Fisher	U.K.	Criterion
1962	Planets Against Us	Mike Williams	U.S.	Walter Manley Enterprises
1962	Death Rays of Dr. Mabuse	Harald Reinl	Germany	Central Cinema Company Film
1962	Eegah	Arch Hall Sr	U.S.	Fairway International Pictures
1962	Night of the Eagle	Sidney Hayers	U.K.	Independent Artists
1962	The Carpet of Horror	Harald Reinl	Germany	International Germania Film
1962	The Devil's Hand	William J. Hole	U.S.	Rex Carlton Productions
1962	The Creation of the Humanoids	Wesley Barry	U.S.	Emerson Film Enterprises
1962	Tower of London	Roger Corman	U.S.	United Artists
1962	Curse of the Blood Ghouls	Roberto Mauri	Italy	Mercury
1962	The Day of The Triffids	Steve Sekely	U.K.	Security Pictures

Year Film Produced	Title	Director	Country of Origin	Studio
1962	Gorath	Ishirō Honda	Japan	Toho
1962	The Brain That Wouldn't Die	Joseph Green	U.S.	American International
1962	The Awful Dr. Orloff	Jesús Franco	Spain	Sigma III
1962	Terror of the Bloodhunters	Jerry Warren	U.S.	ADP
1962	The Violent and the Damned	Jerry Warren	U.S.	Jerry Warren Productions
1963	The Crawling Hand	Herbert L Strock	U.S.	Donald J. Hansen Enterprises
1963	The Slime People	Robert Hutton	U.S.	Donald J. Hansen Enterprises
1963	Voyage to the End of the Universe	Jindřich Polák	U.S.	American International
1963	Invisible Terror	Raphael Nussbaum	U.S.	Aero Film
1963	The Terror	Roger Corman	U.S.	American International
1963	Attack of the Mushroom People	Ishirō Honda	Japan	Toho
1963	Atragon	Ishirō Honda	Japan	Toho
1963	Twice-Told Tales	Sidney Salkow	U.S.	United Artists
1963	Ride of Terror	Ron Winston	U.S.	NBC
1963	Terror in the Crypt	Camillo Mastrocinque	Spain	American International
1963	Tombs of Terror	Antonio Boccacci	Italy	Filmar
1963	The Curse of the Yellow Snake	Franz Josef Gottlieb	Germany	Central Cinema Company Film
1963	Fire Monster vs. Son of Hercules	Guido Malatesta	Italy	Euro International

Year Film Produced	Title	Director	Country of Origin	Studio
1963	Black Sabbath	Mario Bava	Italy	American International
1963	Black Zoo	Robert Gordon	U.S.	Allied Artists
1963	The Blancheville Monster	Alberto De Martino	Spain	American International
1963	Blood Feast	Herschell Gordon Lewis	U.S.	Box Office Spectaculars
1963	The Ghost	Riccardo Freda	Italy	Scope
1963	The Kiss of The Vampire	Don Sharp	U.K.	Hammer Films
1963	Matango	Ishirō Honda	Japan	Toho
1964	Mark of the Tortoise	Alfred Vohrer	Germany	Rialto Film
1964	The Ghost of Sierra De Cobra	Joseph Stefano	U.S.	United Artists
1964	Atomic Rulers of the World	Koreyoshi Akasaka	Japan	Shintoho Film Distribution Committee
1964	The Human Duplicators	Hugo Grimaldi	U.S.	Woolner Brothers
1964	Attack from Outer Space	Teruo Ishii	Japan	Shintoho Film Distribution Committee
1964	Evil Brain from Outer Space	Koreyoshi Akasaka	U.S.	Walter Manley Enterprises
1964	Invaders from Space	Teruo Ishii	U.S.	Walter Manley Enterprises
1964	The Time Travelers	Ib Melchior	U.S.	American International
1964	Sounds of Horror	José Antonio Nieves Conde	Spain	Columbia
1964	Space Monster	Burt Topper	U.S.	American International
1964	Hercules Against the Moon Men	Giacomo Gentilomo	Italy	Nike Cinematografica

Year Film Produced	Title	Director	Country of Origin	Studio
1964	Godzilla versus the Thing	Ishirō Honda	Japan	Toho
1964	Dagora, the Space Monster	Ishirō Honda	Japan	Toho
1964	The Incredibly Strange Creatures Who Stopped Living and Became Mixed-Up Zombies!!?	Ray Dennis Steckler	U.S.	Fairway International Pictures
1964	Honeymoon of Horror	Irwin Meyer	U.S.	Flamingo
1964	The Inn on Dartmoor	Rudolf Zehetgruber	Germany	Arca-Winston Films Corp
1964	The Madmen of Mandoras	David Bradley	U.S.	Sans-S
1964	The Horror of Party Beach	Del Tenney	U.S.	20th Century-Fox
1964	Black Torment	Robert Hartford-Davis	U.K.	Compton Films
1964	The Last Man on Earth	Ubaldo Ragona	Italy	Associated Producers
1964	The Masque of the Red Death	Roger Corman	U.S.	Alta Vista Productions
1964	Moonwolf	George Freedland	Germany	
1964	The Flesh Eaters	Jack Curtis	U.S.	Vulcan Productions
1964	Attack of the Mayan Mummy	Rafael Portillo	Mexico	Jerry Warren Productions
1964	The Curse of the Living Corpse	Del Tenney	U.S.	20th Century–Fox
1964	The Evil of Frankenstein	Freddie Francis	U.K.	Hammer Films
1964	2000 Maniacs	Herschell Gordon Lewis	U.S.	Box Office Spectaculars
1964	Castle of Blood	Antonio Margheriti	Italy	Woolner Brothers Pictures Inc.

Year Film Produced	Title	Director	Country of Origin	Studio
1964	The Creeping Terror	Art J. Nelson	U.S.	Teledyn/Metropolitan Int
1964	Dr. Orloff's Monster	Jesús Franco	Austria	American International
1964	Dungeon of Harrow	Pat Boyette	U.S.	Herts-Lion
1964	Face of the Screaming Werewolf	Jerry Warren	U.S.	Jerry Warren Productions
1964	Ghidorah, the Three-Headed Monster	Ishirō Honda	Japan	Toho
1964	Monstrosity	Joseph Mascelli	U.S.	Emerson
1964	Pyro	Julio Coll	U.S.	S.W.P. Productions
1964	War of the Zombies	Giuseppe Vari	Italy	American International
1964	Witchcraft	Don Sharp	U.K.	20th Century-Fox
1965	Day of the Nightmare	John A. Bushelman	U.S.	Screen Group
1965	Mutiny in Outer Space	Hugo Grimaldi	U.S.	Hugo Grimaldi Productions
1965	The Demon Planet	Mario Bava	Italy	Italian International Film
1965	Invasion	Alan Bridges	U.K.	Anglo-Amalgamated Films
1965	Voodoo Horror	Freddie Francis	U.K.	Amicus Productions
1965	The Night Caller	John Gilling	U.K.	Armatage Films
1965	Monster from the Surf	Jon Hall	U.S.	U.S. Films
1965	Die, Monster, Die!	Daniel Haller	U.S.	American International
1965	The Nanny	Seth Holt	U.S.	20th Century–Fox

Year Film Produced	Title	Director	Country of Origin	Studio
1965	The Eye Creatures	Larry Buchanan	U.S.	American International Television
1965	Curse of the Stone Hand	Jerry Warren	U.S.	ADP Pictures
1965	House of the Black Death	Harold Daniels	U.S.	
1965	Creature of the Walking Dead	Jerry Warren	U.S.	ADP Pictures
1965	Orgy of the Dead	Stephen C. Apostolof	U.S.	Astra
1965	Bloody Pit of Horror	Massimo Pupillo	Italy	Pacemaker Int
1965	The Beach Girls and the Monster	Jon Hall	U.S.	American International
1965	The Beast That Killed Women	Barry Mahon	U.S.	Mahon
1965	Color Me Blood Red	Herschell Gordon Lewis	U.S.	Box Office Spectaculars
1965	Curse of Simba	Lindsay Shonteff	U.S.	Allied Artists
1965	Dark Intruder	Harvey Hart	U.S.	Universal
1965	Devils of Darkness	Lance Comfort	U.K.	Fox
1965	The Embalmer	Dino Tavella	Italy	Europix/ Gondola
1965	Fanatic	Silvio Narizzano	U.K.	Hammer Films
1965	Gamera: The Giant Monster	Noriaki Yuasa	Japan	Daiei Film
1965	Incubus	Leslie Stevens	U.S.	Daystar
1965	Invasion of Astro-Monster	Ishirō Honda	Japan	Toho
1965	Monster a Go-Go	Herschell Gordon Lewis	U.S.	B.I. & L.

Year Film Produced	Title	Director	Country of Origin	Studio
1965	Monsters Crash the Pajama Party	David L. Hewitt	U.S.	Brandon
1965	Nightmare Castle	Mario Caiano	Italy	Allied Artists
1965	The She Wolf	Rafael Baledón	Mexico	Sotomayor
1965	The Skull	Freddie Francis	U.K.	Amicus Productions
1965	Terror-Creatures from the Grave	Massimo Pupillo	Italy	Pacemaker Int
1966	Retik the Moon Menace	Fred C. Brannon	U.S.	Republic
1966	Sharad of Atlantis	B. Reeves Eason	U.S.	Republic
1966	D-Day on Mars	Spencer Gordon Bennet, Fred C. Brannon	U.S.	Republic
1966	But You Were Dead	Gianni Vernuccio	Italy	Mercurfin Italiana
1966	Kill, Baby, Kill	Mario Bava	Italy	Europix
1966	Slaves of the Invisible Monster	Fred C. Brannon	U.S.	Republic
1966	The Sound of Horror	José Antonio Nieves Conde	Spain	Zurbano Films
1966	Captain Mephisto and the Transformation Machine	Various	U.S.	Republic
1966	Naked Evil	Stanley Goulder	U.K.	Gibraltar
1966	Daimajin	Kimiyoshi Yasuda	Japan	Daiei Film
1966	Strangler in the Tower	Hans Mehringer	Germany	Interopa Film
1966	The Witch	Damiano Damiani	Italy	Arco Film
1966	The Navy vs. the Night Monsters	Michael A. Hoey	U.S.	Realart Pictures

Year Film Produced	Title	Director	Country of Origin	Studio
1966	Operation White Shark	Stanley Lewis	Italy	Madison Film
1966	Godzilla versus the Sea Monster	Jun Fukuda	Japan	Toho
1966	Women of the Prehistoric Planet	Arthur C. Pierce	U.S.	Realart Pictures
1966	The Projected Man	Ian Curteis	U.K.	Compton Films
1966	Portrait in Terror	Jack Hill	U.S.	American International
1966	The Return of the Giant Majin	Kenji Misumi	Japan	Daiei Film
1966	The Big Gundown	Sergio Sollima	Italy	PEA
1966	An Angel for Satan	Camillo Mastrocinque	Italy	Discobolo
1966	Death Curse of Tartu	William Grefe	U.S.	Thunderbird Int.
1966	Nightmare	Freddie Francis	U.K.	Hammer Films
1966	Queen of Blood	Curtis Harrington	U.S.	American International
1966	The Black Cat	Harold Hoffman	U.S.	Hemisphere
1966	Blood Bath	Stephanie Rothman, Jack Hill	U.S.	American International
1966	The Blood Drinkers	Gerardo de León	Philippines	Hemisphere/ Falcon
1966	The Diabolical Dr. Z	Jesús Franco	Spain	U.S. Films
1966	The Empire of Dracula	Federico Curiel	Mexico	Vergara
1966	Gamera vs. Barugon	Shigeo Tanaka	Japan	Daiei Film
1966	It!	Herbert J. Leder	U.S.	Gold Star Productions

Year Film Produced	Title	Director	Country of Origin	Studio
1966	The Magic Serpent	Tetsuya Yamauchi	Japan	Toei Company
1966	Manos: The Hands of Fate	Hal P. Warren	U.S.	Sun City Films
1966	The Murder Clinic	Elio Scardamaglia	Italy	Europix
1966	The Painted Skin	Bao Fang	Hong Kong	Feng Huang Motion Pictures
1966	Picture Mommy Dead	Bert I. Gordon	U.S.	Embassy
1966	The Plague of The Zombies	John Gilling	U.K.	Hammer Films
1966	The Reptile	John Gilling	U.K.	Hammer Films
1966	The She Beast	Michael Reeves	U.K.	Leith Productions
1966	Terror Beneath the Sea	Hajime Sato	Japan	K. Fujita Associates Inc
1966	The Undertaker and His Pals	David C. Graham	U.S.	Howco Productions
1966	The Vulture	Lawrence Huntington	U.K.	Homeric Films
1966	The War of the Gargantuas	Ishirō Honda	Japan	Toho
1966	The Witches	Cyril Frankel	U.K.	Hammer Films
1966	Yotsuya Kaidan	Shirō Toyoda	Japan	Daiei Film
1967	Mars Needs Women	Larry Buchanan	U.S.	American International
1967	Son of Godzilla	Jun Fukuda	Japan	Toho
1967	Night of the Big Heat	Terence Fisher	U.K.	Planet Film Productions
1967	Island of Terror	Terence Fisher	U.K.	Planet Film Productions

Year Film Produced	Title	Director	Country of Origin	Studio
1967	Creature of Destruction	Larry Buchanan	U.S.	American International
1967	The Unknown Terror	Charles Marquis Warren	U.S.	Regal Pictures
1967	The Mummy's Shroud	John Gilling	U.S.	Hammer Films
1967	The Terrornauts	Montgomery Tully	U.K.	Amicus Productions
1967	Death Curse of Tartu	William Grefe	U.S.	Thunderbird International
1967	Cyborg 2087	Franklin Adreon	U.S.	Harold Goldman Associates
1967	Yongary: Monster from the Deep	Kim Ki-duk	Korea	Toei Company
1967	The Spirit Is Willing	William Castle	U.S.	Paramount
1967	King Kong Escapes	Ishirō Honda	Japan	Toho
1967	A Taste of Blood	Herschell Gordon Lewis	U.S.	Ajay/ Creative
1967	Castle of the Walking Dead	Harald Reinl	Germany	Constantin Films
1967	Corruption	Robert Hartford-Davis	U.K.	Oakshire Productions
1967	Even the Wind Is Scared	Carlos Enrique Taboada	Mexico	Tauro Films
1967	The Frozen Dead	Herbert J. Leder	U.K.	Gold Star Productions
1967	Gamera vs. Gyaos	Noriaki Yuasa	Japan	Daiei Film
1967	Gappa: The Triphibian Monster	Haruyasu Noguchi	Japan	Nikkatsu
1967	The Gruesome Twosome	Herschell Gordon Lewis	U.S.	Mayflower
1967	Hillbillys in a Haunted House	Jean Yarbrough	U.S.	Woolner Brothers

Year Film Produced	Title	Director	Country of Origin	Studio
1967	Maneater of Hydra	Mel Welles	Spain	Orbita Film
1967	Something Weird	Herschell Gordon Lewis	U.S.	Mayflower
1967	The Sorcerers	Michael Reeves	U.K.	Tony Tenser Films
1967	Succubus	Jesús Franco	Spain	American International
1967	This Night I'll Possess Your Corpse	José Mojica Marins	Brazil	Cinematográfica Calderón
1967	The Touch of Her Flesh	Michael Findlay	U.S.	Rivamarsh
1968	Terror in the Jungle	Andrew Janzack	U.S.	Torres International
1968	Frankenstein	Voytek	U.K.	Thames Television
1968	The Hand of Night	Fredric Goode	U.K.	Associated British Pathé
1968	Destroy All Planets	Noriaki Yuasa	Japan	Daiei Film
1968	Mission Stardust	Primo Zeglio	Germany	P.E.A. Cinematografica
1968	Blood Beast Terror	Vernon Sewell	U.K.	Tigon British
1968	Satanik	Piero Vivarelli	Italy	Copercines/ Rodiacines
1968	House of Evil	Juan Ibañez, Jack Hill	Italy	Azteca Films
1968	The Castle	Rudolf Noelte	Germany	Afa Film Corp
1968	The Strange Case of Dr. Jekyll and Mr. Hyde	Charles Jarrott	U.S.	CBC
1968	The Enigma of Death	Federico Curiel	Mexico	Filmica Vergara
1968	Fangs of the Living Dead	Amando de Ossorio	Spain	Cobra Films

Year Film Produced	Title	Director	Country of Origin	Studio
1968	The Fear Chamber	Juan Ibañez, Jack Hill	Mexico	Azteca Films
1968	The Ghastly Ones	Andy Milligan	U.S.	JER Pictures
1968	The Joy of Torture	Teruo Ishii	Japan	Toei Company
1968	Kuroneko	Kaneto Shindo	Japan	Toho
1968	The Living Skeleton	Hiroshi Matsuno	Japan	Shochiku
1968	The Mad Doctor of Blood Island	Eddie Romero	Philippines	Hemisphere
1968	The Mark of the Werewolf	Enrique López Eguiluz	Spain	Maxper
1968	Nights of the Werewolf	René Govar	Spain	Kin Films
1968	Snake Woman's Curse	Nobuo Nakagawa	Japan	Toei Company
1968	Snow Ghost	Tokuzo Tanaka	Japan	Daiei Film
1968	The Strange World of Coffin Joe	José Mojica Marins	Brazil	Iberia Filmes
1968	Trilogy of Terror	José Mojica Marins	Brazil	PNF
1969	The Monsters of Terror	Tulio Demicheli	Spain	Eichberg-Film
1969	It's Alive	Larry Buchanan	U.S.	American International
1969	Malenka, Niece of the Vampire	Armando de Ossorio	Italy	Cobra Films
1969	Latitude Zero	Ishirō Honda	Japan	Toho
1969	All Monsters Attack	Ishirō Honda	Japan	Toho
1969	Blind Beast	Yasuzo Masumura	Japan	Daiei Film

Year Film Produced	Title	Director	Country of Origin	Studio
1969	Blood of Dracula's Castle	Al Adamson	U.S.	A&E Film Corp.
1969	The Corpse	Viktors Ritelis	U.K.	Gabrielle Beaumont
1969	Gamera vs. Guiron	Noriaki Yuasa	Japan	Daei Film
1969	Hiroku Kaibyoden	Tokuzo Tanaka	Japan	Daei Film
1969	Horrors of Malformed Men	Teruo Ishii	Japan	Toei Company
1969	Inferno of Torture	Teruo Ishii	Japan	Toei Company
1969	Night of Bloody Horror	Joy N. Houck Jr.	U.S.	Cinema IV
1970	Yog, Monster from Space	Ishirō Honda	Japan	Toho
1970	Horror of the Blood Monsters	Al Adamson	U.S.	Independent-International
1970	Monster from Space	Ishirō Honda	Japan	Toho
1970	Gamera vs. Monster X	Noriaki Yuasa	Japan	Daei Film
1970	Taste the Blood of Dracula	Peter Sasdy	U.K.	Hammer Films[59]
1970	Bigfoot	Robert F. Slatzer	U.S.	Gemini-American Productions
1970	Assignment Terror	Tulio Demicheli	Spain	Eichberg-Film
1970	The Evils of Dorian Gray	Massimo Dallamano	Italy	Sargon Film
1970	Blind Woman's Curse	Teruo Ishii	Japan	Nikkatsu
1970	The Blood Rose	Claude Mulot	France	Transatlantic Productions
1970	The Bloody Judge	Jesús Franco	U.K.	Fénix Films

Year Film Produced	Title	Director	Country of Origin	Studio
1970	Count Dracula	Jesús Franco	Spain	Hemdale
1970	Flesh Feast	Brad F. Grinter	Canada	Viking International Pictures
1970	Incense for the Damned	Robert Hartford-Davis	U.K.	Lucinda Films
1970	Jonathan	Hans Geissendorfer	Germany	Iduna Film
1970	Monster Zero	Ishirō Honda	Japan	Toho
1970	Mumsy, Nanny, Sonny, and Girly	Freddie Francis	U.K.	Ronald J. Kahn Productions
1970	The Revenge of Dr. X	Norman Earl Thomson	U.S.	Toei Company
1970	The Wizard of Gore	Herschell Gordon Lewis	U.S.	Mayflower
1971	The Deadly Dream	Alf Kjelin	U.S.	Universal International
1971	The Night of The Damned	Filippo Walter	Italy	Primax
1971	The Touch of Satan	Bruce Kessler	U.S.	Futurama International
1971	Blood Thirst	Newton Arnold	Philippines	Journey Productions
1971	The House That Screamed	Narciso Ibáñez Serrador	Spain	American International
1971	Black Noon	Bernard L. Kowalski	U.S.	Andrew J. Fenady Productions
1971	Octaman	Harry Essex	U.S.	Filmers Guild
1971	Blood and Lace	Philip S. Gilbert	U.S.	American International
1971	She Killed in Ecstasy	Jesús Franco	Spain	Telecine Film
1971	And the World Was Made Flesh	Dusan Marek	Australia	Dusan Marek

Year Film Produced	Title	Director	Country of Origin	Studio
1971	Burke and Hare	Vernon Sewell	U.K.	Armitage Films
1971	The Butcher of Binbrook	Miguel Madrid	Spain	Films Internacionales (FISA)
1971	The Cat o' Nine Tales	Dario Argento	Italy	Mondial Te.Fi.
1971	The Curse of The Vampyr	José Maria Elorietta	Spain	Seseña Films
1971	The Devil's Nightmare	Jean Brismée	Belgium	Cetelci S.A.
1971	The Devil's Widow	Roddy McDowall	U.K.	Commonwealth United Entertainment
1971	The Headless Eyes	Kent Bateman	U.S.	Laviniaque Films
1971	The Mad Butcher	Guido Zurli	Italy	Hi Fi Stereo
1971	The Night God Screamed	Lee Madden	U.S.	Cinemation Industries
1971	Night Hair Child	James Kelley	U.K.	Cemo Films
1971	Queens of Evil	Tonino Cervi	Italy	Carlton Film Export
1971	The Sadist with Red Teeth	Jean-Louis van Belle	France	Cinévision
1971	Scream of the Demon Lover	José Luis Merino	Italy	Hispamer Films
1971	Seven Murders for Scotland Yard	José Luis Madrid	Italy	Hispamer Films
1971	The Shiver of The Vampires	Jean Rollin	France	Les Films
1971	Short Night of Glass Dolls	Aldo Lado	Italy	Dieter Geissler Filmproduktion
1971	They Have Changed Their Face	Corrado Farina	Italy	Filmsettanta S.r.l
1971	Twitch of the Death Nerve	Mario Bava	Italy	Nuova Linea Cinematografica

Year Film Produced	Title	Director	Country of Origin	Studio
1971	Vampyros Lesbos	Jesús Franco	Spain	Fénix Films
1971	Venom	Peter Sykes	U.S.	Action Plus Productions
1971	Web of the Spider	Antonio Margheriti	Italy	Produzione D.C.7
1972	Eulogy for a Vampire	Don McDougall	U.S.	William Castle Productions
1972	The Dead We Leave Behind	Paul Stanley	U.S.	William Castle Productions
1972	The Concrete Captain	Richard Donner	U.S.	William Castle Productions
1972	Legend of Horror	Bill Davis	U.S.	General Film Corporation
1972	Beware! The Blob	Larry Hagman	U.S.	Jack H. Harris Enterprises
1972	Godzilla vs. the Smog Monster	Yoshimitsu Banno	Japan	Toho
1972	Demons of the Mind	Peter Sykes	U.K.	Hammer Films
1972	Blood Freak	Steve Hawkes, Brad F. Grinter	U.S.	Sampson Motion Picture Production Company
1972	Daigoro vs Goliath	Toshihiro Iijima	Japan	Toho
1972	Death Line	Gary Sherman	U.K.	American International
1972	The Fiend	Robert Hartford-Davis	U.K.	World Arts Media
1972	Nothing But the Night	Peter Sasdy	U.K.	Charlemagne Productions
1973	Death's Head	James Neilson	U.S.	William Castle Productions
1973	Dark Vengeance	Herschel Daugherty	U.S.	William Castle Productions
1973	Doorway to Death	Daryl Duke	U.S.	William Castle Productions

Year Film Produced	Title	Director	Country of Origin	Studio
1973	Phantom of Herald Square	James H. Brown	U.S.	William Castle Productions
1973	Spare Parts	Charles Dubin	U.S.	William Castle Productions
1973	The Ghost of Potter's Field	Don McDougall	U.S.	William Castle Productions
1973	Clones	Lamar Card	U.S.	Filmmakers International
1973	And Now the Screaming Starts!	Roy Ward Baker	U.K.	Amicus Productions

Pictures Unsuitable for Exhibition to Native Races, 1931–1950

The following films were "unsuitable for exhibition before Aboriginal and Native Races" by the Chief Censor. This unique form of censorship existed in the Northern Territory, with a focus on the few cinemas in Darwin. Films were banned under the guise of containing stories or scenes "likely to influence the Aboriginal towards conflict with the white race."

This did not mean that the film was banned from general release, only that Aboriginal and other non-whites were prohibited from viewing it. Fines and penalties were in effect for any exhibitor or manager who breached these rules.

Darwin was twice bombed by the Japanese on February 19, 1942, in what was the largest single attack ever mounted by an enemy in Australia. Two hundred forty-two planes dropped more bombs on the harbor and Darwin itself than Pearl Harbor, resulting in an estimated 292 people dead, scores wounded, and the city effectively eliminated. After the attacks, the town was evacuated and, with the resulting war and the follow-up attacks, cinemas were closed for the duration. Film only entered Darwin, on a regular basis, after infrastructure had been rebuilt post-war, at which time the Chief Protector had all but ceased banning films from exhibition.

Although the practice continued, officially, until 1950, it was effectively discontinued once the first bomb hit in February 1942.

Films that were deemed unsuitable are as follows, with the year the decision was made.

Year Released	Title	Director	Country of Origin	Studio
1931	Danger Island	Ray Taylor	U.S.	Universal
1931	Dr. Jekyll and Mr. Hyde	Rouben Mamoulian	U.S.	Paramount

Year Released	Title	Director	Country of Origin	Studio
1931	Frankenstein	James Whale	U.S.	Universal
1932	Afraid to Talk	Edward L. Chan	U.S.	Universal
1932	Back Street	John M. Stahl	U.S.	Universal
1932	Freaks	Tod Browning	U.S.	MGM
1932	Kongo	William J. Cowen	U.S.	MGM
1932	Murders in the Rue Morgue	Robert Florey	U.S.	Universal
1932	Night World	Hobart Henley	U.S.	Universal
1932	The Mummy	Karl Freund	U.S.	Universal
1932	The Old Dark House	James Whale	U.S.	Universal
1932	White Zombie	Victor Halperin	U.S.	United Artists
1933	Destination Unknown	Tay Garnett	U.S.	Universal
1933	The Greeks Had a Word for Them	Lowell Sherman	U.S.	United Artists
1933	The Kiss Before the Mirror	James Whale	U.S.	Universal
1933	Ladies Must Love	E.A. Dupont	U.S.	Universal
1933	The Lost Patrol	John Ford	U.S.	RKO
1933	Runt Page	Ray Nazarro	U.S.	Universal
1933	Island of Lost Souls	Erle C. Kenton	U.S.	Paramount
1932	The Unshod Maiden	Albert DeMond	U.S.	Universal
1934	Green Hell	Randall Faye	U.S.	Universal

Year Released	Title	Director	Country of Origin	Studio
1935	Bride of Frankenstein	James Whale	U.S.	Universal
1935	King Solomon of Broadway	Alan Crosland	U.S.	Universal
1935	Remember Last Night?	James Whale	U.S.	Universal
1934	Shock	Roy Pomeroy	U.S.	Monogram
1936	Parole	Lew Landers	U.S.	Universal
1936	The Invisible Ray	Lambert Hillyer	U.S.	Universal
1938	Air Devils	John Rawlins	U.S.	Universal
1939	Mutiny on the Blackhawk	Christy Cabanne	U.S.	Universal
1940	South to Karanga	Harold Schuster	U.S.	Universal
1941	Invisible Ghost	Joseph H. Lewis	U.S.	Monogram
1941	The Mad Doctor of Market Street	Joseph H. Lewis	U.S.	Universal

Films Shown on Television, 1957–2014

This list gives the first run of all 1923-73 horror and science fiction movies seen on Australian television between 1957 to 2014 and what city it debuted in.

In some cases, the titles that were used for television screenings in Australia were not the same as the cinematic release. An example of this is *Dr. Terror's House of Horror*, which was shown on television in Australia under the title *Voodoo Horror*. One reason for the use of alternate titles was to get around any issues with a film being banned at the time of screening.

When faced with an alternate title for a film, I have used the actual title that appears in the contemporaneous listings from TV Guides, newspapers and advertisements.

Notes: Films in BOLD text were *not* given a full cinema release in Australia (or none at all), prior to the film being shown on television.

Films in *italics* were shown on television while being officially banned from cinematic release at the time. In almost all cases, these bans were lifted *after* the film had been seen on TV.

City	TV Package	
ADL: Adelaide MEL: Melbourne SYD: Sydney BRI: Brisbane CAN: Canberra	AT: Adult Theatre BC: Bill Collins Golden Years of Hollywood CF: Creature Feature DE: Awful Movies with Deadly Earnest Frightful Movies with… Deadly Earnest	FM: Frightful Movies with Professor McCarb GS: Ghost Story MI: Mystery and Imagination NO: Nightmare Owl Theatre SFT: Science Fiction Thriller/Theatre SM: Shock Movie TT: Theatre of Thrills

Television Air Date (YYYY-MM)	Year Produced	Title	Director	Original Studio/Producer	Country of Origin	City	Channel	TV Package
1957–03	1948	**The Monkey's Paw**	Norman Lee	Butcher's Empire Films	U.K.	MEL	ABV-2	
1957–12	1945	The Woman Who Came Back	Walter Colmes	Republic	U.S.	MEL	HSV-7	
1958–04	1945	The Phantom Speaks	John English	Republic	U.S.	SYD	TCN-9	
1958–05	1944	The Girl Who Dared	Howard Bretherton	Republic	U.S.	SYD	TCN-9	
1958–08	1939	The Return of Doctor X	Vincent Sherman	Warner Brothers	U.S.	SYD	TCN-9	
1959–05	1939	The Hunchback of Notre Dame	William Dieterle	RKO	U.S.	MEL	ABV-2	
1959–06	1946	Bedlam	Mark Robson	RKO	U.S.	MEL	HSV-7	
1959–11	1946	**The Catman of Paris**	Lesley Selander	Republic	U.S.	SYD	TCN-9	
1961–01	1923	The Hunchback of Notre Dame	Wallace Worsley	Universal	U.S.	SYD	ABV-2	
1961–11	1942	The Night Has Eyes	Leslie Arliss	Pathé Pictures	U.K.	MEL	ABV-2	
1962–01	1951	**Lost Planet Airmen**	Fred C. Brannon	Republic	U.S.	SYD	ATN-7	CF
1962–01	1940	Dr. Cyclops	Ernest B. Schoedsack	Paramount	U.S.	ADL	NWS-9	MT
1962–01	1953	Invaders from Mars	William Cameron Menzies	20th Century-Fox	U.S.	ADL	ADS-7	
1962–01	1954	Tobor the Great	Lee Sholem	Dudley Pictures	U.S.	MEL	GTV-9	

Filmography, 1897–1973

Television Air Date (YYYY-MM)	Year Produced	Title	Director	Original Studio/Producer	Country of Origin	City	Channel	TV Package
1962–04	1945	The Picture of Dorian Gray	Albert Lewin	MGM	U.S.	MEL	HSV-7	
1962–10	1939	The Man They Could Not Hang	Nick Grinde	Columbia	U.S.	MEL	HSV-7	AT
1962–10	1946	The Devil's Mask	Henry Levin	Columbia	U.S.	MEL	HSV-7	AT
1962–10	1948	**The Amazing Mr. X**	Bernard Vorhaus	Eagle Lion	U.S.	MEL	HSV-7	AT
1962–11	1940	The Man with Nine Lives	Nick Grinde	Columbia	U.S.	MEL	HSV-7	AT
1962–11	1941	The Face Behind the Mask	Robert Florey	Columbia	U.S.	MEL	HSV-7	AT
1962–12	1949	The Dark Past	Rudolph Maté	Columbia	U.S.	MEL	HSV-7	AT
1963–01	1944	The Lady and the Monster	George Sherman	Republic	U.S.	MEL	HSV-7	AT
1963–04	1953	The Beast from 20,000 Fathoms	Eugene Lourie	Warner Brothers	U.S.	MEL	HSV-7	AT
1963–04	1947	**Scared to Death**	Christy Cabanne	Golden Gate Pictures	U.S.	MEL	HSV-7	AT
1963–04	1951	The Stolen Face	Terence Fisher	Hammer Films	U.K.	SYD	TCN-9	
1963–05	1936	The Devil-Doll	Tod Browning	MGM	U.S.	MEL	HSV-7	AT
1963–06	1957	**Enemy from Space**	Val Guest	Hammer Films	U.K.	SYD	ATN-7	SFT
1963–07	1935	The Black Room	Roy William Neill	Columbia	U.S.	MEL	HSV-7	AT
1963–07	1953	House of Wax	Andre DeToth	Warner Brothers	U.S.	MEL	HSV-7	AT

Television Air Date (YYYY-MM)	Year Produced	Title	Director	Original Studio/Producer	Country of Origin	City	Channel	TV Package
1963-09	1941	Dr. Jekyll and Mr. Hyde	Victor Fleming	MGM	U.S.	SYD	ATN-7	
1963-11	1957	The Abominable Snowman	Val Guest	Hammer Films	U.K.	SYD	TCN-9	
1963-11	1954	Phantom of the Rue Morgue	Roy Del Ruth	Warner Brothers	U.S.	MEL	HSV-7	AT
1964-03	1957	The Monster That Challenged the World	Arnold Laven	Gramercy Pictures	U.S.	ADL	NWS-9	SFT
1964-04	1946	**Spook Busters**	William Beaudine	Monogram	U.S.	SYD	TCN-9	
1964-04	1958	The Flame Barrier	Paul Landres	Gramercy Pictures	U.S.	ADL	NWS-9	SFT
1964-05	1943	The Mysterious Doctor	Ben Stoloff	Warner Brothers	U.S.	MEL	HSV-7	
1964-08	1943	Phantom of the Opera	Arthur Lubin	Universal	U.S.	MEL	HSV-7	
1964-08	1936	Things to Come	William Cameron Menzies	London Film Productions	U.S.	ADL	ADS-7	SFT
1964-08	1959	First Man into Space	Robert Day	Amalgamated Productions	U.K.	ADL	ADS-7	SFT
1964-08	1958	The Spaniard's Curse	Ralph Kemplen	Independent Film Distributors	U.K.	SYD	ATN-7	
1964-08	1957	The Mysterians	Ishirō Honda	Toho	Japan	ADL	ADS-7	SFT
1964-09	1953	The Magnetic Monster	Curt Siodmak	United Artists	U.S.	ADL	ADS-7	SFT
1964-09	1936	The Invisible Ray	Lambert Hillyer	Universal	U.S.	SYD	ATN-7	TT
1964-09	1935	Mad Love	Karl Freund	MGM	U.S.	MEL	HSV-7	AT

Television Air Date (YYYY-MM)	Year Produced	Title	Director	Original Studio/ Producer	Country of Origin	City	Channel	TV Package
1964–09	1942	The Captive	Edward Dmytryk	Universal	U.S.	SYD	ATN-7	TT
1964–10	1955	This Island Earth	Joseph Newman	Universal International	U.S.	SYD	ATN-7	TT
1964–10	1955	Tarantula	Jack Arnold	Universal International	U.S.	ADL	ADS-7	SFT
1964–10	1954	It Came from Outer Space	Jack Arnold	Universal International	U.S.	SYD	ATN-7	TT
1964–10	1944	The Man in Half Moon Street	Ralph Murphy	Paramount	U.S.	SYD	ATN-7	TT
1964–11	1942	Fingers at the Window	Charles Lederer	MGM	U.S.	SYD	ATN-7	TT
1964–11	1940	Black Friday	Arthur Lubin	Universal	U.S.	ADL	ADS-7	SFT
1964–11	1953	City Beneath the Sea	Budd Boetticher	Universal International	U.S.	SYD	ATN-7	TT
1964–12	1954	Them!	Gordon Douglas	Warner Brothers	U.S.	ADL	ADS-7	
1964–12	1948	Abbott and Costello Meet Frankenstein	Charles T. Barton	Universal International	U.S.	MEL	HSV-7	AT
1965–01	1944	Dead Man's Eyes	Reginald LeBorg	Universal	U.S.	MEL	HSV-7	AT
1965–03	1945	The Frozen Ghost	Harold Young	Universal	U.S.	MEL	HSV-7	AT
1965–04	1958	Screaming Mimi	Gerd Oswald	Sage Productions	U.S.	SYD	TEN-10	
1965–05	1951	Old Mother Riley Meets the Vampire	John Gilling	Fernwood Productions	U.K.	MEL	GTV-9	
1965–06	1944	Ghost Catchers	Edward F. Cline	Universal	U.S.	SYD	ATN-7	

Television Air Date (YYYY-MM)	Year Produced	Title	Director	Original Studio/Producer	Country of Origin	City	Channel	TV Package
1965-06	1944	Cobra Woman	Robert Siodmak	Universal	U.S.	MEL	HSV-7	
1965-07	1957	Zombies of Mora Tau	Edward L Cahn	Columbia	U.S.	SYD	TEN-10	SM
1965-07	1947	Uncle Silas	Charles Frank	Two Cities Films	U.K.	SYD	ABN-2	CF
1965-07	1932	The Mummy	Karl Freund	Universal	U.S.	SYD	ATN-7	TT
1965-07	1946	The Cat Creeps	Erle C. Kenton	Universal	U.S.	SYD	ATN-7	TT
1965-07	1934	The Black Cat	Edgar G. Ulmer	Universal	U.S.	SYD	ATN-7	TT
1965-08	1932	Murders in the Rue Morgue	Robert Florey	Universal	U.S.	SYD	ATN-7	TT
1965-08	1959	The Tingler	William Castle	Columbia	U.S.	SYD	TEN-10	SM
1965-08	1943	**Calling Dr. Death**	Reginald LeBorg	Universal	U.S.	SYD	ATN-7	TT
1965-08	1958	Space Master X-7	Edward Bernds	Regal Pictures	U.S.	SYD	TEN-10	SM
1965-08	1952	**Crow Hollow**	Michael McCarthy	Eros Films	U.K.	SYD	ATV-0	
1965-08	1960	Battle in Outer Space	Ishirō Honda	Toho	U.S.	SYD	TEN-10	SM
1965-09	1943	Revenge of the Zombies	Steve Sekely	Monogram	U.S.	SYD	TEN-10	SM
1965-09	1958	**The Strange World of Planet X**	Gilbert Gunn	Eros Films	U.K.	SYD	TEN-10	SM
1965-09	1958	The Space Children	Jack Arnold	Paramount	U.S.	SYD	TEN-10	SM

Filmography, 1897–1973 247

Television Air Date (YYYY-MM)	Year Produced	Title	Director	Original Studio/Producer	Country of Origin	City	Channel	TV Package
1965–10	1939	Tower of London	Rowland V Lee	Universal	U.S.	MEL	HSV-7	
1965–11	1961	Homicidal	William Castle	Columbia	U.S.	MEL	ABV-2	
1965–12	1949	Murder at the Windmill	Val Guest	Monogram	U.S.	SYD	ABN-2	
1965–12	1963	The Old Dark House	William Castle	Hammer Films	U.S.	SYD	ABN-2	
1966–01	1957	The Incredible Shrinking Man	Jack Arnold	Universal International	U.S.	MEL	GTV-9	SFT
1966–01	1957	The Deadly Mantis	Nathan Juran	Universal International	U.S.	MEL	GTV-9	SFT
1966–03	1953	**Port Sinister**	Harold Daniels	RKO	U.S.	SYD	TEN-10	
1966–04	1939	The Cat and The Canary	Elliott Nugent	Paramount	U.S.	MEL	GTV-9	
1966–05	1959	**The Cosmic Man**	Herbert Greene	Futura Productions	U.S.	MEL	GTV-9	
1966–07	1962	**Varan the Unbelievable**	Ishirō Honda	Toho	Japan/U.S.	SYD	TEN-10	DE
1966–07	1959	The Man Who Could Cheat Death	Terence Fisher	Hammer Films	U.K.	SYD	TEN-10	DE
1966–08	1955	Conquest of Space	Byron Haskin	Paramount	U.S.	SYD	TEN-10	DE
1966–08	1959	Behemoth the Sea Monster	Eugene Lourie	Allied Artists	U.S.	SYD	TEN-10	DE
1966–08	1960	Macumba Love	Douglas Fowley	United Artists	U.S.	SYD	TEN-10	DE
1966–08	1957	The Giant Claw	Fred F. Sears	Columbia	U.S.	SYD	TEN-10	DE

Television Air Date (YYYY-MM)	Year Produced	Title	Director	Original Studio/Producer	Country of Origin	City	Channel	TV Package
1966-09	1956	Satellite in the Sky	Paul Dickson	New Elstree	U.K.	SYD	TEN-10	DE
1966-09	1951	The Thing from Another World	Christian Nyby	RKO	U.S.	SYD	TEN-10	DE
1966-09	1960	The Stranglers of Bombay	Terence Fisher	Hammer Films	U.K.	SYD	TEN-10	DE
1966-10	1962	Carnival of Souls	Herk Harvey	Harcourt Productions	U.S.	SYD	TEN-10	DE
1966-10	1957	The Vampire	Paul Landres	United Artists	U.S.	SYD	TEN-10	DE
1966-10	1940	The Ape	William Nigh	Monogram	U.S.	SYD	TEN-10	DE
1966-11	1958	**Attack of the Puppet People**	Bert I. Gordon	American International	U.S.	SYD	TEN-10	DE
1966-11	1953	The War of The Worlds	George Pal	Paramount	U.S.	SYD	TEN-10	DE
1966-11	1955	**The Beast with a Million Eyes**	David Kramarsky	American International	U.S.	SYD	TEN-10	DE
1966-11	1956	Invasion of the Body Snatchers	Don Siegel	Allied Artists	U.S.	ADL	NWS-9	
1966-12	1957	The 27th Day	William Asher	Columbia	U.S.	SYD	TEN-10	DE
1966-12	1959	Gigantis, the Fire Monster	Motoyoshi Oda	Toho	Japan	SYD	TEN-10	DE
1967-01	1961	**The Snake Woman**	Sidney J. Furie	Caralan Productions	U.K.	SYD	TEN-10	DE
1967-01	1958	The Lost Missile	Lester William Berke	United Artists	U.S.	SYD	TEN-10	DE
1967-01	1946	She-Wolf of London	Jean Yarbrough	Universal	U.S.	MEL	HSV-7	

Filmography, 1897–1973

Television Air Date (YYYY-MM)	Year Produced	Title	Director	Original Studio/Producer	Country of Origin	City	Channel	TV Package
1967–01	1956	The Creature Walks Among Us	John Sherwood	Universal International	U.S.	MEL	HSV-7	
1967–01	1948	Corridors of Mirrors	Terence Young	Apollo	U.S.	SYD	TEN-10	DE
1967–02	1956	**Warning from Space**	Koji Shima	Daiei Film	Japan	SYD	TEN-10	DE
1967–02	1936	The Walking Dead	Michael Curtiz	Warner Brothers	U.S.	MEL	HSV-7	
1967–02	1960	13 Ghosts	William Castle	Columbia	U.S.	SYD	TEN-10	DE
1967–02	1960	**First Spaceship on Venus**	Kurt Maetzig	Roter Kreis	Germany	SYD	TEN-10	DE
1967–02	1962	Most Dangerous Man Alive	Allan Dwan	Columbia	U.S.	SYD	TEN-10	DE
1967–02	1942	The Mad Doctor of Market Street	Joseph H. Lewis	Universal	U.S.	MEL	HSV-7	
1967–03	1951	When Worlds Collide	Rudolph Maté	Paramount	U.S.	SYD	TEN-10	DE
1967–03	1958	I Married a Monster from Outer Space	Gene Fowler Jr.	Paramount	U.S.	SYD	TEN-10	DE
1967–03	1960	**The Angry Red Planet**	Ib Melchior	American International	U.S.	MEL	HSV-7	NOT
1967–03	1957	Kronos	Kurt Neumann	Regal Pictures	U.S.	SYD	TEN-10	DE
1967–03	1956	The Mole People	Virgil W. Vogel	Universal International	U.S.	MEL	HSV-7	NOT
1967–03	1945	The Strange Mr. Gregory	Phil Rosen	Monogram	U.S.	SYD	TEN-10	DE
1967–04	1942	**The Man with Two Lives**	Phil Rosen	A.W. Hackel Productions	U.S.	SYD	TEN-10	DE

Television Air Date (YYYY-MM)	Year Produced	Title	Director	Original Studio/Producer	Country of Origin	City	Channel	TV Package
1967–04	1954	Devil Girl from Mars	David MacDonald	Danziger Productions	U.S.	MEL	HSV-7	NOT
1967–04	1957	The Land Unknown	Virgil W. Vogel	Universal International	U.S.	MEL	GTV-9	
1967–04	1943	The Seventh Victim	Mark Robson	RKO	U.S.	SYD	TEN-10	DE
1967–04	1941	King of the Zombies	Jean Yarbrough	Monogram	U.S.	SYD	TEN-10	DE
1967–04	1961	Voyage to the Bottom of the Sea	Irwin Allen	20th Century–Fox	U.S.	SYD	TEN-10	DE
1967–04	1955	Cult of the Cobra	Francis D Lyon	Universal International	U.S.	MEL	HSV-7	
1967–04	1959	**The Man Who Liked Funerals**	David Eady	Pennington Eady	U.K.	SYD	TEN-10	DE
1967–05	1961	Blood and Roses	Roger Vadim	Films EGE	U.K.	SYD	TEN-10	DE
1967–05	1964	**Mark of the Tortoise**	Alfred Vohrer	Rialto Film	Germany	MEL	ATV-0	DE
1967–05	1936	The Man Who Could Work Miracles	Lothar Mendes	United Artists	U.S.	SYD	TEN-10	DE
1967–05	1952	The Voice of Merrill	John Gilling	Tempean Films	U.K.	BRI	TVQ-10	DE
1967–05	1958	Curse of the Faceless Man	Edward L. Cahn	United Artists	U.S.	SYD	TEN-10	DE
1967–05	1956	Fire Maidens from Outer Space	Cy Roth	Criterion Films	U.K.	BRI	TVQ-10	DE
1967–05	1953	The Black Castle	Nathan Juran	Universal International	U.S.	MEL	HSV-7	
1967–05	1962	**Hands of a Stranger**	Newton Arnold	Allied Artists	U.S.	MEL	GTV-9	NOT

Television Air Date (YYYY-MM)	Year Produced	Title	Director	Original Studio/ Producer	Country of Origin	City	Channel	TV Package
1967–05	1958	It! The Terror from Beyond Space	Edward L. Cahn	United Artists	U.S.	SYD	TEN-10	DE
1967–06	1955	Abbott and Costello Meet the Mummy	Charles Lamont	Universal International	U.S.	MEL	HSV-7	
1967–07	1959	Jack the Ripper	Robert S Baker	Midcentury	U.K.	BRI	TVQ-10	DE
1967–07	1959	**The Headless Ghost**	Peter Graham Scott	Anglo-Amalgamated Films	U.K.	BRI	TVQ-10	DE
1967–07	1944	Weird Woman	Reginald LeBorg	Universal	U.S.	MEL	HSV-7	
1967–08	1965	**Day of the Nightmare**	John A. Bushelman	Screen Group	U.S.	SYD	TEN-10	DE
1967–08	1958	The Mugger	William Berke	Barbizon Productions Inc	U.S.	BRI	TVQ-10	DE
1967–08	1959	The Four Skulls of Jonathan Drake	Edward L. Cahn	United Artists	U.S.	SYD	TEN-10	DE
1967–08	1953	The Limping Man	Cy Endfield	Eros Films	U.K.	BRI	TVQ-10	DE
1967–08	1957	**The Cyclops**	Bert I. Gordon	Allied Artists	U.S.	SYD	TEN-10	DE
1967–08	1953	Abbott and Costello Meet Dr. Jekyll and Mr. Hyde	Charles Lamont	Universal International	U.S.	ADL	ADS-7	
1967–09	1959	Invisible Invaders	Edward L. Cahn	United Artists	U.S.	SYD	TEN-10	DE
1967–09	1957	Curse of the Demon	Jacques Tourneur	Columbia	U.S.	SYD	TEN-10	DE
1967–09	1958	The Long Knife	Montgomery Tully	Merton Park Studios	U.K.	BRI	TVQ-10	DE

Television Air Date (YYYY-MM)	Year Produced	Title	Director	Original Studio/ Producer	Country of Origin	City	Channel	TV Package
1967–10	1959	Killers of Kilimanjaro	Richard Thorpe	Columbia	U.S.	MEL	ATV-0	DE
1967–10	1963	**The Crawling Hand**	Herbert L. Strock	Donald J. Hansen Enterprises	U.S.	SYD	TEN-10	DE
1967–10	1961	Mothra	Ishirō Honda	Toho	Japan	BRI	TVQ-10	DE
1967–10	1961	Doctor Blood's Coffin	Sidney J. Furie	Caralan Productions	U.K.	BRI	TVQ-10	DE
1967–10	1942	The Living Ghost	William Beaudine	Monogram	U.S.	BRI	TVQ-10	DE
1967–10	1964	**The Ghost of Sierra De Cobra**	Joseph Stefano	United Artists	U.S.	SYD	TEN-10	DE
1967–10	1957	Man on the Prowl	Art Napoleon	United Artists	U.S.	BRI	TVQ-10	DE
1967–11	1963	**The Slime People**	Robert Hutton	Donald J. Hansen Enterprises	U.S.	SYD	TEN-10	DE
1967–11	1958	Machete	Kurt Neumann	United Artists	U.S.	BRI	TVQ-10	DE
1967–11	1954	Gog	Herbert L. Strock	United Artists	U.S.	SYD	TEN-10	DE
1967–11	1958	Woman of Mystery	Ernest Morris	Danziger Productions	U.K.	BRI	TVQ-10	DE
1967–11	1961	So Evil, So Young	Godfrey Grayson	Danziger Productions	U.K.	BRI	TVQ-10	DE
1967–12	1946	**Fear**	Alfred Zeiser	Monogram	U.S.	BRI	TVQ-10	DE
1967–12	1961	The Flight That Disappeared	Reginald LeBorg	Harvard Film Corp	U.K.	BRI	TVQ-10	DE
1967–12	1934	**Lost in the Stratosphere**	Melville W. Brown	Monogram	U.S.	MEL	ATV-0	DE

Filmography, 1897–1973

Television Air Date (YYYY-MM)	Year Produced	Title	Director	Original Studio/Producer	Country of Origin	City	Channel	TV Package
1968–01	1960	Three Came to Kill	Edward L. Cahn	United Artists	U.S.	BRI	TVQ-10	DE
1968–01	1954	Creature from the Black Lagoon	Jack Arnold	Universal International	U.S.	ADL	ADS-7	
1968–01	1953	**Nine Steps to the Gallows**	John Gilling	Eros Films	U.K.	BRI	TVQ-10	DE
1968–01	1934	*The Ghost Walks*	Frank R Strayer	Invincible Pictures Corp	U.S.	MEL	ATV-0	DE
1968–01	1942	The Man Who Returned to Life	Lew Landers	Columbia	U.S.	ADL	SAS-10	DE
1968–01	1941	Nine Lives Are Not Enough	A. Edward Sutherland	Warner Brothers	U.S.	BRI	TVQ-10	DE
1968–02	1958	**Teenage Cave Man**	Roger Corman	American International	U.S.	SYD	TEN-10	DE
1968–02	1954	Radio Cab Murder	Vernon Sewell	Eros Films	U.K.	BRI	TVQ-10	DE
1968–02	1964	The Gorgon	Terence Fisher	Hammer Films	U.K.	SYD	TEN-10	DE
1968–02	1954	The Scarlet Web	Charles Saunders	Fortress Film Productions	U.K.	BRI	TVQ-10	DE
1968–02	1957	20 Million Miles to Earth	Nathan Juran	Morningside Productions	U.S.	MEL	ATV-0	DE
1968–02	1962	**Invasion of the Star Creatures**	Bruno Ve Sota	American International	U.S.	SYD	ATN-7	CF
1968–02	1960	Psycho	Alfred Hitchcock	Paramount	U.K.	BRI	TVQ-10	FM
1968–02	1962	The Magic Sword	Bert I. Gordon	United Artists	U.S.	SYD	TEN-10	DE
1968–03	1959	The 30 Foot Bride of Candy Rock	Sidney Miller	Columbia	U.S.	SYD	TEN-10	DE

Television Air Date (YYYY-MM)	Year Produced	Title	Director	Original Studio/Producer	Country of Origin	City	Channel	TV Package
1968–03	1959	The Hound of the Baskervilles	Terence Fisher	Hammer Films	U.K.	SYD	TEN-10	DE
1968–03	1960	**The Pusher**	Gene Milford	United Artists	U.K.	BRI	TVQ-10	FM
1968–03	1957	Voodoo Island	Reginald LeBorg	Bel-Air	U.S.	MEL	ATV-0	DE
1968–03	1960	**Beyond the Time Barrier**	Edgar G. Ulmer	American International	U.S.	SYD	ATN-7	CF
1968–03	1966	**Retik the Moon Menace**	Fred C. Brannon	Republic	U.S.	SYD	TEN-10	DE
1968–03	1952	Red Planet Mars	Harry Horner	Melaby Pictures	U.S.	MEL	ATV-0	DE
1968–03	1958	**The Day the Sky Exploded**	Paolo Heusch	Lux Film	Italy	SYD	ATN-7	CF
1968–03	1961	The Devil's Messenger	Herbert L. Strock	Herts-Lion International	U.S.	SYD	TEN-10	DE
1968–04	1961	**Invasion of the Neptune Men**	Koji Ota	Toei Company	Japan	SYD	ATN-7	CF
1968–04	1959	The Giant Gila Monster	Ray Kellogg	McLendon-Radio Pictures	U.S.	SYD	TEN-10	DE
1968–04	1952	**Ghost Ship**	Vernon Sewell	Vernon Sewell Productions	U.S.	BRI	TVQ-10	FM
1968–04	1964	**Atomic Rulers of the World**	Koreyoshi Akasaka	Shintoho Film Distribution Committee	Japan	MEL	HSV-7	
1968–04	1933	**The Son of Kong**	Ernest B. Schoedsack	RKO	U.S.	BRI	TVQ-10	FM
1968–04	1962	**The Invisible Dr. Mabuse**	Harald Reinl	Central Cinema Company Film	Germany	SYD	ATN-7	CF
1968–04	1953	The Maze	William Cameron Menzies	Allied Artists	U.S.	SYD	ATN-7	CF

Television Air Date (YYYY-MM)	Year Produced	Title	Director	Original Studio/ Producer	Country of Origin	City	Channel	TV Package
1968–05	1942	The Boogie Man Will Get You	Lew Landers	Columbia	U.S.	ADL	SAS-10	DE
1968–05	1955	Revenge of the Creature	Jack Arnold	Universal International	U.S.	SYD	ATN-7	CF
1968–05	1960	**Unstoppable Man**	Terry Bishop	Anglo-Amalgamated Films	U.K.	BRI	TVQ-10	FM
1968–05	1959	**Prince of Space**	Eijirō Waka-bayashi	Toei Company	Japan	SYD	ATN-7	CF
1968–05	1957	Lure of the Swamp	Herbert Cornfield	Regal Pictures	U.S.	ADL	SAS-10	DE
1968–05	1958	I Bury the Living	Albert Band	United Artists	U.S.	MEL	ATV-0	DE
1968–05	1961	Flight of the Lost Balloon	Nathan Juran	American International	U.S.	SYD	ATN-7	CF
1968–05	1944	The Mask of Dimitrios	Jean Negulesco	Warner Brothers	U.S.	BRI	TVQ-10	FM
1968–05	1964	**The Human Duplicators**	Hugo Grimaldi	Woolner Brothers	U.S.	SYD	ATN-7	CF
1968–06	1958	Monster on the Campus	Jack Arnold	Universal International	U.S.	SYD	TEN-10	DE
1968–06	1957	**Voodoo Woman**	Edward L. Cahn	American International	U.S.	BRI	TVQ-10	FM
1968–06	1954	The Mad Magician	John Brahm	Columbia	U.S.	SYD	TEN-10	DE
1968–06	1940	Doomed to Die	William Nigh	Monogram	U.S.	ADL	SAS-10	DE
1968–06	1956	Curucu, Beast of the Amazon	Curt Siodmak	Universal International	U.S.	SYD	TEN-10	DE
1968–06	1945	Pillow of Death	Wallace Fox	Universal	U.S.	MEL	HSV-7	

Television Air Date (YYYY-MM)	Year Produced	Title	Director	Original Studio/Producer	Country of Origin	City	Channel	TV Package
1968-06	1965	City Under the Sea	Jacques Tourneur	Anglo-Amalgamated Films	U.S.	MEL	HSV-7	
1968-06	1957	Pharaoh's Curse	Lee Sholem	Schenck-Koch Productions	U.S.	SYD	TEN-10	DE
1968-06	1962	**Sherlock Holmes and the Necklace of Death**	Terence Fisher	Criterion	U.K.	SYD	TEN-10	
1968-06	1964	**Attack from Outer Space**	Teruo Ishii	Shintoho Film Distribution Committee	Japan	SYD	ATN-7	CF
1968-06	1966	**Sharad of Atlantis**	B. Reeves Eason	Republic	U.S.	SYD	TEN-10	DE
1968-07	1962	**Planets Against Us**	Mike Williams	Walter Manley Enterprises	U.S.	SYD	ATN-7	CF
1968-07	1957	The Monolith Monsters	John Sherwood	Universal International	U.S.	SYD	TEN-10	DE
1968-07	1951	The Strange Door	Joseph Pevney	Universal International	U.S.	SYD	ATN-7	CF
1968-07	1960	12 to the Moon	David Bradley	Columbia	U.S.	MEL	ATV-0	DE
1968-08	1965	**Mutiny in Outer Space**	Hugo Grimaldi	Hugo Grimaldi Productions	U.S.	SYD	ATN-7	CF
1968-08	1957	The Invisible Boy	Herman Hoffman	MGM	U.S.	SYD	ATN-7	CF
1968-08	1945	The Brighton Strangler	Max Nosseck	RKO	U.S.	SYD	TEN-10	DE
1968-08	1945	**Zombies on Broadway**	Gordon Douglas	RKO	U.S.	SYD	TEN-10	DE
1968-08	1956	The Beast of Hollow Mountain	Edward Nassour	United Artists	U.S.	MEL	ATV-0	DE

Filmography, 1897–1973

Television Air Date (YYYY-MM)	Year Produced	Title	Director	Original Studio/ Producer	Country of Origin	City	Channel	TV Package
1968–08	1955	It Came from Beneath the Sea	Robert Gordon	Columbia	U.S.	SYD	TEN-10	DE
1968–08	1960	**Face of Terror**	Isidoro M. Ferry	Documento Films	Italy	SYD	TEN-10	DE
1968–09	1961	**Battle of the Worlds**	Antonio Margheriti	Ultra Film	Italy	SYD	ATN-7	CF
1968–09	1956	Earth vs. the Flying Saucers	Fred F. Sears	Columbia	U.S.	MEL	ATV-0	DE
1968–09	1964	**Evil Brain from Outer Space**	Koreyoshi Akasaka	Walter Manley Enterprises	U.S.	SYD	ATN-7	CF
1968–09	1960	The Leech Woman	Edward Dein	Universal International	U.S.	SYD	TEN-10	DE
1968–10	1962	**Death Rays of Dr. Mabuse**	Harald Reinl	Central Cinema Company Film	Germany	SYD	ATN-7	CF
1968–10	1945	The Body Snatcher	Robert Wise	RKO	U.S.	SYD	TEN-10	DE
1968–10	1951	Flight to Mars	Lesley Selander	Monogram	U.S.	MEL	ATV-0	DE
1968–10	1961	The Day the Earth Caught Fire	Val Guest	Val Guest Productions	U.K.	SYD	ATN-7	CF
1968–10	1967	Rocket to the Moon	Don Sharp	American International	U.S.	SYD	ATN-7	CF
1968–10	1960	The Hypnotic Eye	George Blair	Allied Artists	U.S.	SYD	TEN-10	DE
1968–11	1964	**Invaders from Space**	Teruo Ishii	Walter Manley Enterprises	U.S.	SYD	ATN-7	CF
1968–11	1966	D-Day on Mars	Spencer Gordon Bennet, Fred C. Brannon	Republic	U.S.	SYD	TEN-10	DE

Filmography, 1897–1973

Television Air Date (YYYY-MM)	Year Produced	Title	Director	Original Studio/Producer	Country of Origin	City	Channel	TV Package
1968-11	1961	**Journey Beneath the Desert**	Giuseppe Masini	Compagnia Cinematografica Mondiale	Italy	SYD	ATN-7	CF
1968-11	1959	**Missile to The Moon**	Richard E. Cunha	Layton Film Productions	U.S.	SYD	ATN-7	CF
1968-11	1945	Dead of Night	Alberto Cavalcanti	Ealing Studios	U.K.	SYD	TEN-10	DE
1968-11	1959	**Giant from the Unknown**	Richard E. Cunha	Astor Pictures	U.S.	SYD	TEN-10	DE
1968-11	1955	Moonfleet	Fritz Lang	MGM	U.S.	SYD	ATN-7	CF
1968-12	1931	The Mad Genius	Michael Curtiz	Warner Brothers	U.S.	ADL	SAS-10	
1969-02	1940	The Invisible Woman	A. Edward Sutherland	Universal	U.S.	SYD	ATN-7	CF
1969-02	1953	**Robot Monster**	Phil Tucker	Astor Pictures	U.S.	MEL	ATV-0	DE
1969-02	1942	Cat People	Jacques Tourneur	RKO	U.S.	SYD	TEN-10	DE
1969-02	1943	I Walked with a Zombie	Jacques Tourneur	RKO	U.S.	SYD	TEN-10	DE
1969-03	1944	The Curse of the Cat People	Robert Wise	RKO	U.S.	SYD	TEN-10	DE
1969-03	1964	**The Time Travelers**	Ib Melchior	American International	U.S.	SYD	TEN-10	DE
1969-03	1963	**Voyage to the End of the Universe**	Jindřich Polák	American International	U.S.	SYD	TEN-10	DE
1969-04	1963	**Invisible Terror**	Raphael Nussbaum	Aero Film	U.S.	SYD	TEN-10	DE
1969-04	1954	**Monster from the Ocean Floor**	Wyott Ordung	Palo Alto	Italy	MEL	ATV-0	DE

Filmography, 1897–1973

Television Air Date (YYYY-MM)	Year Produced	Title	Director	Original Studio/Producer	Country of Origin	City	Channel	TV Package
1969–04	1962	The Phantom Planet	William Marshall	Four Crown Productions	U.S.	SYD	ATN-7	CF
1969–04	1967	**Mars Needs Women**	Larry Buchanan	American International	U.S.	SYD	TEN-10	DE
1969–04	1965	**The Demon Planet**	Mario Bava	Italian International Film	Italy	SYD	TEN-10	DE
1969–04	1962	Journey to the Seventh Planet	Sid Pink	American International	U.S.	ADL	SAS-10	
1969–05	1948	Queen of Spades	Thorold Dickinson	Associated British Picture Corporation	U.K.	SYD	TEN-10	DE
1969–05	1943	The Leopard Man	Jacques Tourneur	RKO	U.S.	SYD	TEN-10	DE
1969–05	1953	**Project Moon Base**	Richard Talmadge	Galaxy Pictures	U.S.	MEL	ATV-0	DE
1969–05	1964	**Sounds of Horror**	José Antonio Nieves Conde	Columbia	Spain	SYD	ATN-7	CF
1969–05	1961	The Innocents	Jack Clayton	Achilles Film Productions	U.S.	MEL	GTV-9	MI
1969–05	1962	The Phantom of the Opera	Terence Fisher	Hammer Films	U.K.	SYD	TEN-10	
1969–05	1942	The Strange Case of Doctor Rx	William Nigh	Universal	U.S.	SYD	ATN-7	CF
1969–05	1963	**The Terror**	Roger Corman	American International	U.S.	MEL	GTV-9	MI
1969–06	1951	The Son of Dr. Jekyll	Seymour Friedman	Columbia	U.S.	SYD	TCN-9	
1969–06	1954	**Serpent Island**	Tom Gries	Z-A Productions	U.S.	MEL	ATV-0	DE
1969–06	1961	Reptilicus	Sidney Pink	American International	U.S.	SYD	TEN-10	DE

Television Air Date (YYYY-MM)	Year Produced	Title	Director	Original Studio/Producer	Country of Origin	City	Channel	TV Package
1969–06	1966	**But You Were Dead**	Gianni Vernuccio	Mercurfin Italiana	Italy	SYD	ATN-7	
1969–06	1957	The Night Runner	Abner Biberman	Universal International	U.S.	SYD	TEN-10	DE
1969–06	1966	**Kill, Baby, Kill**	Mario Bava	Europix	Italy	SYD	TEN-10	
1969–06	1958	**Teenage Monster**	Jacques R. Marquette	Marquette Productions	U.S.	ADL	SAS-10	DE
1969–06	1962	Panic in Year Zero!	Ray Milland	American International	U.S.	MEL	GTV-9	
1969–06	1942	I Married a Witch	Rene Clair	United Artists	U.S.	SYD	TEN-10	DE
1969–07	1960	**The Amazing Transparent Man**	Edgar G Ulmer	American International	U.S.	SYD	TEN-10	DE
1969–07	1964	**Space Monster**	Burt Topper	American International	U.S.	SYD	TEN-10	DE
1969–08	1961	Master of the World	William Witney	American International	U.S.	SYD	TEN-10	DE
1969–08	1966	**Slaves of the Invisible Monster**	Fred C Brannon	Republic	U.S.	SYD	TEN-10	DE
1969–08	1963	**Attack of the Mushroom People**	Ishirō Honda	Toho	Japan	SYD	ATN-7	CF
1969–08	1965	Invasion	Alan Bridges	Anglo-Amalgamated Films	U.K.	MEL	ATV-0	DE
1969–08	1967	**Son of Godzilla**	Jun Fukuda	Toho	Japan	SYD	ATN-7	CF
1969–09	1964	**Hercules Against the Moon Men**	Giacomo Gentilomo	Nike Cinematografica	Italy	SYD	ATN-7	CF
1969–09	1966	The Ghost in the Invisible Bikini	Don Weis	American International	U.S.	MEL	ATV-0	DE

Filmography, 1897–1973

Television Air Date (YYYY-MM)	Year Produced	Title	Director	Original Studio/ Producer	Country of Origin	City	Channel	TV Package
1969–09	1963	The Birds	Alfred Hitchcock	Universal	U.S.	MEL	TCN-9	
1969–09	1960	**Secret of the Telegian**	Jun Fukuda	Toho	Japan	SYD	ATN-7	CF
1969–10	1960	Dinosaurus!	Irvin Yeaworth	Fairview Productions	U.S.	SYD	ATN-7	CF
1969–10	1959	**Ghost of Dragstrip Hollow**	William J. Hole Jr.	Alta Vista Productions	U.S.	SYD	ABN-2	
1969–10	1958	The Blob	Irvin S. Yeaworth Jr.	Fairview Productions	U.S.	ADL	ADS-7	
1969–10	1960	The Hands of Orlac	Edmond T. Gréville	Britannia Films	U.K.	SYD	ATN-7	CF
1969–10	1963	**Atragon**	Ishirō Honda	Toho	Japan	MEL	GTV-9	NOT
1969–10	1940	Stranger on the Third Floor	Boris Ingster	RKO	U.S.	SYD	TEN-10	DE
1969–10	1959	**Attack of the Giant Leeches**	Bernard L. Kowalski	American International	U.S.	SYD	ATN-7	CF
1969–10	1952	The Ringer	Guy Hamilton	London Film Productions	U.K.	ADL	SAS-10	DE
1969–11	1966	**The Sound of Horror**	José Antonio Nieves Conde	Zurbano Films	Spain	MEL	HSV-7	CF
1969–11	1959	4D Man	Irvin Yeaworth	Fairview Productions	U.S.	ADL	ADS-7	
1969–11	1958	**Terror from the Year 5000**	Robert J. Gurney Jr.	American International	U.S.	SYD	ATN-7	CF
1969–12	1960	**Minotaur Wild Beast of Crete**	Silvio Amadio	Gino Mordini	U.S.	SYD	TEN-10	DE
1969–12	1962	**Eegah**	Arch Hall Sr	Fairway International Pictures	Italy	SYD	TEN-10	DE

Television Air Date (YYYY-MM)	Year Produced	Title	Director	Original Studio/ Producer	Country of Origin	City	Channel	TV Package
1970-01	1965	**Voodoo Horror**	Freddie Francis	Amicus Productions	U.S.	SYD	TEN-10	
1970-01	1966	**Captain Mephisto and the Transformation Machine**	Various	Republic	U.K.	SYD	TEN-10	DE
1970-01	1963	Night Tide	Curtis Harrigan	Virgo Productions	U.S.	SYD	TEN-10	DE
1970-01	1967	**Night of the Big Heat**	Terence Fisher	Planet Film Productions	U.S.	MEL	HSV-7	
1970-02	1967	**Island of Terror**	Terence Fisher	Planet Film Productions	U.K.	SYD	TEN-10	DE
1970-02	1967	**Creature of Destruction**	Larry Buchanan	American International	U.K.	MEL	HSV-7	
1970-02	1944	Dark Waters	Andre DeToth	United Artists	U.S.	SYD	TEN-10	DE
1970-03	1965	**The Night Caller**	John Gilling	Armatage Films	U.S.	SYD	TEN-10	DE
1970-03	1966	**Naked Evil**	Stanley Goulder	Gibraltar	U.K.	SYD	TEN-10	DE
1970-03	1958	The Fiend Who Walked the West	Gordon Douglas	20th Century-Fox	U.K.	SYD	TEN-10	DE
1970-04	1944	The Scarlet Claw	Roy William Neill	Universal	U.S.	ADL	SAS-10	DE
1970-04	1953	**The War of the Worlds**	Byron Haskin	Paramount	U.S.	ADL	ADS-7	
1970-04	1958	**How to Make a Monster**	Herbert L. Strock	American International	U.S.	MEL	HSV-7	CF
1970-05	1957	**The Amazing Colossal Man**	Bert I. Gordon	American International	U.S.	SYD	TEN-10	DE

Television Air Date (YYYY-MM)	Year Produced	Title	Director	Original Studio/Producer	Country of Origin	City	Channel	TV Package
1970–05	1956	The She-Creature	Edward L. Cahn	American International	U.S.	SYD	TEN-10	DE
1970–06	1957	The Undead	Roger Corman	American International	U.S.	SYD	TEN-10	DE
1970–06	1962	The Day Mars Invaded Earth	Maury Dexter	20th Century–Fox	U.S.	SYD	TEN-10	DE
1970–06	1965	**Monster from the Surf**	Jon Hall	U.S. Films	U.S.	MEL	GTV-9	
1970–07	1960	The Spider's Web	Godfrey Grayson	Danziger Productions	U.S.	SYD	TEN-10	DE
1970–07	1954	Gorilla at Large	Harmon Jones	Panoramic Productions	U.K.	MEL	HSV-7	
1970–07	1963	**Twice-Told Tales**	Sidney Salkow	United Artists	U.S.	MEL	HSV-7	CF
1970–07	1941	Horror Island	George Waggner	Universal	U.S.	MEL	GTV-9	
1970–08	1963	Diary of a Madman	Reginald LeBorg	Robert E. Kent Productions	U.S.	SYD	ATN-7	CF
1970–08	1965	**Die, Monster, Die!**	Daniel Haller	American International	U.S.	MEL	HSV-7	CF
1970–08	1967	**The Unknown Terror**	Charles Marquis Warren	Regal Pictures	U.S.	SYD	TEN-10	MI
1970–08	1958	From the Earth to the Moon	Byron Haskin	RKO	U.S.	ADL	SAS-10	NOT
1970–08	1954	An Inspector Calls	Guy Hamilton	British Lion Film Corp	U.S.	SYD	ATN-7	CF
1970–09	1964	**Godzilla versus the Thing**	Ishirō Honda	Toho	U.K.	SYD	ATN-7	MI
1970–09	1962	**Night of the Eagle**	Sidney Hayers	Independent Artists	Japan	SYD	ATN-7	CF

Television Air Date (YYYY-MM)	Year Produced	Title	Director	Original Studio/ Producer	Country of Origin	City	Channel	TV Package
1970-09	1956	The Day the Earth Froze	Aleksandr Ptushko	American International	U.S.	MEL	HSV-7	
1970-10	1958	Man Eater	Compton Bennett	Beaconsfield Productions	Russia	SYD	ATN-7	CF
1970-10	1944	Bluebeard	Edgar G. Ulmer	Producers Releasing Corporation	U.S.	MEL	HSV-7	CF
1970-10	1962	The Carpet of Horror	Harald Reinl	International Germania Film	U.S.	MEL	HSV-7	
1970-11	1964	Dagora, the Space Monster	Ishirō Honda	Toho	Germany	MEL	HSV-7	
1970-11	1964	The Incredibly Strange Creatures Who Stopped Living and Became Mixed-Up Zombies!!?	Ray Dennis Steckler	Fairway International Pictures	Japan	SYD	ATN-7	CF
1970-11	1933	Night of Terror	Benjamin Stoloff	Columbia	U.S.	ADL	SAS-10	DE
1970-11	1964	Frankenstein Conquers the World	Ishirō Honda	Toho	U.S.	ADL	NWS-9	
1970-07	1964	Honeymoon of Horror	Irwin Meyer	Flamingo	Japan	SYD	ATN-7	
1970-11	1967	The Mummy's Shroud	John Gilling	Hammer Films	U.S.	ADL	SAS-10	DE
1970-11	1962	The Devil's Hand	William J. Hole	Rex Carlton Productions	U.S.	SYD	ATN-7	
1970-11	1960	The Lost World	Irwin Allen	20th Century-Fox	U.S.	ADL	SAS-10	DE
1971-01	1942	The Undying Monster	John Brahm	20th Century-Fox	U.S.	ADL	NWS-9	

Filmography, 1897–1973

Television Air Date (YYYY-MM)	Year Produced	Title	Director	Original Studio/Producer	Country of Origin	City	Channel	TV Package
1971–02	1954	Killers from Space	W. Lee Wilder	Planet Films	U.S.	SYD	TCN-9	BC
1971–02	1968	**Terror in the Jungle**	Andrew Janzack	Torres International	U.S.	SYD	ATN-7	
1971–03	1964	Moro Witch Doctor	Eddie Romero	Associated Producers International	U.S.	ADL	SAS-10	DE
1971–05	1964	The Masque of the Red Death	Roger Corman	American International	U.S.	ADL	SAS-10	DE
1971–05	1963	The Haunted and the Hunted	Francis Ford Coppola	American International	U.S.	ADL	SAS-10	DE
1971–05	1964	**The Curse of the Black Widow**	Dan Curtis	ABC Films	U.S.	SYD	TCN-9	
1971–05	1960	**The Terrible People**	Harald Reinl	Rialto Film	U.S.	ADL	SAS-10	DE
1971–06	1961	**The Black Abbot**	F.J. Gottlieb	Central Cinema Company Film	Germany	ADL	SAS-10	DE
1971–07	1954	The Snow Creature	W. Lee Wilder	Planet Filmways Inc	Germany	ADL	SAS-10	DE
1971–08	1964	**The Inn on Dartmoor**	Rudolf Zehetgruber	Arca-Winston Films Corp	U.S.	SYD	ATN-7	
1971–08	1951	The Day the Earth Stood Still	Robert Wise	20th Century–Fox	Germany	ADL	SAS-10	DE
1971–08	1966	**Daimajin**	Kimiyoshi Yasuda	Daiei Film	U.S.	SYD	TEN-10	MI
1971–08	1969	**The Monsters of Terror**	Tulio Demicheli	Eichberg-Film	Japan	SYD	ATN-7	
1971–09	1965	The Face of Fu Manchu	Don Sharp	Anglo-Amalgamated Films	Spain	SYD	ATN-7	
1971–09	1941	**Tower of Terror**	Lawrence Huntington	Associated British Picture Corporation	U.K.	MEL	GTV-9	

Television Air Date (YYYY-MM)	Year Produced	Title	Director	Original Studio/Producer	Country of Origin	City	Channel	TV Package
1971–09	1959	The Wasp Woman	Roger Corman	Allied Artists	U.K.	ADL	SAS-10	DE
1971–09	1962	The Creation of the Humanoids	Wesley Barry	Emerson Film Enterprises	U.S.	SYD	ATN-7	
1971–09	1960	Sweetheart of the Gods	Gottfried Reinhardt	Central Cinema Company Film	U.S.	SYD	ATN-7	
1971–09	1966	Strangler in the Tower	Hans Mehringer	Interopa Film	Germany	SYD	ATN-7	
1971–10	1969	It's Alive	Larry Buchanan	American International	Germany	ADL	SAS-10	DE
1971–10	1966	The Witch	Damiano Damiani	Arco Film	U.S.	MEL	HSV-7	DE
1971–11	1964	The Madmen of Mandoras	David Bradley	Sans-S	Italy	ADL	SAS-10	DE
1971–11	1963	The Haunting	Roger Corman	American International	U.S.	ADL	SAS-10	DE
1971–11	1966	Carry on Screaming!	Gerald Thomas	Anglo-Amalgamated Films	U.S.	ADL	ADS-7	
1972–01	1967	Five Million Years to Earth	Roy Ward Baker	Hammer Films	U.K.	SYD	TEN-10	
1972–01	1936	The Man Who Lived Twice	Harry Lachman	Columbia	U.K.	SYD	TEN-10	DE
1972–02	1963	Ride of Terror	Ron Winston	NBC	U.S.	ADL	SAS-10	DE
1972–02	1960	The Little Shop of Horrors	Roger Corman	Filmgroup	U.S.	SYD	TEN-10	DE
1972–03	1958	The Screaming Skull	Alex Nicol	Madera Productions	U.S.	SYD	ATN-7	DE
1972–03	1960	The Fall of The House of Usher	Roger Corman	American International	U.S.	SYD	ATN-7	DE

Television Air Date (YYYY-MM)	Year Produced	Title	Director	Original Studio/Producer	Country of Origin	City	Channel	TV Package
1972–03	1967	The Terrornauts	Montgomery Tully	Amicus Productions	U.S.	ADL	SAS-10	DE
1972–03	1958	Dracula	Anthony Hinds	Hammer Films	U.K.	ADL	ADS-7	CF
1972–03	1964	The Curse of the Mummy's Tomb	Michael Carreras	Hammer Films	U.K.	SYD	TEN-10	MI
1972–04	1940	The Ghost Breakers	George Marshall	Paramount	U.K.	SYD	TEN-10	MI
1972–04	1960	Warlord of Crete	Silvio Amadio	Gino Mordini	U.S.	MEL	HSV-7	DE
1972–04	1956	The Phantom from 10,000 Leagues	Dan Milner	Milner Bros. Productions	Italy	ADL	SAS-10	DE
1972–04	1966	Sting of Death	William Grefe	Essen Productions Inc.	U.S.	ADL	SAS-10	DE
1972–04	1968	Frankenstein	Voytek	Thames Television	U.S.	MEL	HSV-7	DE
1972–04	1966	Rasputin the Mad Monk	Don Sharp	Hammer Films	U.K.	SYD	TEN-10	MI
1972–04	1965	Two on a Guillotine	William Conrad	Warner Brothers	U.K.	MEL	HSV-7	CF
1972–05	1971	The Deadly Dream	Alf Kjelin	Universal International	U.S.	SYD	TCN-9	
1972–05	1936	Suicide Club	J. Walter Ruben	MGM	U.S.	SYD	ATN-7	
1972–05	1965	The Nanny	Seth Holt	20th Century–Fox	U.S.	SYD	TEN-10	MI
1972–05	1968	The Hand of Night	Fredric Goode	Associated British Pathé	U.S.	SYD	ATN-7	MI
1972–05	1941	The Mad Doctor	Tim Whelan	Paramount	U.K.	MEL	HSV-7	MI

Television Air Date (YYYY-MM)	Year Produced	Title	Director	Original Studio/Producer	Country of Origin	City	Channel	TV Package
1972-05	1965	Where the Spies Are	Val Guest	MGM	U.S.	MEL	HSV-7	MI
1972-05	1969	Eye of the Cat	David Lowell Rich	Universal	U.K.	SYD	ATN-7	MI
1972-06	1960	**The Fiends**	John Gilling	Tempean Films	U.S.	SYD	TCN-9	
1972-07	1959	**The H-Man**	Ishirō Honda	Toho	U.K.	SYD	TEN-10	CF
1972-07	1967	Eye of the Devil	J. Lee Thompson	Filmways Productions	Japan	ADL	SAS-10	DE
1972-07	1953	Phantom from Space	W. Lee Wilder	United Artists	U.K.	SYD	ATN-7	
1972-07	1965	Dr. Who and the Daleks	Gordon Flemyng	AARU	U.S.	SYD	ATN-7	
1972-08	1963	Paranoiac	Freddie Francis	Hammer Films	U.K.	SYD	TEN-10	CF
1972-08	1964	**The Horror of Party Beach**	Del Tenney	20th Century–Fox	U.K.	SYD	TEN-10	
1972-08	1965	**The Eye Creatures**	Larry Buchanan	American International Television	U.S.	ADL	SAS-10	DE
1972-08	1961	The Shadow of the Cat	John Gilling	BHP Films	U.S.	MEL	HSV-7	
1972-09	1958	**The Brain from Planet Arous**	Nathan Juran	Howco International	U.K.	ADL	SAS-10	DE
1972-10	1966	**The Navy vs. the Night Monsters**	Michael A. Hoey	Realart Pictures	U.S.	ADL	SAS-10	DE
1972-10	1963	X—The Man with the X-Ray Eyes	Roger Corman	American International	U.S.	SYD	ATN-7	CF
1972-10	1965	**Curse of the Stone Hand**	Jerry Waren	A.D.P Pictures Inc	U.S.	ADL	SAS-10	DE

Filmography, 1897–1973

Television Air Date (YYYY-MM)	Year Produced	Title	Director	Original Studio/ Producer	Country of Origin	City	Channel	TV Package
1972–10	1967	Berserk!	Jim O'Connolly	Columbia	U.S.	ADL	SAS-10	DE
1972–10	1956	It Conquered the World	Roger Corman	American International	U.K.	SYD	ATN-7	
1972–10	1963	The Comedy of Terrors	Jacques Tourneur	American International	U.S.	SYD	ATN-7	CF
1972–10	1966	Operation White Shark	Stanley Lewis	Madison Film	U.S.	SYD	ATN-7	CF
1972–11	1958	Terror in the Haunted House	Harold Daniels	Howco International	Italy	ADL	SAS-10	DE
1972–11	1960	Vampire and the Ballerina	Renato Polselli	Consorzio Italiano	U.S.	SYD	ATN-7	CF
1972–11	1966	Godzilla versus the Sea Monster	Jun Fukuda	Toho	Italy	SYD	ATN-7	CF
1972–12	1933	King Kong	Merian C Cooper, Ernest B. Schoedsack	RKO	Japan	SYD	ATN-7	CF
1973–02	1964	Black Torment	Robert Hartford-Davis	Compton Films	U.S.	SYD	ATN-7	CF
1973–02	1931	Dracula	Tod Browning	Universal	U.K.	MEL	HSV-7	
1973–02	1942	The Mummy's Tomb	Harold Young	Universal	U.S.	SYD	ATN-7	
1973–02	1962	Tower of London	Roger Corman	United Artists	U.S.	SYD	ATN-7	
1973–02	1966	Women of the Prehistoric Planet	Arthur C. Pierce	Realart Pictures	U.S.	SYD	TCN-9	
1973–02	1971	The Night of The Damned	Filippo Walter	Primax	U.S.	ADL	SAS-10	DE

Television Air Date (YYYY-MM)	Year Produced	Title	Director	Original Studio/Producer	Country of Origin	City	Channel	TV Package
1973-02	1972	Eulogy for a Vampire	Don McDougall	William Castle Productions	Italy	SYD	TEN-10	
1973-02	1935	The Raven	Lew Landers	Universal	U.S.	SYD	ATN-7	GS
1973-02	1962	Curse of the Blood Ghouls	Roberto Mauri	Mercury	U.S.	SYD	ATN-7	CF
1973-02	1972	The Dead We Leave Behind	Paul Stanley	William Castle Productions	U.S.	SYD	TEN-10	
1973-02	1951	Bride of the Gorilla	Curt Siodmak	Realart Pictures	U.S.	SYD	ATN-7	GS
1973-03	1972	The Concrete Captain	Richard Donner	William Castle Productions	U.S.	ADL	SAS-10	DE
1973-03	1966	The Projected Man	Ian Curteis	Compton Films	U.S.	SYD	ATN-7	GS
1973-03	1943	The Mad Ghoul	James P. Hogan	Universal	U.K.	ADL	SAS-10	DE
1973-03	1972	Cry of the Cat	Arnold Laven	William Castle Productions	U.S.	SYD	ATN-7	CF
1973-03	1972	Alter-Ego	David Lowell Rich	William Castle Productions	U.S.	SYD	ATN-7	GS
1973-03	1948	The Creeper	Jean Yarbrough	Reliance Pictures	U.S.	SYD	ATN-7	GS
1973-03	1954	Svengali	Noel Langley	Renown Pictures	U.S.	ADL	SAS-10	
1973-04	1941	The Wolf Man	George Waggner	Universal	U.S.	ADL	SAS-10	DE
1973-04	1972	Touch of Madness	Robert Day	William Castle Productions	U.S.	SYD	ATN-7	CF
1973-04	1958	The Haunted Strangler	Robert Day	Amalgamated Productions	U.S.	SYD	ATN-7	GS

Filmography, 1897–1973

Television Air Date (YYYY-MM)	Year Produced	Title	Director	Original Studio/Producer	Country of Origin	City	Channel	TV Package
1973–04	1972	**Creatures of the Canyon**	Walter Doniger	William Castle Productions	U.K.	SYD	TEN-10	
1973–04	1967	Theatre of Death	Samuel Gallu	Pennea Productions	U.S.	SYD	ATN-7	GS
1973–04	1962	Corridors of Blood	Robert Day	Amalgamated Productions	U.K.	MEL	GTV-9	
1973–04	1940	The Mummy's Hand	Christy Cabanne	Universal	U.S.	ADL	SAS-10	DE
1973–04	1972	**The New House**	John Llewellyn Moxey	William Castle Productions	U.S.	SYD	ATN-7	
1973–04	1966	**Portrait in Terror**	Jack Hill	American International	U.S.	SYD	ATN-7	GS
1973–05	1963	**Terror in the Crypt**	Camillo Mastrocinque	American International	U.S.	SYD	ATN-7	CF
1973–05	1972	**The Summer House**	Leo Penn	William Castle Productions	Spain	SYD	ATN-7	CF
1973–05	1967	**Death Curse of Tartu**	William Grefe	Thunderbird International	U.S.	SYD	ATN-7	GS
1973–05	1968	Torture Garden	Freddie Francis	Amicus Productions	U.S.	SYD	TEN-10	
1973–05	1972	**Half a Death**	Leslie H. Martinson	William Castle Productions	U.K.	SYD	ATN-7	CF
1973–05	1931	Frankenstein	James Whale	Universal	U.S.	SYD	ATN-7	GS
1973–05	1942	Night Monster	Ford Beebe	Universal	U.S.	SYD	ATN-7	
1973–05	1972	**House of Evil**	Daryl Duke	William Castle Productions	U.S.	SYD	ATN-7	CF
1973–05	1941	Man Made Monster	George Waggner	Universal	U.S.	SYD	ATN-7	GS

Filmography, 1897–1973

Television Air Date (YYYY-MM)	Year Produced	Title	Director	Original Studio/Producer	Country of Origin	City	Channel	TV Package
1973-05	1960	Village of the Damned	Wolf Rilla	MGM	U.S.	SYD	ATN-7	CF
1973-05	1963	House of the Damned	Maury Dexter	20th Century-Fox	U.K.	SYD	ATN-7	CF
1973-05	1972	**At the Cradle Foot**	Don McDougall	William Castle Productions	U.S.	SYD	ATN-7	
1973-05	1964	The Secret of Blood Island	Quentin Lawrence	Hammer Films	U.S.	SYD	ATN-7	GS
1973-05	1964	**The Last Man on Earth**	Ubaldo Ragona	Associated Producers International	U.K.	SYD	TEN-10	
1973-06	1972	**Bad Connection**	Walter Doniger	William Castle Productions	Italy	SYD	ATN-7	CF
1973-06	1956	*The Black Sleep*	Reginald LeBorg	United Artists	U.S.	SYD	ATN-7	GS
1973-06	1968	**Destroy All Planets**	Noriaki Yuasa	Daiei Film	U.S.	SYD	ATN-7	CF
1973-06	1972	**Time of Terror**	Robert Day	William Castle Productions	Japan	SYD	ATN-7	CF
1973-06	1957	**Fiend Without a Face**	Arthur Crabtree	Amalgamated Productions	U.S.	SYD	ATN-7	GS
1973-06	1945	House of Dracula	Erle C. Kenton	Universal	U.K.	ADL	SAS-10	DE
1973-06	1973	**Death's Head**	James Neilson	William Castle Productions	U.S.	SYD	ATN-7	CF
1973-06	1953	The Neanderthal Man	E.A. Dupont	United Artists	U.S.	SYD	ATN-7	GS
1973-07	1973	**Dark Vengeance**	Herschel Daugherty	William Castle Productions	U.S.	SYD	ATN-7	CF
1973-07	1956	The Sorceress	André Michel	Films Metzger et Woog	U.S.	SYD	ATN-7	GS

Filmography, 1897–1973

Television Air Date (YYYY-MM)	Year Produced	Title	Director	Original Studio/Producer	Country of Origin	City	Channel	TV Package
1973–07	1973	**Doorway to Death**	Daryl Duke	William Castle Productions	Italy	ADL	SAS-10	DE
1973–07	1962	The Premature Burial	Roger Corman	American International	U.S.	SYD	ATN-7	GS
1973–07	1973	**Phantom of Herald Square**	James H. Brown	William Castle Productions	U.S.	SYD	ATN-7	
1973–07	1973	**Spare Parts**	Charles Dubin	William Castle Productions	U.S.	SYD	ATN-7	GS
1973–07	1970	**Yog, Monster from Space**	Ishirō Honda	Toho	U.S.	SYD	ATN-7	GS
1973–07	1973	**The Ghost of Potter's Field**	Don McDougall	William Castle Productions	Japan	SYD	ATN-7	CF
1973–07	1963	**Tombs of Terror**	Antonio Boccacci	Filmar	U.S.	SYD	ATN-7	GS
1973–07	1963	The Haunted Palace	Roger Corman	American International	Italy	SYD	ATN-7	CF
1973–08	1968	**Mission Stardust**	Primo Zeglio	P.E.A. Cinematografica	U.S.	MEL	HSV-7	
1973–08	1962	The Cabinet of Caligari	Roger Kay	20th Century–Fox	Germany	ADL	SAS-10	DE
1973–08	1964	Children of the Damned	Anton M. Leader	MGM	U.S.	ADL	SAS-10	DE
1973–08	1960	**The Flesh and the Fiends**	John Gilling	Regal Film Distributors	U.K.	SYD	ATN-7	CF
1973–09	1958	**The Brain Eaters**	Bruno Ve Sota	American International	U.K.	ADL	SAS-10	DE
1973–10	1958	The Brain from Planet Arous	Nathan Hertz	Howco International	U.S.	SYD	ATN-7	CF
1973–10	1962	Tales of Terror	Roger Corman	American International	U.S.	BRI	TVQ-10	DE

Television Air Date (YYYY-MM)	Year Produced	Title	Director	Original Studio/ Producer	Country of Origin	City	Channel	TV Package
1973–10	1964	Devil Doll	Lindsay Shonteff	Gordon/ Associated/ Galaworld	U.S.	SYD	ATN-7	
1973–10	1964	The Maqsque of the Red Death	Roger Corman	Alta Vista Productions	U.K.	SYD	ATN-7	
1973–11	1965	House of the Black Death	Harold Daniels		U.S.	SYD	ATN-7	CF
1973–11	1970	Horror of the Blood Monsters	Al Adamson	Independent-International	U.S.	SYD	ATN-7	CF
1973–12	1935	WereWolf of London	Stuart Walker	Universal	U.S.	SYD	ATN-7	CF
1973–12	1964	Moonwolf	George Freedland		U.S.	SYD	ATN-7	CF
1974–01	1944	House of Frankenstein	Erle C. Kenton	Universal	Germany	ADL	SAS-10	DE
1974–01	1959	The Mummy	Terence Fisher	Hammer Films	U.S.	MEL	HSV-7	
1974–01	1966	The Deadly Bees	Freddie Francis	Amicus Productions	U.K.	SYD	TCN-9	
1974–01	1963	The Curse of the Yellow Snake	Franz Josef Gottlieb	Central Cinema Company Film	U.K.	MEL	GTV-9	
1974–01	1959	Fellowship of the Frog	Harold Reinl	Rialto Film	Germany	ADL	SAS-10	DE
1974–01	1970	Monster from Space	Ishirō Honda	Toho	U.S.	ADL	SAS-10	DE
1974–02	1971	The Touch of Satan	Bruce Kessler	Futurama International Pictures	Japan	ADL	SAS-10	DE
1974–02	1963	Fire Monster vs Son of Hercules	Guido Malatesta	Euro International	U.S.	SYD	TEN-10	
1974–02	1970	Gamera vs. Monster X	Noriaki Yuasa	Daiei Film	Italy	ADL	SAS-10	DE

Filmography, 1897–1973

Television Air Date (YYYY-MM)	Year Produced	Title	Director	Original Studio/Producer	Country of Origin	City	Channel	TV Package
1974–02	1959	Invasion of the Animal People	Virgil W. Vogel	Jerry Warren Productions	Japan	ADL	SAS-10	DE
1974–02	1965	Creature of the Walking Dead	Jerry Warren	A.D.P Pictures Inc	Sweden	SYD	ATN-7	CF
1974–03	1964	The Tomb of Ligeia	Roger Corman	American International	U.S.	ADL	SAS-10	DE
1974–03	1957	The Manbeast	Val Guest	Hammer Films	U.K.	SYD	ATN-7	
1974–03	1962	The Day of The Triffids	Steve Sekely	Security Pictures	U.K.	ADL	SAS-10	DE
1974–04	1961	Pit and The Pendulum	Roger Corman	American International	U.K.	SYD	TEN-10	
1974–04	1964	The Flesh Eaters	Jack Curtis	Vulcan Productions	U.S.	ADL	SAS-10	DE
1974–04	1943	Frankenstein Meets the Wolf Man	Roy William Neill	Universal	U.S.	ADL	SAS-10	DE
1974–04	1951	Cry, the Beloved Country	Zoltán Korda	London Film Productions	U.S.	SYD	ATN-7	CF
1974–04	1954	The Tomb of Ligeia	Roger Corman	Alta Vista Productions	U.K.	ADL	SAS-10	DE
1974–05	1959	House on Haunted Hill	William Castle	William Castle Productions	U.K.	MEL	HSV-7	
1974–05	1939	Son of Frankenstein	Rowland V. Lee	Universal	U.S.	ADL	SAS-10	DE
1974–05	1964	Attack of the Mayan Mummy	Rafael Portillo	Jerry Warren Productions	U.S.	MEL	HSV-7	
1974–05	1935	Bride of Frankenstein	James Whale	Universal	Mexico	ADL	SAS-10	DE
1974–05	1946	House of Horrors	Jean Yarbrough	Universal	U.S.	SYD	ATN-7	

Television Air Date (YYYY-MM)	Year Produced	Title	Director	Original Studio/ Producer	Country of Origin	City	Channel	TV Package
1974–05	1968	The Green Slime	Kinji Fukasaku	MGM	U.S.	SYD	ATN-7	
1974–06	1971	**Blood Thirst**	Newton Arnold	Journey Productions	Japan	SYD	ATN-7	
1974–06	1966	**The Return of the Giant Majin**	Kenji Misumi	Daiei Film	Philippines	ADL	SAS-10	DE
1974–06	1967	The She-Freak	Byron Mabe	Lion Dog	Japan	ADL	SAS-10	DE
1974–06	1968	Destroy All Monsters	Ishirō Honda	Toho	U.S.	ADL	SAS-10	DE
1974–07	1966	**The Big Gundown**	Sergio Sollima	PEA	Japan	SYD	ATN-7	CF
1974–07	1956	**Night of the Damned**	Filippo Ratti	Primax	Italy	SYD	ATN-7	CF
1974–07	1954	**Island Monster**	Roberto Bianchi Montero	Romana Film	Italy	ADL	SAS-10	DE
1974–07	1967	Blood Beast Terror	Vernon Sewell	Tigon British	Italy	SYD	ATN-7	CF
1974–07	1972	**Legend of Horror**	Bill Davis	General Film Corporation	U.K.	ADL	SAS-10	DE
1974–08	1965	The Night Walker	William Castle	Universal International	U.S.	ADL	SAS-10	DE
1974–08	1961	**The Bacchantes**	Giorgio Ferroni	Lyre Films	U.S.	ADL	SAS-10	DE
1974–08	1968	Submarine X-1	William Graham	United Artists	Italy	ADL	SAS-10	DE
1974–08	1962	King Kong vs Godzilla	Ishirō Honda	Toho	U.K.	ADL	SAS-10	DE
1974–09	1959	Floods of Fear	Charles Circhton	Universal Studios	Japan	SYD	HSV-7	

Filmography, 1897–1973

Television Air Date (YYYY-MM)	Year Produced	Title	Director	Original Studio/ Producer	Country of Origin	City	Channel	TV Package
1974–09	1966	**An Angel for Satan**	Camillo Mastro-cinque	Discobolo	U.K.	ADL	SAS-10	DE
1974–09	1942	The Ghost of Frankenstein	Erle C. Kenton	Universal	Italy	SYD	ATN-7	CF
1974–09	1944	The Mummy's Curse	Leslie Goodwins	Universal	U.S.	SYD	ATN-7	
1974–09	1964	**The Curse of The Living Corpse**	Del Tenney	20th Century–Fox	U.S.	SYD	ATN-7	
1974–12	1968	**Blood Beast Terror**	Vernon Sewell	Tigon British	U.S.	MEL	ATV-0	
1974–12	1958	*Frankenstein's Daughter*	Richard E. Cunha	Astor/ Layton	U.K.	SYD	TEN-10	
1975–02	1952	**Bela Lugosi Meets a Brooklyn Gorilla**	William Beaudine	Realart Pictures	U.S.	SYD	TEN-10	
1975–03	1969	Frankenstein Must Be Destroyed	Terence Fisher	Hammer Films	U.S.	MEL	HSV-7	
1975–03	1940	Chamber of Horrors	Norman Lee	Rialto Film	U.K.	MEL	ATV-0	
1975–03	1958	The Fly	Kurt Neumann	20th Century-Fox	U.S.	ADL	SAS-10	DE
1975–04	1962	**Gorath**	Ishirō Honda	Toho	U.S.	ADL	SAS-10	DE
1975–05	1969	Scream and Scream Again	Gordon Hessler	Amicus Productions	Japan	SYD	ATN-7	
1975–05	1953	Donovan's Brain	Felix E. Feist	Dowling Productions	U.K.	ADL	SAS-10	DE
1975–05	1966	**Death Curse of Tartu**	William Grefe	Thunderbird Int	U.S.	ADL	SAS-10	DE
1975–06	1967	Cyborg 2087	Franklin Adreon	Harold Goldman Associates	U.S.	SYD	TEN-10	

Television Air Date (YYYY-MM)	Year Produced	Title	Director	Original Studio/ Producer	Country of Origin	City	Channel	TV Package
1975–07	1968	**Satanik**	Piero Vivarelli	Copercines/ Rodiacines	U.S.	ADL	SAS-10	DE
1975–08	1958	The Revenge of Frankenstein	Terence Fisher	Hammer Films	Italy	SYD	TEN-10	
1975–08	1960	Two Faces of Dr. Jekyll	Terence Fisher	Hammer Films	U.K.	MEL	GTV-9	
1975–09	1970	Trog	Freddie Francis	Herman Cohen Productions	U.K.	MEL	GTV-9	
1975–10	1970	Count Yorga, Vampire	Bob Kelljan	American International	U.K.	SYD	TEN-10	
1975–10	1944	The Mummy's Ghost	Reginald LeBorg	Universal	U.S.	SYD	ATN-7	
1975–10	1968	Rosemary's Baby	Roman Polanski	Paramount	U.S.	SYD	ATN-7	BC
1975–11	1946	The Spider Woman Strikes Back	Arthur Lubin	Universal	U.S.	MEL	GTV-9	
1975–12	1943	Son of Dracula	Robert Siodmak	Universal	U.S.	SYD	ATN-7	BC
1976–02	1966	Jesse James Meets Frankenstein's Daughter	William Beaudine	Embassy	U.S.	SYD	ATN-7	BC
1976–03	1968	**House of Evil**	Juan Ibañez	Azteca Films	U.S.	MEL	HSV-7	
1976–03	1970	The Dunwich Horror	Daniel Haller	American International	Italy	SYD	TEN-10	
1976–04	1972	The Creeping Flesh	Freddie Francis	World Film Service	U.S.	SYD	ATN-7	
1976–04	1971	Creatures the World Forgot	Don Chaffey	Hammer Films	U.K.	SYD	TEN-10	
1976–05	1931	Dr. Jekyll and Mr. Hyde	Rouben Mamoulian	Paramount	U.K.	MEL	GTV-9	

Filmography, 1897–1973

Television Air Date (YYYY-MM)	Year Produced	Title	Director	Original Studio/Producer	Country of Origin	City	Channel	TV Package
1976–05	1971	The Return of Count Yorga	Bob Kelljan	American International	U.S.	MEL	HSV-7	
1976–06	1971	The House That Dripped Blood	Peter Duffell	Amicus Productions	U.S.	SYD	TEN-10	
1976–06	1957	**Attack of the Crab Monsters**	Roger Corman	Allied Artists	U.K.	SYD	TEN-10	
1976–06	1960	Circus of Horrors	Sidney Hayers	Hammer Films	U.S.	MEL	ATV-0	
1976–06	1956	**Indestructible Man**	Jack Pollexfen	Allied Artists	U.K.	MEL	GTV-9	
1976–06	1958	*Frankenstein 1970*	Howard W. Koch	Allied Artists	U.S.	MEL	ATV-0	
1976–06	1970	*Taste the Blood of Dracula*	Peter Sasdy	Hammer Films	U.S.	MEL	ATV-0	
1976–07	1959	*The Alligator People*	Roy Del Ruth	20th Century–Fox	U.K.	SYD	TEN-10	
1976–07	1972	**Beware! The Blob**	Larry Hagman	Jack H. Harris Enterprises	U.S.	SYD	TEN-10	
1976–08	1971	The **House That Screamed**	Narciso Ibáñez Serrador	American International	U.S.	SYD	TEN-10	
1976–10	1971	A Reflection of Fear	William A. Fraker	Columbia	Spain	SYD	ATN-7	
1977–01	1966	Munster, Go Home![60]	Earl Bellamy	Universal International	U.S.	SYD	ATN-7	
1977–02	1970	Equinox	Jack Woods	Tonylyn Productions	U.S.	SYD	ATN-7	
1977–03	1971	Night of Dark Shadows	Dan Curtis	MGM	U.S.	SYD	TEN-10	
1977–03	1971	The Abominable Dr. Phibes	Robert Fuest	American International	U.S.	SYD	ATN-7	

Television Air Date (YYYY-MM)	Year Produced	Title	Director	Original Studio/ Producer	Country of Origin	City	Channel	TV Package
1977–06	1961	**Creature from the Haunted Sea**	Roger Corman	Roger Corman Productions	U.S.	ADL	SAS-10	DE
1977–07	1970	The Vampire Lovers	Roy Ward Baker	Hammer Films	U.S.	SYD	TCN-9	
1977–07	1933	Lost Patrol	John Ford	RKO	U.K.	SYD	ATN-7	
1977–08	1972	Night of the Lepus	William F. Claxton	A.C. Lyles Productions	U.S.	SYD	ATN-7	BC
1977–08	1970	Goodbye Gemini	Alan Gibson	Joseph Shaftel Productions	U.S.	SYD	TCN-9	
1977–09	1970	**Bigfoot**	Robert F. Slatzer	Gemini-American Productions	U.K.	SYD	TEN-10	
1977–09	1957	The Black Scorpion	Edward Ludwig	Warner Brothers	U.S.	SYD	ATN-7	
1977–11	1971	The Brotherhood of Satan	Bernard McEveety	Columbia	U.S.	SYD	TEN-10	
1978–01	1972	The Deathmaster	Ray Danton	R.F. Brown Productions	U.S.	ADL	NWS-9	
1978–02	1966	Billy the Kid versus Dracula	William Beaudine	Circle Productions	U.S.	SYD	TEN-10	
1978–02	1972	Dracula A.D. 1972	Alan Gibson	Hammer Films	U.S.	MEL	HSV-7	
1978–03	1974	**The Spectre of Edgar Allan Poe**	Mohydeen Quandour	Cintrel	U.K.	SYD	TCN-9	
1978–03	1970	*Cry of the Banshee*	Gordon Hessler	American International	U.S.	SYD	TEN-10	
1978–04	1970	**Assignment Terror**	Tulio Demicheli	Eichberg-Film	U.S.	ADL	SAS-10	DE
1978–04	1971	Willard	Daniel Mann	Bing Crosby Productions	Spain	ADL	SAS-10	DE

Television Air Date (YYYY-MM)	Year Produced	Title	Director	Original Studio/ Producer	Country of Origin	City	Channel	TV Package
1978-04	1968	The Castle	Rudolf Noelte	Afa Film Corp	U.S.	SYD	TEN-10	
1978-05	1966	Nightmare	Freddie Francis	Hammer Films	Germany	ADL	SAS-10	DE
1978-05	1968	The Strange Case of Dr. Jekyll and Mr. Hyde	Charles Jarrott	CBC	U.K.	ADL	SAS-10	DE
1978-06	1968	The Curse of the Crimson Altar	Vernon Sewell	Trigon Films	U.S.	ADL	SAS-10	DE
1978-06	1970	The Evils of Dorian Grey	Massimo Dallamano	Sargon Film	U.K.	ADL	SAS-10	DE
1978-06	DE	Dr. Phibes Rises Again	Robert Fuest	American International	Italy	ADL	SAS-10	DE
1978-06	1973	The Clones	Lamar Card	Filmmakers International	U.K.	ADL	SAS-10	DE
1978-07	1971	Crucible of Terror	Ted Hooker	Glendale Film Productions	U.S.	ADL	SAS-10	DE
1978-07	1971	Black Noon	Bernard L. Kowalski	Andrew J. Fenady Productions	U.K.	ADL	SAS-10	DE
1978-08	1972	The Thing with Two Heads	Lee Frost	American International	U.S.	ADL	SAS-10	DE
1978-08	1969	Malenka, Niece of the Vampire	Armando de Ossorio	Cobra Films	U.S.	ADL	SAS-10	DE
1978-09	1962	What Ever Happened to Baby Jane?	Robert Aldrich	Warner Brothers	Italy	ADL	SAS-10	DE
1978-09	1967	The Fearless Vampire Killers	Roman Polanski	MGM	U.S.	ADL	SAS-10	DE
1978-10	1968	Dracula Has Risen from the Grave	Freddie Francis	Hammer Films	U.K.	SYD	ATN-7	

Television Air Date (YYYY-MM)	Year Produced	Title	Director	Original Studio/ Producer	Country of Origin	City	Channel	TV Package
1978–10	1957	The Curse of Frankenstein	Terence Fisher	Hammer Films	U.K.	ADL	SAS-10	DE
1978–10	1956	**Bride of the Monster**	Ed Wood	Rolling M. Productions	U.K.	ADL	SAS-10	DE
1978–10	1970	The Horror of Frankenstein	Jimmy Sangster	Hammer Films	U.S.	SYD	ATN-7	
1978–10	1970	Scars of Dracula	Roy Ward Baker	Hammer Films	U.K.	SYD	TEN-10	
1978–10	1967	**Yongary: Monster from the Deep**	Kim Ki-duk	Toei Company	U.K.	SYD	TEN-10	
1978–11	1973	**And Now the Screaming Starts!**	Roy Ward Baker	Amicus Productions	Korea	SYD	ATN-7	
1978–11	1967	**The Spirit Is Willing**	William Castle	Paramount	U.K.	ADL	SAS-10	DE
1978–12	1971	**Octaman**	Harry Essex	Filmers Guild	U.S.	MEL	GTV-9	
1978–12	1968	The Devil Rides Out	Terence Fisher	Hammer Films	U.S.	SYD	ATN-7	
1979–01	1939	The Dark Eyes of London	Walter Summers	Argyle Film	U.K.	MEL	ATV-0	
1979–02	1969	**Latitude Zero**	Ishirō Honda	Toho	U.K.	SYD	TCN-9	
1979–03	1970	And Soon the Darkness	Robert Fuest	Associated British Picture Corporation	Japan	MEL	HSV-7	
1979–07	1945	Isle of the Dead	Mark Robson	RKO	U.K.	MEL	GTV-9	
1979–08	1972	Fear in the Night	Jimmy Sangster	Hammer Films	U.S.	SYD	ATN-7	
1980–07	1969	The Haunted House of Horror	Michael Armstrong	Tigon/ AIP	U.K.	SYD	TCN-9	

Filmography, 1897–1973

Television Air Date (YYYY-MM)	Year Produced	Title	Director	Original Studio/ Producer	Country of Origin	City	Channel	TV Package
1980–09	1932	Freaks	Tod Browning	MGM	U.K.	SYD	TEN-10	
1981–06	1971	Who Slew Auntie Roo?	Curtis Harrington	Hemdale	U.S.	SYD	ATN-7	CF
1981–07	1972	**Godzilla vs. the Smog Monster**	Yoshimitsu Banno	Toho	U.K.	MEL	HSV-7	
1982–08	1953	Abbott and Costello Meet the Invisible Man	Charles Lamont	Universal International	Japan	SYD	ATN-7	
1983–01	1961	The Curse of the Werewolf	Terence Fisher	Hammer Films	U.S.	SYD	ATN-7	
1983–02	1940	The Invisible Man Returns	Joe May	Universal	U.K.	SYD	ATN-7	
1983–02	1944	The Invisible Man's Revenge	Ford Beebe	Universal	U.S.	SYD	TCN-9	
1983–03	1942	Invisible Agent	Edwin L. Marin	Universal	U.S.	SYD	TCN-9	
1984–04	1965	**Orgy of the Dead**	Stephen C. Apostolof	Astra	U.S.	SYD	TCN-9	
1984–05	1972	**Demons of the Mind**	Peter Sykes	Hammer Films	U.S.	SYD	ATV-0	
1984–08	1946	The Beast with Five Fingers	Robert Florey	Warner Brothers	U.K.	MEL	GTV-9	
1984–12	1972	The Man from Deep River	Umberto Lenzi	Roas Produzioni	U.S.	SYD	TEN-10	
1985–01	1933	The Ghoul	T. Hayes Hunter	Gaumont	Italy	SYD	TCN-9	
1985–01	1971	Blood from the Mummy's Tomb	Seth Holt	Hammer Films	U.K.	MEL	ATV-0	

Filmography, 1897–1973

Television Air Date (YYYY-MM)	Year Produced	Title	Director	Original Studio/ Producer	Country of Origin	City	Channel	TV Package
1985–09	1971	Dr. Jekyll and Sister Hyde	Roy Ward Baker	Hammer Films	U.K.	SYD	TCN-9	
1985–10	1977	**Tarantulas: The Deadly Cargo**	Stuart Hagmann	Alan Lansburg Productions	U.K.	SYD	TCN-9	
1986–01	1964	*The Evil of Frankenstein*	Freddie Francis	Hammer Films	U.S.	SYD	ATN-7	
1987–03	1967	**King Kong Escapes**	Ishirō Honda	Toho	U.K.	SYD	TCN-9	
1987–07	1971	Dracula vs. Frankenstein	Al Adamson	Independent International	Japan	SYD	TCN-9	
1987–11	1960	*The Brides of Dracula*	Terence Fisher	Hammer Films	Spain	SYD	HSV-7	
1990–04	1967	The Shuttered Room	David Greene	Troy-Schenck Productions	U.K.	SYD	ATN-7	
1990–06	1971	Twins of Evil	John Hough	Hammer Films	U.K.	SYD	TCN-9	
1990–06	1972	Tales from the Crypt	Freddie Francis	Hammer Films	U.K.	CAN	Capitol-10	
1991–08	1966	**Queen of Blood**	Curtis Harrington	American International	U.K.	SYD	TCN-9	
1991–08	1967	**Zontar, the Thing from Venus**	Larry Buchanan	American International	U.S.	SYD	TCN-9	
1991–09	1962	**The Brain That Wouldn't Die**	Joseph Green	American International	U.S.	SYD	TEN-10	
1993–07	1971	*Blood and Lace*	Philip S. Gilbert	American International	U.S.	SYD	TEN-10	
1994–05	1936	The Man Who Changed His Mind	Robert Stevenson	Gainsborough Pictures	U.S.	MEL	ATV-0	
1995–02	1972	The Possession of Joel Delaney	Waris Hussein	Haworth Productions	U.K.	MEL	ABC-2	

Filmography, 1897–1973

Television Air Date (YYYY-MM)	Year Produced	Title	Director	Original Studio/ Producer	Country of Origin	City	Channel	TV Package
1995–03	1972	Vampire Circus	Robert Young	Hammer Films	U.S.	SYD	ATN-7	
1996–01	1971	Hands of the Ripper	Peter Sasdy	Hammer Films	U.K.	SYD	ABC-2	
1996–11	1962	**The Awful Dr. Orloff**	Jesús Franco	Sigma III	U.K.	SYD	ABC-2	
1999–11	1932	White Zombie	Victor Halperin	Victor Halperin/ United Artists	Spain	SYD	SBS	
2000–07	1971	**She Killed in Ecstasy**	Jesús Franco	Telecine Film	U.S.	SYD	TEN-10	
2000–09	1965	**Bloody Pit of Horror**	Massimo Pupillo	Pacemaker Int	Spain	MEL	SBS	
2014–07	1964	Blood and Black Lace	Mario Bava	Emmepi Cinematografica	Italy	SYD	SBS	
	1971	Lust for a Vampire	Jimmy Sangster	Hammer Films	Italy	MEL	SAS-10	
					U.K.	Queensland	QLD-9	

Chapter Notes

Introduction

1. "Coroner Condemns 'Horror' Films," *Sun* (NSW), 20 July 1912.

Chapter 1

1. *The Sydney Morning Herald*, 23 November 1894.
2. The films were *Annabelle's "Skirt Dance," Juan Caicedo Dancing on the High Wire, A Cock Fight, A Blacksmith Shoeing a Horse,* and *Comical Barbershop Scene*.
3. The sixteen films included such titles as *Professor Weston's Boxing Cats, Eugene Sandow in Muscular Display* and *J.K Emmett and His Wrestling Dog*.
4. *Northern Miner*, Charters Towers, 14 September 1895.
5. At Edison Electric Parlour, 162 Pitt Street, Sydney.
6. Robert W. Paul (3 October 1869–28 March 1943) was an English electrician, scientific instrument maker and early pioneer of British film. He discovered that Edison had not placed a patent upon the Kinetoscope, so he bought one, took it apart and reversed engineered it, ultimately claiming it as his own.
7. Worth approximately $1,800,000 in 2017 money.
8. Oral history interview tape recorded with A.J. Perier around 1955, probably by Keast Burke.
9. The date of August 17 was reported by *The Free-Lance* and *The Age*. Both newspapers had journalists in attendance at this screening.
10. "The Play," *The Free-Lance*, 22 August 1896.
11. "On and Off the Stage," *Table Talk*, 21 August 1896.
12. Descriptions of Madame Jessica were not kind. Champion, when reviewing the show on August 9, 1896, described her as such. "The latest attraction at the Opera House is Madame Jessica, a very massive, serpentine, wire walking lady. She is a success, but whether on account of her massiveness or her wire-walking it were a nice point to determine [sic]."
13. "On and Off the Stage," *Table Talk*, 28 August 1896.
14. "Amusements," *The Leader*, 29 August 1896.
15. *The Bulletin* (Sydney), 21 November 1896.
16. 21 November 1896, *The Bulletin*.
17. 14 November 1896, *The Australasian*.
18. 24 September 1896, *The Sydney Morning Herald*.
19. The "Salon Lumière" was pulled down decades ago. The site now houses a Hilton hotel and parking lot.
20. This film is commonly mistaken as being the 1896 Melbourne Cup.
21. The first such lecture film was *Social Salvation* (1898–99).
22. A famous image of the Christians about to be fed to a waiting lion is widely believed to be taken from the 1909 remake, *Heroes of the Cross*. In both cases, the lions were very real and were hired from Wirth's circus.

Chapter 2

1. It is worth noting that, in 1897 when film began to grip the nation, future American president Herbert Hoover moved to Australia to work in the mining sector of Western Australia. He left in 1899. An Australian flag was hoisted at Hoover's 1929 inauguration, a serious breach of protocol as only the American flag can be displayed at the event. Hoover saw the flag and insisted that it remain where it was, the only time a flag of a foreign country has been flown at a presidential inauguration.
2. Alexander "Sawney" Bean was said to be the head of a 48-member clan in Scotland anywhere between the 13th and 16th centuries, reportedly executed for the mass murder and cannibalisation of over 1,000 people.
3. "West's Pictures," *Western Mail*, 16 June 1910.
4. "Lyric Theatre, Bunbury," *Southern Times*, 23 July 1910.
5. Brother of the better-known stage and screen actor Sir Guy Standing.
6. 12 February 1912, *The Sydney Morning Herald*.
7. 12 April 1912, *South Coast Times*.
8. Universal Studios was originally called Universal Film Manufacturing Company and was founded by Carl Laemmle, Pat Powers, David

Horsley, William Swanson, Mark Dintenfass, Charles Baumann, Robert H. Cochrane, Adam Kessel and Jules Brulatour.

9. Herc McIntyre was born in 1890 and passed away in 1976.

10. The company that they worked for demanded all its staff become naturalized Americans. In typical fashion, the McIntyre brothers responded to this demand by quitting on the spot, packing up and leaving, but they decided to take a short holiday through America before returning home.

11. Most other directors of companies at the time were into their 50s.

12. This percentage was never revealed in public, but it is no secret that Herc McIntyre became a very rich man as a result.

13. This percentage was never revealed in public, but it is no secret that Herc McIntyre became a very rich man as a result.

14. "Interview with Carl Laemmle," *The Sunday Sun* (NSW), 12 November 1935.

15. "Picture Censorship," *Newcastle Morning Herald and Miners' Advocate*, 23 November 1912.

16. "Movie Censors," *Newcastle Sun*, 17 January 1919.

17. Commissions, Boards, and Committees, House of Representatives Hansard, 16 December 1918.

18. "Films," 1 November 1920, *Picture Show* (NSW).

19. For a detailed account of the Guyra Ghost haunting, refer to *Filming the Guyra Ghost*, Monster! #31, Wildside-Kronos Publishing, November 2016.

20. "Nigger Minstrels" Advertisement, 29 April 1921, *Inverell Times* (NSW).

21. "Harry Clay's Famous Bargain Vaudeville" Advertisement, 9 May 1921, *The Sun* (NSW).

22. "The Great Theodore" Advertisement, 2 May 1921, *Newcastle Morning Herald* (NSW).

23. Sloggett billed himself as "the Man Who Could Not Be Hanged."

24. "The Incomparable Sloggett" Advertisement, 11 July1923, *Daily Mercury* (Qld).

25. "The Guyra Ghost and Roofing Tiles" Advertisement, 4 September 1922, *The Sun* (NSW).

26. "Local and General News," 14 May 1921, *Armidale Chronicle* (NSW).

27. "Filming the Guyra Spook," 20 May 1921, *Richmond River Herald* (NSW).

28. "Exploiting a Spook," 4 June 1921, *Bundaberg Mail* (Qld).

29. "Filming the Guyra Ghost. How It Was Done," 18 June 1921, *Tweed Daily* (NSW).

30. Ibid.

31. Cosgrove paid a small sum for the exhibition of *The House of Fear* for the initial run of *The Guyra Ghost Mystery* but, in typical Cosgrove style, he promptly laid claim to complete, worldwide ownership of the movie.

32. "The Guyra Ghost" Advertisement, 19 June 1921, *Truth* (NSW).

33. "The Guyra Ghost Mystery" Advertisement, 15 July1921, *National Advocate* (NSW).

34. "The Guyra Ghost" Advertisement, 25 July1921, *Lithgow Mercury*.

35. "A Great Sensation, The Guyra Ghost" Advertisement, 28 July1921, *Guyra Argus* (NSW).

36. "The Guyra Ghost Sensation" Advertisement, 13 August 1921, *Nepean Times* (NSW).

37. "The Guyra Ghost" Advertisement, 10 September 1921, *Port Macquarie News* (NSW).

38. *Everyone's*, 12 December 1922.

39. *Everyone's*, 24 January 1923.

40. *Everyone's*, 4 June 1923.

41. Correspondence between the author and David J. Skal, December 6, 2015.

42. Billed as the "Funniest Hebrew Comedians in the World."

43. Noted for their associations with Georges Méliès and the Lumière brothers.

44. Browning had directed Lugosi a year earlier in *The Thirteenth Chair* (1929).

45. Despite claims at the time, and since, Lovely never took up American citizenship, stating so under oath before the Royal Commission into the Motion Picture Industry in Australia in June 1927.

46. By the time she left Australia Lovely had been known by many names. In addition to Louise Alberti, she was also known as Louise Welch, Louise Carbasse, Louisa Lovely and, in one memorable misspelling, Louise Lovel.

47. The Lon Chaney short "autobiography" was probably ghost written.

48. *The Truth* (NSW), 7 November 1925.

49. *Everyone's*, 26 August 1925.

50. Chaney's real name was Leonidas Frank Chaney. Newspapers reporting his death gave his name as Alonzo, which was the name of the character that he'd played in *The Unknown* (1927).

51. Fisher's name was also reported as "Frederic."

52. George Worrall's name has also been spelled "Worral," "Wurrell" and "Wurel." In most reports, his name is spelled Worrall, which is the spelling I will use here.

53. Government Notice, *Sydney Gazette and New South Wales Advertiser* (NSW), 21 September 1826.

54. *Monitor* (NSW), Saturday, 3 February 1827. Seemingly nobody was alarmed that Gilbert knew what white man's fat tasted like.

55. According to author Robert Hughes, in his landmark work *The Fatal Shore*, it wasn't uncommon for priests and reverends in colonial Australia to elicit such confessions from condemned men by telling them that they would go to Hell if they didn't bare their souls. No confession, no last rites, no salvation.

56. "Execution," *Sydney Gazette and New South Wales Advertiser* (NSW), 6 February 1827.

57. "Fisher's Ghost," *Sydney Gazette and New South Wales Advertiser* (NSW), 5 March 1836.

58. "To The Editors," *Sydney Herald* (NSW), 26 July1841.

59. "Felix" was more than likely the pen name

of one James Riley (ca. 1795–1860), Irish-born ex-convict, "bush tutor" and associate of the Hume family, early explorers and settlers of the southern districts of New South Wales.

60. *Bell's Life* (NSW), 27 June 1846.

61. Born Raymond John Walter Hollis Longford (23 September 1878–2 April 1959).

62. Born Charlotte Edith Cox (23 February 1890–21 December 1925).

63. Longford-Lyell's first movie together was *The Fatal Wedding* (1911). The pair had performed the title roles on stage. Costing an estimated £600, the film went on to gross £16,000 in both Australia and England.

64. *Smith's Weekly* (NSW), 22 July 1922.

65. The first movie that is credited as being directed solely by Lyell was *The Blue Mountains Mystery* in 1921.

66. Australia, *Royal Commission on the Moving Picture Industry in Australia*, Walter Moffitt Marks, *Minutes of Evidence* (Canberra: Government Printer, 1927).

67. NAA: A1336, 12588.

68. "Fisher's Ghost," *Daily Telegraph* (NSW), 18 June 1927.

69. Later to become Greater Union Theatres.

70. Spencer's life had a bizarre end. He bought a ranch in Canada and settled down but was financially ruined in the 1929 stock market crash. In September 1930, he went insane and shot and killed his storeman, Howard Smith, and wounded another man, Walter Stoddart, so severely that his arm had to be amputated. Spencer then vanished in the wilds of Vancouver, triggering a hunt by a posse of an estimated 50 men. Six weeks after his disappearance his body was discovered in a lake where he had drowned himself. He left behind an estate valued at over £60,000.

71. Doyle claimed, at the Royal Commission, that he had no idea how Hoyts would have known about the Combine's rejection. He felt that Longford had told them.

72. Australia, *Royal Commission on the Moving Picture Industry in Australia*, Walter Moffitt Marks, *Minutes of Evidence* (Canberra: Government Printer, 1927).

73. "Fisher's Ghost in London," *Everyone's*, 4 March 1925.

74. "Condescending, very!" *Everyone's*, 8 April 1925.

75. *Ibid.*

76. "Death of Lottie Lyell," *Everyone's*, 23 December 1925.

77. National Film and Sound Archive Australia Title No. 392164, *Raymond Longford: Documentation: Assorted papers including correspondence, invitations and unrealized scripts.*

78. "The Man Who Met Raymond Longford," Tony Buckley, *Metro* #135.

79. "Worries of Movie Directors," *Sunday Times* (NSW), 29 April 1923. "For this particular scene it was necessary for Miss Lottie Lyell and Mr Raymond Longford, the *directors*, to photograph Arthur Tauchert, who plays the Bloke" (emphasis added).

80. "The Man Who Met Raymond Longford," Tony Buckley, *Metro* #135.

81. Australia, *Royal Commission on the Moving Picture Industry in Australia*, Walter Moffitt Marks, *Minutes of Evidence* (Canberra: Government Printer, 1927).

82. *Ibid.*

83. *Ibid.*

84. *Ibid.*

85. *The Herald* (Vic), 1 November 1924.

86. *Brisbane Courier* (Qld) 17 December 1924.

87. *Daily Mail* (Qld), 17 December 1924.

88. *Newcastle Morning Herald* (NSW), 30 December 1924.

89. *Mercury* (Tas), 10 February 1925.

90. Worth approximately $2,905,385 in 2017.

91. Worth approximately $726,288 in 2017.

92. In the 1925 Annual Report it was noted that 322 films were passed unconditionally, 331 were passed after eliminations and 68 films were rejected outright.

93. Compton Coutts, John F. Gavin, Louise Lovely, Wendy Macdonald Osborne and Dunstan Michael Webb.

94. Franklyn Barrett, Charles Chauvel, Herbert Finlay, Gerald Hayle, Frank Hurley, Percy Juchau, Herbert Kirwan, Raymond Longford, Alexander Macdonald, Vaughan Marshall, Isabel McDonagh, John McGeorge, Frederick Murphy and Albert Segerberg.

95. McIntyre stated that 1,382,315 feet of film were passed and only 2,226 rejected, representing a total of 1.6% of the total film submitted.

96. Represented by William Gibson, Albert Kruger and William Lyall.

97. Represented by Horace Wotton and Leonard Roach.

98. Represented by Leslie Keally.

99. Represented by James Sixsmith.

100. Represented by Sergeant Gambier and John Jones.

101. Represented by Stanley Crick, Jean Adams and Elton Wild.

102. Represented by Norman Freeman, Henry Brodziak and Thomas Ferguson.

103. Represented by Charles Nelson.

104. Represented by Ralph Doyle.

105. Represented by Frank Holdaway, Herbert McCrae and Hercules MacIntyre.

106. Australia, *Royal Commission on the Moving Picture Industry in Australia*, Walter Moffitt Marks, *Minutes of Evidence* (Canberra: Government Printer, 1927).

107. *Ibid.*

108. *Ibid.*

109. *Ibid.*

110. *Ibid.*

111. Principal Medical Officer, Education Department, South Australia.

112. *The Guyra Ghost Mystery* (1921). Directed by John Cosgrove.

Notes—Chapter 3

113. Graham Shirley, "Doyle, Stuart Frank (1887–1945)," *Australian Dictionary of Biography*, National Centre of Biography, Australian National University.

Chapter 3

1. Three shillings in 1929 is worth approximately $11.00 in 2015; £8,500 in 1929 is worth approximately $647,854 in 2015.
2. A popular insult of the era was that Americans spoke the English language like they hated it.
3. "An Advertising Stunt," *Traralgon Record* (Vic), 26 May 1930.
4. "Free Trip Offer," *Newcastle Sun*, 29 September 1930.
5. "African Jungle Life," *Daily Mercury* (Qld), 14 August 1930.
6.
7. Letter dated 4 August 1931 from C.E. Cook, Chief Protector of Aboriginals, to the Administrator, Department of Trade and Customs.
8. "Cinema Proprietors Problems," *The Sydney Morning Herald* (NSW), 30 July 1936.
9. "Aborigines And the Cinema," *Barrier Miner* (NSW), 30 January 1930.
10. *The Two Frank Thrings*, Peter Fitzpatrick, 2012, Monash University Publishing.
11. Ina Bertrand, *Australian Film Studies* 7, p. 19.
12. "Literary Notes," *The Australasian*, 19 April 1930.
13. "Lon Chaney's Place," *Western Mail*, 10 September 1931.
14. "The White Panther," 23 July 1924
15. "Universal Pictures," *The Sydney Morning Herald*, 13 February 1932.
16. *Everyone's*, April 27, 1932.
17. *Ibid*.
18. "Why Film Is Banned" *The News*, 8 June 1932.
19. *Everyone's*, 2 March 1932.
20. *Everyone's*, 18 May 1932.
21. Worth an estimated $164,000 in 2017.
22. *Everyone's*, 18 May 1932.
23. The main street of Melbourne.
24. "Frankenstein Banned," *The Argus*, 8 June 1932.
25. "Why Film Is Banned," *The News*, 8 June 1932.
26. "The Box Office Value of Horror," Gayne Dexter, *Everyone's*, 27 April 1932.
27. In typical fashion Dexter got Karloff's name wrong, billing him as "Karloff Boris."
28. McIntyre to *Everyone's*, 4 May 1932.
29. Note from the Film Censorship Board, undated.
30. *Ingagi* was banned due to it being considered fraudulent, not due to content.
31. Born William Henry Pratt on 23 November 1887, in Camberwell, London, England.
32. Born Béla Ferenc Dezső Blaskó on 20 October 1882, Lugosi was originally from the town of Lugos, Kingdom of Hungary, Austria-Hungary (now Lugoj, Romania).
33. There was a good reason for Karloff's silence about his Anglo-Indian heritage—prejudice. Anglo-Indians were, at the time, considered to be half-castes and thus inferior to so-called "normal" Anglos or English people. It's the same reason why Merle Oberon, also an Anglo-Indian, born in Bombay, would always insist that she was Tasmanian by birth, even though no records ever existed of her even living there, let alone being born there. After her passing in 1979, authors Charles Higham and Roy Moseley published their work, *Princess Merle: The Romantic Life of Merle Oberon*, in which they debunked her Tasmanian connections and established her real place of birth—Bombay, India. Thus, Karloff and Oberon, the former by heritage and the latter by birth and heritage, were the first Southern Asian stars in Hollywood.
34. Karloff was born into privilege. The son of a diplomat, he was sent to private schools, leading him to King's College, London, where he studied to enter the British government's Consular Service. He dropped out of university in 1909.
35. Born Elisabeth Johann on July 14, 1904, near Temesvar, Hungary (now Timisoara, Romania).
36. Reports stated that he passed out due to the bandages and make-up covering every part of his body, literally suffocating him.
37. "Make More Faces," *Sun* (NSW), 12 February 1933.
38. *Ibid*.
39. "The Mummy," *Smith's Weekly* (NSW), 18 February 1933.
40. *The News* (SA), 8 May 1933.
41. "The Mummy," *Table Talk* (Vic), 16 March 1933.
42. "King Kong in Sydney," *The West Australian* (WA), 30 June 1933.
43. Ad for King Kong, *Newcastle Morning Herald* (NSW), 17 August 1933.
44. Ad for King Kong, *The Examiner* (Tas), 6 October 1933.
45. Ad for King Kong, *Newcastle Sun* (NSW), 18 August 1933.
46. Stations that are known to have broadcast the serial and the fifteen minutes of live *King Kong* dialogue are 3UZ (Victoria, starting 10 July 1933) 2KO (New South Wales, starting 14 August 1933), 5AD and 5KA (South Australia, starting 1 September 1933) and 4BC (Queensland, starting 2 October 1933). There is no record of any station in Western Australia, Northern Territory or Tasmania carrying the serial.
47. "King Kong," *The Sydney Morning Herald* (NSW), 21 August 1933.
48. "The Thought occurred to me…," *The Emerald* (Vic), 7 October 1933.
49. Letter dated 17 July 1935 from W. Cresswell O'Reilly to Universal Film Mfg.
50. Letter dated 20 July 1935 from Vic Hislop (Universal Film Mfg.) to W. Creswell O'Reilly

51. Letter dated 29 August 1935 from Cresswell O'Reilly to Edwin Abbott (comptroller-general of Customs).
52. Letter dated 12 September 1935 from Edwin Abbott to Sir Victor Wilson, Motion Pictures Distributor's Association.
53. Letter dated 15 October 1935 Sir Victor Wilson to studio managers.
54. Letter dated 15 October 1935 Sir Victor Wilson to Edwin Abbott.
55. Letter dated 17 October 1935 from Vic Heslop to Sir Victor Wilson.
56. Letter dated 5 November 1935 from Edwin Abbott to Sir Victor Wilson. The original letter is now lost, the remaining copy has the handwritten notations by Abbott and O'Reilly and still exists.
57. Advertisement for *Werewolf of London*, 1932.
58. "The Werewolf claims his prey!" *The West Australian* (WA), 7 September 1935.
59. An African American actor, best known for playing Stepin' Fetchit–type roles, William Best (1916–1962) was originally billed as "Sleep n' Eat." He was often called upon to play stereotypically lazy, illiterate, and/or simple-minded characters, such as waiters, porters, shoe-shine boys and elevator operators. Best was an expert at bugging his eyes out and uttering phrases such as "Lawdy!" He deserved better than he got.
60. Samuel Horwitz (1895–1955) was a founder (with brother Moe Howard and Larry Fine) of Three Stooges. He left the Stooges in 1932 and returned to the trio in 1947, where he remained until his death in 1955.
61. "Monogram Arrives," *Smith's Weekly* (NSW), 9 February 1935.
62. J. Albert and Sons were music publishers. One son, Edward "Ted" Albert, would help found the Alberts record label, and combined with Alberts Studio, would foster the careers of music acts such as AC/DC, The Angels and many others via their long association with producers/song writers George Young and Harry Vanda (formerly of the Easybeats, another Albert-connected act).
63. Interview with Carl Laemmle, *The Argus* (Vic), 15 June 1936.
64. "Universal Films," *Sun* (NSW), 2 April 1936.
65. "Picture Films—Censorship and Control," *The Sydney Morning Herald*, 9 August 1938.
66. Noted in both Sydney and Perth newspapers.
67. Noted in Brisbane, Sydney and Perth newspapers.
68. He was billed as Creighton Chaney until late 1937 in Australia.
69. "Of Mice and Men Banned," *The Sydney Morning Herald*, 27 February 1940.
70. "Of Mice and Men," 9 March 1940, *Evening News* (Brisbane).
71. Also referred to as "Karis" and "Claris" in Australian newspapers.
72. "Eerie Horror Film," *Sunday Times* (WA), 23 February 1941.
73. "Films of the Week," *Sun* (NSW), 3 February 1941.
74. Cecil Lawriston Kellaway, born 22 August 1880 and died 28 February 1973.
75. "Films of the Week," *Sun* (NSW), 3 February 1941.
76. "Eerie Horror Film," *Sunday Times* (WA), 23 February 1941.
77. *The Sunday Sun* (NSW), 2 February 1941.
78. "Box Office Prophecies." *Smith's Weekly* (NSW), 30 November 1940.
79. "*The Mummy's Hand*," *Smith's Weekly* (NSW), 8 February 1941.
80. With typical Australian dry humor, the evacuation became known as the Adelaide River Stakes. This was due to the high number of people racing for the relative safety of Adelaide River, a township around 70 miles from Darwin, with most making the journey on foot.
81. "Leonski Hanged—Murderer of Three Women," *The Age* (Vic), 10 November 1942.
82. "Can You Sit Up with a Monster at Midnight?" *The Mercury* (Hobart, Tasmania), 23 July 1942.
83. 24 July 1942, *The Mercury* (Hobart, Tasmania).
84. 10 March 1943, *The News* (Adelaide, South Australia).
85. *Daily News* (WA), 4 December 1942.
86. "His Majesty's," *Voice* (Tas), 20 March 1943.
87. "Horror Films," *Catholic Weekly*, 28 August 1947.
88. "Horrors Enliven School Holidays." *Sun* (NSW), 21 August 1947.
89. *Telegraph* (Qld), 25 May 1945.
90. *After the Reich*, Giles MacDonogh, John McMurray (London), 2007.
91. Mixed in with genuine refugees were a number of Nazi war criminals. In 1986, it was estimated that at least 841 people accused of war crimes were still alive in Australia. Only one was charged with war crimes. In January 1990, Adelaide resident Ivan Polyukhovicht was arrested and brought to trial after being implicated in a massacre of more than 800 people in Serniki, Ukraine. After a trial, he was acquitted. In 2002 the Simon Wiesenthal Centre passed on a list of 22 Nazi war criminals that it believed were still alive in Australia. None were tracked down, let alone charged.
92. *Daily Telegraph* (NSW), 29 May 1945.
93. *Ibid.*
94. "Hanging of Nazi Shown in Film," *The News* (SA), 3 December 1945.
95. *Ibid.*
96. Passed 29 October 1947, Queensland Legislative Council.
97. Letter dated 16 April 1948, from J.O. Alexander to the Secretary, Motion Pictures Distributors Australia
98. "Uniform Film Censorship in Four States," *Daily Mercury* (QLD), 2 February 1949.
99. Notably "Censors' Axe Falls on Horror Film," *The Sydney Morning Herald* (NSW), 29 April

1948, and "Horror Film Now Banned," *Courier Mail* (Qld), 23 April 1948.
100. "Exit the Ghouls," *Film Weekly*, 29 April 1948.
101. "The Passing of the Horror Film," *The Argus Week-End Magazine* (Victoria), 8 May 1948.
102. "Screamy-Weamies Can be So Funny,' *The Sydney Morning Herald* (New South Wales), 22 May 1948.
103. *"Meet the Ghosts," The News* (Adelaide), 7 July1949.
104. *"Abbott & Costello Meet the Killer, Boris Karloff,"* Albany Advertiser (NSW), 4 December 1950.
105. *"Meet the Killer," Canberra Times* (ACT), 14 March 1950.
106. *"Meet the Killers," Barrier Miner* (NSW), 8 January 1951.
107. The review began: "Here is a Jekyl [sic]-and-Hyde sort of story—BORIS KARLOFF and BELA LUGOSI in the poster-news—but only KARLOFF and the director doing any sort of original work." The review pointed out that Lugosi was largely absent from the film and ended by calling it "good average entertainment." *"Back Friday," Smith's Weekly* (NSW), 25 May 1940.
108. *"Dracula," Smith's Weekly* (NSW), 27 February 1932.
109. *"The Mummy," Smith's Weekly* (NSW), 18 February 1933.
110. *"The Walking Dead," Smith's Weekly*, 25 April 1936.
111. *"Dracula's Daughter," Smith's Weekly*, 22 August 1936.
112. "Blood-and-Thunder Storms Box Office," *Smith's Weekly* (NSW), 16 April 1932.
113. *"Frankenstein," Smith's Weekly* (NSW), 21 May 1932.
114. "No More Cowboys and Indians," *Smith's Weekly* (NSW), 21 October 1944.
115. "Horror Films Banned," *Smith's Weekly* (NSW), 1 May 1948.

Chapter 4

1. "Just What Does the Censor Stop Us Seeing?" *The West Australian* (WA), 21 July1953. This article, with the by-line of "A. Special" (correspondent) quotes the censor's office in saying that only 25 horror movies were available for general screening at cinemas. It could be presumed that these 25 movies were all sound versions; silent movies, such as Lon Chaney's classics *Phantom of the Opera, Hunchback of Notre Dame, London After Midnight* and others, still in circulation, were not counted.
2. "Too Much for Dracula," *Daily Mercury*, 31 May 1948.
3. *Variety*, 3 October 1951.
4. "Lured Girl to Kill Her, Police Say," *Newcastle Morning Herald* (NSW), 9 December 1950.
5. *Ibid.*
6. *Ibid.*
7. "Horror Film Talk in Murder Case.," *Sun* (NSW), 1 February 1951.
8. *Ibid.*
9. Also known as St, Vincent's Boys Home, or the Hell Hole by the boys, Westmead was rife with abuse. Those who lived and were raised there talk of physical, emotional, mental and sexual abuse happening on a daily basis. Some of the wards spoke of escaping the home in the hopes that they would be placed in an adult jail where, they believed, they would be safe from the Marist Brothers who ran Westmead. The all too few who reported the sexual assaults and rapes were not believed and sent back to Westmead where further, and, at times, worse abuse awaited them. The media, and the courts for that matter, often dismissed any adverse reports of Westmead as being lies told by boys who could not be trusted.
10. Although it was not mentioned at the time, Cunningham's behavior is consistent with a person having been abused as a child.
11. "New Film," *The Advertiser* (SA), 29 May 1952.
12. This would equate to roughly $115,000 in 2015 money (http://www.rba.gov.au/calculator/annualPreDecimal.html).
13. "King Kong Found Dead," *The Sydney Morning Herald*, 30 October 1968.
14. "Making a Monster," *Sun-Herald* (NSW), 21 March 1954.
15. For example, even a black and white film such as *The Blob* (1958) starring Steve McQueen was still being shown at drive-ins in 1975.
16. "Shakespeare in 3-D," *The Mercury* (Tas), 21 August 1953.
17. *The Advertiser* (SA) 10 June 1953.
18. "3-D Viewers Will Not Spread Disease," *Western Mail* (WA), 9 July1953.
19. "What's on in Town," *Mirror* (WA), 21 January 1956.
20. P. and C. Council Reviews, *Canberra Times* (ACT), 4 February 1956.
21. William Alexander "Bud" Abbott (October 2, 1897–April 24, 1974) was an alcoholic for most of his adult life. He suffered from epilepsy and drank to deal with seizures.
22. Born Louis Francis Cristillo (March 6, 1906–March 3, 1959).
23. *The Sydney Morning Herald*, 31 October 1956.
24. "Boy Dies of Fright in Theatre," *The Sydney Morning Herald* (NSW), 31 October 1956.
25. *Ibid.*
26. *Ibid.*
27. "Odds & Ends," *The Chronicle* (SA), 23 July1953.
28. "New Films in Sydney," *The Sydney Morning Herald* (NSW), 4 November 1956.
29. "Question Film Censorship Speech," Australian Senate, Thursday, 8 November 1956.
30. *The Argus*, 21 December 1951.
31. *The Age*, 17 March 1958.
32. *Ibid.*

33. *The Age*, 20 March 1958.
34. *Ibid.*
35. *The Age*, 31 March 1958.
36. *Hansard* 41 CA V257.
37. One such letter read, "As you are doubtless aware, it has become the practice of suburban picture theatres to present midnight screenings of 'horror' films. The unanimous feeling of the council of the Brunswick Technical School is that these screenings should be prohibited, or at least transferred to more suitable times and then very strictly controlled. I am instructed to bring to your notice the fact that young children and adolescents attend these shows in large numbers. From the standpoints of morality, health, and plain common sense they are most undesirable, and your support is sought for any legislation which will deal with a growing social evil."
38. *Hansard* 41 CA V257.
39. "Horror Gets a New Look," *The Sydney Morning Herald* (NSW), 15 December 1957.
40. In the period between 1963 to 1965 the following movies were all recorded as being rejected by the Censorship Board: *Nightmare*, *Curse of the Mummy's Tomb*, *Kiss of the Vampire* (Hammer), *The Day of the Triffids* (Rank), *Shock Corridor*, *Twice Told Tales* (United Artists), *Konga* (Regent), *Dr. Terror's House of Horrors* (Amicus), *Curse of the Fly* (20th Century Fox) and *Devils of Darkness* (Planet Films).
41. "Question Film Censorship," *Senate Hansard*, Parl No. 22, Thursday, 28 August 1958.
42. "The Mummy," *The Sydney Morning Herald* (NSW), 1 May 1960.
43. "Faces on the Cutting Room Floor," *The Bulletin*, 20 November 1965.
44. "Censorship," *Film Digest* #25, John Baxter, 1966.
45. *Film Digest* #10, p. 4.
46. Shown at both cinemas and drive-ins from September 1969.
47. Season began on the 19 May 1970.
48. Shown on the 29 July 1970, Union Theatre, Parramatta (NSW).
49. ATN 7, 30 September 1970 (NSW).
50. Chipp foreshadowed the reforms in a very lengthy speech given to Federal Parliament on 11 June 1970.

Chapter 5

1. According to Gerald Stone in his book *Compulsive Viewing: The Inside Story of Packer's 9 Network*, the footage of this historic event was lost. What exists now is a recreation done before a film camera in 1957.
2. Worth approximately $6,330 in 2019.
3. At the same time, the American version of the play, produced for the series *Your Jeweler's Showcase*, and featuring Walter Kingsford and Una Merkle, began to air on radio. There is no record of it ever appearing on television.
4. Barbara Toy, 1908–2001. Toy became a famous travel writer, known for her solitary travels around the globe. In most cases she travelled to places that women rarely, if ever, travelled alone, such as Libya, Baghdad, Saudi Arabia and Tripoli and is known as a pioneer in the travel field.
5. "A Censors Lot Is Not a Happy One," *Australian Women's Weekly*, 22 October 1958.
6. "Monsters You're Forbidden to See on Television," *TV Week* (SA), 2 November 1963.
7. The *Blue Book* was an annual report, so named because its cover was a deep blue.
8. "Horror Ban," *TV Week* (SA), 31 October 1964.
9. *The Age*, 16 June 1965.
10. "King Kong Rides Again," *Canberra Times*, 9 June 1969.
11. *Ibid.*
12. "Horror Ban," *TV Week* (SA), 31 October 1964.
13. A Toho Studios production directed by Ishirō Honda; the film was also known as *Giant Monster Baran*.
14. No relation to the more widely known Elvira, Cassandra Peterson.
15. *The Amazing Transparent Man*, *Attack of the Puppet People*, *The Beast with 1,000,000 Eyes*, *The Ghost in the Invisible Bikini*, *Journey to the Seventh Planet*, *Mars Needs Women*, *Master of the World*, *Reptilicus*, *Teenage Caveman*, *The Terror*, *The Time Travellers*, *Voodoo Woman* and *Voyage to the End of the Universe*.
16. *Battle in Outer Space*, *Gigantis the Fire Monster (aka Godzilla Raids Again)*, *Mothra*, *Space Monster* and *Varan the Unbelievable*.
17. *D-Day on Mars*, *Retik the Moon Menace*, *Sharad of Atlantis* and *Slaves of the Invisible Monster*.
18. *The Ape*, *Doomed to Die*, *Flight to Mars*, *King of the Zombies*, *The Living Ghost*, *Lost in the Stratosphere*, *Murder at the Windmill*, *Revenge of the Zombies* and *The Strange Mr Gregory*.
19. *Curucu Beast of the Amazon*, *Monster on the Campus*, *The Night Runner*, *The Frozen Ghost*, *The Leech Woman* and *The Monolith Monsters*.
20. *The Body Snatcher*, *The Brain Machine*, *The Brighton Strangler*, *The Cat People*, *The Curse of the Cat People*, *The Hunchback of Notre Dame*, *I Walked with a Zombie*, *The Leopard Man*, *Port Sinister*, *The Seventh Victim*, *Son of Kong*, *Stranger on the Third Floor*, *The Thing from Another World* and *Zombies on Broadway*.
21. *13 Ghosts*, *The 27th Day: The 30 Foot Bride of Candy Rock*, *The Boogie Man Will Get You*, *Curse of a Demon*, *Earth Versus the Flying Saucers*, *The Giant Claw*, *It Came from Beneath the Sea*, *Killers of Kilimanjaro*, *The Mad Magician*, *The Man Who Returned to Life*, *The Man with Nine Lives*, *The Most Dangerous Man Alive*, *The Tingler*, *Twelve to the Moon* and *Zombies of Mora Tau*.
22. *First Space Ship On Venus* (1960, dir. Kurt Maetzig).
23. ATN 7, 3 February 1973 (NSW).
24. "Ghouls and Ghosts Dust off The Cobwebs,"

The Sydney Morning Herald (NSW), 11 February 1973.

25. ATN 7, 5 November 1973 (NSW).

26. Ironically *Frankenstein* was originally banned in South Australia cinemas for 21 years and then again for another 21 years from television.

27. In the television version, as screened in Australia, the exchange between Victor Moritz and Henry Frankenstein ("Henry—In the name of God!"; "Oh, in the name of God! Now I know what it feels like to be God!") was simply muted, leaving the two actors clearly speaking but with no words coming from their mouths.

28. Died 29 May 1957.
29. Died 2 February 1969.
30. Died 25 June 1937.
31. Died 7 November 1943.
32. Died 27 February 1969.
33. Died 3 May 1933.
34. Died 30 January 1953.
35. Died 6 March 1964.

Chapter 6

1. An example of this is Pier Paolo Passolini's *Salò, or the 120 Days of Sodom*. *Salò* was banned from exhibition from 1976 to 1993, after which it was classified as R18+. The restriction was overturned in 1998 and banned once more. The ban was finally lifted in 2010 when it was classified R18+ once again.

2. *Horror of Dracula* had 18 seconds of "extreme violence" cut.

3. Although cited by some as the first Australian horror film since the silent era, *Wake in Fright* falls into the category of thriller. The film does contain disturbing moments, but they are generally of a psychological manner.

4. NIDA's alumni includes Academy Award winners Cate Blanchett, Catherine Martin, Mel Gibson and Baz Luhrmann, and counts Toni Collette, Judy Davis, Colin Friels, Jacqueline Mackenzie, Steve Bisley, Garry McDonald, Hugh Sheridan, Sam Worthington, Hugo Weaving, Jim Sharman, Richard Roxburgh, Miranda Otto and Susie Porter among its graduates.

5. Born in Victoria, 9 April 1940–29 June 2002.

6. Bourke later claimed it was $300,000, a very sizable amount for a cadet's journalist to raise.

7. The Internet Movie Database lists two Production Assistants for the film, Maurice Zuberano and Alan Callow, with Callow not being credited in the film. As the IMDB often credits people who worked on films and were not credited on screen, but does not mention Bourke, it means that Bourke might have inflated his role to impress others (https://www.imdb.com/title/tt0060934/fullcredits).

8. Adrian Danks, Stephen Gaunson, and Peter C. Kunze, eds., *American-Australian Cinema: Transnational Connections* (Cham, Switzerland: Palgrave Macmillan, 2018).

9. "Remembering Aussie Pioneer Terry Bourke by Richard Harris," February 7, 2017, https://www.filmink.com.au/remembering-aussie-pioneer-terry-bourke/.

10. Norman Yemm (23 March 1933–3 February 2015) won three races in the prestigious Stawell Gift and played professional football with Victorian Football Association Club Port Melbourne before turning to acting.

11. "Norm Hits the Right Note," *Australian Women's Weekly*, 9 December 1981.

12. *The Sydney Morning Herald*, 28 May 1972.

13. Dorsey also handled publicity for acts as varied as Acker Bilk and The Yardbirds.

14. Unless otherwise stated, all of Terry Bourke's quotes are taken from *Lumiere*, June 1973.

15. *The Age*, 10 May 1972.

16. Mark David Ryan, *A Dark New World: Anatomy of Australian Horror Films*, Ph.D. thesis (Brisbane: Queensland University of Technology, 2008).

17. The closest international analogy would be the shock of seeing Henry Fonda shooting a child in the back in *Once Upon a Time in the West*.

18. Banned on the grounds of being blasphemous, indecent and obscene.

19. *The Sydney Morning Herald*, 10 November 1972.

20. Unless otherwise noted, all of Rod Hay's comments are taken from the commentary track of the *Night of Fear* DVD.

21. The films shown to the Board as proof that *Night of Fear* should be granted a classification were *The Godfather*, *The Music Lovers*, *A Clockwork Orange*, *Prime Cut*, *The Devils* and the Mexican horror *El Diablo*.

22. *The Sydney Morning Herald*, 5 December 1972.

23. *The Man with Two Heads*. The plot was best summed up by Alan Frank in his *Horror Film Handbook* (B.T. Batsford, 1982). "Dying of cancer, a bigoted white doctor has his head grafted on to the body of a black convict and the resulting monster goes on a rampage. Bizarrely cast and recalling the 'B' pictures of the fifties, it is directed with such zest that it becomes thoroughly enjoy able on its own hokum level."

24. *The Sydney Morning Herald*, 11 March 1973.

25. Ibid.

26. *Canberra Times*, 27 March 1973.

27. *The Sydney Morning Herald*, 18 March 1973.

28. *The Sydney Morning Herald*, 19 March 1973.

29. *The Age*, 20 July 1973.

30. *The Sydney Morning Herald*, 19 June 1973.

31. He appeared in the flops *Welcome to Arrow Beach* and *Crazy Mama* instead.

32. John Meillon (1934–1989), a gifted character actor known to many Americans as Walter "Wally" Reilly, Mick "Crocodile" Dundee's offsider, had a wicked drinking problem, which led to the joke that it was dangerous to light a match near him in the afternoon in case he erupted into flame. This problem that would ultimately lead to his death from cirrhosis of the liver in August 1989 at the

age of 55. At the time of his death, he looked thirty years older than he really was.

Bourke told writer Richard Harris how he and Meillon clashed during the making of *Inn of the Damned* over Meillon's tendency to be hopelessly drunk by noon, no matter if he was required to perform or not. The shoot had run smoothly until a day where Meillon showed up so drunk that he slurred his lines and couldn't stand up. Bourke propped Meillon up against a nearby tree and threatened to beat him up if he didn't get his act together. Never a physical person, Meillon walked back to the set and delivered his lines perfectly. Bourke yelled cut and Meillon staggered back to the tree where he promptly passed out and remained sleeping for the remainder of the day.

33. *The Sydney Morning Herald*, 18 November 1975.

34. David Stratton, *The Avocado Plantation: Boom and Bust in The Australian Film Industry* (Chippendale, NSW Pan Macmillan 1990).

35. Ward is best known as Mel Gibson's boss, Captain Fifi Macaffee, in the film *Mad Max*.

36. "The History of *Brothers*," Roger Ward, *The Death Rattle*, November 22, 2011.

37. *Ibid*.

38. Bourke attacking Ward's script so angered Ward that he (Ward) allegedly told Bourke that he (Ward) would sleep with his (Bourke's) wife as a punishment. Ward went on to claim that he did just that.

39. Although banned from television, it was cleared for cinema viewing on November 1, 1975, and afforded a PG (Parental Guidance) rating and a running time of 68 minutes

40. "Exorcism role 'bit of a giggle,'" *The Sydney Morning Herald* (NSW), 2 July 1974.

41. Such was the popularity of Vincent Price in Australia at the time that anything he appeared in would be Movie of the Week, no matter how bad it was.

42. ATN 7, Sydney. The movie screened at 10:30 p.m. Of interest is that the film was designated a repeat, meaning it had been shown previously. A search has not turned up any trace of the film before this date, meaning that the repeat designation was an error. Even better was the name afforded to Bela's co-star, *Thor* Johnson!

43. *The Sydney Morning Herald* (NSW), 5 November 1981.

44. "Stereotypes, Clichés, Confusion," *The Sydney Morning Herald* (NSW), 17 February 1982.

45. *The Sydney Morning Herald* (NSW), 11 November 1989.

46. This time the film was described as a "truly awful and unintentionally funny fantasy comedy about a man trying to tell his fiancé that he has a yen to wear her clothes." *The Sydney Morning Herald* (NSW), 7 March 1993.

47. Other movies that had this kind of treatment included *Gone with the Wind* and the two *Godfather* films.

Filmography—Films Released: 1897–1973

1. Aka *Le Cake-walk infernal*.
2. Screened once in its entirety.
3. Censor cuts. Was also screened, uncut, under the title "*The Monk and the Woman*," creating confusion with the 1912 film *The Monk and the Woman*.
4. Censor cuts.
5. Aka *Maciste all'inferno*.
6. Censor cuts.
7. Re-released in January 1929 as a talking picture.
8. Known to have screened at least once in Lithgow (NSW) for an amateur film club called the Camera Club.
9. Banned in South Australia.
10. Banned in Victoria and Tasmania.
11. Censor cuts.
12. Aka *Chamber of Horrors*.
13. Cut to 61 minutes and retitled *The Sinister Shadow*. In the Australian version Rondo Hatton was not called "The Creeper"; he was called "The Shadow."
14. Cut by two minutes, not released as 3-D.
15. Cut to 78 minutes.
16. Cut to 63 minutes.
17. Retitled *Mother Riley Meets the Vampire*.
18. Censor cut 16 scenes.
19. Retitled *Phantom of the Circus*.
20. Censor cut 11 scenes.
21. Rejected and resubmitted to the censor. Passed with cuts.
22. Screened at the 10th Sydney Film Festival.
23. Cut to 80 minutes.
24. Cut to 62 minutes.
25. Advertised as the first Roger Vadim film not to be banned.
26. Cut to 71 minutes.
27. Aka *Dementia 13*.
28. Banned, then cleared with cuts.
29. Promoted as being the first Hammer Dracula to be released at the cinema, and the first Dracula film released for the past 24 years in Australia.
30. Censor cuts.
31. Banned. Released with 4 1/2 minutes of cuts.
32. Censor cuts.
33. Censor cuts.
34. Censor cuts.
35. Banned, released with cuts.
36. Censor cuts (3 minutes).
37. Censor cuts.
38. Originally banned on grounds of indecency. Cleared with cuts.
39. Submitted for review June 1972, 88 minutes, rejected. Submitted September 1972, 85 minutes, rejected. Submitted for review February 1973, 86 minutes, passed, rated R18+.
40. Banned for 15 years.
41. Banned for 43 years. Cut to 68 minutes.
42. Banned for 33 years.
43. Banned for 32 years.

44. Banned for 26 years.
45. Banned for 29 years.
46. Banned for 23 years.
47. Banned for 24 years.
48. Announced for release for 25 August 1923 (*Everyone's*). Not released.
49. Sheet music was released for theme and was popular. Film not released.
50. Spanish language version.
51. The Censor Board calls the film "the most repulsive picture screened before this Board." Ban would remain in effect for 43 years.
52. Announced as being released in April 1933 in *Everyone's* (01/03/1933). Also mentioned in *Everyone's* (15/02/1933).
53. Aka *Japanese King Kong*.
54. Mentioned in *Everyone's*. Not released. Released to television 1968.
55. Newspaper critics claimed this film as one of the best pictures of 1935, but it never screened.
56. Mentioned as being released in *The Newcastle and Maitland Catholic Sentinel* in 1945, but no evidence of release.
57. Gazetted 26/07/1946, not released.
58. Banned due to death in the USA.
59. Banned 1970. Indecent and violent
60. Was screened over two nights on television for its first run, then as a single movie.

Bibliography

Books

Australia. *Royal Commission on the Moving Picture Industry in Australia.*
Bertrand, Ina. *Cinema in Australia: A Documentary History.* Kensington, NSW: NSWU Press, 1989.
Edmondson, Ray, Andrew Pike, and National Library of Australia. *Australia's Lost Films: The Loss and Rescue of Australia's Silent Cinema.* Canberra: National Library of Australia, 1982.
Hertz, Carl. *A Modern Mystery Merchant: The Trials, Tricks and Travels of Carl Hertz, the Famous American Illusionist.* London: Hutchinson, 1924.
Marks, Walter Moffitt. *Report of the Royal Commission on the Moving Picture Industry in Australia.* Canberra: H.J. Green, government printer, 1928.

Archives

National Archives of Australia
AP5/1, 40/926A
AP5/1, 1944/2481
AP5/1, 1944/4546
AP5/1, 1946/6114
AP5/1, 1947/3754
AP5/1, 1947/10500
AP5/1, 1947/10512
AP5/1, 1947/10520
NAA: SP6/1, A32/116

Newspapers

New South Wales

The Armidale Chronicle
Barrier Miner
Braidwood Dispatch
Cessnock Eagle and South Maitland Recorder
Daily Advertiser
Newcastle Morning Herald and Miners Advocate
The Newsletter—an Australian Paper for Australian People
Northern Star
Southern Record
Sunday Times

Queensland

Daily Mercury
Daily Standard
Gympie Times
Morning Bulletin
Pittsworth Sentinel
Truth
Warwick Examiner and Times

South Australia

The Advertiser
Daily Herald
Kapunda Herald
News
Peterborough Advertiser
The Recorder
The Register
Sunday Journal

Tasmania

The Examiner
The Mercury
The North Western Advocate

Victoria

The Advocate
The Age
The Argus
Frankston Standard
Punch
Table Talk

Western Australia

Daily News
Geraldton Guardian
Kalgoorlie Miner
Mirror
Sunday Times
The West Australian

New Zealand

Auckland Star
Evening Post
Hutt News
New Zealand Herald

Index

Abbott, Bud 119, 120
Abbott, Edwin 81, 82
Abbott and Costello Meet Frankenstein (1948) 101, 108, 140; see also *Meet the Ghosts*
Abbott and Costello Meet the Killer, Boris Karloff (1949) 101, 102, 119
Abbott and Costello Meet the Mummy (1955) 119
The Abominable Dr. Phibes (1971) 148
The Abominable Snowman of the Himalayas (1957) 140
Academy Awards 84, 89, 159, 160
Ace of Scotland Yard (1929) 55, 56
The Adventures of Robin Hood (1938) 87
The Amazing Mr. X (1948) 138
The Ape (1940) 93
The Ape Man (1943) 85
atrocity films 96–99
Atwill, Lionel 31, 84, 95, 120
Australasian Films (film company) 37, 38, 40, 45, 51, 64, 68

Balcon, Michael 79
banned 1, 17–19, 30, 31, 48, 54, 57, 60, 64–66, 68–72, 80, 85, 86, 88, 89, 95, 97, 99–102, 104, 106, 108, 121, 122, 124, 127, 128, 131, 132, 135, 137, 139–45, 147, 155, 156, 159, 165, 166
Bannerman, Ian 143, 144
Barrymore, Lionel 31
Baxter, John 131, 132
The Beast from 20,000 Fathoms (1953) 138
The Beast with Five Fingers (1943) 98
Bedlam (1946) 56, 61, 138
Behets, Briony 151–55
Bertram, Ina 62
Billy the Kid Versus Dracula (1966) 148
Biograph 13, 15, 16, 27, 61
The Black Cat (1934) 86, 103, 140
Black Friday (1940) 103, 140
The Black Sleep (1956) 120–22
Black Sunday (1960) 148
Blacula (1972) 148
Blatty, William Peter 160
Boris Karloff's Thriller (television show) 139
Bourke, Terry 2, 149, 150, 152–59
Bride of Frankenstein (1935) 60, 68, 69, 80, 82, 83, 86, 87, 91, 103
Bride of the Monster (1955) 162
Broderick, Fred 67, 83

Browning, Tod 21, 26, 27, 31, 32, 57, 69, 71, 86, 132, 140, 159

Carradine, John 84, 122, 148
The Cat Creeps 140
Cat People (1942) 93
The Catholic Weekly (newspaper) 92, 93, 100, 113
censorship 13, 16–18, 43–47, 49, 53, 54, 60, 61, 66, 72, 77, 81, 82, 85, 87, 92, 93, 97, 99, 101–3, 112, 114, 122, 131, 132, 135, 138, 142, 143, 149, 155–57
Chaney, Lon 15, 26–28, 31, 50, 63, 82, 88, 91, 92, 101, 102, 112, 122, 139
Chaney, Lon, Jr. 15, 82, 88, 91, 92, 101, 102, 112, 122
Chaplin's 24, 31, 50, 139
Clive, Colin 66, 69, 120, 146
Columbia 1, 55, 84, 143, 145
Commonwealth Film Censorship Board 17, 18, 77
Corman, Roger 145, 149
Costello, Lou 101, 119, 120
Count Yorga, Vampire (1970) 134, 148
Creature from the Black Lagoon (1954) 1, 108, 114, 115, 128
The Creature Walks Among Us (1956) 125
The Creeping Unknown (1955) 120–22, 125; see also *The Quatermass Xperiment*
Cullen, Headly 143, 144
Cunningham, John Eric 111
The Curse of Frankenstein (1957) 127
The Curse of the Fly (1965) 147
The Curse of the Mummy's Tomb (1964) 130, 147
Cushing, Peter 127–29
cut films 48, 49, 69, 71, 77, 78, 80, 85, 95, 101, 131, 132, 135, 137, 139, 142, 147, 148, 153

Deadly Earnest 142–45, 149
Doyle, Stuart 21, 23, 26, 37–41, 45, 46, 51, 52, 78
Dracula (1931) 26, 27, 31, 32, 57–60, 63, 66, 68, 69, 72, 73, 75, 78, 82, 86–88, 93, 96, 101, 103, 109, 112, 115, 120, 123, 127, 128, 132, 133, 140, 146–48, 160, 166
Dracula AD 1972 (1972) 148
Dracula Has Risen from the Grave (1968) 132, 133, 147
Dracula vs. Frankenstein (1971) 148
Dracula's Daughter (1936) 58, 63, 86, 87, 103, 123

Efftee (film studio) 61
Essanay (film studio) 13

299

Index

Everyone's (magazine) 25, 26, 38, 39, 51, 58, 60, 63, 65, 67–69, 71
The Exorcist (1973) 159, 160

The Face at the Window (1919) 18, 19, 50
Face of Marble (1946) 85
Film Weekly (magazine) 71, 80, 98, 100, 112, 116, 133
Fisher's Ghost (1924) 32, 34–41, 46, 49, 50, 148, 159
Frankenstein (1910) 14
Frankenstein (1931) 13, 14, 60, 63–66, 68, 69, 71, 72, 76, 77, 80–83, 85–91, 93, 96, 98, 101, 103, 104, 108, 111, 112, 114, 119, 120, 123, 126–28, 130, 132, 134, 140, 141, 146–48
Frankenstein Meets the Wolf Man (1943) 88, 93, 96, 119
Frankenstein Must Be Destroyed (1969) 132, 134, 147, 148
Freaks (1932) 21, 26, 31, 32, 69, 71, 72, 86, 132, 140, 159
Freund, Karl 73, 119, 120

Geach, Edwin 10, 34
Ghost of Frankenstein (1942) 90, 91, 93, 96, 123
The Ghoul (1933) 61, 79, 82, 86, 93, 95, 103
Glen or Glenda (1953) 162, 163
Godzilla (1953) 77, 115
The Golem: How He Came into the World (1920) 25, 26, 73
Gorilla at Large (1954) 118
Guyra (town/haunting) 19–24, 50
The Guyra Ghost Mystery (1921) 19–21, 24

Hatton, Rondo 95
The Haunted Barn (1931) 50, 61–63
The Haunted Castle (1921) 9, 10
Hertz, Carl 3–10
Higham, Charles 131
Hitchcock, Alfred 137, 159
Hollywood 90, 135
The Hordern Mystery (1920) 19, 20, 50
horror ban 1, 2, 85, 100, 101, 104, 108, 109, 111, 112, 128, 132, 133, 139, 147
Horror of Dracula (1958) 127, 132, 147, 148
House of Dark Shadows (1970) 148, 165
House of Dracula (1945) 88, 132
House of Frankenstein (1944) 88, 96, 98, 123, 130
House of Wax (1953) 112, 113, 118, 138
House on Haunted Hill (1959) 108
Hoyts 37–40, 45, 46, 51, 61, 73, 78, 113, 114, 125
Hull, Henry 82, 83, 146
The Hunchback of Notre Dame (1923) 28–31, 50, 87, 139

Ingagi (1930) 56, 57
Invisible Ghost (1941) 61
The Invisible Man (1933) 69, 70, 79, 86, 93, 101
The Invisible Man Returns (1940) 93
The Invisible Ray (1936) 60, 86, 103, 140, 142
The Invisible Woman (1940) 93

Jesse James Meets Frankenstein's Daughter (1966) 148, 165
Johann, Zita 73, 76, 119

Karloff, Boris 15, 61, 63, 64, 66–68, 72–77, 79, 81, 84, 86–89, 91, 92, 96, 102, 108, 111, 115, 119, 132, 135, 138–42, 146
King Kong (1933) 57, 77–80, 86, 113, 114, 118, 141, 142, 157, 163
King Kong (1977) 163

Laemmle, Carl (Sr) 16, 28, 72, 85, 103, 120
Lee, Christopher 127–29, 146
London After Midnight (1927) 27, 30, 31, 58, 86, 87
Longford, Raymond 32, 34, 35, 37–41, 44–46
Longford-Lyell 35, 37, 38, 40, 45, 46, 50
Lord of the Flies (1963) 123
The Lost Patrol (1934) 61
The Lost World (1925) 51, 78
Lugosi, Bela 15, 25, 27, 31, 57–60, 63, 72, 73, 84, 86, 87, 101, 108, 109, 112, 119, 120, 122, 127, 135, 146, 162, 163

MacMahon, Joseph 7, 8
The Mad Ghoul (1943) 93, 95
Mad Love (1935) 86
McIntyre, Hercules Christian 16, 41, 42, 45, 54, 55, 58, 60, 63, 65, 66, 68, 69, 86
Meet the Ghosts 101, 109; see also *Abbott and Costello Meet Frankenstein*
Méliès, Georges 9, 10
Metropolis (1927) 25, 73
Mighty Joe Young (1949) 109, 110, 113
Monogram (film studio) 84, 85
Morgan, Ronald 84, 93, 94
The Mummy (1932) 1, 60, 61, 72–77, 79, 82, 86, 89, 92, 93, 95, 96, 101, 103, 112, 119, 120, 128–30, 140, 146, 147
The Mummy's Curse (1944) 95, 98, 123
The Mummy's Ghost (1944) 93, 94
The Mummy's Hand (1940) 89, 90, 92, 93
The Mummy's Tomb (1942) 92, 130, 146, 147
The Munsters 140, 141
Murder by the Clock (1931) 58, 60, 68

New South Wales (censorship and banning) 17–20, 22, 24, 31, 56, 83, 90, 96, 97, 100
New Zealand 8–10, 14, 21, 34, 38, 39, 58, 86, 89, 128
Night of Fear (1972) 2, 50, 148–58
Night of the Living Dead (1968) 148, 161
Nosferatu (1922) 25, 58, 132, 139

O'Reilly, Cresswell (censor) 18, 43, 48, 54, 77, 82, 89, 95
The Outer Limits 137, 142, 145, 149

The Phantom of the Opera (1925) 30, 42, 50, 93, 139, 147
Phantom of the Rue Morgue (1954) 138
The Phantom Speaks (1945) 138
Pickford, Mary 28, 139
Plan Nine from Outer Space (1958) 162–163
Planet of the Apes (1968) 80, 142, 148
Poverty Row (studios) 83–85, 145

Queensland (censorship and banning) 3, 56, 65, 99, 105, 156

Index

Republic (film studio) 1, 79, 84, 85, 138, 143
The Return of Doctor X (1939) 138
Return of the Ape Man (1944) 85
The Revenge of Frankenstein (1958) 147
Revenge of the Zombies (1943) 96
Rickard, Harry 5, 7, 9, 10
RKO (film studio) 61, 77, 80, 84, 86, 109, 113, 114, 138, 141, 143, 163
Royal Commission on The Moving Picture Industry of Australia 13, 35, 38–41, 44, 46, 48, 49, 51, 53, 60, 105, 131
Russell, Charles 150, 152
Rydge, Sir Norman 52
Rylah, Arthur 125

The Sealed Room (1909) 13, 85, 122
Sestier, Marius 7–9
Smith's Weekly (newspaper) 76, 90, 102, 103
Soldiers of the Cross (1900) 10, 11, 21, 96, 97, 99, 102, 124
Son of Dracula (1943) 93, 96, 112
Son of Frankenstein (1939) 68, 86, 87, 103
Son of Kong (1933) 80, 142
South Australia (censorship and banning) 8, 17, 18, 59, 60, 66, 68, 69, 81, 90, 92, 94, 97, 99, 100, 111
Strange, Glenn 101
The Strangler's Grip (1912) 14, 15, 50
Sydney Morning Herald (newspaper) 81, 101, 121, 151, 157, 158, 160, 162

Table Talk (newspaper) 5, 6, 77
Tasmania (censorship and banning) 4, 5, 10, 30, 56, 61, 64, 72, 87, 91, 96, 107
Taste the Blood of Dracula (1970) 148
television 60, 80, 101, 105, 119, 120, 122, 125, 127, 130, 132, 135–46, 148–50, 152, 153, 158–63
Terryrod Productions 150, 153

Toho (film studio) 143–45
Toy, Barbara 137
The Twilight Zone 137, 142
The Twins (1921) 24, 25

UFA (film studio) 25
United Artists (film studio) 25, 45, 49, 58, 84, 89, 121, 145
Universal Films Ltd. (Australia) (film studio) 15
Universal Studios (USA) (film studio) 1, 15, 16, 27, 28, 30, 31, 41–43, 45, 47, 54, 55, 58, 60, 63–66, 69, 72–77, 79, 81–87, 93, 94, 96, 99–101, 103, 109, 112, 114, 115, 119, 120, 124, 128, 130, 139–43, 145, 146, 148, 161

The Valley of Gwangi (1969) 133
Valley of the Zombies (1946) 85
Vampira 143, 144
Vampire Lovers (1970) 148
The Vanishing Lady (1896) 4, 9, 21, 88, 112
Van Sloan, Edward 73, 120, 146
Victoria (censorship and banning) 7–9, 11, 15, 30, 43, 49, 62, 65, 82, 87, 97, 104, 124, 125, 137
Vitagraph (film studio) 13

Warner Brothers (film studio) 69, 84, 86, 138
Weir, Peter 148, 159
Werewolf of London (1935) 82, 91, 103, 146
Whale, James 69, 70, 79, 81, 120
White Zombie (1932) 72, 86
Williamson, J.C. 3, 7, 14, 89, 90
The Wolf Man (1941) 88, 92, 93, 96, 101, 102, 112, 119, 140
Wood, Edward 161–163

Zacherley 143
Zucco, George 84